GATECRASHING EUROPE

Kris Mole was born in London, 1983, and grew up in Brighton. He works as a freelance journalist and English teacher, frequently embarking on ambitious travel projects, documenting European countries and the lives lived within them.

He is officially banned from a small town just outside Rome, and played two seasons of semi-professional football in the Slovenian national league.

Gatecrashing Europe

Kris Mole

Valley Press

First published in 2015 by Valley Press
Woodend, The Crescent, Scarborough, YO11 2PW
www.valleypressuk.com

This second edition first published in 2020

ISBN 978-1-912436-24-8
Cat. no. VP0144

A CIP record for this book is available from the British Library.

Cover illustration by Diego Blanco López (diegoblanco.net)

Cover design by Peter Barnfather.
Text design by Jamie McGarry.

Printed and bound in Great Britain by
Ashford Colour Press, Gosport.

Contents

This book is dedicated to the memory of my aunt
Susan Proto 1952 – 2007
for whom I completed the challenge

1. Terry Wogan Plants a Seed

I DON'T LIKE the Eurovision Song Contest. I love it. And despite the loss of Terry Wogan, and despite being a heterosexual male, I always will. You see, for me as a young boy growing up poor – first in South-East London, then Brighton – the Eurovision Song Contest provided me with my only glimpse of what the continent across the water had to offer: jolly fat men with moustaches, and the beautiful girls who loved them. And smiles: big, cheesy and, most importantly, genuine smiles. Europe took on mythical status in my pre-pubescent mind as, come the end of the annual Saturday night's entertainment, I would drift off to sleep with dreams that one day I too might get to experience that Promised Land. I wasn't yet eight years old but already I was a confirmed Europhile – and this in itself was quite some feat because, at that age, my limited vocabulary didn't yet include the word Europhile.

There were no holidays for my family. We couldn't afford a bus ticket to school, never mind a flight to some overcrowded Spanish resort. My sister and I were lucky if we had more than a slice of lettuce to go between the two slices of bread we took to school each day and generously called a sandwich. So the night of the Eurovision Song Contest became my substitute getaway; Terry Wogan my tour guide for the evening, as I travelled the length and breadth of the continent without leaving the comfort of my settee.

Years passed with no decline in my fascination for all things Euro; and then came the afternoon that my mum told me that to make a bit of extra cash through the summer we would be hosting language students from, yep, you guessed it – Europe! This was to be my first interaction with anyone foreign; I had to impress. In the weeks leading up to the arrival of our first guests, I spent hours each night spread out on the living room floor writing down and memorising words from my mum's French and German dictionaries. I instantly found that I was fascinated by foreign language and couldn't wait to start practising on our guests. And then they came. Stefan and Andre: two Germans with long hair and denim jackets; and for two weeks I worshipped these two men. That's right, these were no boys; these were sixteen-year old men. For only men were allowed to go out into town in the evening unaccompanied, mingling with girls and smoking cigarettes; I wasn't even allowed in the front garden on my own after dinner. Stefan and Andre were the perfect guests: polite, intelligent, spoke fluent English, tidied up after themselves, ate whatever they were given and, most importantly of all, were patient with the annoying and curious young boy of the family. Actually, they were more than patient, taking me under their wing and letting me tag along in their free time, hanging out on the beach with their large group of German school friends and playing football in the park. I would look on in awe at Andre while his girlfriend sat on his lap, sharing a smoke or an apple. Europeans ate *fruit!*

The whole group made me feel like a peer rather than the little kid that I was. I was sad the day we dropped Stefan and Andre off at the coach station for their journey home, but comforted by the fact that in a few days' time we would be welcoming some new faces into our house: girls… French girls. Over the next two years we had a regular stream of these exotic young people sharing our roof for a couple of weeks at a time, and a pattern quickly took shape. When we had boys, we would talk about and play football; and when we had girls, I would stare at their beauty and wish that I were older. I would remain sad for a short period after each departure until the coming of new friends lifted my spirits.

At the age of twelve, these summers of European exposure ended, as it was no longer practical for my sister and I to share a bedroom. I spent the next few years in the wilderness – apart from one Saturday evening every twelve months, when Terry would take me away for a few hours. My contact with Europe may have been cut, but the dream lived on. One day I would smile like the Europeans. After all, I was a twelve-year old boy with my whole life ahead of me and was, according to my teachers at least, full of potential. Yet even at this tender age I already had a huge regret in life: that I hadn't been born European; popping out of my mum's body with a bit of designer stubble and a cigarette poking nonchalantly out of the side of my mouth.

When I was sixteen, a dream was fulfilled. A dream I had harboured since long before hair had started sprouting proudly out of previously bald parts. I kissed a girl. I know what you're thinking, but let me stop you in your tracks – this was not my first kiss. I had kissed many girls by the age of sixteen. Okay, not many, but a few. This was, however, my first *European* kiss. The evening had started like any other; three of us schoolmates out in town for a bit of underage drinking in a bar on the promenade that didn't check IDs. A few hours later we were stood at the bus stop, the only natives in a sea of foreign students making their way back to their host families after an evening of activities, just like our students had done each night all those years previously. Only something was different now, something had changed. I wasn't tucked up in bed. I wasn't a little kid. I was a man; for only *men* were allowed to go out into town in the evening unaccompanied, mingling with girls and smoking cigarettes. Well, only one of us smoked – and it wasn't me – and none of us were mingling with any girls, but we were definitely out in town. And we had been drinking beer, and not from a can in the park, but in a bar with other like-minded grown-ups. Yes, we were men. I cleared my throat.

'Men,' I said, 'why are we not mingling with girls?'

There was silence, followed by the shrugging of shoulders. Lee looked down to the ground, James looked down to the ground and I looked down to the ground. We were not men. We were shy little boys who should have been tucked up in bed long ago instead of taking up space that could have been filled by proper men. The number two bus pulled up and, along with a swarm of strange-language-speaking blondes, we boarded, taking the last three available seats upstairs, none of which were next to each other.

If I were a man, I would turn to this beautiful girl sat next to me and say something friendly and intelligent, I thought angrily to myself. *But I am not! I am just a young boy not worthy of such a seat.*

'Hi.'

Yes, I would say hi and from there a beautiful conversation would develop. Hang on, did she just say hi?

I turned my head slightly to the right and my eyes were met by a beaming smile: a Eurovision smile.

'Hi,' I replied, in a squeaky voice that definitely didn't belong to any man. And sure enough a conversation developed. The English language didn't have a word capable of conveying how I felt when I looked into the twinkling eyes of Kristina, this 16-year old from Helsinki. Kristina's host family lived a couple of miles further along the bus route than me, but this didn't stop me from bidding Lee and James farewell for the evening as the bus stopped close to our homes and they jumped off; while I carried on into the next town, locked in deep and meaningful conversation.

'Do you want to walk in the park for a little while?' Kristina asked me as we got off at her stop. 'I don't have to be in until 11:30. We still have half an hour and I am enjoying your company.'

I nodded. Five minutes later, under the glare of streetlights beaming through the trees into the park, we stood with our arms wrapped around each other and our lips locked together; for I was a man.

From that day on I never looked back. Every evening throughout the summer months was spent making friends with the hundreds of students that flooded into the city, and every night ended with a kiss. Every night except one, when I experienced my first European slap round the face, courtesy of a feisty Swede. But that's a story for another day. I had made up my mind. I didn't want a Lisa, a Becky or a Tracey when I now knew I could have a Valentina, a Maria or an Ana. Together with Lee, one of my best mates from school, we worked our way through almost every nationality the continent had to offer, learning in the process about countries I knew almost nothing about: Slovenia, Estonia, Lithuania. I soon found myself more and more attracted to one nationality of girl in particular: Italian. I can't tell you if it was down to the accent, the way they dressed, their long dark silky hair or their curvy figures; there was just something different about the Italian female. There was, though, one slight problem with preferring Italians to the Scandinavians and Germans of this world: their grasp on the English language tended to be well below average, meaning that too many romantic a word went wasted. So I did what (I presume) any man in my position would do: I went to the shop and bought an Italian dictionary, before enrolling in an evening class in the Italian language at a local adult education centre; not caring one little bit that I wasn't actually an adult. It wasn't long before I was conversing nightly in the language I had only just picked up (on a basic level, at least) and, at the age of 18, with the summer period over and with money in my pocket from the job I held in a ceramics showroom, I booked a budget week in Italy's capital. Alone. If it were a film it would be titled *Rome Alone*. But it wasn't a film, it was just my first holiday abroad.

Unfortunately, the week that promised language immersion, culture, history, cuisine and romance took on a completely different shape on the very first day when I stumbled upon Finnegan's, an Irish pub close to the Coliseum. I liked it in Finnegan's. I liked it in there a little too much. After returning to Brighton and embarrassingly explaining to people that all I could really remember of Italy was throwing up on my jeans, falling into a fountain and being the victim of an attempted robbery on the street by a couple of Russian thugs, I vowed to return… and this time for more than just a fleeting visit.

'I'm moving to Rome,' I told Lee one evening whilst sitting in his living room watching *Good Morning Vietnam*, 'Fancy coming along?'

'Yeah, okay. Might as well,' was Lee's surprising response.

So the decision was made. In February 2003, aged 19, I flew to Rome on a one-way ticket along with Lee and another old school friend Matt, with less than £700 in my pocket and no plans in place for when we arrived. Money soon ran out, and after a month we had given up any hopes of finding work. We got kicked out of the apartment we rented in the suburbs when we could no longer afford the weekly rent, and headed into the centre of the city to find a cheap hostel to stay in until we could arrange for someone back in England to transfer us enough money to book a flight home. The hostel we stumbled into was looking for a couple of cleaners and a receptionist, and nine months later I was still running the front desk. Everything had fallen nicely into place and I felt completely at home in Italy's capital, wondering if I would ever want to return to England. Then one day, completely out of the blue, I was called into my boss' office and told that I was surplus to requirements and was being let go. *Oh well,* I thought, *it's been great while it lasted, but I suppose returning to Brighton and getting a proper job wouldn't hurt too much.*

Before making my way home there was somewhere I first

had to see: Slovenia. I had fallen for a colleague in the hostel, a Slovene girl who worked through the summer but had to return home for the resumption of her university studies. I needed to see her one last time before leaving the European mainland. I took a train and spent two weeks in the capital, Ljubljana. When I left, I knew I was in love for the first time in my life; and as luck would have it, the object of my affections, Vanja, seemed pretty smitten with me too. On the way to the airport for my flight home, I bought a Slovenian language course, and as soon as I got back to Brighton I set about learning as much of it as I could, whilst enrolling in a course to get myself qualified as a teacher of English as a second language. It took just a couple of months working a night shift in Marks and Spencer to save enough money to make my next move, and in February 2004, armed with a teaching certificate and £1000 in cash, I flew one-way to Ljubljana where I rented a cheap studio flat. Before long I was playing football for a team in the national league, and had got myself a job at the most prestigious language school in the country… and all because Terry Wogan had planted that seed in my young, impressionable mind.

Slovenia became my home and Vanja, after a couple of years of sharing a flat with me, became my fiancée. England became but a distant memory. I worked mornings in the school; spent evenings with my football team; adapted to the culture and the language; travelled to other ex-Yugoslav republics whenever the opportunity arose and fell in love with the country that had offered me a living. Unfortunately, I also gambled compulsively, and when ankle ligament damage forced me to give up the football, I threw myself more and more into the world of betting. My team trained four days a week and played matches at the weekend. We went on tours together, played in tournaments across the continent and spent a lot of time participating in social activities that brought families, girlfriends and wives into the mix. It was a way of life. So when

I could no longer play I didn't know what to do with myself. Do a university degree? Volunteer for some charity work? Read *War and Peace*? Nah, I know – I'll gamble more.

Three years after moving to Slovenia, I found myself in more debt than I could handle and had to make the difficult decision to once again return to Brighton with my reputation in tatters and my relationship with Vanja – a girl who had given me nothing but love – in ruins, thanks to my destructive addiction.

As I sit here now, I can't help but think back to my childhood, and the posters pasted all over the walls of my school with messages like:

'Alcohol – Just say No!'

'Drugs – Just say No!'

'Cigarettes – Just say No!'

I am amazed that the local police liaison officer didn't have the foresight to campaign on a much more common problem. Where was the poster saying:

'Some intimidating Montenegrin mafia characters are offering you lots of credit to play poker in their illegal games room in the attic of a small unlit bar up a side alley that you would never have known was there unless you were specifically searching for a game you had overheard a degenerate gambler talking to his mate about in the post office – JUST SAY NO!'

Back in Brighton I soon found employment in another language school and after a couple of months Vanja followed me so that we could have one final attempt at making our situation work. It wasn't to be, and in the summer of 2007 she returned to Slovenia; our partnership had failed. To take my mind off of the painful situation I had caused I threw myself into work and getting fit again. I also decided I would go to Palestine for a few months to volunteer with an aid organisation. The only thing delaying my departure was funding; my gambling was out of control, but I would be good to go by October, I had money due to me from the language school. I handed in my notice and worked through the final month in a daze, not knowing what lay ahead of me but feeling more than ever that I needed to get away from it all. After having my independence for so many years abroad, it was now unbearable living back at my family home with my mum and dad.

It was a warm September's evening when I turned up at football training with the local team I had recently joined, ready to participate in my first full session since the injury. Five minutes later, as I lay on the ground screaming in agony, I knew that I had damaged the same problem ligaments in my ankle as before. The physiotherapist had convinced me that I was healed; turns out he wasn't a very reliable physiotherapist. I took the news that I wouldn't be able to play badly, and slipped back into old ways, spending my nights drinking and gambling, flitting my way through the Palestine fund in no time. I had fucked up. The language school had already replaced me, and as the summer was now over there wouldn't be a lot of teaching work on offer anyway. The future looked bleak, I was skint and depressed, until the October evening that changed everything.

As I sat in front of the computer at home playing poker, I received a phone call from a German girl I had worked with in the school, Stefanie. Stefanie and I had had a brief fling towards the end of the summer, but it had quickly fizzled out as we realised we were much better suited as friends. She was out having a few leaving drinks with ex-colleagues; she was due to leave England and return to Germany, and she wanted to meet me afterwards to say goodbye. At first I made my excuses, much preferring the idea of staying in and continuing my gambling session, but after a few moments of thinking I called her back and said I would be there in an hour. I hadn't been out in a while and didn't like how unsocial I had become.

We bought a few bottles of beer and sat on the beach, under the stars, listening to the water gently washing in against the pebbles; and as the alcohol loosened my tongue, I told her how envious I was that she was getting away from Brighton.

'What do you want to do, Kris?' she asked, as I sat sulking like the little kid that I still was.

'I want to get out of here. I want to see new places, meet new people. I wanted to go to Palestine but now I've blown that option through my own stupidity. I lived on the continent for four years in total, and in all that time I only ever saw a small handful of places. I want to know what's out there. I want to smile like they do in the Eurovision Song Contest!'

'The Eurovision Song Contest? Sorry, what?'

'Don't worry. I want to see Europe.'

'Then do it. Go travelling.'

'I can't, can I? I've no money and now no job either. Sometimes I think about just buying a cheap ferry ticket to Calais and seeing how far I can go without cash in my pocket – just walking off into the French horizon,' I told her, honestly.

'You're crazy,' she said, 'but knowing you as I do, I wouldn't be surprised if you tried something that ridiculous.'

I remained silent for a couple of minutes, lost in imagination, before turning to her with a glint in my eye that hadn't been there for quite some time. I mean the glint hadn't been there for quite some time; the eye had been there since birth. Since before birth actually.

'I am going to do it. I am going to go and see Europe. And I am going to do it without any money. Who needs cash anyway?'

Stefanie looked at her watch and saw that it was coming up for four in the morning. She had heard me come out with a thousand and one foolish drunken ideas since we'd met and she knew that after a sleep I would have forgotten all about this one.

'Come on, I'll walk you home,' I said, as we picked up our empties and staggered across the pebbles.

I dropped Stefanie off at her door and set off for home. As I walked I noticed a spring in my step as my mind raced with the thought of really doing what I had said I would. But how would it be possible? I needed a goal. I needed a plan. I needed a wee. So I found an alleyway.

After a few hours' sleep I dragged myself up for the walk down to the bookies before returning home and making some tea and toast. It was like any other Saturday: I would sit on the settee in a pair of shorts, watch Soccer Saturday on Sky Sports, rip up my losing bet slips and tell myself that next weekend would be the one that would set me up properly. Celtic wouldn't give away a 91st minute equaliser to balls up my accumulator and I would be able to start building a roll for myself. Except this wasn't like any other Saturday, because five minutes into the afternoon kick-offs I lost interest in what was going on in stadiums around the country and logged on to the internet to read travel forums and blogs, in search of information about travelling for free. All I found were the usual hitchhiking tales and details of farms that offered accommodation in exchange for hard labour, but that wasn't what I was after. I didn't want to spend my time milking cows or cleaning out horse shit, that wasn't what travelling meant to me. Travelling was not knowing from one day to the next where you would be in 24 hours' time; it was witnessing rituals that were alien to you; crossing borders and having your passport checked. The ideas started flowing. What if I started in the north of France and tried to make it to Turkey? No, wait, a better idea... What if I could find enough money for a flight to Morocco and then try to make my way home over land? No, too boring. What if I tried to get to every country in the European Union? Yes, that's it! No, wait, that's too easy. I knew, for example, that there was a point in the Alps where you could be in Austria, Slovenia and Italy almost simultaneously. And then it came to me:

Every capital city in the European Union.

That evening I went to see my aunt Susan in hospital where she was bravely battling lung cancer. I sat by her bed and watched as the doctors and nurses did their best to keep the patients comfortable, and I felt sad. Sad that so many people around me were dying. And then the light bulb above my head flicked on and I had my final idea. My mission to get to every capital city without any money would be called The Great Euro Freebie Challenge, and in the process of completing it I would raise funds and awareness for Cancer Research UK through sponsorships. I would dedicate the journey to Susan Proto, my battling aunt.

The next week or so was spent in preparation for this, the biggest ordeal I had ever thought of putting myself through. I set up an account on the fundraising website Justgiving.com, who would manage all sponsorships that I received and make sure the money went straight into the coffers of Cancer Research UK. I set up a blog where people would be able to follow my preparations, and eventually the actual journey. I posted on travel forums and Facebook the details of the trip I was planning. I got people interested. I emailed the local papers to ask them to spread the word. I wrote up the official rules that I would live by:

1. No money will be handled by or spent by me.
2. No credit cards will be used.
3. I will visit every European Union capital city on the physical continent.
4. I will say yes to any unplanned opportunities that arise.
5. Donations from people I meet along the way of anything other than cash will be accepted.
6. I will update the blog whenever I get the opportunity.
7. As England is not on the mainland, the challenge will begin in a foreign city.
8. I will not let any woman compromise the challenge.

That was basically it as far as rules were concerned.

Let me explain rule number three in a bit more detail. The European Union consisted at the time of 26 countries, they were: Austria, Belgium, Bulgaria, Cyprus, Czech Republic, Denmark, Estonia, Finland, France, Germany, Greece, Hungary, Ireland, Italy, Latvia, Lithuania, Luxembourg, Netherlands, Poland, Portugal, Romania, Slovakia, Slovenia, Spain, Sweden, and the UK. Three of these countries – the UK, Ireland and Cyprus – were all islands and, as such, not part of what I considered to be 'the continent.' My mission was to see the continent, so these three were taken out of the equation, leaving me with a list of 23 capital cities. As for rule four, say I was standing at the side of the road in the Czech Republic trying to hitch a lift to Prague when a driver pulled over and said, 'I'm not going anywhere near the capital but I am going to a small village that you have never heard of before and I invite you to come along for the ride and to meet my family', I would have to accept this offer. This should lead to interactions and experiences that otherwise would not take place, and would add to the unpredictability of the journey. Onto rule number seven. I would start the journey on the continent. After much deliberation, I decided against beginning my trek in any of Lisbon, Athens or Helsinki and opted instead for the Swedish capital of Stockholm. From there I didn't know whether I would head up and across the Scandinavian north to get round to Helsinki, or south to Denmark and through to Germany. That would be decided once at my starting point. Finally rule number eight. As is probably obvious by now, my initial fascination for all things European was sparked by those dangerous (and wonderful) little creatures: girls. However, The Great Euro Freebie Challenge had to be bigger, stronger and more important than any fling I would potentially have along the way. This was my personal project and I would see it through to the end without any unnecessary complications. For I was a man and this was my calling.

So, the rules were in place and I was ready to go. The last thing I needed now was time to talk myself out of things, so I found a one-way flight to Stockholm with Scandinavian airline SAS for under £50 and booked it immediately. Departure date was set for the 1st of November 2007, which was just a week away. If I spent a couple of days in each capital, I would be home in time for Christmas. That was the plan. One of the local papers, the *Shoreham Herald*, sent a photographer round to take my picture, I went out on one final bender with my mates and I filled my rucksack to the brim with warm clothes and a sleeping bag. A random email from an American student who had stumbled across my blog advised me to have a look at a website called Couchsurfing, which I did. Couchsurfing was an online community with members all over the world who were willing to have complete strangers spend a night or two sleeping on their settee or floor. Members' profiles included a photo, a description of what the guest would be sleeping on, a bit about themselves and, most importantly, references that had been left by other Couchsurfers who had either stayed with or hosted the person. This website would save me having to regularly sleep in train stations, parks and by the roadside. It would also introduce me to people my own age. I quickly created a profile and emailed a couple of Stockholm residents, Philippe and Mia, explaining why I was soon to be in their city and asking if either of them would be able to put me up for a night or two. Positive replies came almost immediately from both, but Mia's came slightly earlier and I accepted her offer. After thanking Philippe for his kind offer and letting him know I was now sorted, he told me to take his mobile number in case something went wrong and I found myself in a desperate situation once there.

I had just one more thing to do before setting off in search of that Eurovision smile. On the evening of the 31st October I went to see Susan one last time. Just as I was leaving and giving her a final kiss on the forehead, she leant in, looked me in the eyes and asked, 'Are you really going to see this challenge through to the end?'

'Yep.'

'Good boy.'

2. Stockholm

Capitals left to visit: Amsterdam, Athens, Berlin, Bratislava, Brussels, Bucharest, Budapest, Copenhagen, Helsinki, Lisbon, Ljubljana, Luxembourg, Madrid, Paris, Prague, Riga, Rome, Sofia, Tallinn, Vienna, Vilnius, Warsaw

Days on the road: 1
Distance travelled: 0 miles
EU capitals visited: 1

STOCKHOLM AIRPORT IN the afternoon smells like cinnamon. There's a piece of valuable information that you won't gain from Lonely Planet.

I was stood at the conveyor belt waiting for my belongings to show up when I spotted it. Surely it wasn't mine. It couldn't be. It was. My sleeping bag, probably the thing that I would need more than anything on a trip with no money, had been slashed from top to bottom and all the fluff was coming out the sides. I picked it up and threw it straight into the bin. The Great Euro Freebie Challenge was off to a flying start.

Tickets for the city bus had to be bought in advance from a little kiosk inside the airport. This was going to be my first blagging challenge of the journey and the thought of it filled me with nerves and trepidation. My apprehension didn't bode too well, considering I was at the very start of a trip in which every little necessity would have to be acquired for free. I approached the woman behind the counter and asked her if she had a couple of minutes for me to tell her a story. She smiled and told me to continue. I quickly explained the basic idea of my journey and I told her about Mia, who was waiting for me in Stockholm proper, and how I was worried that if I didn't get there in time I might not have a place to sleep for the night. As I went through things I could see from her facial expression that I was wasting my breath. I finished up and asked the obvious question of whether it would be possible to get a free ticket for the bus, to which she replied, 'I'm really sorry. It's great what you are doing and I wish you luck, but it is not possible for me to give any tickets away without taking the money. I would get myself into trouble. The only thing that I can suggest is that you try speaking to the driver of the bus. I really am sorry.'

I could tell she was being sincere and I felt embarrassed to have put her in the position I had. I also felt embarrassed to be begging for something. Just as I was thanking the woman for her time I was tapped on the shoulder. I turned around to see a young couple that had been waiting behind me in the queue to buy tickets.

'Excuse me. We heard your story and we can help you. It isn't a lot, but we can offer you a bus ticket to the city centre. Would you accept our offer?' said the Swedish girl with the friendly, round face.

I looked at her boyfriend to make sure that he agreed and when I saw him smiling I knew that they had discussed it and all was fine. I thanked the two of them as the man paid for three tickets; one for each of them and one for me. I had just experienced the first act of selfless kindness of the journey and it left me feeling a strange mix of extreme happiness and slight unease.

The bus ride from the airport to the city took about 40 minutes and dropped me off at the main bus station. I took the little piece of paper that I had written directions to Mia's on, checked the name of the local Metro station I needed to get to, and then set about trying to find the main train station.

It was evening rush hour and when I stumbled through the crowds and into the main terminus I wished I was anywhere else but where I now found myself. It was twice as hectic as London Victoria at the same time of evening and none of the signs were translated into English. I didn't want to ask anyone in a uniform for help, just in case he asked to see my ticket, so I stood in the middle of the bustling crowd and started asking people as they flew past me in all directions, 'Do you speak English?'

No one wanted to give me the time of day. Eventually someone pointed me in the direction of the Metro and, fighting my way against the stream of human traffic, I made my way there. It being rush hour did have its advantages, the main one being that I could slip through, ticketless, with the crowd. I got on the train and spent the entire journey with my face squashed up against the glass, as I listened to disgruntled Swedes tutting at me for blocking their exit paths with my backpack. I wasn't in the running to win any Scandinavian popularity contests.

I got to the station I was supposed to be at, Bandhagen, and walked up the stairs and through the small hall at the top. Waiting in the foyer was the solitary figure of Mia. She had dyed jet-black hair, piercing green eyes and dressed a bit emo. She smiled as she introduced herself. She led the way to her flat, a five minute walk from the station, and on the way we chatted. This was my very first Couchsurfing experience and I wondered if my nerves showed. I was about to pop my Couchsurfing cherry. Mia spoke with an Irish accent as strong as any Dubliner, a result of living and working in the Emerald Isle's capital for a number of years. She had also picked up their unique sense of humour and delivery. I felt immediately comfortable in her presence and in her flat. After a quick bite to eat, she took a phone call and then told me that a friend of hers wanted to meet me and buy me a beer. Who was I to turn down such a request?

We took the Metro to a trendy part of town called Södermalm. Looking around the bar my eyes were met with the sight of far too many good looking people to all be in the same place at the same time. Everyone was just standing around looking cool and Swedish. These were the sort of girls I would expect to see walking around the garden on Hugh Hefner's arm. One thing was blatantly clear looking at the male of the species: the Swedes were into their beards. *It must be the Viking genes,* I thought. Every single man in the bar sported bushy facial hair. Was it a characteristic of the modern Swedish man or had I fallen for the oldest trick in the book: Let's tell our guest we're taking him to a regular pub but really we'll take him to a beard convention?

We've all done it at one time or another.

After a few drinks we called it a night and headed back to the flat. Day one of the Great Euro Freebie Challenge was all but over and I was fed, watered and had a roof over my head. This was going to be a piece of piss.

I woke far too early the next morning, 7 o'clock to be precise. Mia had told me the evening before that she was only able to host me for one night as she had to leave town to visit family, so as soon as the hour was decent I called Philippe, the Stockholm resident who had given me his number before I'd left England, to see about crashing at his place for the night.

'Kris, I'm sorry mate, but I am not going to be in Stockholm tonight. I have to go to Oslo by train. Why don't you come with me? You can stay at my family place there,' he told me.

'I would love to come and see Norway but there's one problem. I am without money so train travel is not an option.'

'That's a shame. Is there no way you can get some money for the ticket?'

'Not possible. I have a budget of zero. But maybe I could persuade the train company to let me go for free.'

As I said it I wondered in my head if it could really be

done. The offer of a place to stay in Oslo was so random and unplanned that rule number four dictated that I accept it. I wanted adventure, I wanted to not know from one day to the next where I would be in 24 hours' time, I wanted to see places that I hadn't thought about when planning my route, I wanted to know that I had a place to sleep that night and I wanted to see Norway. Oslo was calling.

'Meet me at the station at 2 this afternoon. Our train leaves at 2:25. That will give you enough time to try and get on it,' I was instructed.

After thanking Mia for the night's entertainment and hospitality, I took the Metro back to Stockholm's main station, arriving a little bit before the arranged meeting time of 2 o'clock. I went directly to the ticket office and, just like the day before, explained my story to the woman behind the desk with a look of hope rather than expectation in my eyes. The woman didn't have the authority to give out any freebies but told me that it might be worth talking to the train's guard before it left.

'What are my chances of success?' I asked her before walking away.

'Slim,' she replied.

'I like those odds.'

I then went back outside the station to wait for Philippe, managing to publicly disgrace myself in the process. From carrying the heavy bags and having not eaten I was feeling uncomfortable, even more so because my belt wasn't doing a good enough job of holding up my jeans. I decided that I would feel better if I changed into a pair of tracksuit bottoms. None of the public toilets could be entered without paying a small fee so instead I looked around outside for a quiet spot to quickly get changed in. I stumbled upon a deserted little area at the back of the station, where the only person in sight was a well-dressed, middle-aged woman waiting for a coach. Behind her was a little wall that seemed perfectly placed to protect my dignity. I stood behind it, thinking that the woman would have enough interesting things on her mind not to bother paying me any attention. I slightly over estimated the scale of the woman's thoughts though, as rather than pay no attention she did a very bad job of watching me inconspicuously. I didn't care; I just wanted to change as quickly as possible and get back into the warmth of the station. I emptied out all of my pockets onto the cold concrete and then dug around in my little rucksack to find my bottoms, dropping a few bits of fruit onto the floor in the process. I kicked off my shoes and quickly removed my jeans. Then, as I stood in my boxers, bending over to pick up the replacement piece of clothing, I looked up to find the woman still staring at me, no longer bothering to try and look inconspicuous. I made eye contact and was surprised to see a shocked look spreading across her face. Her eyes weren't meeting mine but seemed to be focused on something more captivating. I was curious, so followed her line of vision slowly down my body to the thing that was causing such amazement. I gasped as I saw my penis poking out of my flies and taking a good look around at his surroundings. The phrase, 'like a sitting duck,' springs to mind. The woman quickly disappeared. I hurriedly started pulling my tracksuit bottoms on; panicking that she would return with a policeman, telling him that I had flashed her. Before I had finished pulling up my trousers I looked up and saw that she had indeed returned and was now speaking to me in Swedish. She didn't seem angry, but rather was speaking quite nicely and in a friendly tone. I tried to explain that I didn't understand but she just kept on. Then I got the gist of what she was saying. She was asking me where I was from.

'Romania? Bulgaria? Hungaria?'she suggested.

I know the country is called Hungary and not Hungaria, by the way. It was her who didn't. Anyway, what? Here was a strange looking guy, in an international bus station, all his worldly belongings including an apple and a banana spread out on the floor in front of him, wearing a crappy pair of tracksuit bottoms and he'd just got his knob out. For some reason, she had come to the conclusion that I was a gypsy – or maybe just a Romanian flasher – but either way I had a feeling this wasn't good.

'No, I'm from England. England,' I tried to explain.

'England? No, no, no, no. Romania, yes.'

She shook her head, laughed and walked quickly off. I put my penis away – I had failed to do it whilst protesting my nationality – pulled up my bottoms, picked up my bags and ran in the opposite direction, hiding behind a car as she returned to the spot with a couple of gun-carrying cops. The Great Euro Freebie Challenge was but a day old and already I was a wanted man in a foreign land, and from what I have heard, sex pests are not given the warmest of welcomes in prison in any country.

I waited for Philippe to show up and wondered what I would do if I wasn't able to get to Oslo. I had nowhere to sleep for the night, it was freezing cold, my sleeping bag no longer existed and a police sketch of my ugly mug – and possibly penis – was no doubt already being printed in the thousands to be stuck up on lamp posts all over the city. I wondered if the Stockholm constabulary would at least let me use the image for the front cover of this book. The one of my face. Not the one of my cock.

Philippe arrived ten minutes later and seemed nervous about the idea of crossing an international border with a fugitive. He went to buy his own ticket while I entered the platform and found the waiting train's ticket inspector standing at ease. I tapped him on the shoulder and when I had his attention whipped out the *Shoreham Herald*, open to the page with my picture spread across it, and put it in his hands, explaining that I would be sleeping rough in Stockholm if he didn't let me ride to Oslo. I could barely believe it when he laughed and told me to get on carriage number 15. I was going to Norway. For free.

The train slowly pulled out of the station and I panicked as I realised Philippe hadn't made it in time. I would have to fend for myself in Oslo. Then I saw him traipsing through the completely packed carriage towards me, a look of disbelief on his face that I had sorted out free passage. We managed to find two seats next to each other and we started talking. Philippe was Swedish but of Hungarian parents. He was 34 years old, athletically built with short, brown curly hair, and a medical student studying in Sweden's capital.

Immediately evident about his character was that he was a bit of a sleaze when it came to the female sex. Every single story he told – and there were hundreds – was about his sexual exploits. I found each one harder than the last to believe, as he was hardly an oil painting and also had a way of making me feel quite uncomfortable. He had this habit of just staring, wide-eyed, deeply into your eyes when talking. No blinking, no looking away for a second, just staring. Less than ten minutes into my conversation with Philippe I was given my first taste of what to expect over the next few days.

'Wait here, I have to do something,' he said, standing up and leaving his seat.

I watched as he strolled down the carriage and up to the buffet, I assumed to buy something to eat. After a few minutes, when still no food had been handed over, I realised that he was trying to pull the waitress. He seemed to be doing a good job of it. I sat and waited for about 15 minutes before watching him enter her phone number into his mobile, kiss her hand and then return to his seat. He said nothing but threw me a smug look that said, 'That's how I roll.' He then slept for a few hours before waking at around 6:30pm and dragging himself lethargically up the carriage towards the toilets. He returned a few minutes later buzzing, full of a newly acquired energy.

'There are two gorgeous blonde girls sitting up there watching a film on their laptop. We should go and talk to them,' he enthused.

I told him that I really didn't feel like chatting to anyone and that they probably wanted to be left alone to enjoy the film. He seemed disappointed in me and also adamant that they were sitting there waiting for us to make our move, but after a few minutes of unsuccessful attempts at changing my mind he gave up and sat quietly again. This was going to be a long couple of days. A few minutes later the two girls walked past us and down to the buffet. Philippe had been right about one thing: they weren't harsh on the eye. They bought a couple of cans of beer and as they walked past us and back to their seats Philippe did what I hoped he wouldn't.

'Excuse me girls,' for some strange reason he chose to speak in English. 'I noticed before that you were watching a DVD. I was just wondering if my friend and I could join you as we are pretty bored.'

I sat, staring out of the window, embarrassed by his technique.

'The batteries died, so we can't watch it anymore,' replied one of the girls, before asking him in Swedish if he could speak Swedish.

He told her that of course he could but that he preferred if we all spoke English so that everyone present – meaning me – would be able to follow the conversation. The girls then asked me where I was from and seemed quite impressed by the mere fact that I was English. Why is anyone's guess. Still embarrassed by Philippe's style, I kept my eyes on the window.

'Why don't you come and sit with us,' one of the girls then said.

'Great,' said Philippe, 'first though, I'll go and get us a couple of beers.'

The girls walked back to their seats while Philippe winked at me. I knew that to get on well with this guy I was going to have to get used to his one-track mind. We joined the girls and got talking. Philippe seemed to want to use my story for his own gain and immediately started explaining to them about my journey and how he was the guy I had chosen to help me through my time in Sweden and Norway. Our new friends didn't know what to make of my challenge; the only conclusion they were able to come to was that I must be mad. I quickly found myself talking to one of the girls about her time in Brighton – she had spent a month there as a language student some years previous. I tried to remember if I had pulled her during my youth – while Philippe's interactions with the opposite sex continued to leave me feeling uneasy. I watched out of the corner of my eye as he invaded the personal space of the girl he was talking to, asked her far too many personal questions and also freaked her out with that habit of opening his eyes really wide, as if he were either constantly surprised or just a plain old psychopath. As our train approached Oslo Philippe took both girls' numbers in his mobile and also gave them his. They told us that they were going to a party the following evening and that they might be able to pull a few strings to get us invited. It was obvious that they were just being polite to keep Philippe from pestering them. As we walked back to our seats to get our stuff together he said, 'Did you see how badly they wanted us? Your story's a winner. It is going get us so much action over these next few days.'

I didn't say anything. I didn't know what to say.

Our train pulled into Oslo's main station at 9:03pm, almost seven hours after leaving Stockholm.

Welcome to Oslo.

3. Oslo

As we walked through the station towards the main exit, Philippe spotted an attractive girl working behind the counter of a tobacco shop and decided he would…?

If you answered: 'Acknowledge her beauty with a little inward smile and then walk on by,' you haven't been paying attention and need to go back and read the last chapter again. If, however, you answered: 'Try to pull her', give yourself a pat on the back.

Philippe stuck with his usual technique of just chatting utter bollocks, and again for some reason spoke in English. The poor girl did everything she could to express her lack of interest until eventually her huge musclebound boss appeared from behind a door and told my host that if he wasn't going to buy anything then he would have to vacate the premises. Sheepishly, Philippe did as he was told.

'Why did you speak English to her?' I asked. 'We're in Oslo, not London.'

'Because if I spoke to her in Norwegian she would tell from my accent that I am Swedish, and I don't want her to know that.'

'Okay, but did you know that when you speak English to these girls you speak with a really strong accent? And I don't mean a Scandinavian one. You sound like an Indian. But when you speak to me, you are completely accentless. You have two different versions of English.'

What I was saying was true. He had been educated at a private school in England and could speak perfect English without even a hint of a foreign twang, but somehow felt the need to change the way he spoke when communicating with non-mother tongue speakers. To listen to him speaking to me and then to a Scandinavian was like listening to Hugh Grant morph into Apu from the Simpsons.

Once outside in the open air we had a decision to make. Philippe's nan's house – the place where we would be spending the next few nights – was outside the city. If we wanted to go out on the town this evening we wouldn't have time to go home and drop my rucksack off and then come back, and Philippe had his sex-obsessed mind set on meeting girls, so the only option was to find a storage place. The lockers in the train station were expensive and Philippe didn't want to pay for one when he was sure we would be able to find a free alternative.

'Leave them in a hotel,' he suggested.

'How can we leave our bags in a hotel that we are not staying at?'

'The newspaper, of course.'

He answered in a tone that said, 'Do you really have to ask?'

It actually made sense. The newspaper had already secured me a free train journey, it was time to put it to the test and see what else it could provide. The closest hotel was a big 5-star place called The Opera, so off we headed. We walked through the doors and up to the desk where a young lady sat, looking bored. She seemed genuinely happy to have some people to talk to and, after hearing my story, was eager to help. She called for a bus boy to take my bags to the storage room, and handed me a key to a very plush bathroom in which to freshen up and change my clothes for the evening.

My first impression of Norway's capital after leaving the hotel behind and observing the life around me was that it was quite different to Sweden and a lot more similar to England as far as atmosphere and behaviour were concerned. The men were boisterous and aggressive; the girls were drunk and loud. It was Friday night and everyone was out with the same plan: to get well and truly shit-faced. Philippe decided that our best bet if we were to meet local women was to head down into the centre of town, but before doing so we were stopped by a couple of police officers. Everyone entering the main square was being given the once over with a hand-held metal detector as the cops checked for knives and other weapons. It was all a bit different to the passive atmosphere of Stockholm. After not finding anything offensive on me, the policewoman smiled and wished me a pleasant stay in Oslo. The streets were full of young people drinking from bottles and cans. Everybody seemed completely wasted already and the night was still young. Strangely, none of the city's establishments seemed to have any clientele. Philippe explained that the cost of drinking in bars and clubs was so ridiculously sky high that people just couldn't afford it, so instead the custom was to drink from the supermarket, get mullered before entering any place, then to nurse one or two more drinks for the rest of the night. I was taken on a basic tour of the small city and I liked what I saw. Oslo was lively, with little bars spread all over the place. The night air was getting colder and we didn't have any pre-bought alcohol, so we entered the first bar we came across that had more than a small handful of people inside. Philippe got the beers in before marching straight over to a table full of girls, dragging me along for the ride. He introduced himself and then me before proceeding to tell them the story of how his English friend found himself in Norway. I couldn't believe that he was using me so shamelessly, but then I also couldn't believe that they all seemed so interested. I found myself chatting with a girl who made it clear that I wouldn't be pulling her by making sure she mentioned her boyfriend in every other sentence. Not that I was thinking about pulling. I was just happy to be engaging in conversation with someone other than Philippe. Talking of Philippe, he was now going from girl to girl in this group of friends, trying to find out which one would be most likely to let him into her knickers later on in the evening. It was cringe-worthy but also harmless. He was starting to grow on me. The girl I was speaking to was excitable and full of energy and I was enjoying the chat, until I asked her how her day had been.

'Pretty strange actually. I used to go to school with this boy; he was always so nice, quiet and friendly. The kid that everyone liked. I haven't seen him for a few years, but he was in all the newspapers today,' she told me, laughing.

'Cool. What did he do? Something inspiring?'

'He beat his own mum to death with a hammer and is now awaiting sentencing.'

She was still laughing. Nervously, I laughed too. I downed my pint and looked around the room for an escape now that this conversation killer had been dropped. I took a second to look across and check on Philippe's progress and saw the realisation in his eyes that not one of these girls, no matter how much alcohol consumed, was going to give him what he craved. He motioned to me that it was time to leave. It was only 1am but I was well and truly cream crackered and was glad when my suggestion that we call it a night was accepted.

'Are you hungry?' Philippe asked.

'I could eat.'

'Then I'll get us a couple of kebabs before we take the bus. It's a long ride home and there's no food in the flat.'

The kebab house in question was identical to every kebab house on every English high street. A fat guy stood behind the counter, his body covered in dark fur, concealed only partially by a white vest. In his hand was a machete that swung dangerously from left to right as he swayed along to the Turkish music playing out of an old stereo next to the doner meat. I sought rest in a little white plastic chair in the corner, my face squashed up against the glass, sliding down occasionally until the point where something would wake me and I would pick myself back up. Time seemed to slow down as I slipped in and out of dreamland, all the time trying to stay alert enough not to be left behind and forgotten by Philippe. Where was he? I picked my head up from the windowsill and had a quick scan around. He was chatting up another group of girls, and not the most classically good-looking clan either. The one he had picked out for special attention was chubby with a perfectly circular face. She reminded me of a female cherub. Just for a change, Philippe had decided to conduct the conversation in English, and as I was handed my medium doner I wasn't best pleased to hear him agree to join the group in a bar that they had heard good things about. I just wanted to sleep, was that too much to ask? We followed them through the streets and entered this little place where the music was too loud and the patrons too drunk. Philippe didn't want to spend any more money on drinks so he just hovered around the girls, still trying to pull them, while they sipped on cocktails. While all of this was going on I was sat on a chair in the corner of the room, the place where everyone just came and chucked their coat. Everyone in there actually thought I was the cloakroom attendant and would ask me how much it cost to look after their belongings. That didn't really happen. I made it up. Imagine how bored I must have been at the time if even now as I write about it it still bores me so much that I have to resort to making up little stories just for my own amusement. Imagine that level of boredom.

Eventually the girls finished their cocktails and had obviously had enough of Philippe's attentions and so left. I perked up as this meant we could now go home and sleep. Philippe handed me his coat and told me to wait outside with it while he went to relieve himself in the toilets. My head filled with images of a bed, a blanket and a pillow. I couldn't wait.

I had been standing outside in the cold for about ten minutes when I started worrying about Philippe. Where was he now? Even if he had gone for a dump he would have been out a few minutes ago. I came to the conclusion that he had said the wrong thing to a girl and her boyfriend had beaten him up. He was definitely the kind of guy that that sort of thing happened to. I had to go and investigate. I pushed my way through the dancing drunkards and into the toilets. He wasn't there. I came out and back onto the dance floor from where I spotted him standing at the bar drinking a Red Bull. What the hell? He hadn't even bothered to bring me in from the cold. I walked up to him and threw him a disapproving look. That's what English people do when we get angry; we throw a disapproving look. I also made a mental note to remind myself later to send him an angry letter.

'Mate, there you are. Listen, I think I've found a girl. I was talking to her for a bit and she seems up for it. Anyway, we have missed our bus and the next one doesn't leave until 3:30, so there's no point just standing out in the cold. Come and dance,' he said.

I was fuming but what could I do? Philippe was my only point of contact in the city and I had nowhere else to go. He pointed out to me the girl that was the object of his desires: an extremely drunk creature surrounded by three equally grotesque men all trying to get a piece. I reasoned that the only reason she might want to get with Philippe was that she could smell kebab on him.

'Wait here,' Philippe then told me, as he made his way across the floor and into the girl's personal space. This was good, as I knew she would soon reject him and he would pick his coat up and head for the door. No such luck though, as no sooner had that thought crossed my mind than she grabbed him by the hand and led him to the dark corner of the dance floor where she put her arms around him and gave him a grinding. I felt sick, so I went back to looking after people's coats.

3am finally came, and with it closing time.

'Any luck with her?' I asked craftily, knowing full well the answer.

'No, mate. She told me at the end of the night that she had a boyfriend at home.'

'Oh, that's a shame. You wasted a good hour with her.'

I smiled. As we walked to the bus stop I felt like I was at home in England. All around, drunken girls carried their shoes in their hands while people pissed up the side of walls and vomited in the kerb. There were also fights kicking off everywhere. One particularly dramatic confrontation involved chairs being thrown and a bloke getting whacked round the head by someone holding a street sign. Welcome to Norway.

The bus to the town of Asker, 13 miles outside Oslo, took 45 minutes. Philippe's nan's house looked like an antiques shop that no one had taken care of. There were old black and white photos everywhere; hundreds of yellow-paged books on shelves, on the table, on the floor; and in the corner of the room sat an old grand piano. Philippe showed me to my room and I didn't even bother putting a sheet on the bed. I fell asleep immediately. I was woken at 10 the next morning by Philippe telling me to get up as there was a guy coming round in 20 minutes to look at the flat. Philippe's nan had recently been put in an old people's home and so he had come to Oslo to rent the property out on her behalf.

'I'm just going to have a quick tidy up in the living room to make it look a bit nicer. Can you do me a favour?' he asked.

'Of course. What is it?'

'Don't have a shit in the toilet until after he's been and gone. It will make the whole flat stink, as I don't want to open any windows and let the cold in. I really need to go myself, but am just going to have to hold it in. Thanks.'

I nodded.

Later that evening, as we sat relaxing in the living room, an intriguing photo on the wall caught my attention. It was black and white and showed a young, attractive woman breastfeeding a baby. Not your typical living room photo.

‘Who’s the lady in the picture?’ I asked.

‘That’s my nan breastfeeding my mum,’ he told me, matter-of-factly.

‘OK.’

It was Saturday night and Philippe had to go and visit his nan in the home, while I had to return to the city to pick up my stuff from the Opera Hotel. My train pulled in to Asker station and on it I got, making my way directly to the conductor as soon as we had started moving, explaining that I was in Norway with a group of mates on a stag weekend and that we were staying in a hotel in Oslo. We had taken a day-trip out to Asker – why we would go and visit a town that consisted solely of a library and a furniture shop, I didn’t take the time to explain – where my so-called mates had thought it would be hilarious to steal my wallet and train ticket and leave me stranded. I told him that I was desperate to get back to the safety of Oslo as I had no idea where I was and it was now getting dark and cold. The inspector laughed and told me not to worry; he would allow me to finish my journey into the capital. Nice bunch of people, those Scandinavians.

At the Opera Hotel, the male receptionist led me into the storage room where I sprayed myself with some deodorant before putting on a clean shirt. The guy watched me curiously.

‘This is the closest thing I can get to a shower,’ I told him. ‘I’ve not had the chance of a proper wash today.’

I expected either a laugh or for him to turn his nose up at me in disgust, so was pleasantly surprised by his response.

‘Why didn’t you say so? You can use the hotel’s gym to freshen yourself up properly. There’s a shower in there. I will get you the key.’

Yet more unconditional kindness. After showering, I was hungry. It was time to once again test the magical capabilities of the *Shoreham Herald*. I wandered along the side of the water by the marina until I came to a place called Peppes Pizza, which was an Indian curry house. I jest. Peppes Pizza was a pizzeria. I walked in and declined the head waitress's offer of a table for one, instead asking to speak to the manager. She said, 'No problem,' and led me through the diners to an office at the back, where a blonde woman – something of a rarity in Scandinavia – in her twenties was sitting at a desk adding up figures on a calculator. She introduced herself to me as the manager, which surprised me as I had been expecting to come face to face with someone that looked like either of the Super Mario Brothers, and not someone who looked like a contestant on the Eurovision Song Contest. Yes, she had that Eurovision smile. I handed her the Herald before telling her that I hadn't eaten a thing all day and would really appreciate it if she could throw some leftovers my way.

'Would you like a pizza?'

I hadn't been expecting anything more than a couple of garlic dough balls or a slice of inedible, burnt crust. Her offer of a full pizza humbled me. The kindness and friendliness I had so far encountered in the two Scandinavian countries was something quite special.

'A pizza would be very welcome. Thank you so much,' I told her.

'Okay, go with Irene, she will give you a pizza and whatever you want to drink. Good luck with everything and I am going to be following your progress through your blog.'

Irene led me to a table and brought me a glass of cola. Then the pizza was brought out. Hmmm, what to tell you about the pizza? I can honestly say that as far as quality goes, the base was fantastic. And I'm not just saying that to return the favour. If I was, I wouldn't then tell you what happened to the pizza. Well, half of the pizza. This pizza had two different types of topping, one on each half. One half was absolutely delicious: chilli beef and peppers. The second half wasn't as appetising, even after not eating for a day. Thai chicken with pineapple and peanuts. I was faced with a genuine dilemma. On the one hand, I couldn't waste food that had been so generously gifted to me. On the other: pineapple and peanuts.

I slowly ate the good half while my brain went through the options.

'Excuse me, Irene,' I called out.

'Yes? What can I get for you?'

'A doggy bag, please. You see, I won't have any food again tomorrow, so I want to save some of this for breakfast.'

I left the restaurant and handed the bag of food to the first homeless person I saw. It was a woman, and whether or not she ate my present is anyone's guess. I wouldn't hold it against her either way. Pineapple and peanuts; who orders that?

I met Philippe in a square. He had brought with him a ready-mixed bottle of vodka and Sprite, which I downed quickly to loosen me up a bit as I listened to him explain how we were going to use the newspaper to meet women. Walking past a bar, we came across a couple of girls standing outside, smoking. Philippe asked one of them for a light and then proceeded to try and get laid. He introduced me, but this time didn't mention my journey, so at least I didn't feel like I was being used. The girls were actually pretty cool. Philippe, not one to dilly-dally around the important issues, immediately asked them where they were heading and if we could accompany them.

Once again I was embarrassed and didn't know where to look. The girls, feeling like they had been put on the spot, said that we could come if we wanted to but that they didn't know where they were going. That old chestnut. We started walking with them and split into pairs. I ended up with the better looking one of the two whose name I now knew was Kia, and the conversation was flowing nicely until Philippe bumped into a girl that he knew from somewhere else and turned around and started walking in the opposite direction with her instead. He was hedging his bets. By now I was so fed up with this shameless behaviour that I decided I would rather carry on talking to these girls than be led all over the city by my host's penis.

'Do you mind if I come with you for a bit?' I asked. 'I'm not interested in getting into your pants. I just really need a break from that guy.'

They laughed then Kia said, 'I thought he was your friend. My God, he's so creepy. I thought you were the same as him. Isn't this what you two do; walk around the city trying to pick up girls?'

'No, it's not. I've known him since yesterday. He's hosting me here in Norway so I haven't really got much of a choice, but please don't paint me with the same brush.'

'You better come with us then.'

They said they knew a decent bar that we could go to but to get there they wanted to take a ride on a bicycle-taxi. They hailed one and jumped on the back, telling me to do the same. Obviously these things cost money, so I declined the offer and said I would have to give the bar a miss.

'No you won't. Just keep up with us on foot.'

I wondered why anyone would pay for a lift that took just as long to get to the destination as it did to walk, but I didn't air my thoughts on this occasion. I walked alongside the bike, looking like the tightest man outside of Scotland. I looked even tighter a few minutes later at the bar as the girls ordered their cocktails and I asked the waitress to give me a glass of tap water.

Kia, looking a little perplexed, then asked why I couldn't afford a drink and why I hadn't ridden on the taxi with them, so now I felt like I could tell them about my challenge without it looking like I was showing off. I handed her the copy of the Herald and stood sipping my water as she read it.

'Oh my God! That is so cool!' she exclaimed. 'Let me buy you a beer.'

I was gagging for a cold one, so graciously accepted. We sat down at a table and by now Kia really seemed to like me. The feeling was mutual, and I had the feeling that rule number eight was going to prove difficult to abide by. She leant over to the next table and asked a young lad if he would take a photo of us. Both girls then put their arms around me and posed while he took it. The lad's mates returned to their table from the bar, and Kia, who was still excited about my challenge, handed them the newspaper and told them about me. The boys were young, just 17, and were now fascinated by me. So fascinated, in fact, that they came and joined our table. This was not what I wanted but hey, you have to think of your fans. I was having questions thrown at me from all angles and was doing my best to answer all of them but at the same time I could feel Kia's hand rubbing the small of my back and I wanted everyone else at the table to do a disappearing act. Rule number eight was in serious jeopardy. I finished my beer and before I'd put the empty glass on the table, a new full one was put in front of me by one of the boys. *I could get used to this,* I thought. Then Kia's friend whispered something in her ear and both girls started putting their coats on. Kia leaned in and told me that her friend was complaining that she was bored and that she had to go and meet some other friends in another bar, but that she would really like to catch up with me later in the evening when she didn't have to 'babysit' her friend. She typed her number into my phone and told me to call her in about an hour. And just like that I was left with a group of teenage boys. Fantastic. They weren't a bad set of lads, far from it, but they did make me feel old, especially when one of them started trying to impress me by bragging about his 'older woman' girlfriend.

'She's 23!' he proclaimed, '23!'

This old woman was a year younger than me.

One of the boys pulled from his pocket what looked at first

glance to be a small tin of shoe polish.

'What's that?' I enquired.

'Snus,' he said, before putting it under my nose for me to smell.

It looked like a teabag and smelt like a pub's ashtray – during the days before smoking was banned – at closing time.

'You put it under your top lip and then spit out the black residue when you're done,' he explained. 'Here, try it.'

I wanted to say no. But rule number four insisted that I give it a try. It tasted like a teabag that had been sitting in a pub's ashtray until closing time. Just then some young girls that I had noticed watching us from their table for some time came over to greet the boys.

'These are some girls we went to school with,' one of the boys told me, 'They've only come over because they want to find out who you are. You will definitely get lucky,' he smirked.

I was already wanted in Sweden for flashing my penis at a woman in a bus station, I did not want to add improper conduct with a minor to my list of crimes committed on Scandinavian soil, so I told everyone at the table that I had to go and meet a friend and quickly made my escape.

I received a text from Philippe telling me he was in a place called Tiger Tiger, and that I should find it and meet him there, so I started walking the streets, randomly asking passers-by if they knew where this place was but not finding a single person sober enough to utter anything comprehensible. I walked straight into a street brawl between two men in their early twenties; one a Norwegian, the other a Turk. There were people shouting; a girl sitting on the kerb crying, make-up smeared all round her face; another girl was hitting the Turk in the face with one of her shoes and spitting on him, while a circle of spectators gathered round to enjoy the action. The police soon arrived and piled everyone involved into a paddy wagon. Just as the scene was being cleared up, I asked one of the coppers where Tiger Tiger was, and finally I had some proper directions.

The bouncer told me that he couldn't let me in. It was 2:15, the place was due to close at 3 and he said that no more entries were allowed in the final hour. Fair enough. I called Philippe and he came out to see me.

'Listen, I've pulled a hot girl. She's Israeli and I think I might be going back to hers tonight. Take this bus ticket and go home. I will see you in the morning,' were his words to me.

He handed me the ticket and also a set of keys and then headed back inside. I scrolled through the list of numbers on my phone, found Kia's, looked at it for a minute and put it back in my pocket. Rule number eight was not going to be broken tonight.

I was woken later that morning at 9:30 by Philippe knocking loudly on the door to be let into the flat. He stunk; the kind of stink that meant there was no need for me to ask how his night had gone. This didn't stop him from filling me in anyway. I will spare you the details. Once clean, Philippe told me that I could travel with him to Gothenburg, back in Sweden, later that evening in a rental car that he was going to pick up. His parents lived there and he had to take a load of stuff from his nan's to their house. In return for his kind offer I agreed to spend the day helping him clean the flat. We worked on it all day and well into the early evening, filling box after box after box with old clothes, books, photos, and all sorts of other stuff that hadn't been touched in decades. As we slugged away, something unexpected happened. I stopped finding my host annoying. I even started to like him. We bonded and I saw that underneath all his stories of shagging and more shagging, was an intelligent guy with a wicked sense of humour. Maybe I had been too quick to judge him.

It was midnight when we finally pulled out of Asker. The drive to Gothenburg was long and it was cold in the car. I was so tired after the night before that my eyes soon closed and I drifted off to sleep. Philippe was even more exhausted; he hadn't had a wink of sleep with the Israeli. At one frightening point I woke to the loud noise of radio static. I looked across to the driver's seat and saw Philippe nodding off at the wheel.

'Mate, wake up!' I jabbed him in the arm.

'I'm fine. Put some music on the radio,' he mumbled.

I made sure to keep him talking the rest of the way. We arrived at Philippe's parents' house at 3:30am.

Welcome to Gothenburg.

4. Gothenburg

PHILIPPE'S MUM HAD made a feast of different meats cooked to a Hungarian recipe, loads of mashed potatoes and a delicious soup; all of which Philippe now stuck in the microwave to heat. We were both starving and it didn't matter how tired we were or how late it was (or how early in the morning), nobody was going to sleep until we had stuffed ourselves full of home cooked food. As we ate, Philippe reminded me that I had to be up and out of the house by 5:30am to catch the early train as he had to get back to Stockholm early in the morning for a class. I was heading for Denmark's capital Copenhagen and would use the newspaper to secure the free ride. I looked at the clock on the cooker and saw that it was already 4:15. I didn't fancy my chances of waking on time, but said, 'Okay.'

Philippe showed me down to a small spare bedroom in the basement and I fell asleep before I was even under the covers. An hour later the alarm on my phone beeped loudly and I did what anyone else would have done under the same circumstances: turned it off and went back to sleep. I woke again a few minutes later to find Philippe gently slapping my face.

'Come on mate, get up. I really have to go.'

The next thing I remember is jumping to my feet in a panic as beams of sunlight streamed through the cracks in the door. It had not been light a minute ago when Philippe was slapping me.

'Shit! What's the time?' I asked loudly.

Sometimes I speak to myself. I picked my phone up from the floor and saw that it was 9:30. Four hours had passed since Philippe had slapped my face. I panicked, not knowing what to do. I was in the house of strangers and the only person who could explain my presence had left for Stockholm four hours previously. How would the homeowners react when an unshaven man who spoke neither Swedish nor Hungarian made his way up into their kitchen from the basement to join them for breakfast? There was only one way to find out. I crept to the top of the stairs and heard the voices of a man and woman coming from the living room. I tapped gently on the door and pushed it open to find what I assumed was Philippe's dad sitting reading a newspaper, and his mum putting bread in the oven. This was a very awkward situation I now found myself in. It became slightly less comfortable when the bread-baking woman began screaming uncontrollably and the newspaper-reading man jumped to his feet and took a rifle from a bracket on the wall and started waving it at me.

'No! No! Don't shoot! I can explain!' I shouted.

Then, in a moment of genius, I picked up a bread knife from the table in front of me and shouted, 'You think you can hurt me? No need! Nobody can hurt me as well as I hurt myself!' and with that, plunged the knife into my left thigh, before looking the gun-pointing old man in the eye and laughing hysterically. He put the gun down and started laughing with me, and then, seeing her husband at ease, the woman stopped screaming and also joined in this jolly moment whilst handing me a tea towel to wrap around the wound that was now bleeding profusely onto the tiled floor. I then told myself to stop being ridiculous and just open the door.

'Good morning. I am so sorry; I overslept. I am sorry I'm still in your house. I will go now,' I said, heading for the front door.

'No, no. Don't go. Come, join us. We eat now.'

Philippe's mum beckoned for me to take a seat in the kitchen. She spoke fairly decent English and laughed as she told me that Philippe was asleep in his room after getting to the train station five minutes too late and missing his train.

She also told me that he had let her know to expect a foreigner to emerge from the basement, and then asked me to explain about my trip as her son had been very vague in his tired state. As I told her the basics my plate slowly filled with all different varieties of Hungarian salami, cheese and bread. As I ate I asked how it was that they had come to live in Sweden, and found that their story was much more interesting than mine and involved escaping from the Communist regime of Hungary by visiting Sweden as part of a musical orchestra on a short-term visa and then overstaying, eventually being given Swedish citizenship many years later. The couple held hands and smiled at each other as the story was recounted and I felt the love in the room.

I looked up to see Philippe entering the conversation.

'Did you show them the newspaper?' he asked, excitedly.

'I didn't. But I will now.'

I pulled it out of my bag and laid it on the table for his mum to translate to her husband.

It was soon time to leave, but not before giving each member of the family a hug and the warmest of thanks. The kindness

they had shown me had made me emotional and I knew I would never forget these people. But the Great Euro Freebie Challenge needed to continue, and so I lifted my rucksack up onto my back and wobbled down the snow-dusted street (I hadn't actually seen any snow fall yet, this had been there since before my arrival) to the tram stop from where I made it to the central train station. Denmark was my next port of call, even though I'd not had any opportunity to arrange a place to stay once there. The Copenhagen train was already on the platform when I arrived at the station so, just like in Stockholm, I sought out the train's guard and told him the truth about why I had no money and why I needed to get to Denmark. And just like the guard in Stockholm he smiled and told me to get on the train. However, he told me he only had authority as far as the border, and that after we crossed the frontier I would have to seek permission from his Danish counterpart to continue the journey.

The view from the window whilst crossing from Sweden to Denmark was truly exhilarating, as the journey took us across the Oresund Bridge, a magnificent piece of architecture high above the sea, before leading down into a tunnel below the water. Once in Denmark the friendly ticket inspector got off and was replaced by a female railway employee with a stern face. I walked up to her compartment and told her why I was on her train without a ticket, but was met with a different reaction to those which I had experienced in Sweden and Norway. She told me that this simply wouldn't do and that I would have to raise the money somehow to pay for a ticket. She didn't care how I did it – she even suggested I walk up the train asking fellow travellers to donate – but she was adamant that I pay for my ride. I could see that a change of approach was needed. It was time to bring out the big guns. It was time to turn on the trusted Krissy charm. I knew it was cheating, as there was no way any woman could fail to be hypnotised by my magic, but I also knew that Gosh – sorry to break it to you, but there really isn't a God – would only disapprove if I used my gifts for evil. My purpose was pure.

'The inspector in Sweden told me that when I got into Denmark, a beautiful, friendly, understanding, and did I already mention beautiful, lady would get on and take his place. He said that she would be really generous and nice because all Danes are naturally that way. I didn't believe such a woman could exist, but now I see who he was talking about.'

I then waited for the reaction. I didn't have to wait long. She blushed, grinned and told me to sit down and stop being so silly. I pulled into Copenhagen's Central Station at 4:30pm and ticked the second EU capital off of my list. In case you were wondering, Oslo didn't count because Norway wasn't a member state of the European Union at the time. Probably still isn't, but I don't know what year you are reading this book in and what's changed. In fact, I am amazed simply by the fact that someone is reading this book.

Welcome to Copenhagen.

5. Copenhagen

Capitals left to visit: Amsterdam, Athens, Berlin, Bratislava, Brussels, Bucharest, Budapest, Helsinki, Lisbon, Ljubljana, Luxembourg, Madrid, Paris, Prague, Riga, Rome, Sofia, Tallinn, Vienna, Vilnius, Warsaw

Days on the road: 5
Distance travelled: 708 miles
EU capitals visited: 2

THIS WAS GOING to be the hardest challenge of the journey so far. I hadn't arranged a place to stay, I had no contacts in the country I was in, it was already starting to get dark, and on top of all that it was freezing cold and pissing down with rain. Outside the station a girl in a yellow anorak gave me a free lollipop as she tried to promote some product that had absolutely nothing to do with lollipops, and as I sucked on it I spotted a backpacker crossing the road in front of me. He was instantly recognisable as an Australian. That facial expression that gives away one's experience of finding oneself in a strange city at dusk; that look that says, 'Been here before.' An Aussie is never flustered. He can pick up the scent of a youth hostel from 30 miles and will always lead you to safety. It's in the genes. I managed to catch up with the guy and, as we stopped together at another set of traffic lights, I asked him if he knew of a hostel. Of course he did! We walked together and introduced ourselves. My new mate was a native of Melbourne, in his early 30s, who went by the name Greg. Could I have found a more stereotypical Aussie? The only thing missing was the hat with corks on it, and I would have wagered a few quid that he had one lurking somewhere in the depths of his rucksack.

He told me he was quite near the beginning of a year jaunt around the continent and that he hoped to work in London and earn enough money to then take another year or so travelling Asia. After he had finished telling me his story I explained a little about mine. I got the basics through to him, avoiding going into intricate detail at this point as I didn't want to appear too self-indulgent. He seemed quite concerned that I wouldn't be able to blag a free bed in the hostel and that I would end up sleeping outside in the rain. I told him I didn't allow negative thoughts to creep in to my psyche, but that if the worst came to the worst I was big enough and ugly enough to handle a night of sleeping rough, most probably in the train station. The hunger would be an altogether different obstacle, but again it was one that I would cross when I came to it. He said he felt inspired and that he couldn't imagine going anywhere without at least a few dollars in his pocket. He asked if I needed anything. I thanked him but told him I was good. The rain was pouring out of the heavens, the sky was now dark and there was a yellowy blur from where the headlights were morphing into one another as people in cars making their way home from work got caught up in the traffic. It was hard to feel positive as we approached the hostel and even harder once we'd wandered in to the reception lobby and seen the size of the queues of people waiting to check-in. The building Greg had led me to was called Dan Hostel. It was sixteen floors high and held over one thousand beds. Working behind the desk, checking travellers in, were a male hippy and a movie-star-looking blonde girl with piercing blue eyes. Just as they didn't come much more Aussie than Greg, they certainly didn't make them any more Nordic than this girl. Greg suggested that I join the queue in front of her as there would be more chance of me charming a young lady than a male hippy who from his accent we had both now ascertained was from Ireland. Greg stood in the other queue and kept an eye on me to see that things were going well. We arrived at our designated members of staff at pretty much the same time and the first thing I did was ask the blonde if I could show her something. She was intrigued so I pulled out the soggy newspaper and explained to her that it had been a long, hard day, that I had nowhere to sleep and wouldn't be able to offer any money, and that the question I had to put to her was whether they would be so kind as to help me out, even if it meant me sleeping on a couch in the reception area.

'I will have to call my manager,' she said, nervously. 'I can't make any promises, but hopefully I can persuade him.'

I waited for a second and then heard the Irish guy lean over to her and say that it was fine; she should book me in to a dorm. I smiled, she smiled, the Irish guy smiled, Greg smiled, some Korean people who hadn't understood a word of the conversation and therefore had no idea what was going on smiled, everyone on the ground floor smiled and the whole lobby started to resemble the video shoot of REM's 'Shiny Happy People.'

The girl took my passport and filled out all the necessaries before handing me a sheet and a pillowcase and giving me the key to my room up on the 16th floor. Greg came over and congratulated me on blagging a room and I told him I would look out for him later on to see if he wanted to take a wander around town.

In my 8-bed dorm I found just one other guest: a middle-aged and heavily depressed German man. He was stockily built, had a moustache and smelt of body odour. Pretty much your standard German. Joke! Sorry, Germans. Just to be polite I made idle chit-chat with him but his English was as poor as my German. Still, I managed to get out of him that his name was Andreas and that the construction company he worked for in Germany had sent him to Denmark to help complete a project. He complained that he hated his company for being so tight and forcing him to live in a youth hostel, and he told me he had also started to hate Denmark full stop. He had to get up for work every morning at around 5, the same time that many of the guests were just making their way to bed. He found it impossible to get the sleep he needed because whenever he tried to get his head down early it was made pointless due to all the noise of the other guests. He had one of those faces you try not to stare into when talking, for fear of him snapping and smashing you over the head with a glass ashtray, but I felt a pang of pity towards him. He said his contract in Denmark was for six weeks and he had had to leave his wife at home. This made my sympathy for the poor man even stronger. At the very least, surely the company could have put him in a private room. I made my bed, ate a muesli bar whilst enjoying the view over the river, then took a long, hot shower. Under the steaming water I stood and thanked the travel gods for once again seeing to it that I would have a roof over my head for the night.

The rain was battering down against the windows and I knew that on my hunt for food I was going to get wet and cold again. I took a map from reception and strolled out into the bitter air. As well as needing to put something in my stomach I also had to try and find somewhere to use the internet free of charge, as I hadn't arranged anything for the next day. I had decided that I would attempt to make it to Hamburg in Germany, en-route to my next capital city, Berlin.

Finding someone kind enough to let me use a computer was no real challenge at all. A lovely hotel receptionist in the Copenhagen Plaza, next to the train station, showed me to a little internet booth usually reserved for the hotel's guests. I only managed to send out five requests for a place to crash in Hamburg, as there weren't too many potential hosts available.

Back out on the streets and now in search of food, it soon became apparent that the friendliness and generosity found in Sweden and Norway wasn't as prevalent here in Denmark. There was an almost German attitude and behaviour to the people. Don't ever tell them I said that. I went from restaurant to restaurant, each time asking if they could spare any leftovers. Each time I was told that it was impossible to give anything away for free. I was becoming desperate and frustrated. I tried baker's shops, coffee houses, takeaway kiosks, and everywhere in between, but all I found was people telling me to get on my bike. The more desperate I became, the less hopeful I was each time I entered a new place. A pizzeria looked promising when I could see through the glass that all the staff were Italian. Surely they would be friendlier and more generous to someone in need, especially if I explained everything in their mother tongue. After pleading with the restaurant's owner, a guy in his early 30s, I found his response hard to swallow. He explained that he would give me his right arm to help if he could but he couldn't possibly give me any food because his chef was an extremely temperamental character who would be most upset if the food he cooked was given away for free. After the experience with the Italians I gave up. I was too hungry, cold and exhausted to keep walking around the city begging, and I didn't think it would be good for morale if I took any more rejections. I made my way back to the hostel and slowly ate another Muesli bar from my bag. I didn't have many left. That was dinner for the night.

It was getting on for 9pm and all the lights in my bedroom were off as Andreas was tucked up with his head under the blankets, trying to block out the world and get some much-needed sleep. Rather than bother him by attempting to do anything in the dorm, I took the lift downstairs to the lobby area where I got into conversation with the two members of staff on the front desk. It took me right back to the time I spent doing the same job in a hostel in Rome as a 19-year old. It had been the best year of my life.

The blonde receptionist's name was Line and she was 21 years old. The Irish guy was Liam. He was in his late twenties and had moved to Denmark because it was the homeland of his girlfriend. I recognised his predicament only too well. Now that they weren't preoccupied with the duty of checking people in they were both keen to probe me about my challenge and to find out how it was possible to survive under such conditions. I explained how sometimes things came easy and other times not so and I told them of my failed attempts at finding something to eat earlier in the evening.

'That's pretty harsh, man,' said Liam, sympathetically yet also with a laugh. 'I'll tell you what; I will give you a free breakfast ticket now so at least in the morning you will be able to get something to eat here before you head off. On top of that, also have a couple of these.'

He handed me a few little pieces of paper that had the words Free Beer printed on them. Each ticket could be exchanged for a pint at the Scottish pub just down the road. Liam's thought was that if I went down there later in the evening, had a couple of drinks and got talking to people, I might be able to find a fellow traveller heading to Germany the following morning that I could tag along with. I didn't like the idea of heading into the pub alone so asked if either of them would care to join me after their shift finished at 11.

'I'm not sure about that. I'm pretty tired,' Liam said. 'But we do have a few cans of Heineken in the fridge here, so the three of us can sit in the dining area and have a drink if you like.'

I liked.

11 o'clock came around and as arranged my two new friends joined me at a table. Liam immediately got into conversation with a mate of his sitting at a table next to ours so I found myself with only Line to entertain. I would be lying if I said

that I was disappointed. We talked about travelling, education, hobbies, and as the time ticked quickly by I was very aware of a spark between the two of us. We held each other's gaze the whole time and for the first time since I had left Brighton I felt a real connection with another person. Line was confused. She was a university student who had a deep desire to travel and to experience a new way of life but felt trapped in Copenhagen because she couldn't just leave the studies and the obligations to go off for a year and then have to come back with all the challenges of restarting her education, finding accommodation, searching for a new job, adjusting back to reality.

'Every day that you live *is* reality,' I told her, amazing myself at how profound I could be. 'What you see as reality now isn't what you will see as reality tomorrow. If you need to travel, then pack your bags and go. When you wake up on a deserted beach; that will be your reality.'

It was midnight and Liam turned back to us to say goodnight. He was going home to his waiting girlfriend and a hot dinner. I looked at Line, she looked at me.

'Pub?' I asked.

'Pub,' she replied with a nod of the head.

The weather had taken a turn for the worse and the rain smacked hard against our faces, pushed by gale force winds. I pushed Line's bike for her as she led me towards our destination. It was your usual Gaelic establishment. Not too dissimilar from an Irish pub, the main difference being that rather than the walls being pasted with Guinness posters, the celebrated drink was Tennent's Super. The dark blue flag with the white diagonal cross hung high above the bar. The tables were surrounded by small groups of young people roaring loudly under the influence of alcohol, and on the stage in the corner a bloke with a beard shouted rather than sang U2 hits. The name of this Scottish pub was one that some top marketing executive with an absolutely genius wit and imagination had obviously been paid a lot of cash to come up with: The Scottish Pub. I collected our cold malt beverages from the bar as Line found us a little table. I sat myself down opposite her but was immediately told that she didn't like to shout above the music so I should sit next to her instead. It was at this point that I got a sneaky feeling things were going to get a little friendly and that rule number eight was going to be put to the test. The evening flowed and it was as if I was talking to someone I had known since my school days. Every joke I cracked got the laugh. Every story I told got her complete attention. And every subtle compliment I gave received a less subtle one in response. She told me more about herself and I could understand her as well as she could me. I managed to put all of the worries and anxieties of the journey that stood in front of me out of my mind and just felt completely relaxed spending my evening with this beautiful Danish girl. I told her about Philippe and his parents and how ingratiated I felt to them for all they had done for me, at which point she looked me in the eye and said, 'I want to tell you something that you're not supposed to know, but I don't know if it's right for me to say.'

She knew that after a statement like that there was no way I was going to let her get away without spilling the beans.

'You know you have to tell me now, so let's not play the game where I try and persuade you, you say that you can't, I say that you have to, and in the end you finally just blurt it out. That will just be a waste of everybody's time. So what is it?'

'You remember the Australian guy that you walked in with earlier?'

'Greg. What about him?'

'He paid for your bed. He told Liam quietly to charge it to him. That's why we were able to give you a place for the night. He said he didn't want you to know, he just wanted to help you complete your challenge. If you see him, please don't tell him that you know.'

I was gobsmacked. I wanted to cry. Not tears of sadness; not even tears of joy. I just felt so emotional that once again someone had gone out of their way to help me, and the fact that he hadn't sought any sort of recognition for his act of kindness touched me to such an extent that I was silent for about five minutes. I wanted to meet Greg and to thank him, to show him my appreciation. I wanted to do something to help him. I didn't know what he needed help with, but whatever it was I wanted to do it. I felt guilt too. Backpackers tend not to be rich individuals and need to watch the pennies, yet this man that I had only just met at a set of traffic lights outside a train station had dug into his wallet and paid for my bed all of five minutes after being introduced into my life. I stared into the wall and right through it as my head tried to make sense of what was happening to me on this journey. Then Line snapped me back to the present with some words that changed my outlook on life and in so doing also changed the way I would be on my travels.

'You don't need to do anything for Greg. I am a strong believer in treating others as you wish to be treated yourself. You were in need, Greg saw that and so he helped you. There will be times in life when you are in a position to help somebody else that is needy. Take those opportunities and life will balance itself out.'

Wise words.

We carried on chatting until kicking out time, getting through a couple of pints in the process. Line's hand was on my thigh.

It was 2 o'clock in the morning and time for me to say goodnight and farewell before heading back to my bed for a few hours' sleep and contemplation. Or so I thought.

'If you like, I can show you somewhere else. It's an all-night bar where we can carry on the evening.'

Line's suggestion took me slightly by surprise. I was looking like shit, hadn't shaved since starting my travels, was wearing a tracksuit top and was weary to the world, and yet this girl with superstar good looks was more than a little keen to spend these late hours with me.

'I'm up for that,' I responded, as nonchalantly as I could, while inside I performed a Roger Milla goal celebration. If you don't know what that is, YouTube it. 'That is of course if you are happy to pay for the drinks. I would love to buy them, but, you know, I left my wallet at home.'

'Come on!' She laughed and led the way out the door.

We left her bike locked up where it was and walked the five minutes to our next port of call, not quite holding hands but shoulders brushing closely together. Checkout time at the hostel was only seven hours away and yet rather than being on my way back to my dorm to get my head down before what I knew was going to be another long and difficult day, I was on my way to a bar. I will let you in on a little secret: I wasn't thinking about sleep. Inside the dingy, dark, little place that we now found ourselves, the hardcore element of Copenhagen's drinking community was gathered. It was neither loud nor boisterous. This was where people came to discuss political and cultural revolution whilst simultaneously getting rat-arsed. At least, that's what it looked like they were talking about. For all I know, the main topic of the evening could have been which member of Abba would make better meatballs. In case you were wondering, it's Frida. Benny, as hard as he tries, bless him, just can't get the right balance between bite and tenderness.

Facial hair was in abundance, as were coats covered in badges depicting left-wing symbols. I'd always felt at home with this kind of people. I nipped into the toilet and returned to an awaiting pint. This girl was good. She was drinking a cocktail that looked fit for Del Boy. Conversation was clearly getting in the way of other plans. At least that was the message I was now receiving from the pair of eyes staring right into mine and the mouth that had edged its way closer and closer and now waited, slightly open, lips shiny with gloss, about an inch from my face. Inexplicably, panic set in. Inside my head the voice was loud: *'Shit! Should I kiss her? I have to kiss her. I want to kiss her. She wants to be kissed. What if I do and she doesn't want it? What if I don't and she does? Her mouth is waiting. Her eyes are waiting. She's waiting. Hang on a minute, while I'm thinking all of this am I still talking to her out loud and if so, what about? Yes, I checked, I am still talking about something. She's smiling. She knows what I'm thinking. What a game these women play.'*

And then as my mouth uttered something of which I have no recollection, my words were muffled by her lips touching mine. I would have done it eventually, I swear I would have. But she had beaten me to the punch. It was soft, gentle and nice. Rule number eight had been broken.

Agnetha never puts enough flour in her meatballs. They look great going into the pot, but by the time they come out they've turned into a stew. Of course, she will always then explain that her intention all along was to make the Swedish equivalent of broth, to which we will all have a little giggle and tuck right in. She knows that we are laughing with her, not at her. She is nothing if not an entertainer is Agnetha.

Now that we were kissing – me and Line, not me and Agnetha from Abba – there didn't seem to be much to talk about any more. The minutes started to fly by, as they tend to do when you're kissing a beautiful woman, and before we knew it it was quarter to six in the morning. The rain had stopped and the street cleaners were out manoeuvring those little sweeping buggy things that they drive; the ones with the flashing orange light on top that make that annoying beeping noise. Those things are universal. It kind of ruins the moment when you've got a girl backed up against a wall (in a friendly way. I don't mean like in a robbery), you're kissing her, exchanging cute little words with each other, and then you almost get swept under a broom-on-wheels with all the fag ends and polystyrene cups that the city's residents have discarded throughout the previous day. No, let me tell you, that does not enhance the romantic atmosphere in any way, shape, or form. And doesn't the smug looking street cleaner just know it? This is his only bit of joy. It is not yet six in the morning, it's freezing cold, it's still dark, he has struggled to get himself out of bed and in to work at this ungodly hour, his job is to clean up all the muck that people have carelessly chucked on the floor, and then he sees two people who have obviously been up all night having fun and are now finishing things off with a bit of touchy-feely up against the side of a building.

'If only there were some way that I could take away that feeling of contentment from these two and at the same time give myself something to smirk at,' he thinks to himself. 'Hang on a minute…'

And then you turn around with a look of fear in your eyes as he comes to mow you down, grinning like the Joker from the Batman comics.

With the moment well and truly spoilt outside I guessed it was time to find out which bed I would be waking up in later. Would it be my bunk in the hostel or would somewhere more comfortable be offered? It would be my bunk in the hostel.

'No, I really don't think it's a good idea. I have to get some sleep. You have to carry on your journey to Germany later today. I'm not going to get in the way of plans and make things complicated. You need to go back to the hostel.'

That told me.

I walked through the lobby to a look of recognition from the night shift receptionist who had seen me leave with Line many hours earlier. There was a knowing grin on his face as he nodded his greeting. I entered my room to the sounds of light snoring from a lot of people that hadn't been there when I had left the evening before. Andreas was getting dressed for work and threw me a look of contempt as I took off my jeans and shoes and fell into bed. I fell asleep quickly enough; unfortunately I woke quickly enough too. Two hours went just like that. It was 8:30 and I had half an hour before I had to vacate my room. I felt like the cat's arse as I dragged myself to the shower. Ahead of me lay a day in which I had to somehow make my way to Hamburg, find somewhere to sleep when there and also get my hands on something to eat; and all of the above tasks were to be completed whilst carrying some seriously heavy bags. At least the sun was shining, although not warmly. I exchanged my breakfast token for some bread and juice but annoyingly felt too rough to eat anything, then checked out of the hostel, leaving my bags by reception as I jogged down to the Copenhagen Plaza to check my emails to see if anyone in Hamburg had replied to my pleas. They hadn't.

Fuck it, I thought, *I'll make my way to Hamburg regardless.*

I emailed a couple more Hamburgers, – is that the term for someone from Hamburg, or have I just pulled a JFK? – leaving my mobile number with them and asking them to send me a text with details if they were in a position to help me out once I arrived in Germany.

I don't think I've ever seen Bjorn attempt to make anything in the kitchen more risk-free than a few Ryvita Crackers with a bit of herring out of a tube. Frida tells me that when they were younger and on tour in Germany they once found themselves staying in a room with a little kitchenette. After a few drinks Bjorn had told everyone that he'd always fancied attempting to make Bratwurst and had then staggered over to the hob. To cut a long story short, he let the oil get too hot and burnt his hand. After that incident he never went near a cooker again. He doesn't talk about it though, so if you see him, don't probe.

I returned to the hostel to collect my stuff and then made my way to the train station. Getting on the train to Hamburg was easy enough as the friendly Danish conductor said that I could ride as far as the edge of Denmark and then would have to get off and ask his counterpart from across the border for permission to travel on. The ride through Denmark was scenic if you like open fields and wind turbines. And let's face it; who doesn't? To be fair, that wasn't the only thing to be seen. There were some nice parts of the journey in which we went right along the coastline, the stormy sea crashing against the rocks just outside my window. I was just dropping off to sleep when everything suddenly got exciting as the train I was on rode straight onto a boat. I hadn't been expecting this as I hadn't done my research. I had assumed that we would be crossing into Germany over a land border, but no, we were going by sea. On a train! I started to worry a bit at this point, as all the passengers were getting up and getting off the train but leaving their baggage behind. What was going on? Some sort of passport control, or worse, ticket control? Like everyone else I stood up and disembarked.

Fortunately, the people weren't getting off to show any documents but rather to go up on to the deck of the ferry for the duration of the crossing. The water was choppy and I felt sick as a dog so, as people walked around the duty-free shops, I found a nice little row of seats and laid down for a quick nap. The over-water journey only took about 45 minutes and then we were told to go back downstairs and retake our seats on the train. I was in Germany. I was about half an hour into the country when the ticket inspector came to pay me a visit. I told him that the Danish railway company had given me permission to travel for free to Hamburg and that I had been told that they were also going to fill him in on the details.

'Travel for free? Why?' he asked.

I handed him the Herald. He took the time to read the entire article before smiling and commenting that he had never heard of anything like it in his whole life but he was happy enough to allow me to stay on the train to complete my journey. I thanked him profusely. As I was doing so, there was a beep on my phone. I grabbed it from my pocket, excitedly. Could it be that someone was offering me a place to spend the night? Yes it could. A guy named Ollie told me that once in Hamburg I should take a local train to Berliner Tor station and call him when I got there. Things had fallen into place once again.

And before you sit down and write that letter complaining that I spent the chapter on Denmark telling you about the meatball making skills of 70s super band Abba; I am aware that Abba came from Sweden and not Denmark. But hey; tom-ay-to, tom-ar-to.

Welcome to Hamburg.

North Cape
Jan Mayen
(Norway)
NORWEGIAN SEA
Scandinavia
Lapland
SWEDEN
FINLAND
NORWAY
Trondheimsfjorden
Faroe Islands
(Denmark)
Shetland Islands
(UK)
Gulf of Bothnia
Aland
Gulf of Finland
OSLO
STOCKHOLM
HELSINKI
ESTONIA
LATVIA
LITHUANIA
Gotland
BALTIC SEA
NORTH
SEA
Skagerrak
DENMARK
COPENHAGEN
SCOTLAND
UNITED
KINGDOM
British
Isles
IRELAND
DUBLIN
ENGLAND
LONDON
CELTIC SEA
English Channel
NETHERLANDS
Hamburg
BERLIN
POLAND
WARSAW
BELARUS
GERMANY
BELGIUM
PARIS
FRANCE
PRAGUE
CZECH.REP.
SLOVAKIA
Carpathian Mts.
KIEV
MOLDOVA
VIENNA
AUSTRIA
HUNGARY
ROMANIA
SWITZ.
Bay of
Biscay
Massif
Central
Alps
CROATIA
BOSNIA & H
SERBIA
BELGRADE
BUCHAREST
Pyrenees
ITALY
ROME
BULGARIA
SOFIA
MADRID
SPAIN
PORTUGAL
LISBON
Corsica
Sardinia
Sierra Morena
MEDITERRANEAN SEA
ALGIERS
TUNIS
TUNISIA
ALGERIA
MOROCCO
RABAT
Strait of Gibraltar
Sicily
GREECE
ATHENS
Peloponnesus
ALBANIA
Anatolia
Istanbul
ANKARA
CYPRUS
Crete
AEGEAN SEA

6. Hamburg

TAKING THE LOCAL Metro to Berliner Tor without a ticket was as easy to me as scoring a penalty in a World Cup knock-out match is to a German. Once there, I walked out onto the street to find it was grey and raining; a common experience so far on this trip. I had Ollie's number but didn't have any credit on my phone so the first thing I needed to do was find somewhere to make a free call from. An apartment rentals agency seemed like a good enough place to start asking so I walked in and asked the middle aged lady behind the desk if she spoke English. She shook her head and looked extremely flustered. It was the time of evening when local businesses were starting to lock up for the night and just as she was thinking about the Sauerkraut dinner awaiting her at home, stood in front of her was a tired looking young man speaking gibberish. I tried to explain in German that I needed to make a call, but as soon as I started speaking I remembered something fairly important: I don't speak German. I will give the woman credit where due, she didn't panic for too long. She got her head together, gestured with her hand for me to wait, said something in German – which definitely wasn't 'where is the train station?' because I remember that sentence from school – and called out something rather loudly. A couple of seconds later the cavalry arrived in the form of another middle aged woman.

'I speak ein bissien English,' she told me.

I told her about Ollie and she asked for the number, I assumed to make sure I wasn't calling long distance. She dialled and spoke German to someone on the other end before handing the receiver to me. Ollie spoke perfect English with only a small hint of a German accent. He would be along to meet me in 20 minutes. Exactly 20 minutes later – as you would expect from a German – he turned up, we shook hands, and he started to lead me to his block. Instantly I knew he was someone I was going to get on very well with. The reason for his perfect grasp of the English language, and also his surname of Evans, was that his dad hailed from Wales. He had moved here in the 80s as a construction worker (think Auf Wiedersehen Pet) and had met his future wife, learned perfect German, had a couple of sons, and stayed for good. We got to Ollie's student block and, as we trekked up the stairs, we were already talking like we had been mates for a long time. I was starving, so when he asked me if I would like a sandwich I almost bit his hand off. Then I watched him take the food from the cupboard and realised that the sandwich was to be made with black bread. If you are not familiar with this thing that some people on the continent call food, it is not to be confused with brown bread. Brown bread is lovely, soft, and bready. Black bread is none of the above. It's not even bready. Would I get away with using the word 'bready' if we were playing Scrabble? Probably not, but you know I would try. Into the sandwich went some cheese and lettuce, before it was handed to me on a plate. That sounds like a metaphor, but it wasn't intended as one. It was literally handed to me on a plate. What to do? I couldn't eat it; I knew that as soon as I took my first bite. Black bread is like dog poo that has been left to harden in the cold. You chew and chew and chew but you just can't swallow. I will explain later how I am able to confidently make that comparison. By now Ollie was watching me. I had but two options. Either spit the black bread out of my mouth discreetly, or spit it out not so discreetly. Actually, what I did was swallow it. I retched a little bit but I don't think he noticed. I put the rest of it down on the kitchen top and lied, saying that I had a stomach ache.

'That's fine, mate,' Ollie said. 'You can eat it later when you are feeling a bit better.'

'I look forward to it.'

My host then showed me to his bedroom where I would be spending the night on a mattress on the floor. I was told that a little bit later in the evening we were going to be joined by his brother's girlfriend Kimia for a dinner of pancakes and Nutella. Apparently this was Ollie's specialty, or rather the only thing he knew how to make. Before anything else, we had to pay a visit to the supermarket to get the provisions. Waiting for us at the bottom of the stairs was Kimia. She was dark featured, petite and very pretty. She introduced herself but as we walked to the shop I could sense that she didn't particularly like me being around. This was fair enough; I was a stranger with no money. Never one to give up easily, I asked her where her origins were, as she was clearly not of German descent. She said that she was Persian. I then proceeded to tell her the story of how I once tried to teach myself the Persian language of Farsi, and just like that she warmed to me. The three of us then talked like good friends. In case you were wondering, I stopped with the self-taught Farsi lessons once I realised that to be able to use their script you had to be an artist. I am no artist. Call me old fashioned, but I prefer to write my words, not draw them.

Kimia lived in a similar student block just around the corner from Ollie's. Her boyfriend was living and studying in Berlin but having Ollie living locally kept up the family feeling. You could feel the good vibe between the two and I imagined that Ollie's brother was very similar; another person I would most likely get on well with. Later that evening the three of us walked around to Kimia's flat to pick up an inflatable mattress that she was lending me for the night. In her kitchen she took the time to fill up a brown paper bag with all sorts of biscuits, crackers and some tinned fruit for my journey to Berlin the following day. I was touched. We then said goodbye and headed back to Ollie's without her. On the way, he told me that Kimia was notoriously impossible to impress and never liked any of the

Couchsurfers he had staying at his flat.

'And I can't believe she gave you food, too! I am shocked to the core!'

Back in the lobby of his block we stopped to buy a few beers from the vending machine. We took the beers straight into Ollie's room where we started drinking, while I used his computer to search for somewhere to lay my hat in Berlin. Ollie interrupted me.

'My brother lives in Berlin and usually he hates the idea of having any guests; he doesn't agree with the whole Couchsurfing philosophy. But I think he might host you, especially if he has spoken to Kimia already and she has told him that you're cool. Let me call Kimia first, run the idea by her, then we'll see what we can do.'

I liked the fact that he called me cool. I am quite cool. I also liked the idea of going to sleep that evening knowing I had a place to crash the following night.

'I like it!' I said, dramatically giving the thumbs up at the same time.

Kimia's response to Ollie's suggestion was a German translation of, 'Oh my god! I can't believe you called me to suggest that, I was literally just about to phone you because I'd had the same idea!'

Ollie phoned his brother Julian, who had already been briefed on the idea by his girlfriend and was willing to trust his better half's and his brother's instincts and give me a shot. I felt a big responsibility; like I had been vouched for by someone in an important position and their job was now dependent on me being on my best behaviour. I knew the challenge was big, but if anyone could pull it off successfully then it was somebody more responsible than me. But, seeing as there was no one else around, I was going to have to do it anyway.

The rest of the evening turned into a heavy-duty drinking session as we discussed Ollie's two biggest passions in life:

Hitchhiking and Borussia Dortmund Football Club. Ollie hitchhiked everywhere. If he was travelling to his hometown of Dortmund to visit family, he hitchhiked. If he was going to another part of Germany to see friends, he hitchhiked. If he was going to a Couchsurfing camp somewhere in Eastern Europe, he hitchhiked. If he was going to the shop to buy a pint of milk, he, well, he walked. The shop was just around the corner. Anywhere else though, he hitchhiked. My host, surprisingly, was doing his best to convince me that the best way of getting to Berlin the following day was to hitchhike, but the previous few days had instilled in me a confidence in blagging free train rides. On a train I could catch up with writing the diary, I could walk to the toilet if I needed to pee, and I wasn't going to get drugged and raped by a bearded man in a dress and a pair of suspenders. But hey, I can dream.

After finishing the beers and feeling more than a little pissed, it was time to get some kip. Ollie gave me his bed for the night as he spread himself out on the inflatable mattress on the floor. I tried protesting his generous offer but he was having none of it.

'Mate, with all the tough times you're going to go through on this trip, the least I can offer you is a comfortable place to sleep,' he told me.

The rain was beating down heavily the following morning as I left the flat for Berlin. Through the night I had allowed myself to entertain the idea of taking Ollie's suggestion and hitchhiking, but definitely not in this weather. I got to Hamburg station and found that there was one train to Berlin every hour, so I made my way to the correct platform and waited for my chariot to come in. When it did, I tried my by now usual technique of politely asking the guard if I could jump on. I whipped out the newspaper, smiled in a friendly manner and explained that I had to get to Berlin as I had someone waiting for me.

'Ride for free? Are you serious? Not on my train!'

The doors then closed and the train pulled away without me. I was sure I had just come up against a one-off jobsworth. I would have more luck an hour later when the next one came in. No I wouldn't. The exact same scenario played out again. An hour later and it happened for the third time. I was now completely demoralised as I remembered the number one truth about Germans: They follow rules explicitly.

I needed a new plan. The first one I tried was to walk up to the Station Services desk to see if they would give me a ticket. I explained things and tried to look as desperate as possible but the woman behind the desk told me there was nothing she could do to help. She suggested that I go out on to the street and find a place called the Bahnhoffs Mission. She didn't think to tell me what the Bahnhoffs Mission was, just that I should go there. I didn't think to ask either. I just did as I was told, like a good German boy. I found the place. The Bahnhoffs Mission is something like the Salvation Army; a non-profit organisation there to help the tramps that live around the station. They provide food and coffee and a place to go for company and a chat. They also provide train tickets to Germans who haven't got any money on them for whatever reason, but only on the condition that the person pays back what he has borrowed later on. Anyway, this service was only available to people living at a German address. The male worker offered to pay for my ticket out of his own pocket but, as he was working and couldn't leave his desk, he would have to give me the cash and I would have to go and buy the ticket myself. I had to decline his offer and move on, but not before asking a question.

'Say I get on the train anyway, without a ticket or money, and I get caught by the guard halfway through the journey. What will happen to me?'

'They will most probably just detain you in a police cell in Berlin while they figure out what to do with you next,' he said with a shrug.

'So they won't kick me off the train in the middle of nowhere?'

'No. They will take you to Berlin.'

The book could do with an arrest story, I felt, and so it was settled. I was going to Berlin and was going to end up in a cop shop, but at least inside I could tick Germany's capital off of my list. And the police would have to let me go eventually. Or deport me.

The next train to Berlin left at 1:47pm and I was on it, sitting myself down on the floor in between carriages to await my fate. After about half an hour a guard finally approached me. He spoke no English and looked more than a little confused that I wasn't showing him my 'fahrkarte' but was instead rambling away at him in English; so he disappeared, returning a couple of minutes later with an English-speaking colleague who was equally perplexed by my ticketless situation. Remember, I was in Germany, where everyone played by the rules. This was alien territory to these guys. In a friendly enough manner he informed me that he had no choice but to write me out a fine that I would have to pay at a later date, before handing me a blank piece of paper and asking me to write my address on it. The great thing about British passports is that they don't have your home address printed inside them like so many others do. There is the next of kin address handwritten in the back, but that is all. So with a bit of quick thinking I wrote down my name and underneath it I wrote the address of Tottenham Hotspur Football Club – 147 High Road, London, N17 0AP. I handed it to the guard, along with my passport, and sat back down on the floor as he disappeared to his compartment. He returned a few minutes later and, looking me in the eye, asked, 'So, you are a Spurs fan, no?'

I had been rumbled. He had obviously checked the address with the police over the radio and been informed that unless I lived in the stadium I had given him a moody address.

'Yes,' I said, ashamedly and with my eyes pointing to my toes.

'I am a Hertha Berlin fan, myself,' he told me happily.

Why was he telling me this? What kind of trouble was I in? Why the suspense?

'Do you know how I knew you were a fan of the Spurs?'

'Yes.'

I couldn't believe it. He was giving me the Scooby Doo ending. He was going to talk me through his great detective work and then expect me to congratulate him and say something like, 'Fair cop, guv'nor. You caught me good and proper.'

'I am a follower of English football and I know the stadium address of every Premier League team. I learnt them all one afternoon when I was bored. So when I was looking at your passport I recognised your street name but I couldn't remember from where. Then I saw the postcode, N17, and it all came back to me. You live on the same street as White Hart Lane Stadium.'

He was looking very pleased with himself, but little did he know the joke was on him. He had said he knew every address, but clearly he didn't. 147 High Road could not be my home, and I told him as much.

'I'm sorry sir, but you need to spend more time on your homework. White Hart Lane is at 147 High Road. Now look again at my passport and then tell me you know every address. Damn liar! If there's one thing I cannot stand it is deception,' I told him.

To which he replied, 'Here is your fine. You can pay it at any German train station, or post it in from England.'

He handed me a small piece of paper and my passport and then said, 'I wish Spurs a good season!' before walking off down the train. I relaxed for the rest of the journey and got into Berlin at 3:15pm, ticking another capital off of my list but saddened by the fact that I hadn't been locked in a small room with only one phone call allowed. The European arrest would have to wait for another day; hopefully on French soil, as I have always loved the film *Papillon*.

Before closing this chapter I should clear up any confusion. I didn't really pull the guy up on his lack of precise knowledge when it came to street numbers. What I actually said was, 'Wow, that's really impressive. I don't have nearly enough brain capacity to learn such information. You must be a very intelligent man.'

Welcome to Berlin.

7. Berlin

Capitals left to visit: Amsterdam, Athens, Bratislava, Brussels, Bucharest, Budapest, Helsinki, Lisbon, Ljubljana, Luxembourg, Madrid, Paris, Prague, Riga, Rome, Sofia, Tallinn, Vienna, Vilnius, Warsaw

Days on the road: 7
Distance travelled: 1095 miles
EU capitals visited: 3

I MET JULIAN at Alexanderplatz dead on 5pm. He was like his brother, only a bit more grounded. He had no dreams of hitchhiking around the world; he would be happy enough in life to see Borussia Dortmund beat Schalke away every now and then. We took a train back to his flat in the east side of the city, the Soviet sector, but not before stopping off for a crate of beer. I was starting to see a family trait, or perhaps just a German one, and I was all for cultural immersion.

It was a UEFA Champions League night and Julian didn't have a telly, so we went across the street to a replica of Moe's Tavern out of the Simpsons. Depressed middle aged men sat along the bar staring into the bottom of their glasses, while Bart kicked Mr. Burns in the shin and Barney laughed. Julian introduced me to white beer, and that's what we spent the rest of the evening drinking.

I slept that night in a sleeping bag on the wooden floor of Julian's bedroom. I use the term 'slept' lightly, and sleep lightly I certainly did. Morning arrived – and not a moment too soon – and after showering and packing up my stuff, Julian filled my bag with apples and a carton of apple juice. I don't think he liked apples very much. Before leaving the flat, I read an email sent the night before from a girl in the Polish city of Poznan, Karolina, responding positively to my couch request. I had a place to stay for the night; all I needed to do was make it out of the comfort of Western Europe and into the unknown and intimidating East. Julian and I then cemented our new found friendship with an exchanging of precious goods. I gave him a Spurs shirt and in return received a Borussia scarf in the colours of a bumblebee. Before leaving Berlin there was something I had to see: the East Side Gallery – the long stretch of the Berlin Wall that remains intact and is covered in murals by local and international artists. It took me more than two hours to walk the length of the wall on both sides, studying the murals and for the first time on the trip enjoying one of Europe's most important landmarks. I then made my way to East Berlin railway station to catch the 12:47 Warsaw Express to Poznan, a city midway between the capital cities of Germany and Poland. I wasn't feeling great, with painful blisters on my feet and excruciating back pain caused initially from the night on the wood and then not helped by the lugging up and down the Berlin Wall of the backpack. Hunger pains were also starting to kick in, as I hadn't had time for breakfast. I ate an apple and washed it down with some apple juice, before putting an apple flavour Wrigley's into my mouth, given to me by Kimia in Hamburg. Apparently, the loving couple had met at a Mr. Kipling convention.

Waiting on the platform for my train to arrive, I sat and watched the people getting on and off the one that pulled in just before mine, and almost choked on my gum as I witnessed something bordering on surreal. A blind old man, complete with stick, was being escorted along the platform by two station employees, each one holding an arm. Carefully, they took him as far as the train door and then both let go of his arms as he went to board. The old boy took one final step forward and then disappeared from sight. I gasped, rubbed my eyes and looked closer, to see that the poor old boy had missed the step and fallen between the train and edge of the platform; his head and top of his torso the only parts of him now visible. I jumped to my feet and ran to offer my assistance, but was waved away by the two not so helpful helpers as they pulled him back up onto the platform before lifting him onto the train. I was overcome with empathy as I tried to imagine what would go through your head if you were completely without the benefit of sight and felt yourself falling down the side of a train like that. The fear of the unknown must have been terrifying. Even with 20/20 vision I would have shit myself. I was then incredulous to see the two teenage station workers walking away from the scene, doubled up with laughter.

'Oi!' I shouted after them, 'Was that funny? How about I take that old man's stick and make you two violate each other with it. I think that might be funny too. Idiots!'

They turned, looked at me, stopped laughing and hurriedly retreated into the safety of their office.

At 12:47 I took a seat in the last carriage and watched as we moved through the outer suburbs of the city and onward towards Poland. It wasn't long before I was confronted by a female ticket inspector who, after listening to my story, told me, 'Ich verstehe kein Englisch,' before disappearing and then returning a couple of minutes later with a male colleague who could speak my language. I again explained my situation, hoping that my words would find them in good spirits and generous moods. But this wasn't Scandinavia, it was Germany. Friendly wasn't a national characteristic; efficient was.

'You know, if I am in somebody else's country, I don't go around without money or a credit card in my pocket,' the female one told me coldly, revealing that she hadn't been entirely truthful when saying she couldn't speak English.

'Well, you do if that's the whole reason for you being in the country in the first place,' I replied.

She had no answer for this and just stared out of the window for a few seconds.

Checkmate.

'Okay, you can travel as far as Frankfurt Oder. That's the border town,' her male colleague told me, 'Then you will have to get off. In Poland they are not as civilised as us East Germans. They will stop the train and kick you out into the forest if they find you without a ticket.'

Throw me off the train in the forest? I don't like the sound of that one bit. And did he just say East Germans? And there was me believing the propaganda that the Berlin Wall had been bulldozed in 1989 and Germany had been reunified. Whatever. German, East German, at least they were civilised, unlike the Neanderthals I was set to come up against in Poland. Before that moment I hadn't thought about any behavioural differences I might encounter after crossing the old Iron Curtain, but hearing this warning from my East German civilised friends sent a shiver down my spine.

Once at Frankfurt Oder I jumped off and was wished good luck by the two East Germans, who also advised me on the easiest way of making it to Poznan. It didn't involve train travel.

Frankfurt Oder was a completely different world to any I had been in before. I felt like I was playing a starring role in *Back to the Future* part 4, in which the hero – me – takes the DeLorean back to 1980s Communist hell. I walked around the town in a state of amazement. Every man had a mullet and a moustache, every woman had a mullet and a moustache, every man wore cheap denim, and every woman wore cheap denim. Babies dressed like their parents. These people were either vintage Euro porn stars or dedicated members of the East German branch of the David Seaman fan club. The ticket inspectors' main piece of advice had been to walk into

Poland and to hitchhike from there, but they hadn't told me how to find the border crossing. I stopped about 15 people to ask directions but not one of them spoke English, despite the majority of people I asked being under the age of 25.

'Ruski?' they would ask.

'Nein,' I would reply.

Not only did no one speak English but they also looked upon anyone that did with undisguised suspicion and contempt. I was the first Westerner to walk these streets, probably ever, and was clearly a spy. I was getting tired of the hunt and so decided to stop trying to be intricate and to just get back to basics.

'Wo ist Polen?' I would ask while pointing in different directions, waiting for someone to say 'Ja!' when I pointed the right way.

After about an hour of walking around in circles I stumbled accidentally upon the frontier; a bridge over the river Oder. I walked across, having my passport closely scrutinised by the German side for some reason – normally the police of the country you're leaving couldn't care less – and arrived on Polish soil in the town of Słubice. The only difference between this side of the river and the other was that the road signs were written in Polish. The mullets were still on display, but the people on this side looked more hardened. And everybody had an alcoholic drink in his or her hand. I needed to find the nearest motorway so started asking people for directions. This was a lot easier than on the German side as I found that if I asked in Slovenian the Poles would understand my question, and likewise I would understand their Polish response. The first person I asked pointed me onward and told me it was about four kilometres to walk.

After about half an hour, I came across a tiny train station in the middle of nowhere. Speaking again in Slovenian and getting answered in Polish I managed to ascertain that the only train to Poznan was due to depart at 6:45pm. The time now was 3:30pm. My mind was still full of images of me being booted out of a train door and into a bear-infested forest after dark so I decided that trying to take the train would be my last resort if I didn't manage to hitch a lift. I walked a bit more, until I found the motorway and pulled from my bag a piece of cardboard on which I had written in black marker pen the word 'POZNAN'. I had never hitchhiked in my life but I had seen plenty of pictures and films where the hiker had nothing more than a cardboard sign and a dream and they had always been picked up after a few minutes of standing at the side of the road. That was how hitchhiking worked. It was simple.

After standing there watching vehicles fly past me for half an hour a lorry finally pulled over. I started walking towards the passenger door. The driver was leaning out of the window and saying something I couldn't understand. He was also laughing.

This is good, I'm getting a lift from someone with a sense of humour.

Then I cottoned on to what he was saying and what the joke was. I was on the wrong side of the motorway. All of these vehicles were coming *from* Poznan, not going *to* Poznan. I saw the funny side and also took comfort from my mistake; it meant that the only reason I hadn't been picked up was because no one had been going my way. As soon as I got to the other side I would be in the passenger seat and on my way in no time. Dodging traffic in the kind of incident that would usually make it on to an episode of *Police, Camera, Action*, I made it across the four lanes in one piece, dropped my bags on to the grass behind the barrier and stood optimistically holding up my little sign.

My phone had been ringing constantly the whole time I had been standing at the roadside, as Karolina tried to find out if I was going to make it to her city any time in this lifetime, but I was unable to answer as I had no credit left, meaning the call would immediately cut out. I wasn't worried though, as I would soon be in Poznan. Another hour of waiting passed, excruciatingly slowly, as not a single motorist pulled over. Then my luck changed as a lorry driver took pity and parked up just ahead of where I was standing. Excited, I picked up my gear and made my way up to the passenger door, only to realise he'd pulled over to make a phone call and not to give me a lift. Still, he was here now and I knew he would be persuaded to let me in. I stood in front of his cab, held up my sign and gestured towards the passenger seat. He looked at me, shook his head and waved for me to get out of his way. Then he drove off, covering me in dust. I was getting cold and disillusioned when things took a turn for the worse as I looked up and saw walking towards me two heavily built men dressed all in black. The Polish police. As they got closer I became more nervous. I was pretty sure standing by the side of the motorway was illegal. Then it struck me that unless the police in Poland carried bottles of vodka in their hands, these two guys weren't upholders of the law but were in fact just a couple of drunks. Shaven heads, baseball caps, massive hands. Big bastards with lumpy faces who looked like bare-knuckle fighting champions. I started wishing for the police to turn up. The men got close enough to make conversation and then one of them started speaking to me in Polish gibberish. Well, gibberish to me, but probably not to a fellow Pole. I began to understand what he was saying. He was asking me where I was from, to which I replied, 'Anglia.' I wasn't lying, trying to make out like I was some sort of pig farmer from Ipswich or mustard salesman from Norwich; I was simply telling him the Polish word for England. He smiled and then said, 'Pijem!' which from my time living in a Slavic language speaking country I knew meant 'drink!' He pointed to a sign by the side of the road that told of a service station some 2,500 metres in the distance, then waved for me to join the two of them on their pilgrimage to the holy site. I needed to find a way out of this situation but didn't want to risk upsetting these boys, as to do so would most likely lead to an invitation to one of the surrounding fields for a punch-up, and the last thing I wanted was to have to kick seven shades of shit out of these two pleasant gentlemen. But at the same time, it was pretty clear that should we make it to the service station, I would be expected to treat these guys to a drink or two as I was a westerner travelling through their country and would definitely be carrying a wad of cash. I started walking with them, stopping to tie my shoelace after about a minute, realising that they were both intoxicated enough not to notice immediately. They walked on for another minute before one turned round to see me walking back in the opposite direction. He shouted something, to which I pointed at my watch and pulled the international face for: 'Would you look at the time! I really must dash. Sorry!'

He turned back round to his mate for a moment, and when he turned back I had already darted through the oncoming traffic and made it safely to the other side of the road. My first ever attempt at hitchhiking had been a complete failure and so I was going to go back to the tried and tested method of bunking the train.

Darkness had quickly taken over the early evening sky and the little road I had to trek down that cut through the forest had no form of lighting. I tripped in potholes, slipped in mud and sprinted like my life depended on it as animal cries screamed out from both sides of the road. If I slipped and fell I had no doubt that all that would be found of me the following morning would be a skeleton wrapped in the yellow and black Borussia Dortmund scarf that Julian had exchanged with me for a Spurs one. I didn't know whether to take reassurance or enhanced fear the few times a human being passed me walking in the opposite direction; always alone, always drinking hard liquor from a glass bottle. Where the hell were they going? Probably to the service station. I got to the train station an hour before the Poznan train was due in. I was now feeling worse than ever, freezing cold and starving, with no water, in this shit hole of a town full of piss heads, in the pitch black, feet so blistered that I couldn't even stand without feeling the agony, and knowing that there was a very good chance I would wait for the train only to get chucked off a little bit further up the track and fed to the bears; two of which I had already met and knew were waiting for me outside Poland's equivalent of Little Chef. As I sat down on my bag and wondered whether this was all worth it, whether I should just make my way to a police station and then on to the British Embassy to get myself in contact with home and a flight arranged, I was suddenly overcome by a surge of strength and I found myself saying, 'Snap out of it, you fucker! Don't let Poland defeat you. If you end up sleeping in the woods tonight, then so be it. You would sooner die trying to complete this challenge than go home a failure.'

And that was that. I started to use my loaf and came up with a plan to get to Poznan. First of all though, I needed to find a drink. The only building in the area was a tiny little roadside hotel. I entered and asked for a glass of water, not only to lubricate my throat but also because I craved some kind of civilised human contact. The day had been a lonely one so far. Unfortunately no one in the hotel spoke English, so after necking the pint in front of me I went across the road to the station. Standing on the platform were two drunken lads, about 21 years old, one of them drinking straight from a bottle of Martini. 6:45 came and brought with it the train, which I jumped on, relieved to be out of the cold and on my way but wary of being kicked right back out there. The ticket guard came along after about 20 minutes and I immediately started spouting off a story that I had thought up a little bit earlier on whilst in the hotel lobby. I figured it would be easier than attempting to communicate the real reason behind my pecuniary predicament. I told him that I had been invited to drink with two blokes on the motorway, but after we'd parted company I'd reached into my pocket and found that there was an empty space where my wallet had been. My brother was going to be waiting for me at Poznan station and would be able to pay for my ticket when we arrived. After about three minutes of explaining this elaborate story – an explanation that included a very well performed mime of a wallet theft – I realised that the poor old guy didn't understand a word I was saying and was just humouring me. Then my saviour arrived in the form of a young woman who needed to pee. As she passed us on her way to the toilet she noticed my difficulty and asked in English if she could help. I again told my little white lie, this time without the use of mime, and listened as she translated to the old man.

'He says that he will take your passport until we arrive in Poznan. Once there, your brother will have to come and give him the money before he gives you your passport back,' she said.

'Okay, that's fine. Thank you so much. I thought he would stop the train and kick me off into the forest!'

'What? What do you think we are? East Germans? Don't worry, you are in Poland now, we are civilized.'

The relief was immense and I even found a smile for the Germans and their tales of cruelty. Were they merely entertaining themselves at my expense, or did they really believe what they said? Who knew the kind of cross-border scaremongering that went on in these strange little pockets of the continent.

The train I was on travelled at a ridiculously slow pace; perhaps as fast as a milk float on a cobblestone road. As well as being slow, the journey also quickly turned loud and headache inducing as a large group of young soldiers got on, making their way home to see their mums for the weekend. One sat down next to me with a tiny puppy in his arms. On noticing that I was clearly foreign he began trying to engage me in conversation, despite not really being able to speak English. He did manage to get across the story of how he came to be in possession of the dog. He had found him aimlessly wandering around on his own and had decided to give him a home.

'He is my baby,' he told me.

He then asked me to name it, saying he wanted a traditional English dog's name. I offered Rover, Rex, Snoopy and Keith. Keith was to amuse myself. Surprisingly, he shook his head at each of the above and instead christened his new companion Soldier. I felt offended. Why ask me for suggestions if you're not going to use any of them? And the dog definitely looked a lot more like a Keith than a Soldier. Come to think of it, so did the soldier.

Everyone on the train, without exception, was drinking beer. Even the guard. Okay, not the guard. I pulled into Poznan station late in the night and got off the train to find the ticket guard standing on the platform. I needed to get my passport back. On seeing that my brother hadn't turned up – I would have been pretty surprised if he had as I haven't got one – he simply shrugged, handed me my document and patted me on the back in a 'Good luck, son' kind of way. I felt joy as I walked out of the station and into the cold night of Poznan.

Before I close this chapter, I want to tell you the important lesson I learnt on this, the most difficult day of the Great Euro Freebie Challenge so far. It is that the uniform accessory of every self-respecting Polish railway employee is the moustache. The ticket guard that replaced the Germans at the border station had one. The guy in the station's office had one; the old boy on this train had one; the woman operating the signals at Poznan station had one; and I'm not talking about half-arsed attempts, I'm talking proper, full-bodied Tom Selleck jobs.

Welcome to Poznan.

North Cape
Jan Mayen
(Norway)
NORWEGIAN SEA
Scandinavia
Lapland
SWEDEN
FINLAND
NORWAY
Faroe Islands
(Denmark)
Shetland Islands
(UK)
Gulf of Bothnia
HELSINKI
STOCKHOLM
OSLO
Gulf of Finland
ESTONIA
LATVIA
LITHUANIA
NORTH
SEA
Gotland
BALTIC SEA
DENMARK
COPENHAGEN
SCOTLAND
British
Isles
UNITED
KINGDOM
IRELAND
DUBLIN
ENGLAND
LONDON
NETHERLANDS
Hamburg
BERLIN
POLAND
WARSAW
BELARUS
MINSK
GERMANY
BELGIUM
PRAGUE
CZECH.REP.
SLOVAKIA
KIEV
PARIS
FRANCE
VIENNA
AUSTRIA
BUDAPEST
HUNGARY
ROMANIA
MOLDOVA
Carpathians Mts.
SWITZ.
Massif
Central
CROATIA
BOSNIA & H
SERBIA
BELGRADE
BUCHAREST
BULGARIA
SOFIA
ITALY
ROME
Corsica
Sardinia
MONTENEGRO
KOSOVO
ALBANIA
Pyrenees
MADRID
SPAIN
PORTUGAL
LISBON
Sierra Morena
MEDITERRANEAN SEA
ALGIERS
TUNIS
TUNISIA
ALGERIA
MOROCCO
Sicily
GRECCE
ATHENS
Anatolia
MEDITERRANEAN SEA

8. Poznan

Now that I had made it to Poznan I wondered how I was going to find Karolina, as I was unable to call her and didn't have her address written down. I walked speedily past the bus station and across the busy flyover to where the city's skyline started. I made my way into a hotel, past two of the biggest security guards I had ever seen, and up to the reception desk where I pleaded to be allowed to make a quick call. The receptionist obliged – the Poles clearly weren't as mean as the Germans had made out – and dialled the number before handing me the receiver. Karolina answered and spoke with a strong British accent which slightly knocked me off guard. Not that I had any complaints. The thought of having a conversation with someone that could understand me was pleasing. She told me that I had caught her just in time as she had been about to give up any hope of me arriving and turn her phone off before going to bed. I breathed a sigh of relief before writing down the address that she gave me, along with directions for getting there. I asked the receptionist where I could pick up the bus that I needed and she said something in Polish to one of the security guards who took me outside and pointed to a bus stop just up the road. I jumped on the back and sat with my face glued to the window, desperate not to miss my stop. I made it to Karolina's block without problem and rang the buzzer for her to let me in. The door was opened by a smiling blonde with a little black dog standing wagging its tail at her feet. She gave me a quick hug and beckoned me in, asking straight away if I wanted a shower.

'Yes please!'

Smelling less like a compost heap, I returned to the kitchen where Karolina had prepared me some crackers and cheese, and a cup of tea. A man with a ponytail walked into the kitchen to take a beer from the fridge and was introduced to me as Andrzej, Karolina's flatmate. All three of us were roughly the same age and I could tell I was with intelligent people by the way they spoke. The reason for Karolina's British English was that she worked as an English teacher and had been studying the language for the past 20 years, since she was a baby. Andrzej's accent was strong, but he also spoke fluently. He soon went to bed and Karolina escorted me into her bedroom where I was to kip down for the night.

'You have the choice,' she started. 'You can sleep on the floor, but that will mean me having to go and get the mattress from the other room, finding the sheets and pillow cases and then making the bed. Or you can sleep in there with me.'

She pointed to a single bed up against the wall.

'No, it's OK. I will take the floor. I'm not going to come into your home and take up your space. Don't worry about sorting my bedding out for me either, I'll do it,' I told her, feeling slightly uncomfortable.

'Really? Because it's no problem at all. In fact, it's easier if you just sleep in with me.'

What was going on here? She clearly wanted me to share her bed, but it still didn't feel right. Did I now refuse her offer one more time and risk offending her, or did I just jump right in? She seemed comfortable enough so I opted for the latter. I got under the blankets, fully clothed, and then covered my eyes after turning round to see that she had stripped down to a loose fitting t-shirt and a thong. Whoa! I did not know Couchsurfing was *that* kind of website. She climbed in and under the covers and I squeezed myself up against the wall, afraid to even brush my leg against hers as I didn't want her to think I was trying it on.

She turned off the light and we talked for a while – I honestly can't remember about what – and then I felt something stirring down below. No, not that. Further down below. She was stroking my leg with her foot. Unfazed, I carried on chatting, not returning any of her advances as I still feared that she could be simply teasing me only to kick me out on my arse if I tried anything inappropriate. This game of Cat and Mouse carried on for a good 20 minutes until she decided to up the ante.

'I'm actually glad you're here,' she told me, 'because I've been wondering for a while if Andrzej is gay and now someone is here who can tell me if he is or not. You.'

I was confused.

'What do you mean? Why would I be able to tell you?'

'Well, you are gay aren't you? I mean, you've been in bed with me now for almost half an hour, I deliberately stripped down to my underwear in front of you, I've been stroking your leg continuously and you haven't made a single move. It's pretty obvious that you're gay. But don't worry, I'm not homophobic.'

Wow! I had just heard the most genius line of seduction ever used in the history of mankind, or rather womankind. Karolina had put me in a position where on the one hand I could be a gentleman, not have sex with her, but risk making her feel unwanted. Or, on the other, I could sleep with her but worry that it might seem like I had taken advantage of a Couchsurfing host. But wait, I wasn't the one taking advantage here. And she did have an amazing body. Let's be honest, is there an unattached man in his early 20s out there who, put in the same position, would take the option that didn't involve sex with a hot, blonde Polish girl?

'The only reason I didn't make a move is because this is your home and your bed and I'm not that sort of guy,' I told her. 'But, seeing as my reputation as a virile male is on the line, and also taking your very well proportioned body into account, I suppose I can make an exception.'

'Have you got any condoms?' she asked as she lifted my t-shirt over my head.

'In the bag.'

'Get them!'

Now, this isn't the sort of smutty book that women read on the beach so I will spare you the details, but let's just say that after a long and tough day my night went a long way to picking me back up.

The following morning Karolina made me breakfast before leaving me alone in the flat while she went to work. I sat down in her bedroom to check my emails and found one from my mum letting me know that my aunty Susan had passed away that morning. I just sat staring at the screen, wanting to cry but not knowing how to. Andrzej then walked in and, sensing my sadness, asked if I wanted to drink with him as he had a load of bottles of various spirits and felt like having a bit of a session at the kitchen table. I decided that the best way to toast my late aunt's life was to get blind drunk and just remember the good times – the holidays she had taken me on as a kid; the Christmases spent in her living room listening to Elvis; the times she had babysat me over weekends when both my parents had been at work; the football matches that she had travelled all over the south to watch me play in. I had spent a lot of time with Susan and I missed her already.

I sat at the table, head to head with Andrzej, and first ate the pierogi (dumplings) and sauce that he put in front of me before starting on the proper stuff. Andrzej worked in a wine and spirits shop and was a bit of a connoisseur. He pulled a bottle of the Brazilian spirit Cachaca from the top shelf of the cupboard and placed it down on the table next to a couple of whole limes and a pot of sugar. He explained that he had discovered this cocktail whilst travelling around South America and that it was one of his favourites. He sliced the limes, mixed them with the alcohol and also a load of sugar and ice, and handed me the finished article: a glass of Caipirinha. It was sickly and strong. Just what I needed. I poured it down my neck and thought of my family at home, all mourning together the death of someone that had been so close to everyone in my family.

Andrzej was a dedicated drinker who didn't feel the need to make idle chit-chat. I suspected he had a lot on his mind too and this was just a time for two men to sit at opposite ends of the table, drinking and appreciating each other's company without the need for too many words. Each time my glass emptied it was immediately refilled by the host, and after a while I was feeling a bit dizzy. Then the bottle of Cachaca was put away and replaced by a large bottle of Scotch. A few glasses later and Andrzej's brother turned up at the flat. They greeted each other like brothers do, I was introduced, and then the three of us sat in peace to continue the session. A few glasses of Scotch later and I was breaking up inside. Susan's death was affecting me, but I couldn't show any signs of weakness in front of these two serious drinkers. I was representing my country. I carried on drinking, despite feeling pretty sick.

A while later Karolina walked in the door and joined us in the kitchen. By this time the bottle of Scotch had been put away and replaced by a bright green liquid: Absinthe.

Karolina pulled up a chair in front of me and slowly began rubbing my leg under the table but by now I had drunk so much that I was seeing three of her sat in front of me and didn't know which one to look at. I made the conscious (and highly drunk) decision then and there to not allow myself to have sex on this night of mourning, and so just carried on matching the brothers glass for glass until about 11pm when I could sit up straight no longer and so told those sat around me that I needed to go and lie down for a few minutes and would be back to join them in a short while. I staggered out of the kitchen and into Karolina's bedroom. I opened my eyes a few minutes later and was surprised to see sunlight pouring through the window. I was even more surprised to see the clock on the bedside table telling me it was 7am. What had taken place the night before? I had no idea. Karolina wasn't in the bed, which was something, but for some reason I was stark bollock naked and lying on top of the covers. Had I broken my promise to myself and slept with her again? If I had, was I to blame if I knew nothing about it? My head was banging and my mouth was dry so I stood up, put on a pair of boxers and went to the kitchen to get some water. Andrzej's bedroom door was open and I could see Karolina asleep on the mattress on his floor. I felt guilty for having got so drunk and taking her bed. I poured a pint of water down my neck and went back to sleep, waking later at 11 to find no life in the flat. After a long shower, I found Karolina making breakfast in the kitchen.

'Hey. I'm really sorry about last night. I don't know what happened. I don't usually get like that,' I told her.

She laughed and told me not to worry.

'We thought you were in a coma. We tried everything to wake you. Andrzej was even slapping your face quite hard.

You just wouldn't come to. We then tried moving you but we couldn't even do that. You were just spread out on your back on top of the bed. In the end we decided it was best to just leave you.'

'But why did you take off all my clothes?'

'We didn't. You were like that when we came in.'

My mind then conjured up the sorry image of these two trying to lift me while I just lay there with everything out. I could only laugh. And cringe.

'Guess what?' She then asked.

'Go on.'

'Last night, I gathered conclusive evidence that Andrzej is not gay.'

She gave a grin that told me exactly what she meant. I laughed.

I sent a few quick emails to Couchsurfers in Warsaw giving my phone number and asking anyone that could host me that night to text me details as I wouldn't have access to internet and couldn't take calls. I was going to leave Poznan by train at 7 that evening.

Once Karolina was washed and dressed – and had walked around the flat for a couple of minutes in her underwear – we headed out onto the street for my guided tour of the city. The air was crisp and the ground icy as we wandered around the city's Old Town. I was blown away by the beauty of the place. The main square was the prettiest I had visited and there was an overpowering atmosphere of romance.

It was the day before Polish Independence Day and we walked into a large gathering of people that stood watching schoolchildren dressed as World War II soldiers singing the national songs of that era on a hastily constructed stage. It had a Soviet feel to it: maybe it was the songs about camaraderie, maybe it was the uniforms, or maybe it was the high-rise socialist-era blocks of flats on the horizon.

'Come on, I'll show you the Cathedral and then I know this really good hot chocolate place that we can warm up in,' Karolina said.

The Arch Cathedral Basilica of St. Peter and St. Paul, built in the second half of the tenth century, is the oldest cathedral in Poland and also supposedly the place where Poland's first historical ruler Mieszko I was baptised. Karolina had clearly done her research as she was able to educate me at every place we visited. Standing in front of the cathedral, a building that had stood in the same spot for close to 1000 years, it was impossible not to feel the history, and to imagine all that the huge walls had been witness to over the centuries.

After warming up with a hot chocolate, we headed to the city's shopping mall. It was getting dark. I laughed as Karolina demonstrated what she called 'the absurdity of the Polish mindset' by showing me a little hotdog stand that stood outside the huge mall on a street corner. The whole architectural plan of the mall had had to be changed at the last minute and built around this man's stall, as he had refused to sell his tiny plot of land to the developers for any amount of money. He had been selling hotdogs there for years and refused to sell out his values to big business. As funny as it was to actually see, I felt a strong sense of respect for the fast food vendor. We went into the mall, which on the inside looked nothing like a shopping centre but rather an art gallery. Karolina explained that the owners of the complex were two art buffs that had spent fortunes on art and also on the architecture. Half of the mall was made out of metal to represent the new world, while the other half was made out of brick to represent the old. Karolina also explained how only the very top name shops were allowed to have a place in the building. The reason we had come to the mall was so that I could bid my farewell to Andrzej who was working in the wine shop. He looked in pretty good nick considering the fact that he'd carried on drinking after I'd passed out the night before and had also got up early in the morning and worked throughout the day. He told me that he'd woken up so drunk that he could hardly stand and when he'd phoned his boss to say he was running a bit late had actually started the conversation with the words, 'Good evening,' despite it being 8am.

We left the mall and headed out into the snow blizzard that was now in full flow. The first snowfall of the trip. I didn't have much time left in Poznan, just a couple of hours before my train was due to depart, and I still hadn't received any reply from any of the possible hosts I'd contacted in Warsaw. I started worrying. I would be arriving in Poland's capital just after 10 at night and didn't fancy bedding down in the train station, as I had read online stories about the place and it didn't sound like the most hospitable of surroundings. We got back to the flat and Karolina told me that we didn't have to rush as she had arranged for someone to give me a lift to the station.

'Oh, that's great. Thanks. Who is it?'

'My boyfriend.'

I was stunned. In the last two nights Karolina had slept with two different men, neither of whom was her boyfriend. How could she have a boyfriend? Why hadn't she mentioned it? I felt weird. She obviously sensed my discomfort or felt like she needed to explain herself so she started talking.

'His name's Cris. We've been together for a couple of years and I do love him. It's just that, well, I don't feel anything sexual towards him anymore. He is more like my best friend.'

'You don't have to explain anything to me.'

'I know. I just wanted you to know the situation. He doesn't know that I occasionally seek pleasure with other men that I do find attractive. He doesn't need to know. Do you understand?'

'Mmmm.'

Just then the buzzer went and Karolina pressed the button to let Cris in. As I waited to meet him I hoped that he would turn out to be either an arrogant looking guy or someone who looked like he had a lot of women in his life. The door was pushed open and I was greeted by neither of the above. Cris was gentle, polite, average looking and clearly very much in love with his girlfriend. He gave her a kiss and a cuddle and then shook my hand and introduced himself. I was spooning pieces of mackerel into my mouth straight out of the tin that I'd packed before leaving England, and he joked that Karolina was such a good host that her guests had to bring their own food. I liked the guy and felt bad in the knowledge that I had wronged him, despite not knowing it at the time of the act. If I closed my eyes I could still see Karolina naked and kissing me and I wanted to get the image out of my head.

The time came to leave, but just before going down to the car Karolina wrote a note in Polish that I was to give to the ticket inspector when he came along. I had come up with the idea whilst eating the tinned fish. There is certainly merit in the theory that fish is brain food. The note explained that I had been in the station earlier in the day, buying my ticket, when two guys had invited me to a bar to have a drink with them as they wanted to practise their English. They led me to an alleyway and robbed me. I had only been in Poznan visiting a friend but now had to get back to Warsaw where my Polish friends were waiting for me as we had a flight to England the following day. Karolina told me that she didn't think it would work but that anything was worth a try. We drove to the station and I got out of the car and hugged her before waving the two of them on their way. I could sense that Cris was in a rush to get back to the flat where he was obviously planning on getting laid. I shuddered at the thought. Karolina hadn't even changed the sheets.

As I waited on the platform I finally got what I had been wishing for: a text message from someone in Warsaw. It was from an English guy called Jon telling me that I could stay in his flat and that I would have to meet him and his friends in a bar in the centre of the city. He gave me directions and wished me luck in getting there. I jumped on the train and took a seat. It wasn't long before the ticket inspector approached me and I immediately handed him the note. He read it, before saying in perfect English, 'Oh my God! That's terrible. So you have friends waiting for you in Warsaw?'

'Yes. I really need to get there. I didn't know what else to do other than get on the train.'

I did my best to look desperate.

'Okay, don't worry. The best thing I can think to do is to call your friends and arrange for them to come and meet you in the station where they can pay for your ticket. Otherwise, I'm afraid, the fine will multiply and will get very expensive.'

He then handed me his mobile phone and stood watching me. I was shocked; this possible scenario had not crossed my mind. I did some quick thinking and dialled Karolina's number. She answered.

'Hi, Karolina. It's Kris. You know how I'm meant to be meeting you in Warsaw later tonight? Well, I'm going to need you to come and meet me at the station and lend me the money for a ticket because I was robbed in Poznan.'

The inspector then took the phone off me and explained the situation to Karolina in Polish. He hung up and told me that he was going to call Karolina again in an hour to arrange the details of the payment. He then told me to relax and not to worry. I couldn't believe that my plan was working. I sat alone in the carriage as we rolled through the Polish countryside.

After about an hour and ten minutes of sitting quietly I was disturbed by the ticket man who came to tell me that he had been trying to get through to Karolina for the past twenty minutes but that she wasn't answering her phone. Because of this, he was going to have to write me out a fine. He told me to stand up, and led me to his compartment. He was being exceptionally friendly as he wrote down the fake address I gave him. He asked if I liked it in Poland. I told him what he wanted to hear, that I loved the country and its people, and he expressed his regret at the robbery I'd been a victim of.

'I am sorry that this happened to you in my country. I hope you don't think that all Poles are like this. We are well known for being a very welcoming people, usually.'

I wondered then if that's all Karolina had been doing by seducing me – being welcoming.

The inspector handed me my fine, before joking that this was probably the most expensive beer I had ever gone for. What a farce this all was. I thanked him for his help and said goodbye just as we were pulling into Warsaw's central station. It was 10:20pm and I ticked another capital off of my list.

Welcome to Warsaw.

9. Warsaw

Capitals left to visit: Amsterdam, Athens, Bratislava, Brussels, Bucharest, Budapest, Helsinki, Lisbon, Ljubljana, Luxembourg, Madrid, Paris, Prague, Riga, Rome, Sofia, Tallinn, Vienna, Vilnius

Days on the road: 10
Distance travelled: 1457 miles
EU capitals visited: 4

THE NIGHT AIR was ice cold as I walked through a park in the shadow of a gigantic building that resembled Big Ben. It was the Palace of Culture and Science and, as I was later to find out, the second tallest clock tower on the planet. With the help of some local taxi drivers' knowledge I managed to find the pub I was looking for and was greeted on the door by a guy who shook my hand in a way that suggested he had been awaiting my arrival.

'Hi. You must be Kris,' he said warmly.

Either he was a very gifted psychic or he was my host Jon. I couldn't be sure so I decided to test him.

'Yes I am. And you must be a very gifted psychic?' I said; not out loud but in my head.

I gave him a couple of seconds to respond but he said nothing, instead he just looked at me wondering why I was staring him in the eye with a look of intense concentration. He was Jon.

'Yes, I'm Kris. Nice to meet you,' I said out loud.

'There is a guy called Jon waiting for you at the back of the pub. He is with the group of Canadians,' he said, moving out of my way to let me through.

He was neither a very gifted psychic nor Jon. I had not considered all the options.

I made my way inside and introduced myself to the table of English speakers, all aged roughly the same as me. A tall, pale guy with a Home Counties accent stood up, introduced himself as Jon, and then introduced me to Nick and Paul, two Canadian brothers. The rest of the group consisted mainly of Poles. I say mostly, there was also a German girl amongst them. I immediately found myself fielding questions about my day and how I'd made it to Warsaw, and as I spoke the table space in front of me filled up with pints of beer and shots of Polish Vodka. Everyone felt like buying me a drink. I had only eaten a few crackers and a bit of mackerel all day, so I knew that this amount of alcohol would probably have an adverse effect, but everyone else was wasted already and I wasn't going to turn down the opportunity to catch up a bit. I downed everything in front of me and then was told that we were heading off to a club. The only thing I really wanted to do was get to a bed and maybe find something to eat, but I couldn't bring myself to dampen my new friends' spirits so I asked what I should do with my luggage. They spoke to the guy that had met me on the door. He turned out to be the head barman, Max, and he said that I could keep all of my stuff in the downstairs cellar and pick it up the following morning. Apprehensive as I was about leaving all of my possessions with a stranger in a pub, I didn't feel like I had much say in the matter.

As we walked the streets in search of a club that the group had heard was worth checking out, I was told the story of how Jon and the two Canadians had been arrested a few weeks previously for stealing a set of portable traffic lights. They were still waiting for the court date to have their fate determined. I knew that I would get on well with these guys. Anyone who thinks, 'Fuck stealing a traffic cone, let's get the set of lights!' is alright by me.

We got to the club we were looking for, an 80's style mosh-pit of a place inhabited by large men with skinheads and women with punk hairstyles, and we headed inside. The place was so dingy and dirty that it didn't even have a cloakroom. Instead you just chucked your coat over wooden beams supporting the ceiling. Getting drunker by the minute, and feeling loose, we all took up space on the dance floor and I soon found myself in between two ridiculously attractive girls grinding up against me and squeezing various parts of my body.

'Wow, so you are from England. We love English men!' they shouted in unison.

My enjoyment was halted less than a minute after it had begun when a fight broke out between a couple of huge Neanderthals and, as one got knocked to the ground, he almost took the two girls with him. The bouncers quickly ejected the beasts but the mood had already been killed. It had been fun while it lasted. We stayed until the music finished and then before leaving spent a good ten minutes trying to locate our coats. Outside, Jon got talking to a scary looking girl with a Mohawk who he invited back to the flat for a smoke. She said she would just go and find her boyfriend and as she walked off Jon changed his mind about wanting her to come with us and shouted 'Run!' which we all did, as you tend to when someone unexpectedly shouts 'Run!' and then starts running. Five minutes later we stopped, completely out of breath, at a kebab house, where Jon sorted me out with a chicken shawarma and I asked the girl behind the counter to fill a polystyrene cup with tap water for me, which she did, giving me a strange look as she handed it over. I downed it in one and then turned to see Jon giving me the same look I had just received from the girl.

'You didn't just drink tap water, did you?' he asked.

'Yea. Why?'

'Because the tap water in Warsaw isn't really drinkable. Nobody touches it.'

'But I was thirsty.'

I arrived back at the flat with Jon, Nick and Paul, all of whom rented the place, as well as Kim the German girl who had come to stay with the boys for a short period as a Couchsurfer and had ended up living with them for free as she completed her studies in the city. The feelings towards her were mixed, as Jon constantly made fun of her but in a friendly enough way; Nick fancied her and was desperate to get her into bed; and Paul just flat out didn't like her. I didn't like her either, as all night she had gone out of her way to avoid talking to me and when she had looked at me it had been to throw daggers my way. She had also given us a lecture in the kebab house for eating animals. She was a vegan, and just a little bit self-righteous. The flat consisted of two huge bedrooms, a kitchen with balcony, a small bathroom and a separate room with a toilet. There was also a cat that strolled around. The larger of the two bedrooms had nothing more than a double mattress on the floor and a couple of wardrobes around the outside. The other bedroom had three single camper beds and was where the two brothers and the German slept. Jon paid more rent so had the big room to himself, despite the fact that the flat was owned by Nick and Paul's dad, a Pole who had emigrated to Canada before the birth of his sons. We all sat on the double bed and passed around a spliff as the room started to spin and I closed my eyes.

I woke the next day to find myself alone in the room and with no sound coming from anywhere else in the flat. It was 2 in the afternoon and I wondered if everyone had gone out and forgotten I was there. I got up to investigate and found the four of them all asleep in the other room; Jon in bed with Kim. I wanted to shower and brush my teeth but couldn't, as all of my belongings were still in the basement of a pub I had no idea how to reach. I made a cup of tea and was joined in the kitchen by a smug looking Jon who wrote down some directions for me.

An hour of walking later and I was lost in the city centre, going around in circles. People rushed past me in all directions as the snow fell. The streets were choc-a-bloc with people celebrating Polish Independence Day. Soldiers dressed in WWII fatigues paraded up and down the main street; old tanks and cannons lined the side of the road; and all around people drank vodka and toasted national heroes. It was all well and good, but I was only interested in finding my stuff and getting back to the flat for a shower and hopefully something small to eat. I began looking around to see if I could find a taxi driver to point me in the right direction when I felt a tap on my shoulder. I span around to see Max standing there smiling broadly. What were the odds of that? He laughed when I told him I was searching for the bar.

'We are not very close. But I'm going there now, you can walk with me.'

We walked and talked and naturally the subject of why I was in Poland came up. Max loved the story and as soon as we got into the bar he instructed the girl behind the counter, Patricja, to make me a cup of Earl Gray. After I had drunk it Max made me a generous offer.

'I would like to invite you to come and have something to eat with me in a Chinese restaurant close to here,' he said.

I had forgotten that I'd hardly eaten over the past few days. My hunger had been replaced by a numb feeling all over my body. I knew I should eat and this offer was too kind to refuse. We walked to the small restaurant just around the corner and sat down at a little table. There were only a small handful of other diners but everyone seemed to be enjoying the food. Max ordered a couple of starters, a couple of cans of drink and fried chicken with noodles for my main course and then started telling me his story. Originally from Sierra Leone, he had been forced to flee the war-torn country and build a new life for himself in Europe. He had been through so much tragedy and pain that it really put my own struggles into perspective. My own struggles? What struggles?! Max explained his simple philosophy of life to me: 'If you are a good person and have a good heart, you will get what you deserve. If not in this life, then in the next.'

He then gave me a concrete example.

'When I was a young boy in school, I was always kind to everyone in my class. I was popular because I was a good kid. One night years later, when the war was happening in my country, a group of rebel soldiers came and took me away. They beat me badly before holding a gun to my head. They were going to kill me that night. Then the leader of the group turned up. He looked at me and asked, "Max. Is that you?" Through my badly beaten eyes I looked at him but couldn't recognise the face. "Max. It is you. I went to school with you. Remember me? How are you?" The leader then ordered his men to let go of me before saying, "You were so good to me in school. When I had problems with my studies you were always the one to help me. I am so sorry for what my boys have done to you today. Listen, Max, for your own safety you have to get out of Freetown. I can give you a pass to get through. If anyone stops you, you just tell them to call me. But you have to go. It is the only way I can save your life after you helped me so much in school." And that was when I escaped my country and came to Europe.'

I was speechless. Sat in front of me was someone who was so positive about life, so optimistic, worked so hard for so little money but who had seen the worst side of mankind. How was it that he remained so upbeat?

'I told you. If you have a good heart, you will see the good in people and in life.'

The food was brought over and I looked down at it, picked

up a fork and realised I had no appetite at all. My stomach had shrunk and I couldn't eat. I chewed on the first piece of chicken for an eternity as Max demolished his meal in no time at all. I was embarrassed. He had brought me here and spent money on my dinner and now I couldn't eat it. I tried harder to force some down, but it was as if I had forgotten how to swallow. I just felt sick. I apologised and he told me not to worry and that I should take it away in a doggy bag and just try to eat little bits of it slowly throughout the evening. I did and, after a few beers back at the flat, managed to get it all down just before bed.

I spent much of the next day just walking around the city aimlessly. Warsaw had been one of the cities I had most been looking forward to seeing when I first planned my journey.

The main reason for this was the film The Pianist. Roman Polanski's sad tale of life in the Warsaw Ghetto had portrayed a truly beautiful Old Town, a place that I had wanted to see and feel for myself ever since seeing the film. I had romanticised the streets so much in my mind. Now I was here. I was in the place I had dreamt of seeing for years, and I have to be honest with you, I wasn't feeling great. Throughout the five hours that I spent traipsing around, the wet snow didn't stop falling once. The temperature was -7 degrees, and foolishly I had left the flat in the morning without gloves or a scarf. All of the excitement prior to my visit had now been extinguished, but not by the weather alone. There was something else that saddened me, something that I really should have researched before arriving. Warsaw's Old Town wasn't as old as I had imagined.

During the invasion of Poland in 1939, much of the district was badly damaged by the German Luftwaffe, which targeted the city's residential areas and historic landmarks in a campaign of terror bombing. Then, just to cap things off, whatever had been left standing after 1939 was blown up by the German army immediately after the Warsaw Uprising that lasted between August and October of 1944. Warsaw's entire Old Town had been systematically destroyed. The Germans had left nothing intact. So the Old Town that I now stood in was a replica, built after the end of the 2nd World War. Speaking to a Polish friend a couple of months later on in my journey I learnt that Warsaw was nicknamed The Phoenix City after being completely destroyed and then rebuilt from the ashes with the heroic effort of Poland's citizens. I'm not saying that the place isn't beautiful; it really is. But for me, the most wonderful thing about the Old Towns of Central and Eastern Europe is that you can stand in the middle of them and just let your imagination take you back through the centuries. You can look at the buildings and know that 200 years ago a person might have been stood in exactly the same spot and he or she would have had the same view. That's the magic that is lacking in Warsaw's Stare Miasto.

I spent a good few hours strolling the tiny streets of the area, desperate to find something that would make Warsaw special in my mind again, but it wasn't forthcoming and in the end I gave up and made my way back to the flat. The walk home was one of dejection; I didn't want to be on the continent any more. I was tired of the ice cold conditions, of not having food, of not having money. The cold, the tiredness and the hunger were finally grinding me down.

Back at the flat I resolved to get through the rest of the challenge as quickly as possible. I checked the internet for the train times to Lithuania and found that there was just one a day and that it left Warsaw for Vilnius at 7:40 in the morning. I was going to pack my bags, get an early night and be on that train out of Poland the following morning. That was the plan until Nick invited me for a few beers. We got back to the flat at 3am but I was still going to get out of there, so, drunkenly, I packed before falling onto the bed.

I woke at 9:30am and instantly checked to see why my

alarm hadn't gone off when it was supposed to. Conclusion: I had forgotten to set it. I swallowed a couple of paracetamol and went back to sleep. Lithuania would have to wait a day. Later in the day I received an email from the BBC, who had found out about my journey and created a page on their Southern Counties website dedicated to the challenge. They asked if they could interview me live on the radio to talk about how things were going and to try to push up the sponsorships. I also received an email from a guy called Mark who ran a tourist information and bookings company based in Poland called Cracow-Life. His company had grown from humble beginnings in Krakow to become the biggest rival to established organisation In Your Pocket. They produced guide books, maps and online information for cities all over Central and Eastern Europe, and when they had branched out into Slovenia I had written the content and taken the photos for their Ljubljana-Life website with a view to becoming a part of the team. Unfortunately, due to unforeseen circumstances – my gambling – I'd had to leave Slovenia just as things were taking off. Mark, a Zimbabwean of English descent, had paid me a visit in Ljubljana and we had got on very well. He told me by email that the company was making a £250 donation to the cause and had also written about my journey on every one of their websites. He also let me know that he would be more than happy to take care of my stay if I passed through Krakow. I didn't plan on taking that route but it was good to know I had the offer, as maybe on the way back down south from the Baltics my path would take me that way.

Jon and the Canadians told me about an Indian guy living close to the flat who was an ambassador for the website Hospitality Club, an almost identical idea to Couchsurfing. They said that he owned an Indian restaurant in the city and that he enjoyed entertaining foreign guests.

'You should send him an email and let him know about your

challenge. He will probably invite you round for a meal,' they suggested.

Tony also had a profile on Couchsurfing, so I found it and sent him a quick message letting him know of my challenge and asking if he would be able to spare me any leftovers from his restaurant. He replied almost immediately with a much better offer. I was invited round to his flat for a home cooked meal later that evening, just like the boys had presumed would happen.

Middle aged, heavily bearded and wearing a turban, a t-shirt that said "Don't freak, I'm a Sikh" on it, and a pair of jeans, Tony looked a lot more laid back than I had been expecting. He welcomed me in, offered me a glass of water and then disappeared into his bedroom, returning a couple of moments later wearing nothing but a vest, a pair of boxer shorts and his turban. It was a moment of comedy class but it wasn't intended as such, so I held my laughter.

'When I cook, I like to feel comfortable,' he told me. 'I don't like to wear clothes; they make me hot and sweaty.'

What could I do apart from smile nervously and say, 'It's your home.'

He then pulled a little wooden chair from in the living room and put it in the corner of the kitchen.

'Sit. I like it when people watch me cook. It makes it easier to talk.'

I was now starting to wonder if the lads back at the flat were on a wind-up sending me to this guy. Was he in on the joke? Tony asked me about my journey and I told him little bits but never really managed to get far into my sentences before being interrupted by his own tales of travelling. As he talked, he pulled a plastic tub filled with a green paste out of the fridge and then peeled and chopped a load of cucumber, before dipping a slice of it into the paste and handing it to me.

'This is my special chilli mint sauce. It's a bit spicy. You don't mind spicy food, do you?'

'No, I love it,' I said before popping it in my mouth.

No sooner had it touched my tongue than my nose was running and tears were streaming down my face. It was the hottest thing I had ever tasted. Tony looked on with surprise as I ran to the toilet to blow my nose. Still, as hot as it was, it was also incredibly moreish and I found myself eating lots of it, blowing my nose in between bites. Tony's stories soon went from tales of travel to tales of a different nature.

'I moved here a few years ago for a Polish woman I was with. In the end it didn't work out, she dumped me. But it was okay, because I soon had another Polish girlfriend. She was so young, just 19. In the end she dumped me too. But it didn't matter, because after her I found a young Ukrainian girl, she was a student here and was only in her late teens. In the end though, she dumped me.'

I was starting to see a theme but decided against voicing my observation. I just listened.

'The best thing about living in Poland is the girls. I just love young Eastern European girls. They are so beautiful, don't you think?'

'Yea, they're nice. How old are you, Tony?'

'I'm 46 but I feel as if I'm still in my early twenties like you.'

'Right.'

'Anyway, after the Ukrainian girl dumped me, I soon found another one, this time from Belarus. It didn't last long because…'

I could continue, but I think you get the point. There were a lot of these stories; each one involving a young Eastern European girl and each one ending the same way. The question I was asking myself was how he got these girls in the first place. But then I remembered, his restaurant was by all accounts the best Curry House in Warsaw, he made a good living, had a nice flat, etc… So it probably wasn't too hard to impress girls from countries like Ukraine and Belarus, if only for a very short period of time.

A few minutes before dinner was ready Tony told me that it wasn't just going to be the two of us eating, but that he had a Couchsurfing guest staying with him. I wasn't blown away in shock when he told me that it was a young Ukrainian girl. He told me that she had been at his place for the past two nights and was going to be staying for another couple of weeks as she completed some kind of study placement in Poland. My primary thought was whether or not he was going to put some trousers on before she arrived. Don't forget that throughout all of the above conversation I was talking to a man wearing just a vest, a pair of boxer shorts and a turban. And I wasn't allowed to laugh.

Natasha was in her early twenties. She had tight, curly brown hair, dark eyes, and a body as slim as could be without being ill. She had a gentle manner and came across as quite shy. I wondered how comfortable she felt being alone in the flat with Tony, and I got a good indication of her feelings as I was letting her in the front gate and she said with a huge smile, 'Oh, Tony has another guest. I'm so happy!'

I could see she really meant it.

Dinner was quite delicious and very spicy. Tony was still in his underwear, but to my surprise Natasha seemed to find it normal. I guessed that she'd had to get used to it pretty quickly. Personally, I still felt completely weirded out by the whole experience, but hey, I wasn't in a position to turn down a free meal just because the chef was half way to being a nudist in a turban. Throughout the meal the atmosphere became gradually more uncomfortable as Tony 'entertained' us with some of his jokes. His repertoire didn't include any 'knock knock' pieces but did include some very graphic references to both male and female genitalia. By now I really was convinced that this whole night had been set up and I was the victim of a practical joke. I mean, come on, I was having dinner with a half-naked, middle aged Indian who after telling stories of his young Eastern European conquests then introduced me to Natasha, before embarrassing both himself and his guests with a list of shockingly graphic sexual jokes, all the time wearing nothing but a vest, a pair of boxer shorts and a turban. Surely no one could be this outrageous and take themselves so seriously at the same time. After we had finished eating, Natasha went into the bathroom to freshen up, and while she was out of earshot Tony said, 'She's something, huh?'

If this wasn't all a big joke I worried for the poor girl and didn't want to leave her alone with Tony. But what could I do? Natasha rejoined us and then said, 'Tony, listen. I know that I told you I would stay here for a couple of weeks, but earlier on today I found someone else to stay with. I think it will be better.'

Tony didn't take the news so well.

'What do you mean? You told me you wanted to stay here for a couple of weeks, so I made arrangements to accommodate you. I had to cancel some other guests. And now you are telling me that you don't want to be here. I think that's bad etiquette.'

'I'm sorry. I just think I will be more comfortable staying with students that are closer to my age. I will be leaving tomorrow morning.'

'Fine,' was all that Tony could muster in response before switching into sulk mode. He switched on his laptop in silence and booted up a game of online poker. For real money. I couldn't believe what I was seeing. Tony was a fellow degenerate gambler; I could tell by the way he retreated into the game and completely ignored his guests. I sat talking to Natasha for a few minutes until I started getting severe cramps in my stomach.

'Tony, really, thanks for everything. The dinner, the

company, it was great. But I think I'm going to go now,' I said, standing up.

'Oh, really, do you have to? Why don't you stay here a bit longer?'

It was Natasha. She didn't want me to leave. I felt bad for her, but I knew that she was getting out of there the following morning and I also knew that if I didn't leave soon I might embarrass myself.

Tony closed his poker game and filled up a couple of Tupperware tubs with leftovers from dinner and told me to eat it the next day when trying to get to Vilnius. I thanked him and then exchanged phone numbers with Natasha and whispered in her ear that she should call me if she felt uncomfortable and needed to get out of the flat, as I was sure there would be a place for her at Jon's if things got too hard to handle with Tony. She smiled nervously and I left.

As soon as I got out into the falling snow it hit me. Not the snow, the cramps. If I didn't get to a toilet soon I was going to soil myself. I ran at full speed all the way back to the flat, up the stairs, in through the door, straight past the guys and into the bog.

Must be the spicy food, I thought, as I sat on the throne with a look of incredible relief on my face. I then joined Jon, Nick and Paul in the kitchen and found them all grinning.

'What's so funny?'

'Nothing. How was it at Tony's? Did he have a young Eastern European girl there?' Paul asked, while the others smirked away.

'Yes! How did you know?'

'Because he's *always* got a young Eastern European girl there!'

They all burst out laughing.

'That's why we sent you there. We knew it would shock you.'

I told them the story of the evening over a cup of tea and

then they told me a few stories of their own, like how not so long ago they had received an email from a girl asking if she could come and stay with them as she felt uncomfortable at her current place, with Tony. They invited her round and she told them how she had arrived at Tony's late one night and found his flat full of young girls. He was plying them with drink and getting them to play a game of strip poker with him, but when one of the girls refused to take off her bra, Tony went mental and berated her and her friends for being teases and not playing by the rules. Another girl they had met at a Couchsurfing meeting had told them that when she'd arrived at Tony's to find it again full of female guests, Tony had explained to her that the only available place for her to sleep was in his bed with him. She promptly left and had to find last minute accommodation in a hotel.

'He's a pervert. But his restaurant's good. How was the food?'

'It was nice, but I've got a bit of a dicky tummy now.'

They laughed even more.

Just before going to bed I paid another desperate visit to the toilet as the cramps in my stomach intensified. I hoped it would pass before trying to make it to Lithuania the following morning.

My sleep that night was full of tossing and turning as the pains moved me into a state of agony and I became overpowered by a feeling of nausea that left me shivering and sweating at the same time. I was running from the bed to the toilet every 20 minutes or so and in the end even contemplated taking a pillow in with me and trying to get some shuteye on the floor. I decided against this idea for hygiene reasons, but it was a close one. Somehow I managed to make it up and out of bed before 7 the next morning and after creeping around trying not to wake anyone, I lifted my rucksack onto my back and walked down the stairs and out into the freezing dawn air. I wasn't the least bit optimistic about the day that lay ahead. I was in serious pain and I was starting to wonder if it was more than just the after-effects of spicy food. Perhaps I'd got some kind of bacteria. As well as the curry at Tony's, there was also the pint of tap water that I had downed a couple of nights before. I hadn't vomited, which I took as a sign that I wasn't too severely sick, but the diarrhoea was relentless. I squeezed my way onto the tram, packed full of Warsawians (not entirely sure if that's a word, I just took a stab in the dark) making their way to work, school or university. There was no way of sitting down on this journey, so I just stood bent over in pain, my face pushed against the glass as the people around me eyed me curiously. The sheer agony became too much to bear before I was anywhere near the train station and I found myself pushing through the masses and jumping off and out into the fresh air. I had no idea where I was, but a quick scan of the skyline revealed that trusty old clock tower I told you about at the start of the chapter. If I could make it there I remembered how to get to the train station. I got to the park in question and then fell to the floor as sharp, stabbing pains cut across my stomach. I was dying, I was sure of it. I staggered over to a bench and fell onto it, lying there on the wet wood for a few minutes as I waited to see the bright light you hear about in Near Death Experience stories. When it failed to show up, I figured I was probably going to be alright. But my train. Shit, my train. I had about 20 minutes to get to the station and onto the platform before it departed. I couldn't run, so I thought I would try the next best thing: walking briskly. It wasn't as easy as I had hoped, so I soon resorted to the next, next best thing: staggering. Luckily, I was able to pull off the staggering perfectly. I am a good staggerer. I made it to the station with about ten minutes to spare but then a spanner was thrown into the works. I couldn't go any further without first going to the toilet. This was a real emergency. Now I found the ability to run. And run I did; very, very fast.

I got to the public conveniences outside the main entrance of the station and sprinted towards the door of the Gents. I was almost there, almost at the point of relief, when a middle-aged woman in a puffy green coat stepped in front of me.

'Get out of the way, lady!' I screamed.

She didn't budge and started saying something at me in Polish. I had no time to learn the language now; if I didn't make it to the toilet within approximately the next 90 seconds there was going to be a mess that I wouldn't be clearing up.

'Come on! I need to go. Please! Lady, I'm warning you. Oh, come on!' I begged.

She could see that I was doubled up in pain. How hard was it to understand the situation? She rubbed her fingers together in the international gesture for 'money.' She then pointed to a little sign on the door with the cost written on it. I didn't have money and I certainly didn't have time to explain the purpose of my challenge.

I screamed at her, 'Proszę! Proszę!'

I had heard it said a few times since my arrival in Poland and guessed it meant 'please.' Who knows? Either way, the evil lady in front of me wasn't in generous mood, even if I had said the magic word. She shook her head, mumbled a load of gibberish and pointed for me to leave the area. I was in distress. I crawled along the floor, through the snow, back to the park and onto the bench. Tears were streaming down my face as I lay there. The only thing I could think to do was to get back to the flat in as quick a time as possible. I had already missed my train anyway, so what difference would it make? I was stuck in Poland for at least another day, but with my condition as bad as it was, I worried that it would be more than 24 hours before I could be on my way again.

Getting back to the flat should have taken me about 25 minutes. Instead, it took me over two hours as, in my state of diarrhoea-induced confusion, I managed to get on the right number tram but heading in the wrong direction. I took it all the way to the final stop, got off, looked around, didn't recognise a thing and then guessed that I needed to walk up the road a bit. It didn't turn out to be one of my better guesses. After walking – and occasionally crawling – for about 15 minutes I was still no closer to finding a clue as to my whereabouts. I pulled a map of Warsaw out of my bag and looked around for signs of human life. Up in the distance I spied an old lady walking towards me. The speed she was walking at, I estimated that she would reach me some time in the next year. I couldn't wait that long so I tried jogging. I got to her and she looked scared. I took a couple of paces back, trying not to appear aggressive, then pointed to the map and tried pronouncing the street I was looking for. Surprisingly, she didn't understand what I was saying and attempted to carry on walking past me.

'No, old lady, you shall not pass without helping me first,' I told her, boldly.

I believe the Polish translation of that sentence is 'Proszę!' She took the map from me and I pointed to Jon's street that I had circled in biro a couple of days before. Her reaction didn't exactly fill me with joy as she shook her head vigorously whilst saying over and over again, 'Nie, nie, nie, nie.'

She pointed to the two of us and then pointed to a point on completely the other side of the map to my little circled area. Was she telling me I had somehow come to the other side of Warsaw? Yes she was. So I walked the long distance back to the tram stop, still in severe agony, and jumped on the tram. At least one thing was for sure: I couldn't go in the wrong direction this time. It wasn't direction that was heaviest on my mind, but rather ticket inspectors: I had to make it the whole way across the city without any getting on and checking me. The nervous feeling that I experienced throughout the ride back to Jon's place was what I would usually refer to as 'squeaky bum time', however I don't feel the term is appropriate in this case as if I had allowed my bum to so much as let out the tiniest of squeaks it would have caused an international incident and no doubt would have led to the British Embassy in Poland being forced to make an apology on my behalf. I didn't think I could handle that scale of embarrassment, so I put all thoughts of such a scenario to the back of my mind and tried to think about something else. In this case I chose Thomas the Tank Engine. I used to love Thomas as a kid. And then in my mind I heard the slow voice of Ringo Starr say, 'And then the Fat Controller shat his pants.'

Miraculously, I made it back to the flat without incident. I rang the bell to the flat and waited for what seemed like an eternity for someone to answer. Eventually Paul let me in and complained that I had woken him up. The whole flat was still in slumber.

'No time to explain!'

I pushed past my Canadian friend and straight into the toilet. I spent the rest of the day in bed, my pain growing by the hour.

The BBC had sent me an email telling me to expect a call from them the following morning at 8:50 for an interview live on air. That evening, still in pain but not needing the toilet as often, I accompanied Nick and Paul to a Sheesha bar, where I was introduced to a friend of theirs, Noam, and a friend of his, Domča. Noam was 21 years old and from Belgium. He looked the archetypal liberal: beard, long hair held in place by a brightly-coloured band, and baggy clothes. The son of Polish parents, he had studied at the University of Bristol and spoke in a British way, although couldn't speak Polish. Domča was from Slovakia, 19 years old, dark haired and olive skinned. She was in Poland for a few days to meet with Noam and to help plan an upcoming conference for a student organisation that they were both a part of, AIESEC. We all sat around a small table on cushions on the floor, drinking tea and smoking the apple flavoured Sheesha. Noam and Domča were the two most overly enthusiastic people I had ever met, but despite this, I liked both of them a lot. They each had a million questions about my challenge, and were both amazed by my story. To be fair, they were the type of people who would be amazed by a well-made cheese sandwich. Or a hat. Or by any colour. Or shape. What I'm saying is they were able to see the positive side of every little thing and expressed this with words such as, 'awesome', 'amazing' and 'brilliant'. They told me a little bit about AIESEC, but it all went over my head. I gathered that it was a non-profit organisation that had branches in universities all over Europe, but if you asked me what they actually did I didn't have the foggiest. I would find out later. Noam told me that he was going to be chairing the conference down in Slovakia in just under a week's time and that they would love to have me there to act as a motivational speaker to the attendees. My story was so inspirational, he told me, that it had to be shared with others to help them realise that anything was possible if you put your mind to it. I still had no idea what the organisation was or why they would want to listen to someone like me, but when Noam finished his pitch with the sentence, 'You will meet loads of interesting people and will also have free accommodation and food,' I couldn't really turn him down.

If I was going to be in Slovakia in a weeks' time then I was going to have to completely change my planned route and head south from Warsaw instead of north into the Baltics. This was another opportunity to put the 'Never Say No' rule into practice. Throughout the evening I had been doing my best to disguise the pain I was in, but as the night drew to a close the cramps became severe and I worried that I would be caught short again. Eventually the waitress asked us to leave as she was closing for the night. I could have kissed her. One person I couldn't have kissed was Domča, who, in an act of Eastern

European brutal honesty that I had never completely got used to, told me after leaving the bar, 'You're different outside to how you were in the bar. In there you were fun, friendly, and you looked good. Out here, you look haggard and rough. You don't look good now.'

I wanted to say, 'If you were as sick as I am, as dehydrated as I am, as tired as I am, as hungry as I am, as in pain as I am, and on the journey that I am, you might not look as good as you do right now, either.'

But as I didn't want to cause a scene, all I came up with was, 'Thanks for pointing it out.'

'See you in Slovakia, mate,' Noam said as he and Domča jumped off the tram a few stops before us. Nick and I got back to the flat just before 4 and I checked my emails before going to bed. There was one from Mark in Krakow, who had read on my blog that I was ill and felt that it would be a good idea for me to head down to Krakow where he could get me to a doctor and where I could rest until I felt well enough to move on. He told me that his company would be able to provide me with my own apartment for as long as I needed, free of charge. Krakow was on the way to Slovakia and would be the perfect halfway point. It was also probably necessary for me to get a diagnosis from a medically trained professional, just in case I wasn't going to get better without medicine. I emailed him back telling him to expect me later that day. I finally got into bed just after 4, knowing that I had to be up a few hours later for the BBC.

The interview went well and shortly after I watched as a few donations from strangers came in to the Justgiving page. I was pleased. Just before my train to Krakow was due to leave, we met up with Paul in the station who wanted to buy me a Big Mac before I left. I didn't think it was the best idea with my stomach being in the condition that it was, but I had hardly eaten over the past few days and the thought of some shit food was exciting. After devouring my meal I made my way to the platform with the two Canadian brothers. My train was already there, so I hugged the lads, thanked them for all that they had done for me over the past few days and climbed aboard the train.

Within minutes of the train pulling out of the station, as I stood nervously in the area between carriages, I was confronted by a woman who had clearly stumbled upon a time machine in her previous era of 1985 and had used it to escape her oppressed life as an Eastern Bloc Olympic triple jumper to seek political asylum in 2007, where she'd managed to find work as a ticket inspector. She was obviously a new arrival as she still sported the short spiky haircut with the mullet going down the back of her neck, a little moustache caused by all those performance enhancing drugs the state had pumped into her, as well as that constant expression of arrogance in her face, a result of continuously being told by her coaches that she was unbeatable. Tall and lean, she was a fearsome foe.

She spoke no English and wouldn't be convinced that I was in fact from England, despite me holding my passport up in her face and saying, 'British!' over and over again. She relentlessly shouted at me in Polish to the point where I was wiping bits of chewed sauerkraut off of my face. The fury in her grew as she switched to what I assumed was her attempt at speaking English but could also have been Polish for: 'I'm going to break your bones.'

'Tick-et! Tick-et! Tick-et!' She roared.

'Nie-mam! Nie-mam! Nie-mam!' I said back as I imitated her tone. *'I don't have! I don't have! I don't have!'*

After a while of getting nowhere with this conversation she gave up, sighed in a way that I understood meant, 'This isn't over!' then disappeared up the train, muttering expletives under her breath and leaving me standing alone, wondering what punishment awaited me. She returned a few minutes later with an increased look of insanity in her eyes. Thankfully, she was accompanied by a male colleague who looked a lot more controlled. I would even go as far as to say he looked amicable, although next to her Joseph Stalin would look like the sort of guy you could share a vodka with. He spoke English – her male colleague, not Stalin – and he asked me why I didn't have a ticket. I pretty much used the same story that I'd used on my previous two train journeys in Poland. The inspector then translated my story for the triple jumper and they started arguing. He clearly wanted to believe me, she clearly did not. He took my passport out of my hand and flicked through the pages, paying special attention to the ones in the middle.

'Why do you have so many stamps from Slovenia, Croatia and Bosnia?' he asked.

I had no idea how this was relevant to the situation but decided I would turn my tiny lie into a much bigger one. Just for fun.

'I work for the BBC News website,' I explained, 'writing about the new EU members and candidates for entry. I base myself in Ljubljana but I am in Poland today because the BBC wants a real life story about the Polish people and their everyday lives. I want to paint a good picture of the Poles for all the British readers.'

I thought this lie was genius, even if I do say so myself, because I was basically telling him that he was representing his country now and had a very good opportunity to help Anglo-Polish relations by being nice to me. Whatever he did or didn't do was going to be read by thousands of people. I could hardly believe my luck when I realised that he actually bought my story.

'I am so sorry that this has happened to you in our country. I don't know exactly what we should do. I need to speak with my colleague about it,' he said.

I looked at her and she scowled. I checked that her colleague wasn't watching then threw her a grin. The battle had taken a turn.

'Come with us.'

They led me through the train to their own private compartment and told me to stand outside in the corridor. They didn't return my passport. I spent the next two and a half hours doubled up in agony as the stabbing pains hit me hard in the stomach. Just at the end of the corridor was the train's only toilet, which meant that I had to endure the verbal abuse of every passenger that had to squeeze past me and my luggage on the way to and from relieving themselves.

'Why don't you go and sit in a carriage instead of standing here blocking the route?' was the clean version of what they were saying.

Up and down the train people poured vodka and beer into paper cups, sang boisterously and even danced. As far as I could tell, there was virtually no difference between the 3:05pm Warsaw to Krakow Express and the streets of Brighton at chucking out time on a Friday night. That meant a lot of toilet visits. Add to that the fact that the small space just outside the toilet was also used as the smoking area and you might begin to understand my strategic faux pas. Well, technically it wasn't *my* mistake, but the people weren't to know that. As far as they were concerned, I was enemy number one.

At around 5:30pm we were moving through Krakow's suburbs and towards the central station. Outside, a thick layer of snow lay on the ground, being added to every second as huge flakes fell from the skies. If I thought it had been cold and wintry in Warsaw, I was in for a shock to the system in Krakow. This was a whole new level of freezing. Finally we pulled into the main station and I stood and watched as the jovial Poles staggered out of their compartments and off onto the platform. What was going to happen to me? Was I going to be met by police and a representative from the British consulate? Perhaps I was going to be taken into a little room and tied to a chair while the mulleted woman poured acid in my face and said, 'So you thought you could pull the wool over my eyes and get away with it? Think again.' Or maybe they were just going to write out a simple fine and send it to the fake address written in the back of my passport. I didn't have to wait long for my answer, as the two railway employees came out of their compartment, one smiling, the other grimacing as if in pain. The man handed me my passport and said simply, 'Be more careful next time. Have a pleasant stay in Krakow.'

'Thank you.'

I smiled and shook his hand before winking at his colleague.

Welcome to Krakow.

10. Krakow

ONCE OUTSIDE THE station I called Dana, one of Mark's employees, who gave me directions to the flat. My stomach still killing, I was relieved to have made it to a city where I had English-speaking friends who would see to it that I got the medical attention I needed.

After walking through a picturesque park, lined with snow-covered Christmas trees, I found Dana waiting for me outside the building, wrapped up in a thick coat, scarf, hat and gloves. She was in her twenties, and had a red nose that was doing a lot of sniffing.

'Sorry, I've got a bit of a cold,' she told me.

She led me through the huge wooden door into a courtyard, where we quickly turned left through another big wooden door and then climbed a dark, narrow staircase. The building was three floors high and my flat was on the top level. Dana showed me in, showed me how everything worked and then told me that Mark would call me later in the evening to invite me to dinner. She then wished me a speedy recovery and left. The flat overlooked a mini square down below that had as its centrepiece a small green where people walked their dogs and had snowball fights.

Shortly after Dana left, while I lay crumpled in a heap on the bed, I received a call from Mark letting me know that his son would be round to collect me in about half an hour to take me to theirs for dinner. Some 30 minutes later there was a buzz at the door and I followed the 13-year old boy up the street to his father's place.

Mark was in his mid-thirties, casually dressed in a woolly jumper and jeans and spoke with an upper middle class accent.

Born to English parents and brought up on a farm in Zimbabwe, he'd been forced to leave the country some years previously after his family's farm was repossessed by Mugabe's men. He had since made a very good life for himself, building Cracow-Life from a small information website into a huge enterprise with employees in countries all over Europe. He invited me to sit down at the kitchen table while he poured us a couple of cold beers. Mark's wife, who also worked for the company, was away on business and so dinner was something that his childminder had rustled up: a typically Eastern European dish, Barley and Potato soup followed by roast chicken. Frustration followed when, after putting away the last of the soup, the stabbing pains struck me down once again, leaving me unable to eat more than a couple of mouthfuls of the delicious meat that sat so invitingly in front of me. I had to get back to the flat quickly, so apologised for my health and ran all the way. I spent the rest of the night sweating profusely and shivering as though I were in an icebox. I was running to the toilet every half an hour or so and was drifting in and out of sleep. I even hallucinated, at one point seeing the serene figure of an old lady looking over me and wiping my brow. Thank fuck I don't believe in ghosts!

When I woke the next morning still in agony, I was sure that whatever was wrong with me was not just going to clear up naturally. Mark was worried when he met me later that day and so got one of his employees, Oksana, to book me in to see a doctor. Mark was unable to come with me due to work obligations, so later that afternoon put me in a taxi, paid the driver and told him where to take me and to wait for me outside and bring me back again.

A beautiful receptionist, who couldn't have been older than 20, told me to take a seat and wait for the doctor. I made an attempt at producing a nice smile for her, but the reality was that I looked like I had been raped by a gorilla. A couple of minutes later the doctor came and led me into the examination room. Now, this doctor wasn't what I had been expecting or hoping for. I had prepared myself for a balding old man with a patterned jumper who smelt like tea; the kind of GP that I was used to. I felt comfortable with this kind of man. There was no embarrassment, whether he was giving you something for a rash, feeling your balls or discussing your sad mood. You knew where you stood with this kind of GP. You were a patient who knew nothing, he was a wise old man qualified both academically and also in the school of life and whatever he said you took note of. He had seen it all before and had bought the t-shirt, the pencil sharpener and even the souvenir photo. The doctor that now sat at the desk in front of me, however, was neither old, wearing a patterned jumper or smelt of tea. She wasn't even a man. Looking into my eyes was an absolute stunner of a woman with a white medical coat unbuttoned to half way down her chest, from where the most shapely – and surgically enhanced – pair of assets peeked out and demanded all attention. She looked like an adult movie actress about to shoot a doctors and nurses scene. She was in her early thirties and had long, dark hair. She wore the most delicate of perfumes and had a smile that you would happily frame and put on your wall. Unfortunately, she spoke not a word of English, and so began by asking me in Polish to describe my symptoms. At least this is what I guessed she was asking me. I responded in a mixture of English and Slovenian, but the doctor put her finger to her lips to indicate for me to be quiet, before calling in a translator. Enter the beautiful receptionist. Could this get any more embarrassing? I spent the next five minutes answering in great detail questions such as: 'How often do you need to go to the toilet?' 'Is the stool hard or runny?' and my personal favourite: 'Have you noticed any blood in what you've passed?' The questions were posed in Polish to the receptionist, then in English to me, I would then reply to the receptionist in English, she would nod and double check every sentence, repeating my every word to make sure she'd understood correctly before translating my responses back into Polish for the doc to make her assessment. The worst part of this whole ordeal was that it sounded even more detailed in Polish. I was sure I hadn't used that many words. Eventually my ordeal came to an end and it was explained to me that I had a bad strain of bacterial poisoning that would clear with the aid of medicine. I was to take 16 doses a day of various prescriptions as well as having to drink three litres of water. Back at the Cracow-Life offices I emailed Noam to let him know I was still on for the conference in Slovakia, while Mark went to pick up my prescriptions from the chemist. I shuddered at the thought of what would have happened had I made it to Lithuania instead of Krakow.

The following night, after having been stuck in bed for 32 hours putting nothing into my body but water and tablets, and with Mark away at his weekend home somewhere in the mountains, I found myself sitting in the corner of the room unable to focus on the book I was reading due to hunger. Just as I was wondering how long I could go without nourishment, there was a ring at my doorbell. I opened the door to find Oksana, the girl from Mark's office, standing with a fresh loaf of bread and some dried bread with raisins in that she told me was good for the stomach. She said she had been worrying about me all day and figured that without any money I probably didn't have any food. Once again I was being treated to a completely selfless act of kindness from someone who didn't even really know me. How many times would I be humbled on this journey? I asked her in for a cup of tea but she declined my offer, saying she had to be somewhere. To be fair, I wouldn't have wanted to come in and sit with me either. Later that night, at about 9, I was without the cramps for the first time in I couldn't remember how long and was craving something hot to eat. The bread had only acted to bring my appetite back, and I'd only eaten half of it as I needed to make sure I had some left for the following day. So like a fox going through the gardens at night, I locked up the flat and with steely determination made my way out in search of food. Only the last bit was like a fox. The first bit, where I locked up the flat, that's not really something a fox would do.

It was a Saturday night and the streets of Krakow were heaving with revellers, mostly foreign. The natives were all packed into pubs watching the Polish national team playing in a European Championships qualifier against Belgium. A win for the Poles would secure qualification to the finals. You could feel the tension in the city, and with every near miss, hard tackle and disputed refereeing decision, the screams, shouts and whistles of the masses would flow out of the pub doors and meet in the town square like the chorus to a classic song being murdered by a Scottish alcoholic on a park bench. Every pub was showing the game, but as much as I tried to squeeze into any of them with the hope of disappearing into the middle of the crowd, I was either stopped at the door and told there was no room or I was approached by a waitress asking me what I wanted to order and then escorted out by her two large shaven headed colleagues in black bomber jackets. At least I was fraternising with the locals. I gave up trying to catch any of the game and set my concentration back to what it was I had left the flat for in the first place: finding dinner. I paced up and down the busy streets, scanning both sides of the road with my eyes, searching for somewhere, anywhere, that looked like they might be able to provide me with a hand-out. All around me, pissed-up Englishmen on Stag weekends bustled past with kebabs, burgers and slices of pizza in their hands, grease running down their chins. Did they have any idea what they were doing to me? Of course they didn't. Why would they? That was a ridiculous rhetorical question. They weren't even eating everything they had. Bits of pita bread and pizza crust were thrown into the kerb. I watched every crumb; where it ended up. I checked that I wasn't being watched, trying to work out if a big deal would be made if I scavenged some of their leftovers from the ground. Would I be ignored, mocked or perhaps even started on? I was feeling more desperate by the second. I fought the urge to grab a passing Yorkshireman by his scarf and lick chilli sauce from his face. I didn't want to go down like that. That's not the way I wanted it to end. Without thinking, I walked into an Italian restaurant, Carlito, and asked the attending waitress if I could speak to the manager. Just like in the Pizzeria in Oslo it wasn't a Super Mario Brother that approached me, but rather a local woman, in this case a strong looking Pole in her late twenties. The expression on her face said: 'I don't mess around, and people don't mess me around. I get things done.' But at the same time there was something in the roundness of her features that screamed out: 'I'm not really as hard as I seem. On the inside I'm soft and gooey like a chocolate brownie.'

'Yes? What can I do for you?' she asked in English, looking impatiently at her watch.

I gave her the briefest version of my story, explained about the food poisoning and told her how long it had been since I'd eaten anything proper. Then I got to the big question.

'So, really, I was just wondering if you might be able to spare some leftovers.'

'Do you eat meat?' she asked, still showing no emotion.

It was like talking to Stephen Hawking. Except she walked, talked without aid, probably couldn't teach me much about Quantum Gravity, and worked in a restaurant.

'I eat anything.'

'Okay, wait here,' she said, before disappearing through a door.

She returned a few minutes later with a little polystyrene box that she handed to me, which contained some cold Lasagne.

I thanked her and told her that if I ever wrote the story of my time in Poland, I would be sure to tell the readers about her restaurant. So, if by any chance you ever find yourself in Krakow and you're feeling hungry, get along to Carlito on Florianska Street. Job done.

I took my 'kill' back to the flat and opened up the box on the little table. The lasagne looked good enough, but there was one thought flashing brightly in my mind's eye like a neon motel sign in an American road movie:

'COLD MEAT. COLD EGG PRODUCE. DANGER. DANGER. DANGER.'

I was scared. Two weeks previously I would have wolfed down that cold Lasagne quicker than you could say, 'Sam and Ella, who are they?' But now I looked at it like a session of Russian roulette. In the end I thought, *Fuck it*, and ate it all anyway. That's just the kind of guy I am.

The following day Mark was back in Krakow and he called me to let me know I was being moved into a different flat, one that had a cooker in, so that I could speed my recovery along with some hot meals. Dana showed me to my new residence that overlooked the city's walls and was a lot warmer than the previous flat. My stomach was starting to feel better and I didn't expect to be in Krakow for any longer than a couple more days. Mark had filled the cupboards with pasta and tins of tomatoes, so I was also able to start building up my strength for the next part of the journey down to Slovakia.

Before leaving Krakow I wanted to see a bit of the city so, on a particularly foggy and overcast afternoon, I set out in search of the historical centre and the Jewish quarter. I didn't find any of the sites I was looking for, thanks to the thick fog that engulfed the city, but I did walk around aimlessly for a good few hours and got a feel for the city.

The next morning I went along to the bus and train stations to check out my options for getting out of Krakow. There was no bus for a couple of days but there was a train leaving for Bratislava the following morning at 6:50. I decided I would jump on it and see how far I got. Later, when I told Mark of my plan, he insisted on taking me back round to the station and buying me a ticket to Žilina, a small Slovakian city just across the border en-route to Bratislava.

So the time had come for me to leave Poland and head for pastures new. I dragged myself out of bed at 5:50am and got myself under the shower. Nothing was going to stop me making the 6:50 to Žilina. From there I would be able to bunk the rest of the way to the capital. I had received an email from Domča telling me to meet her in Bratislava at 8:45pm, from where we would take the bus together to her home in the city of Nitra, and then on to the conference that I was due to speak at the following day in a small village out in the sticks. After hastily chucking all of my stuff into the backpack and wrapping a scarf around my neck, I closed the door to the flat behind me at 6:30, giving me plenty of time to get to the station. I did as I had been instructed to do by Mark and popped the keys to the flat in the post box next to the door and then skipped – not literally – down the stairs. My skipping was halted at the bottom, however, when I found that the staircase had a gate. I hadn't noticed this on any of my previous trips up and down the stairs, but that's because during the daytime it had always been open. Now it was locked. And I had just put the key that opened it into a post box that was also locked. I was trapped. I couldn't get back into the flat and I couldn't get out of the building. I was in apartment limbo. Panic set in. I had just 15 minutes to catch my train or else I would be stuck in Krakow with a wasted ticket and no means of getting to the conference in Slovakia, as Domča would be in Bratislava to meet me for one day only. I ran back up the stairs to the top floor and then proceeded to bang on every other door in the building, in the hope that someone, anyone, would get out of bed and release me. But not one person answered their door. Not one. I then resorted to Plan B. I called Dana on her mobile. I hated ringing her at such an hour, but I could see no other alternative. Sleepily, she told me that she would be there in half an hour to let me out. It no longer mattered if she came in ten minutes, half an hour or three days, the train was already out of the equation. I sat down on the freezing cold stairs and waited, before being released into the ice-cold morning air and having nowhere to go.

I went to the station and tried explaining my situation to the lady behind the ticket desk in the hope of being able to exchange my ticket for a train leaving later in the day, but the woman turned out to be not very nice and told me to either buy a new ticket or bugger off. I buggered off. It was still only 7:45am and nobody would be arriving at the Cracow-Life offices for well over an hour, so I had nowhere warm to go and nowhere to put my bags. I sat on a frosty bench in the main square and watched the locals going about their business. My bum froze. Whilst sitting there, I decided that I would jump on a train to Slovakia later that day without a ticket and just push my luck. I was due some, surely. Once Mark's office was open for the day I sent an email to Domča explaining my predicament, and she replied instructing me to make my way to Žilina where a couple of people she knew would meet me and put me up for the night. I headed back to the station to try my luck on the 11:45 train to the southern Polish town of Katowice. As I walked past the ticket desk I looked across and saw that an old lady behind the window was beckoning me over. I did as I was told and found that she was the same lady who had sold the ticket to Mark the previous day. She recognised me and asked why I was still in Krakow when I should have been well on my way to Slovakia by then. I told her of my misfortune and of her not-so-friendly colleague, and she asked me to hand her my ticket. She took it and changed it for a new one without charge. What a nice lady.

My train pulled into the station of Katowice at 1:15pm. Katowice, as you approach it by train, looks the same as South London does as you approach by train on the Brighton line: rows of dirty terraced houses backing on to the railway, with dirty, old blocks of flats behind them. The information board told me that my connecting train didn't leave for Žilina for another two hours. I walked out of the station and set off to explore the town. For the first time in Eastern Europe I felt in a place not completely safe. I definitely wasn't going to venture too far away from the station with all of my belongings strapped to my back. The streets were lined with Del Boys, selling all sorts of crap on the streets; battery-operated Chinese shit, mostly. The inhabitants looked just like the Polish manual workers living all over England. Every man sported short cropped hair covered by a baseball cap and had a menacing look in the eye, like he would enjoy nothing more than to welcome you to his city with a head-butt. I decided to leave the streets of Katowice behind me and went back to the station to wait on the platform. Once on my train, I called Noam to find out about my mystery accommodation. He told me he was currently on the train to Žilina from Katowice. We were on the same train. This was perfect. I was in the front carriage, while he told me he was in the back one. I walked the length of the train to meet him. I didn't find him there, but instead came face to face with a group of male gypsies in their 30s trying to lock themselves into the toilet. It turned out Noam was on a train three hours ahead of mine. After a few hours I started to wonder whether I was actually on the right train at all. Looking out of the window I had seen nothing but dark forest for what seemed like a hundred miles, and there had been no announcements made over the speakers. Then out of nowhere the Slovakian border appeared and the train filled with intimidating men in dark gloves, shining torches in faces. After entry into Slovakia, a ticket guard came and I asked him what time we were due to arrive in Žilina. Although he spoke not a word of English, I was happy to find that the Slovak for '7:30' sounded almost identical to its Slovene equivalent. 'Pol ôsmej' in Slovakian; 'pol osmih,' in Slovene.

And just past 7:30pm my train pulled into my target destination. I still had no idea if I had a place to spend the night, and I could no longer make any calls from my phone as I had run out of credit. Noam sent me a text to let me know he was working on it. I had no choice other than to trust him. I stood for half an hour in the cold outside Žilina station before being picked up by Vlad, a young AIESEC member, who drove me back to a large student residential building, treated me to dinner in the canteen and then offered a spare bed in his dorm. He told me of the time he had been backpacking around England and found himself stranded in a small village without any money for accommodation. He had walked into the village church in search of help. The vicar called around a few of the parishioners and eventually found someone able to put him up for a couple of nights. My host now felt privileged to be able to return the favour to an Englishman.

The following morning he bought my ticket and put me on the bus out of the city. It was just before 3 in the afternoon when I jumped off of the packed bus on a narrow road surrounded on all sides by woodland. Standing waiting for me at the bus stop was Daša, a dark haired girl with Coke bottle glasses, who led me up a path to the school where everything was happening.

Welcome to Kl'ačno.

11. Kl'ačno & Nitra

I WAS LED through the double doors and into the main lobby where a couple of students were sat behind a desk, handing out name badges.

'Ah Kris, we've been expecting you! So glad you made it!' said one of the girls as she ticked my name off on a list. 'Are you looking forward to it?'

'If I knew what I was here to do, I might be,' I told her, honestly.

At this, everyone started laughing as if I had just cracked the best joke of the afternoon.

'Ah, Kris, Noam told us you were funny,' said the girl, through her laughter.

Nobody believed that I had turned up in a small Slovakian village in the middle of the forest without first asking what it was I would be doing. Instead, they just thought I was a joker. I hoped I wasn't there to perform stand-up comedy in the evenings. Before I had time to find out any information, an effeminate guy with blond hair who introduced himself as Fubus took my bags from me and I followed him up to the third floor and down a corridor where I was shown to my bedroom. My own bedroom. We were in a boarding school. On the stairs we passed a couple of girls who, on seeing me for the first time, said, 'Hi, glad you made it. How are you?' like they knew me from somewhere. It was all a bit weird. I put my bags on the bed and then followed Fubus down to the second floor and into a large hall where Noam was leading some kind of ice-breaking ceremony for about 15 people. He was standing at the front of the room on a chair explaining the rules of silly games to these young adults who really were too old to be playing silly games.

'Right, I want you all to sit in a circle,' Noam shouted, and then he walked round giving everyone a number. 'I will call two numbers, and if your number is called you have to get up and run around the circle and back to your place quicker than the other person.'

There was an excited look on the faces of the participants that made me wonder if I'd been invited to a retreat for people with learning difficulties. Noam spotted me standing in the corner looking bemused and waved me over. He picked someone out of the circle to take over the number calling and then he gave me a big hug that didn't exactly lessen my apprehension at being there.

'Noam, what is this place? Why am I here? Who are these people?' I blurted out all the questions at once.

Noam laughed.

'Well, Kris, this is an AIESEC retreat. Everybody here is an AIESEC member. Half of the people are here to train to become trainers, the other half are here to take part in some workshops and listen to some speakers, so that they can learn and become more confident for when AIESEC sends them abroad to continue their studies. They just need preparation and that's what we do. You are here to inspire them with your stories. They can't have any fears about being in a different culture once they've heard how you have survived! Not everyone's here yet, we are expecting about 30.'

'But why will they listen to me?' I asked, still not sure about the whole thing.

'Because you are the motivational speaker!'

He turned to face the group.

'Listen up, guys. Listen up!' Noam called and everyone in the room stopped what they were doing and looked towards us. 'This is Kris. He is here to inspire you over this weekend. If ever you want to talk to him about anything, just find him and I'm sure he will be happy to speak to you, won't you Kris?'

What the hell is going on?

'Um, yes. Yes, of course I will.'

'Kris is currently in the middle of a crazy challenge that I'm sure will inspire you all. Kris, why don't you tell everyone what you are doing at the moment.'

What? No! Don't put me on the spot like this!

'Hi guys, I'm Kris, as you now know. Um, I'm currently on a mission…'

I told the shortest version possible of the Great Euro Freebie Challenge, fearful of boring everyone. These people wouldn't want to hear my story. I was just a strange man with no money. But as I spoke the last of the words, expecting everyone to just go back to playing their game or for Noam to have to give them some more instructions, people started putting their hands up like children in class; a class in which I was the teacher.

'Yes, you, the boy with the striped shirt.'

I found myself pointing to people as questions flew in from all corners of the room.

'What's been the most difficult country to be in so far?'

'What's been the best moment?'

'How long do you think it will take to finish?'

'What home comfort do you miss the most?'

Everyone in the room had a question to ask. Everyone in the room also had a glazed look in their eyes and spoke slowly and creepily. Eventually the questions ceased and I followed the group downstairs to the canteen for dinner. Every time I passed someone on the corridor or even as I queued up for my dollop of mashed potatoes and chicken, they would look dopily into my eyes and say, 'Hi Kris. How are you?' I would say, 'Fine, thanks. How are you?' to which they would reply, 'Great!' before walking away.

Domča arrived just as we were sitting down to eat, and joined Noam and me at a table. All around us people chatted excitedly about AIESEC. I ate silently. Later that evening after everyone had completed their workshops and I had wandered around the outside of the building a few times, a party took place in the main hall. It had everything you would expect of a party: music, dancing, people coupling up, and everyone in a great mood. Only something was missing; I just couldn't figure out what. To find the answer I would need a strong drink to clear my mind. I walked up to the refreshments table, picked up a polystyrene cup and poured myself a large… *apple juice?*

'Noam, is the alcohol all gone?'

'No mate. No alcohol tonight. Everyone's got a busy day ahead tomorrow,' he said, as he knocked back a shot of lemonade.

'No alcohol? But how come everyone looks so drunk? I mean, people are doing the Macarena out there.'

'I guess they are just drunk on happiness and positive energy. Let yourself go and you might have fun too.'

This was too much for me. I had to escape to my room.

At around midnight the party was over and I found myself sat outside the building on a swing sharing a spliff with Domča and Noam. It was at this point that I decided that Noam wasn't really Noam but was in fact Hollywood actor Sean Penn.

'Has anyone ever told you you're a ringer for Hollywood actor Sean Penn?' I asked.

'Who's Hollywood actor Sean Penn?'

'You are Hollywood actor Sean Penn. From this day forward, no longer will you go by the name Noam. Noam is dead, long live Hollywood actor Sean Penn.'

And so it was official.

The three of us sat up until 6:45 in the morning; Hollywood actor Sean Penn working on a presentation on his laptop, whilst Domča and I chatted.

Breakfast was served at 8. I walked into the canteen, took one look at everyone and walked out again. People were smiling, singing and greeting each other. Even Hollywood actor Sean Penn and Domča were happy. I went back to bed, sleeping through the day until 4. What a motivational speaker! when I woke up to shower, I couldn't find my towel and then remembered that I had left it on a radiator in Žilina. Chucking everything out of my bag onto the bed, the only thing that looked capable of replacing the missing towel was a cotton vest. May I take this opportunity to give you my tip of the chapter: a cotton vest does not really work as a towel.

That evening I was still a bit wet when I joined everyone in the main hall for an event they were calling Global Village. All around the room small groups had set up tables on which were placed bottles of alcohol and bowls of food from a particular country. The idea was that you would visit each table, learn something about that nation and sample the food and drink. I spent the entire night on the Slovakia table knocking back shot after shot of Slivovica. At about 2 in the morning, as I made my way back to the main room from the toilet, I passed a girl in the corridor that I'd caught myself stealing glances at all evening.

'I'm not the only one who thinks this is creepy, am I? You think this is weird, too. I can see it,' she said from behind me.

That was why I had been watching her. I could see that she was uncomfortable in this cult-like environment. She was also the best-looking girl in the building. But that's not why I was looking at her, you understand?

'It is a little strange, I agree,' I turned round to look. 'But why are you here if you don't like it?'

'I need AIESEC because I want to go to study abroad. I'm not Slovakian, and so that makes it more difficult for me to get a placement. But if I'm a member of AIESEC things become easier,' she explained.

'Where are you from?'

'Another European country. It doesn't matter which one. My parents moved us here when I was a child.'

She spoke slowly and with nonchalance.

'Which country?'

'One that I'm not proud of. It doesn't matter.'

Her evasiveness annoyed me.

'Can I guess?'

'You can try.'

'Romania,' I said, confidently.

'How did you know?'

'Lucky guess.'

It really was, too.

'You are more interesting than anyone else here,' she said, as she looked at me with an enticing smile that drew me in.

'Likewise,' I replied.

'You want to drink with me?' she asked. 'I can go grab a bottle of vodka.'

I liked where this was going.

'Yea, I guess.'

We sat outside on the swings and worked our way through the bottle, chatting like two old cynics waiting for the Post Office to open. Catalina was the first Romanian I had ever had a conversation with. As the hours disappeared, we got more wasted. At 5:30am my new friend pulled herself up and announced that she was going to bed. I walked with her to her room and stood next to her as she put the key in the door and opened it. I knew she was going to invite me in. I just knew it.

'Well, good night,' she said, a playful look in her eye.

She leaned forward, kissed me softly on the side of the mouth and closed the door behind her. I walked to my room with a huge grin across my face. I had enjoyed the evening with Catalina immensely, and liked her even more for the way it had ended. She had had me right at her command. Still, I knew all along that she wasn't going to invite me in.

I woke later that morning at 10 to the sight of a female backside bending over at the end of my bed. I couldn't remember much from the night before, but I was pretty sure I hadn't brought Catalina back with me. Or had I? Slowly the woman unbent herself and turned around to look at me.

Damn, I'm never drinking again, I thought as I looked into the old, yellow eyes of the 50-year old woman with a scarf wrapped around her head.

'Catalina?' I asked.

How was I going to tell her that last night had been one big mistake? She pointed at me and then at the corner of the room.

'You want me to stand in the corner? But why?'

She said nothing but continued to point. I stood up and walked to the corner. Catalina was a lot firmer and scarier than I remembered her. I didn't want to piss her off. She then stripped my bed, threw the dirty pillow case and sheet into a green bag and left me alone.

After showering and drying myself off with the vest, I staggered into the main hall where I found people hugging each other and saying what a pleasure it had been to spend a weekend with them. In the corner, sat alone, was the real Catalina. She looked at me, smiled and then looked away. Hollywood actor Sean Penn then stood up on a chair and announced that it was time for the coffee chat.

'Kris is going to talk to you all now about his adventures so far and take questions from you. So go and get yourself a coffee and then take a seat,' he told them.

How had I not been expecting this? I was at an AIESEC conference as a motivational speaker, had been there for two days, everything was now being packed up and people were getting ready to go home, and yet I hadn't at any point done any motivational speaking. In fact, the night before had been passed doing the exact opposite with Catalina. I must have known this moment was coming. I sipped at a cup of tea – I don't like coffee; it's for grown-ups – and looked out into the hopeful faces that stared back at me. Right at the back, looking at me with an expression that said, 'Remember, I know you're a fraud,' was a grinning Catalina. An hour later I was hugging people I didn't know as they thanked me for opening their eyes and wished me luck on the rest of my journey. What can I say? You've either got it or you haven't.

Slowly the building emptied as people left and headed back to cities and towns all over Slovakia. As I stood alone, Catalina walked up and said, 'Well, I guess this is goodbye,' before giving me one final smile and disappearing out of my life. Meanwhile, it dawned on me that I had no idea where I was going next. How was I even going to get out of the forest? No one had told me anything and I hadn't thought to ask. I didn't need to worry though, as Domča found me and said that some of the AIESEC members had had a whip-round and were going to take me by bus to the town of Nitra, where some of them were students. I could spend the night there in the AIESEC office, and then take the bus the following day with Domča to Bratislava.

Just before leaving I gave Hollywood actor Sean Penn a hug – this time I instigated it – and then stood and waited while he passionately kissed Domča. I was a bit surprised, as I hadn't seen the signs, but if two people can both feel as happy as they did at 8 in the morning after just an hour's sleep then they belong together. I joined the group on the Nitra bus and after a two and a half hour drive we arrived in the town. Domča went to stay at a family member's place, leaving me with Fubus, who took me into AIESEC's office that just happened to be on the same floor in the same building as his student dorm.

'Wait here,' he told me, as he left me alone on the couch in the office.

He returned a few minutes later to tell me that his roommate was away, meaning that I could sleep in his room with him. I preferred the idea of the office, but didn't want to be rude.

'Great!' Fubus said, clapping his hands like a schoolgirl who had just been told she could have a slumber party.

I made my bed for the night and then went off to the communal bathroom at the end of the hall. As I stood, weeing into the urinal, in walked an attractive girl carrying in her hand a roll of toilet paper. She smiled a greeting to me as she passed and then went into a cubicle, shut the door, sat down on the toilet and let out a little squeak of a fart. She knew I was standing there. She had just smiled a greeting at me. She definitely knew I was there! How did she feel it appropriate to let me hear that? I washed my hands and left before she emerged from the cubicle as, strangely, I was the one feeling embarrassed. This was all wrong. As I jogged back up the corridor to the bedroom, three more girls passed me, each one carrying a toilet roll. I opened the bedroom door and quickly entered, shutting it behind me, hoping that that would mark the end of the awkward situations for the evening. I looked up and saw Fubus, standing and looking at himself in a full-sized mirror... wearing a pair of Spiderman pyjamas.

I met Domča the following afternoon and she bought me a bus ticket to Bratislava. We took the bus together but as I got on I still hadn't arranged a place to sleep. Domča couldn't host me because of a lack of space at her family home and nobody had replied to any Couchsurfing requests I'd sent a couple of days earlier. I'd had one reply from a girl called Zuzana, but she had said she couldn't host me but would like to treat me to a dinner one evening. I had her number and texted her from the bus asking if she knew of anyone with a free couch and, luckily, just a few minutes before I arrived in Slovakia's capital, she replied saying that she would be able to put me up for the night after all. At just after 9pm my bus pulled into the bus station and I ticked another capital off of my list.

Welcome to Bratislava.

12. Bratislava

Capitals left to visit: Amsterdam, Athens, Brussels, Bucharest, Budapest, Helsinki, Lisbon, Ljubljana, Luxembourg, Madrid, Paris, Prague, Riga, Rome, Sofia, Tallinn, Vienna, Vilnius

Days on the road: 26
Distance travelled: 1963 miles
EU capitals visited: 5

After a long bus ride followed by a few minutes on a tram I found myself standing on the corner of the street where I was supposed to meet Zuzana. She arrived shortly, and the first thing that struck me about her was her height; she was well over 6ft.

'Hi, Kris. I'm glad you made it. Listen, I have to warn you before we go into the house that I've had a bit of an argument with my mum and dad today, so if they're in a bad mood or rude in any way, they don't mean it,' were the first words she said.

I was expecting the worst, but was pleasantly surprised when we walked through the door of the expensive house and into the living room where I was greeted warmly by Zuzana's parents, as well as her brother and his girlfriend. I was quickly ushered into an armchair, my bags were taken from me and put in the corner of the room and a plate of chicken and potatoes was dropped into my lap. I felt a little awkward eating while everyone watched, but I was starving. Zuzana's brother and his girlfriend soon left, leaving me sitting with the rest of the family, trying to make conversation through the language barrier. Zuzana's English was fine, but her parents struggled.

Well, her father, a bearded, relaxed looking man in a sleeveless t-shirt didn't speak a word, but her mother, a blonde lady with an infectious smile, could speak a little but was only let down by her own lack of confidence. That and the fact that every time she tried to say anything, Zuzana would interrupt her and start interpreting.

'It's fine, Zuzana, really. I understand your mum perfectly when she speaks,' I said.

But Zuzana couldn't help herself. She was a lawyer in her late twenties, and I wondered if her daily environment had anything to do with her need to dominate. The middle-aged couple were looking through brochures, trying to find the right deal for a skiing trip they planned to take, so I felt it best to stop talking and just let them be. It was only a few minutes though before the dad stood up, walked out of the room and returned with four glasses and a bottle of clear liquid. I recognised it immediately: Slivovica, the potent, homemade plum brandy. That was where the rest of the evening went, the language barrier no longer a problem.

My bed for the night was in the spare room and came complete with its own bathroom. Zuzana provided me with toiletries and towels, leaving me feeling like I was in a hotel. I couldn't have asked for more.

The next morning was an early one. I was up and showered by 6:30, was eating breakfast with Zuzana by 7, and was dropped off in the city centre before 8, as Zuzana had to go to work for the day. I had no plans other than to explore the city, but before I could start that I had to find a toilet for my daily ritual. I made my way back to the city's bus station and towards the public facilities, when I noticed that a lot of the people going in were carrying their own toilet paper.

How bizarre, I thought to myself, and then I recalled what I had seen in Nitra. Oh yea, now I remember.

I went in and panicked when I saw that none of the cubicles

had paper in. I didn't know what to do, so went back outside and by chance found a cleaning lady walking around holding a roll of tissue. I asked her for some. Just as the woman was unravelling the exact amount that she thought I would need, a beautiful girl of about 20 walked right in through the door and saw the whole thing. I instantly turned a dark shade of purple, until I noticed that in her hand she too was carrying her own toilet paper. This was Slovakia, a country where people were not embarrassed by things that should not be embarrassing. We can learn a lot from the Slovaks. I took my paper with a smile and even asked for a couple of extra sheets. I felt liberated.

I couldn't have picked a better day for just wandering around. The sun was shining brightly, which reflected off of the thin layer of snow still left on the ground from the previous day's fall, giving the impression of a spring morning rather than one in the middle of winter. The first place I headed to was the castle, simply because it was visible from all over the city and I thought I would use it as a viewing point from which to be able to draw up a virtual map of the city in my mind. After a long walk uphill I made it there along with some Japanese tourists and some courting local young couples. The view out over the city and the Danube river was pleasant.

There was a Christmas Market taking place in the Old Town, with the centrepiece a giant Christmas tree still being decorated. A group of carol singers congregated in one corner of the square, practicing for their night-time performance, while people walked past sipping mulled wine and gorging on greasy sausages in thick bread rolls. Stall after stall sold different variations of what was being marketed as *gypsy food*. I walked for hours, people-watching. Bratislava's population, on this day, seemed young and happy. I sat on a bench, watching starry-eyed young lovers feeding each other pretzels, and I thought about the scene in the film *EuroTrip* in which the Americans find themselves in Bratislava with just a dollar to their name but are able to live like kings in the miserable, depressed, dark city. I wanted to make a video, to put it on YouTube, to show Americans the real beauty of Bratislava in the winter.

I received a text from Domča inviting me to lunch over by her university on the other side of the river in the borough of Petržalka. The name was familiar to me thanks to the relative success in the Champions' League the previous season of the local football team of the same name. Earlier that morning, before going our separate ways, Zuzana had handed me some paper vouchers which could be exchanged at any student restaurant for food. As we sat down to eat in the pizzeria, Domča told me that she wanted to buy me a bus ticket to Vienna for the next part of my journey, and that I shouldn't think anything of it because the prices were cheap. It was at this point that I remembered the vouchers in my pocket, which I handed to Domča, telling her to use a couple of them to pay for our food and to put the remaining couple in her pocket as a thank you.

That evening I met Zuzana after she finished work and we watched the turning on of the Christmas tree lights. The carollers I had seen earlier in the morning were now well-rehearsed and belting out some beauties, and it seemed as though the same people who had been enjoying the mulled wine in the morning were still around, slipping in the snow and telling strangers they loved them. We headed back to the flat where I sat up drinking with Zuzana's parents long after Zuzana had decided to call it a night at 9:30.

Early the next morning I was dropped off by Zuzana for the last time in the city, before I walked for an hour to the bus station in an area of the city called Novi Most. I handed my ticket over to the driver and my coach pulled out of Bratislava's bus station at 9:45am. Ten minutes later and we had crossed into Austria. Until then I had no idea that Bratislava was so close to the border. As we drove on into Austria, Bratislava's castle still stood proudly in view. Each little village we passed through was a replica of the last: little colourful cottages on one side of the road, fields on the other, always a large crucifix with Jesus on it as you entered the village, and always a little church with a red roof as you exited. It was all very Catholic. My bus parked up at 11am and I ticked another capital city off of my list.

Welcome to Vienna.

13. Vienna

Capitals left to visit: Amsterdam, Athens, Brussels, Bucharest, Budapest, Helsinki, Lisbon, Ljubljana, Luxembourg, Madrid, Paris, Prague, Riga, Rome, Sofia, Tallinn, Vilnius

Days on the road: 28
Distance travelled: 2012 miles
EU capitals visited: 6

I GOT OFF the bus at Vienna's international bus station at 11:20am and took the Metro to the large square, Steffansplatz, where I had a quick look around, doing my best to impersonate an interested tourist. It was no good though, as all I could think about was the fact that I had nowhere to spend the night, nowhere to go and nothing to eat. At least I had made it to Vienna. There was nothing in the rules that said I had to stay there any longer, so I decided my best option would be to hitchhike back to Bratislava where I would have a place to stay while I plotted the next leg of my journey. Then I thought, *hang on a minute, things were far too easy in Slovakia. You need more of a challenge to keep things interesting.*

I knew what I had to do: Ljubljana, capital of Slovenia – a 235-mile journey.

I walked into Steffansplatz' Tourist Information Centre to ask where the city's main train station was, only to be told that there was no one main train station of Vienna.

'So where would I go to get a train heading south?' I asked.

'Sudbahnhof,' (South train station) was the answer. Obviously.

I took a tram to another of the city's big squares, Karlsplatz, from where I was told I could pick up a tram to Sudbahnhof. What I found at Karlsplatz was a disgusting Metro station where, despite it being midday, everyone was walking around with a can of beer in his or her hand. I dodged my way in and out of the drunks, before witnessing a fistfight. Between two women. Well, I say women. If I also say they were wearing steal capped Doctor Martins, you should get a better picture in your mind. Station security broke up the fracas. I got out of there quickly and found my way to Sudbahnhof, which housed no better quality of person than that found at Karlsplatz. There was a train leaving for Venice at 12:57pm, which would stop off at a place called Bruck an der Mur, two hours south of Vienna, from where I could pick up a connecting train to Graz, and from there a train to Maribor in the east of Slovenia. An even better scenario would be if I managed to stay on the train all the way to the Southern Austrian town of Villach, close to the Slovene border but on the western side of the country, meaning I wouldn't even have to go through Maribor. But I didn't expect to get that lucky. I sat and passed away the minutes on a bench inside the station terminal next to an old drunk who fought over bread with the pigeons. He lost.

By now I was tired of jumping on trains and waiting under emotional duress for the authority figure to come and find me. I needed a new technique. My train, an expensively priced Eurostar service, pulled into the station and on it I jumped. Three minutes after the train started moving I got up from my seat and went to find the inspector. I was going to take my fight directly to my opponent.

'Hello. Listen, I don't know what to do. I just put my hand in my pocket to get my ticket out of my wallet only to realise that my pocket is empty. Oh my God! I don't know what to do now. Please, take my details and fine me, but I have to somehow make it to Villach today.'

'It's okay. Don't worry. Go and sit down, of course you can stay on my train, but I can't allow you to go all the way to Villach. There is a police station at Bruck an der Mur. You can ride as far as there and then you will have to get off and report your situation to the police,' said the inspector, sympathetically.

I got to Bruck an der Mur at 2:58pm and then sprinted across to the next platform for the 3:02pm train to Graz. Once on it I went for the old adage of 'If it ain't broke…' and used the same technique. It worked a treat and I was soon in Graz. Unfortunately I arrived one minute too late for the train to Maribor, so I asked when the next train going anywhere near the border was. The man at the information desk told me there was one leaving at 4:20pm going to a border village called Spielfeld. I took it, using the same technique and having the same success.

I got to Spielfeld, which I had been told was a crossing point into Slovenia, but all I found was a deserted, unstaffed station that led out onto a little shit-hole of a village, also deserted. It was dark and I was in the middle of nowhere, so I decided I would just walk to Slovenia. How hard could it be? I entered the village's little pub, the only place showing any signs of life, and found that nobody spoke either English or Slovenian. I also found that the people of Spielfeld mated with their siblings; at least that was the conclusion I came to from the amount of cross-eyed mutants with webbed hands frequenting the place. I asked, 'Wo ist Slowenien?' and many hands pointed in the general direction I needed to take. So off I trekked. I quickly found myself on the motorway and noticed that most of the cars driving past had Slovenian or Croatian plates. I carried on walking up the side of the busy road for about 20 minutes and then came to a little lay-by full of parked, empty Croatian lorries. There was a restaurant – more of a Greasy Spoon than a Ritz – and the sign in the window said they served Burek, Ćevapi, and Pljeskavica. Basically, hot meat and cheese pastries, grilled meat balls and burgers. It didn't take much brain power to figure out where the Croatian lorry drivers were hiding. I went inside and was greeted by the young waitress. She spoke no English, so I resorted to my not-bad not-great Croatian and asked her if she knew of anyone who might give me a lift over the border. She said she would ask. She came back and said nobody wanted to take me and that it was only 200 metres to the crossing point but that I probably couldn't just walk over without a car. I got chatting to her and I mentioned how good the Burek smelt. I had already told her that I had been walking for hours – an exaggeration – and that I had no money because everything I owned was in Slovenia and that I had been left on the motorway after having an argument with my girlfriend who was driving. She asked if I preferred the meat or cheese version. I told her cheese. I couldn't believe my luck when she called to the guy in the kitchen for a 'Sirnica' (hot cheese pastry) and handed it to me on a plate. I thanked her profusely and we chatted as I ate. After finishing, I went outside and spoke to a Croatian lorry driver, then a Slovene one, but neither of them wanted to drive me anywhere. So I thought, *Jebiga!* – Google it, or wait for me to reveal what it means in Chapter 17 – and started walking towards Slovenia.

The look on the Slovene border guard's face was a picture as he watched me approaching his booth, side by side with all the cars and lorries.

'Where are you going?' he asked whilst checking my passport.

'Ljubljana.'

I laughed. I could only laugh at the situation. We were about 100 miles from Slovenia's capital. He looked at me, not knowing what to say, before telling me it was about 2km to the nearest Slovene town and that on the way I should stay safe by walking on the left side of the motorway.

Being back in Slovenia felt good straight away. After the years

I had spent living there, it felt like a homecoming. I walked for about another 45 minutes, following a railway line, until I stumbled upon the tiny train station of Šentilj. The time was about 7pm and the one guy manning the station told me there was a train to Maribor at 8. I checked the timetables posted on the walls and saw that if all went to plan I would be in Maribor at 8:17pm and should then be able to run and catch the 8:20 to Ljubljana. I waited in the cold waiting room and jumped on the train when it came in. I was the only person on it; there wasn't even a ticket guard. At Maribor I got on the 8:20 but it was only going as far as Zidani Most; half way to Ljubljana. I went to the ticket guy and used the same technique as earlier in the day in Austria. He told me to sit down and not to worry, commenting that it was usual to have your wallet stolen in Austria, as they are a known nation of thieves. Once again cross-border myths took precedence over the truth, and once again it tickled me. I got to Zidani Most at 9:40pm and then had to wait until 10:35 for the train to Ljubljana. I sat in the 1940's style waiting room with two old ladies on their way to Belgrade and one teenage boy with pink hair. The train was delayed by half an hour. Once on it I tried explaining to the two inspectors in Slovene that I had lost my wallet and could pay in Ljubljana but, as they contemplated, the girl that was sitting to my left leant over and said that she would pay the small amount for me. I told her there was no need but, judging by the facial expressions of the two guards, in fact there probably was a need. As he was issuing my ticket, one of the guards complimented me on how well I spoke Slovene, then after he'd gone the girl turned to me laughing and said, 'How would he know how good your Slovene is? He's hardly in a position to judge; you speak better Slovene than him!'

The two guards had both been what the Slovenes call, when they are being polite, 'Southerners,' and when being rude, Čefurji'; a derogatory term used to describe immigrants from the ex-Yugoslav republics. I got into Ljubljana at midnight and found Vanja, my ex-fiancée, waiting for me on the platform.

Welcome to Ljubljana.

14. Ljubljana

Capitals left to visit: Amsterdam, Athens, Brussels, Bucharest, Budapest, Helsinki, Lisbon, Luxembourg, Madrid, Paris, Prague, Riga, Rome, Sofia, Tallinn, Vilnius

Days on the road: 29
Distance travelled: 2253 miles
EU capitals visited: 7

My first day back in Ljubljana since leaving almost a year earlier under such difficult circumstances was spent catching up with a couple of old friends, Steve and Dave, both of whom I'd worked with in the language school. Steve, an Australian who had recently married a Slovene woman, bought me lunch in a Bosnian restaurant opposite the main train station; a place where we had eaten many a time over the years. He had to rush back to work before we had even finished digesting, so from there I headed down to the Cutty Sark pub where I knew I would find Dave, a Yorkshireman in his late twenties who refused to ever accept that he was an adult. Dave looked like a poor man's Charlie Sheen, always had a beer in his hand, was always surrounded by people – usually because he owed them money – and never had a worry in the world. He had gone from teaching job to teaching job, always lasting as long as it took for his bosses to realise that despite his claims, he couldn't actually speak English. To be fair to Dave, though, he was fluent in Yorkshire. Every single story I ever heard Dave tell started with the words, 'I were int bar t'oova night,' and ended with, 'it were a right laff, it were.'

Sure enough, there he was sitting outside the pub with his pork-pie hat on his head, a cold beer in his right hand and a cigarette in his left. He treated me to a few cold ones as we sat outside, forgetting that it was a freezing December's day, and took the piss out of each other. It was like I had never been away.

The next few days were spent sitting around just enjoying Vanja's company and wondering where it had all gone wrong for us. The three and a half years we had spent sharing a flat, a bed and a life seemed such a distant memory now, but if I had just had a little more self-control things could have turned out so differently. I know it's not good to sit and think, "What if?" but sometimes you just can't help yourself. She still looked as beautiful as ever, she was still as funny and sharp as ever, and she was still as caring towards me as ever, but we just weren't the same two people we had been in the past. While I was sat around thinking these thoughts and resting myself as I prepared for the next bout of ticketless travel, people back home and abroad were starting to become aware of my journey. I received an email from Brighton's local paper *The Argus* asking if they could feature me in a double-page spread in their weekend edition. I also received an email from Julian in Berlin with a link to a German magazine article that had been published about my journey, written by his flatmate. On top of that, the BBC wanted to do a follow-up interview with me on Southern Counties Radio. It was all good and I hoped it would lead to a boost in sponsorships. Sabrina, a German girl who had become a good friend when we worked together on the reception of the youth hostel in Rome many years earlier, also sent me an email inviting me to stay at her flat in Rome when I headed down there some time in the next few days.

Soon enough the day came when I had to bring my resting period to an end and move out of Ljubljana and down towards Italy's capital Rome. The school I used to work at made a donation to the cause by providing me with a train ticket to Mestre, close to Venice up in Italy's northeast. From there I would be left to my own devices to somehow make it the 330 miles south to The Eternal City.

My train got me in to Mestre at 2:10 in the afternoon and, despite there being no sun in the sky, I failed to find a single person standing on the platform not wearing sunglasses. Welcome to Italy. The information board told me there was a Eurostar leaving for Rome at 2:50pm and I planned to be on it. Shortly after we pulled out of the station I went and sought out the ticket inspector, explaining to him in Italian that I had been robbed outside the station and needed to get to my office in Rome, from where I could take care of any penalty fare. I handed him my passport. Unfortunately, I hadn't come up against the most sympathetic of characters on this particular afternoon, and the typically Northern Italian looking man with long, silver hair and a pointy goatee on his chin, shrugged his shoulders and told me that it wasn't his problem and that I had to get off at the next stop, Padova.

'But what will I do? I'm screwed,' I pleaded.

'I don't know and I don't care. But whatever it is, it won't be on my train.'

I didn't contemplate dragging the conversation on any longer. I would just have to try again from Padova. Inside me though, burned a fury, simply because had I really been the victim of an unfortunate incident, this guy would have just made my life all the more difficult. As it was, I was lying, so no harm done. But still!

The station's clock showed 3:08pm and the station's information board told me that the next fast train leaving Padova went as far as Bologna and left at 3:38pm. From Bologna there would be more trains Romeward bound.

Romeward bound... Did you see what I did there? Brilliant.

3:38pm came and went and I found myself still at Padova station. There had been a slight change of plan. Well, not so much a slight change of plan as a monumental domino effect. It all started when, whilst waiting for the train, I walked up to the station's information desk and explained to the guy manning it that I had had my wallet stolen and needed to get to Rome. I just wanted to know if there was any way I could get on the train here and then have someone meet me and pay for my ticket when I arrived in the country's capital. I didn't quite know why, but after he came from behind his desk saying, 'Vieni con me,' I found myself trailing him like a doomed child following the Pied Piper of Hamelin, half expecting him to take me to an office where I would be handed some sort of permit to travel. I followed him through the hall, up the platform and into the little office, but this was no free ticket boutique; I was in a mini police station, stood in front of a bored copper who now had something to do to pass the time. Some 45 minutes later I had given a full police statement describing in detail when, where, and by whom I had been robbed. I actually had to describe the two thieves; right down to the clothes they had been wearing. My memory was impeccable. In case you were wondering, my assailants were a 4'11' mother with an arched back and wearing green rags, and her 12-year old son who also wore rags, but stood upright. They had three plastic carrier bags with them, and I felt that the theft had taken place just outside McDonalds in front of the station, but I couldn't be sure. I had to think on my toes, as the policeman's questions became more and more detailed and my lie became more and more elaborate. The mother and son double act had come up to me asking for bread or money, I had politely told them to clear off, and then a few minutes later I had found that my wallet was missing from my pocket. I told the copper that I wasn't certain they had stolen it and that perhaps it was just coincidence. I didn't want to get anyone in to trouble, after all. He replied with a bitter smile, 'Trust me, the gypsies stole it. Gypsies are thieves.'

After the last of the questions had been asked and the report had been officially stamped, I was just about to leave the office when I was told to sit and wait for a few minutes. 15 minutes later in walked a smug looking policeman, dragging behind him two gypsies matching perfectly my description. I almost choked on my tongue in shock. He held them both by the scruffs of their necks as he asked me if they were the culprits. I looked into the confused eyes of the mother, gulped and nodded my head.

'Yes, officer. It was them.'

What else could I do? I needed to get to Rome, and to do that I needed to see my lie through to the end. They would be let out onto the streets again after a little beating in the back room.

Okay, that didn't really happen. I just wanted to picture your face when confronted with such a cold-blooded account. Most of it was true. I mean, I did give the report and all, and I did describe the thieves exactly as I told it to you, but fortunately the police didn't drag any innocent gypsies into the office. All that happened was they gave me a carbon copy of the report and sent me on my way.

The police kicked me out the door, leaving me wondering what I had gained from the last 45 minutes. The answer was nothing. In fact, I was actually in a worse situation because I had now missed the Bologna train. I stopped in the doorway and turned back to the policeman.

'Hang on a minute,' I said, 'but how am I going to get to Rome? I thought you would help me.'

'That is a dilemma,' he replied, stroking his chin. 'I suppose you could just jump on the train and try to explain the situation to the inspector. They might kick you off at the next stop, but then you just get on another train and try again.'

The Italian police were telling me to do exactly what I had

been doing all along: break the law. I decided I best do as I was told. I got on the 4:08 Eurostar from Padova to Rome and rather than seek the inspector out, I took a seat at the back of the train and waited to see how far I could get. He didn't come for 45 minutes, and when he did finally approach me I asked if he spoke English. He did. I decided to play the poor foreigner who spoke no Italian and I showed him the police report, telling him that the policeman had told me I could get on the train. He showed sympathy and muttered something about gypsies being the cause of all of Italy's problems. He told me I could go as far as Florence with him, where he would then speak to his replacement to try and persuade him to let me carry on to Rome. We got to Florence and I got off of the train with the inspector. On hearing my story, the new guy didn't say anything; he just gesticulated for me to get back on the train. Italians love a bit of the old gesticulation. The original inspector shook my hand and wished me luck.

My train got into the station at 8:20pm and I called Sabrina.

I ticked another capital city off of my list.

Welcome to Rome.

North Cape
Jan Mayen
(Norway)
NORWEGIAN SEA
Scandinavia
Lapland
SWEDEN
FINLAND
NORWAY
Faroe Islands
(Denmark)
Shetland Islands
(UK)
Orkney Islands
Isle of Lewis
Hebrides
British
Isles
SCOTLAND
UNITED
KINGDOM
IRELAND
DUBLIN
ENGLAND
WALES
LONDON
CELTIC SEA
English Channel
NORTH
SEA
DENMARK
COPENHAGEN
Gulf of Bothnia
Gulf of Finland
HELSINKI
STOCKHOLM
OSLO
TALLINN
ESTONIA
LATVIA
RIGA
LITHUANIA
VILNIUS
KALININGRAD
(RUSSIAN FED.)
BALTIC SEA
Gotland
Skagerrak
NETHERLANDS
AMSTERDAM
BELGIUM
BRUSSELS
LUX.
GERMANY
BERLIN
Hamburg
POLAND
WARSAW
BELARUS
MINSK
KIEV
CZECH.REP.
PRAGUE
SLOVAKIA
BRATISLAVA
VIENNA
AUSTRIA
HUNGARY
BUDAPEST
Carpathians Mts.
ROMANIA
BUCHAREST
MOLDOVA
FRANCE
PARIS
Bay of
Biscay
Massif
Central
SWITZ.
LIECHT.
SLOVENIA
LJUBLJANA
ZAGREB
CROATIA
BOSNIA & H
SARAJEVO
SERBIA
BELGRADE
MONTENEGRO
KOSOVO
F.Y.R.O.M.
ALBANIA
TIRANA
BULGARIA
SOFIA
GREECE
ATHENS
Peloponnesus
AEGEAN SEA
Crete
ITALY
ROME
Naples
Corsica
Sardinia
Sicily
Pyrenees
SPAIN
MADRID
PORTUGAL
LISBON
Sierra Morena
Balearic Is.
MEDITERRANEAN SEA
Strait of Gibraltar
MOROCCO
RABAT
ALGERIA
ALGIERS
TUNISIA
TUNIS
VALLETTA
MALTA
Anatolia
CYPRUS
Istanbul

15. Rome

Capitals left to visit: Amsterdam, Athens, Brussels, Bucharest, Budapest, Helsinki, Lisbon, Luxembourg, Madrid, Paris, Prague, Riga, Sofia, Tallinn, Vilnius

Days on the road: 35
Distance travelled: 2721 miles
EU capitals visited: 8

I WAS BACK in Rome, the city I felt I had owned for a year four years earlier. As it was now clear that my initial presumption that I would have finished the whole trip by Christmas had been a little misplaced, I decided that I would start trying to spend a little bit more time in each place I stopped off at, to be able to see a few more things and also rest up a bit more. Rome was the perfect place to put this change of plan into action.

Exiting the station out on to Via Marsala, past the junkies and tramps that lined the outside wall, the smell of street rubbish and takeaway pizza hit me in the face and infected me with a sense of nostalgia as I remembered the times I'd walked this street in the early hours of the morning, struggling to keep my balance and stay on my feet. 2003 had been a great year. But it wasn't 2003 anymore and I wasn't here to reminisce. I strolled the 15 minutes to Sabrina's flat in the San Lorenzo area of the city, stopping to remember only briefly the time I accidentally ripped off a drug dealer for 20 Euros inside the park I now passed.

Sabrina hadn't changed a bit since I had last seen her, and she greeted me at the door with a hug and then introduced me to the two English girls sitting on her settee sharing a spliff, Amy and Jema. Over the next couple of smokes I learnt that Sabrina's two guests were as different as The Queen and Freddie Mercury. Amy was a well-spoken girl from London with classical good looks; every bit the English rose. Jema, on the other hand, wore a vest, sported a thick, dark moustache and was every bit the showman. Both were in their early twenties but both had ended up in Rome after following slightly different paths. Amy was the girlfriend of Declan, who owned one of the most popular Irish pubs in the city. Jema worked as a dominatrix, stubbing out cigarettes on businessmen's chests and walking in heels over their bollocks. Amy hailed from Greenwich, the place of my own birth, and spoke like Kiera Knightly. Jema hailed from Bolton and spoke like Peter Kay. Jema scared me, if not for the fact that she spat into men's eyes for a living then because before moving to Rome she had spent a couple of years working as a bouncer on the door of one of Manchester's roughest clubs. After a while we were joined in the living room by Sabrina's Albanian flatmate Sid, and Pumbaa the pug dog, who I was sure I recognised from the film Men in Black, but didn't want to say just in case it wasn't him and he got annoyed. Sid wore his hair in a ponytail and had a beard. He was a colleague of Sabrina's in the Yellow Hostel that she now managed. After sharing a load of takeaway pizza, the living room cleared of people as Jema and Amy went home and Sid and Sabrina went to their bedrooms, leaving me to sleep on the settee with a couple of cushions and a blanket. Ordinarily I would have been more than pleased with this set-up, but ordinarily I wouldn't have, five minutes before going to bed, watched an over-excited pug vomit on the settee. Sabrina had cleaned it up thoroughly but somehow the image (and the probably imagined smell) remained.

I woke the next morning to an empty flat and a cold, sunny day. I showered and headed out the door with the plan to just walk and walk and walk, taking in all the places that had once been so familiar. At one point in the day, however, I got a little tired of walking and decided to take the Metro for a couple of stops. This didn't go as smoothly as I had hoped, as I found myself sprinting away from a couple of sunglasses-wearing security guards in hot pursuit, after being seen jumping a ticket barrier at the Spanish Steps station. I managed to evade capture by joining a large group of Middle Eastern holidaymakers on a guided tour of the area. I find I can pass quite easily for an Arab. Even the tour guide failed to notice that I was in fact a stowaway.

A few nights into my stay in Rome Sid invited me over to the bar of the Yellow Hostel for an evening of drinking; all rounds on him. We took our pints from the English barman and ventured downstairs into the basement room where the table-tennis table was being used for a drinking game I was soon to find out was the most popular sport among Americans at the time: Beer Pong. The rules of the game were fairly simple. One team of two players stood at the end of each table and lay out in front of them 10 cups in the shape of a diamond. Each cup was then half-filled with beer. Each team took turns to have two throws of a table-tennis ball (one throw for each player) with the aim being to sink the ball into one of the opposing team's cups. If a successful shot was made, the contents of that cup were to be drunk by one of the receiving team's players and the cup then removed from the game. The winning team was the first to successfully eliminate all of the enemy's cups. The losing team then had to drink the remaining beer left on the winning team's side and then vacate the table so that the next team of challengers could take their shot at defeating the remaining champs. The challenging team always had to buy the beer for the game. I immediately worked out the reason why I had never seen this game played at home and why it would never take off: The losing team is the one that has to drink everything.

'Excuse me,' I said politely, tapping a baseball cap wearing American on the shoulder, 'but would you mind explaining to me what the point of winning is?'

'What do you mean, brother? Winning is the bomb! Who doesn't want to win, man? Can I get a 'Hell Yea!?'

And at this, a large shout of 'Hell Yea!' went up into the air from all around.

'I can see that winning is important to you, but can you not see that the aim of the game is to pay for a load of beers and then to watch some other guys drink those beers that you have just paid for?'

A confused look came over his face. A confused look came over everybody in the room's face. Then after a couple of moments of awkward silence he smiled, then laughed and said, 'Man! You almost had me there! You Brits with your dry sense of humour. Now if you'll excuse me, I've got a game of Beer Pong to win! Hell yea, motherfucker!'

I sighed, downed my Jack and then in partnership with Sid took on the reigning champs at this newly discovered game. We had just lost our second match, when in through the door walked a couple of young American guys with big arms and crew cuts. Both had obviously been drinking for a good few hours, and one in particular – who could have been Wayne Rooney's long lost twin brother, separated at birth and shipped across the Atlantic – seemed a little worse for wear as he banged into doorways and tables and spilt beer as he walked.

'Can I play, please?' he asked, with surprising politeness.

Before I knew it, Sid and one of the place's barmen, Zack – a rich, cocky Californian frat boy – were setting up the table and a ball was placed in my hand. With this drunken oaf on my team there was no way we would be suffering a victory.

'You go first, mate,' I encouraged my teammate and then watched as he lost his grip on the ball and let it drop and roll along the floor and under the table. He dropped to his knees to retrieve it. A full minute later, he had failed to return to his feet.

'Can't you find it?' I asked, bending over to offer my assistance.

There was no reply. His head was bowed and his eyes were still pointing to the ground. Without warning he grabbed my legs tightly and pushed his face into my knees and I realised that he was sobbing. Uncontrollably.

'It should have been me! It should have been me!' he kept shouting, still holding tightly to my legs.

I looked around for support but only found Zack and some other Americans laughing.

'Do you know what it's like to have people trying to kill you every single day?' he asked through tears. 'War is fucking hell. It should have been me!'

'Bullshit!' laughed Zack. 'I've shot a gun. I'm from the hood; people get shot all the time. You're not special!'

I couldn't believe what I was hearing. This cocky little teenager who hadn't even started shaving yet was mocking this soldier, just back from war where he had obviously experienced some kind of trauma, and telling him he was no different to some kids in California.

'Hey Zack, why don't you shut the fuck up?' I snapped, before picking the soldier up off the floor and lugging him over to a bench up against the wall, all the time looking around the room for the friends that he'd arrived with. They were nowhere to be seen.

'It should have been me. It should have been me driving that day. It should have been me that lost his legs! It shouldn't have been Mitchell! It should have been me!' The soldier continued screaming whilst crying onto my shoulder.

'What's your name?' I asked, seeing as we had now broken the ice enough for it to leave me with a soaking wet shirt and a patch on my crotch.

'Pete,' he wailed. 'And Mitchell is my best friend. Those bastards put an IED under his tank. He lost both his legs. It should have been me! I should have died there that day. They were trying to kill me every day for 15 months. I can't sleep. Why am I still alive? If I hear a loud noise or see a flash I break down with fear. I'm broken, man, I'm broken!'

I could do nothing but hold Pete in my arms and let him outpour his pain. I could have done with some support, especially from someone who knew him better than I did, which, let's face it, wasn't that well at all. But all around I saw only sniggering Americans. Zack was showing off to the assembled girls by threatening to throw Pete out if he didn't pull himself together, and in the corner of the room a young Eminem-wannabe with a huge gold-plated chain around his neck, an oversized baseball cap on his head and an embarrassing attempt at a gangster moustache above his top lip was making noise about how he came from a war zone: Detroit. Never mind the fact that this was clearly a spoilt little rich kid travelling Europe on daddy's credit card; he was pure ghetto. Pete continued to cry – now that the floodgates had been opened there didn't seem any way to slow down the flow – and Zack decided that it was time to remove him from the premises. I couldn't argue with the decision; after all, Pete wasn't really doing the atmosphere of the place any favours, but I did step in to prevent Zack and the Australian barman from physically carrying him up the stairs and through the curious, laughing crowd of onlookers. I put Pete's arm over my shoulder and led the way as he stumbled up the stairs, stopping at the top to ask if he could first zip up his jacket before being put out the door.

'You can zip up when you get outside!' Zack said with a smirk. 'Just get out. We don't need your kind in here!'

Pete then put his hands up to the back of his head, surrendering completely. The poor guy was completely submissive, didn't want to cause any trouble, was clearly traumatised from the things he had seen and had only come here tonight to try and relax with some Army friends and a few drinks. It had turned bad, but even now after this humiliation he was still completely cooperating with the staff who were throwing him out simply because he had been brainwashed into believing that volunteering for his country was a good choice, and had then been given a shitty job to do that had left him mentally scarred. Whether you agree with any of the wars that we fight or not – and not that it matters, but most of them I don't – the soldiers aren't the ones to blame; they are generally just poorly-informed working-class kids short on options, who get preyed upon by governments, with their greed and lack of value on human life. It could've been me.

Pete's mate, a Mexican-American called Oscar, then materialised. When I say he materialised, I don't mean he just appeared out of thin air. Oscar was no ghost. I mean that he returned from the toilet and found the drama that was unfolding outside.

'Oh, not again,' he sighed. 'It's like I have to be his babysitter every time we go out now. He's been through some tough shit.'

I explained to him what had happened and he said he would take care of it and see him back to the hostel they were both staying in.

'But can you do something for me first?' he asked. 'Before Pete let his guard down a bit, we were both talking to some of the people in there and they were really cool. I would like to keep in touch with them and I think Pete would to. Would you mind going in and getting their email addresses for me?'

I didn't fancy Oscar's chances much of getting many responses, as it looked to me as if a lot of the guests had been making polite conversation rather than really bonding with the two GIs, but I wasn't going to say no. So, armed with a piece of paper and a pen picked up from behind the bar, I re-entered the Beer Pong room, which was now eerily quiet, despite being full of Americans.

'Listen up, guys. I'm not looking for any smart remarks or showing off, but Oscar has asked if any of you would like to keep in touch with him or Pete to write your contact details on this piece of paper,' I announced, holding up the sheet of paper.

There was silence, until the Eminem-wannabe felt bold and shouted out, 'You gotta be kidding me. Those guys are losers, man!'

'What did I just say?'

'Yea, well, I'm just saying, they're pussies. That guy nearly spilt beer on me. I should have kicked his ass.'

'Right, I've had just about enough of you. Sit down and shut up.'

I was losing my temper.

'Or what?'

'Ask me again.'

'Okay, man, okay. I ain't got no beef with you,' he then said, before sitting down and shutting up.

Meanwhile I was left wondering why he had brought meat into the conversation. A couple of girls came forward and wrote down their particulars, which I took back upstairs and outside, where Pete was now banging his head against a brick wall, still screaming.

'Thanks, buddy,' Oscar said as I handed him the paper.

'Yea no worries. Now, you better get him out of here and to bed before the police turn up. The Roman constabulary isn't overly fond of drunken English speakers. I should know.'

That was the end of the night for me. I truly hope that Pete, wherever he may be now, has been given the right kind of therapy and is getting on with his life. More than that, I hope he is out of the armed forces. I hope he's still alive.

My time in Rome had run its course and it was now time to get back to Ljubljana, where I would spend the Christmas period, before plotting my course south to cover the capital cities of Serbia (despite not being in the EU), Bulgaria and Romania.

Hopping trains all the way, I was thrown off at Florence, Bologna, Ferrara, and then purposely at Venice, from where I managed to get across the border and all the way to Ljubljana after explaining to the Slovenian inspector that I was on my way to seeing my fiancée as a surprise Christmas visit, and that I had hitchhiked all the way from England to Italy but couldn't stand being out in the cold anymore. In good holiday spirits he told me to sit down and put my feet up. This kind of rule breaking is not something to usually expect of Slovenian people in uniform, so I wouldn't advise trying the same stunt.

So, all in all, the journey from Rome to Ljubljana was simple, if not short. The only squeaky bum moment came on the Rome to Florence express when, half way through the journey, after I had already explained to the inspector that I'd been robbed by gypsies at the station, I noticed that working in the back end of the train was the very same inspector that had so kindly let me ride for free from Padova to Florence on my original journey down through Italy. If he came across me again, travelling back up through the country with the same fictional tale, I would surely have some tough questions to answer. Fortunately, he stayed in his end of the train. As I travelled north that day, I felt sadness at leaving my old friend Sabrina behind. It had been great catching up with her after the years. I also felt that Sid, Amy and Jema were new friends that would remain in my life.

Oh, and just to clarify: Jema didn't really wear a vest. And she didn't have a moustache, either. And she wasn't every bit the showman. She might have been every bit the show woman, I don't know; I didn't take in one of her concerts. I don't think she did concerts. If you missed the Freddy Mercury reference from the start, it is probably because you are younger than me. Not your fault.

Welcome back to Ljubljana.

16. Ljubljana

CHRISTMAS WAS A relaxing period as I went out to the mountain resort of Kranjska Gora for a few days rest and recuperation with Vanja, staying in a little cabin that her family rented. We walked around for days in the snow, chatting and remembering old times. We slept in late in the mornings, watched the telly and enjoyed each other's company. New Year's Eve was spent with Vanja's family, standing on the balcony of their home watching the fireworks and thinking about the struggle that lay ahead. I spent the few days after Christmas plotting my route south and decided that Greece would be put on hold as instead I would make my way down to Bulgaria via the ex-Yugoslav countries, before making my way back up in a loop through Romania and Hungary, getting back to Slovenia, from where I would take the journey westward towards France and Spain. Another of the language schools that I used to work for donated a bus ticket to Belgrade, so I set about trying to find somewhere to bed down in what was once the capital of the whole of Yugoslavia. I sent out emails to 15 people in Belgrade but, as I would be arriving during Orthodox Christmas, finding someone with space for me proved extremely difficult, until a singer called Miroslav answered my pleas. Arranging a place in Bulgaria wasn't as tough. I received a reply within ten minutes of sending my request from a guy called Chavdar. I was all sorted for my next two ports of call.

It was Thursday 3rd January 2008 and I was up early. Vanja wrapped up some sandwiches for me, as I squeezed the last of my things into my backpack whilst pouring a half-litre carton of chocolate milk down my throat – just the chocolate milk, not the actual cardboard carton – and then we crammed on to the packed bus to the centre of the city. It was a crisply cold yet bright and sunny day: the kind of cold that'll freeze the ears right off the side of your head. There were only about nine or ten other people waiting to get on the 10am coach to Belgrade. I was happy with this because I had been expecting to have to sit for eight hours with my face squashed up against the glass as the abnormally large Serb next to me stuffed his face with barbecued meat, grease collecting in his beard, whilst shooting his gun into the air and singing nationalist songs boisterously with a busload of his fellow compatriots. Not that I let stereotypes influence my expectations.

I took my seat and we left on time. I had been expecting there to be at least one Slovene on the bus, or maybe an Australian or American backpacker, but no, I found myself the only non-Serb on the vehicle. No guns though. Not even any barbecued meat; just nine or ten other people, the majority of whom were already asleep.

Getting out of the city and onto the motorway was like entering a winter wonderland scene straight off of a Christmas card. Snow-covered hills reached high up into the clouds on both sides as tiny white villages sat at their feet. The puritan would argue that this beautiful vision was slightly spoilt by the fact that someone with a great sense of humour had travelled the whole distance of the stretch of motorway between Ljubljana and Novo Mesto and sprayed the words 'Fuck You' and 'Fuck Off' in huge green letters on almost every sign and bridge along the way. The schoolboy in me giggled every time we passed a new one.

The further we drove from Ljubljana, the thicker the snow on the ground outside became. The sun still shone brightly though, it was a perfect day for a drive. About an hour after leaving Ljubljana we got to the town of Novo Mesto. I had never been there before, but that was mostly because every Slovene that I had ever heard mention the place had included the word 'shit' quickly followed by the word 'hole' in their description. As I looked out the window I could understand why. Every wall had been daubed with Slovene nationalist slogans and racial slurs aimed at the other ex-Yugoslav communities. The swastika was also bandied about quite liberally. As we sat in the bus station another fifteen or so Serbs boarded the coach. It couldn't be such a terrible place here, could it? This was Slovenia, after all; a land that encompasses beauty in some form or other wherever you happen to look. I stared out of the window, scanning the area, trying to find that something nice; that thing that would make me go away and say, 'You know what? Novo Mesto might not be the nicest place on the planet, but it's still not as bad as they say. At least they have that beautiful (insert item of beauty here)'; that little something that would make the place that little bit less crap. My hopes were dashed though, as my eyes fell upon two small, pasty-faced, pony-tailed, skinny lads in their early twenties, marching up and down the concourse in Dr. Martin boots, grey camouflaged trousers and black bomber jackets covered in sewn-on White Power badges. I let them catch me grinning at them. They looked away. I wanted to feel anger at them, but all I could muster was pity as they were clearly the kids who had been picked on in school and hadn't lived enough of life yet to know any better. Just idiots, not worthy of any reaction. Someone had taught them the rubbish they believed.

The driver took us out of Novo Mesto and I didn't look back. The next stop would be the Croatian border before setting off earlier in the day. As we approached the outer edges of Slovenia and got nearer to their Southern neighbour I was starting to feel the pressure of the half a litre of chocolate milk on my bladder. I was starting to feel it pretty strongly. We got to the border at 12 and I got excited when we were told that we all had to get off of the coach to walk through passport control on the Slovene side. There would be a toilet there for me to nip in to, surely, right? Wrong. Oh well, even standing up for a few minutes meant some of the pressure was taken off of my now aching kidneys.

I always get nervous when crossing from Slovenia into Croatia and this day was no different. I had had problems or at the very least special attention on every occasion prior and the last thing I wanted or needed now, as I danced to keep from pissing myself, was any kind of delay in getting through. The reason I always have difficulties? It's partly because there's a bit of an air bubble underneath my passport picture that seems to arise an itsy-bitsy bit of suspicion in border guards' minds; but it's mostly because in that picture I look more like a Bosnian or an Albanian than 95 per cent of all Bosnians and Albanians. We all got off the bus and formed an orderly queue to file past the little booth that housed the Slovene officer. As my turn came, I kept my eyes firmly down as I shuffled along and handed her my passport.

'Kris?'

Oh dear, question time.

'Where are you going?'

'To Belgrade,' I replied sheepishly.

'Kris.'

There was a pause as I still refused to look at my interrogator.

'You don't remember me, do you?' she then asked.

What? Now I looked up, taken aback by the question. She was smiling at me. I knew her from somewhere, but couldn't place the face. Then it clicked. She was an ex-student of mine, somebody I had taught English to for three hours a week over a course of a year in Ljubljana. All the times I had given her shit for not doing her homework, tested her in front of the class and told her I expected a better effort, and now how the power had shifted. She started chatting, asking me loads of questions about what I was doing and what I had been up to over the past year or so. She didn't seem to care in the slightest about the impatient queue of Serbs forming behind me, none of whom could speak English and all of whom were now trying to work out whether I was in trouble with the authorities or if I was trying to chat up a policewoman. I don't know which would have given me more kudos in their eyes. After a couple of minutes we said goodbye and shook hands. The Serbs would eye me suspiciously for the rest of the journey.

At 12:30 we pulled into a service station in Croatia and by now I was almost in tears from the pressure on my bladder. I jumped off the bus and sprinted into the garage building, only to find that I would have to pay 2 Kunas or 30 cents to use the amenities. I ran outside as quickly as I had run in, found myself a tree and proceeded to write my name in the deep snow. Well, it started as my name but then went on to include date of birth, followed by the first two chapters of my autobiography.

We drove through Croatia and into Serbia, arriving at the border at about 4pm. The guard got on and stamped my passport and then we proceeded into his country. The clear conditions of Slovenia had long since disappeared and been replaced by a fog that just got deeper and deeper the further south we drove. I couldn't even see the side of the road when I looked out the window. It was literally just a haze of white, as the snow on the ground mixed with the fog in the air. Every now and then you would catch a blob of light; a cry for help from a streetlamp, begging you not to forgot him.

'When you get off of the bus at the other end, tell them there were some you left behind!' it whispered.

The snow outside was so deep that the trees in the fields either side of the road were buried; their cold heads trying to stay above the line.

After what seemed like an eternity on the coach we pulled into Belgrade bus station at 5:45pm. I wasn't in the EU, so no need to tick anything off of my list, but I was in another capital city.

Welcome to Belgrade.

17. Belgrade

I GOT OFF the bus and had an intense stretch. It was freezing and I was knee deep in snow. I had Miroslav's address written on my phone, so I walked around a bit looking for someone to ask for directions, until a voice disturbed my concentration.

'Kris?'

I turned around quickly, convinced that I had misheard. Who in Belgrade knew me? It was Miroslav. He'd come to meet me at the bus station, and had recognised me from the photo on Couchsurfing. I handed him some of my bags and we started the leisurely walk to his flat. My host talked almost in a whisper, making it difficult to pay attention to the conversation, but I did manage to find out that he was in university studying to become a fully trained classical singer, and not, as I had first assumed, a turbo folk performer. It was the photo on his Couchsurfing profile that had led me to this false assumption. He just looked like the kind of guy you would see performing in pubs up and down the Balkans. We got to the flat on Balkanska Street and I was led up the stairs and into the warmth. Like any good host, the first thing Miroslav did as soon as our shoes were off was offer me a cup of tea, and like any true Serbian man, when I accepted his offer he called through to the woman in the kitchen to do the honours. Jasna was Miroslav's sister. She had short red hair, a pale face, and a cheeky look about her that gave away her sense of humour. She introduced herself and welcomed me to their home. She was at university studying English and on a completely unrelated note I can also tell you she made a lovely cup of English breakfast tea.

'Hvala,' I thanked her in Serbian as she handed me the hot drink.

The living room was small and cosy. There was no telly; instead there were two bookcases filled to breaking point with literature in Serbian and English. In the corner of the room sat a small piano that both siblings could play. I was shown to my own room. Actually it was Miroslav's room, but for the time I was here he was going to sleep on the settee in the living room; an act which filled me with gratitude.

'After dinner I'm going sledding with my girlfriend up at the medieval fort. Do you want to join us?' Miroslav asked me.

The previous night had brought the city's first delivery of snow that winter, and it hadn't been a scrimp and save job; it was the most snow they had had in one night for years. We walked out the door at 10pm. Jasna wasn't coming, as she had a bit of a cold, so was going to take the time to catch up on some studying. Miroslav led me on a walk through the pretty streets of the Old Town until we got to a park where we waited for his girlfriend to show up.

Luna was an olive-skinned girl who spoke perfect English. She arrived carrying the sled and we walked through the park, through the fort, through the free open-air military museum and up to the top of the hill that offered a view over Belgrade by night. Coming from different directions the distinct sound of Serbian folk music was being blasted out from clubs all over the city. It was exactly how I had imagined Belgrade to sound. It doesn't surprise me anymore but it always used to how the capital cities of the ex-Yugoslav republics are so different from one another. Ljubljana, Sarajevo, Belgrade and Zagreb have very little in common. It's not like in England where most city high streets are just clones of one another. In the ex-Yugoslavia you really know you've crossed a border when you travel between the above mentioned cities. Ljubljana is like a little Alpine village; Zagreb looks up to and imitates Vienna; Sarajevo is Turkish in character, what with the call to prayer and the carpet sellers; and Belgrade is in your face, loud and proud.

We spent a good couple of hours sliding down the steep hill at great speed, before getting thrown off of the sled and into a tree at the bottom, getting up, brushing ourselves down and climbing the hill to do it all again. Snow was in my hat, in my gloves, in my shoes, inside my coat. My body hurt from the cold, but it didn't matter because I was sliding down a hill at high speed like a child. The walk home was slow and uncomfortable as the snow that had infiltrated my clothes started to melt.

Above: In the middle of the sister and brother duo.

I slept well on my first night in Serbia, despite feeling a little bad that Miroslav and Luna were both sleeping on the small settee. I had told them before I went to bed that they should take the room and I would have the couch, but they told me to shut up and go to sleep. The following morning I joined Jasna on a trip to the shops to buy bread and cheese. There was a right old gossip going on in the busy bakery. I couldn't follow too well what was being said, but the old women were certainly enjoying themselves. Whatever the subject was, I knew it was juicy because at one point they all gasped in sync. Outside, Jasna told me what had set off the gasp: 'Do you all know that young Hadžić is gay?'

In front of the whole bakery, one little old lady had just outed poor old Hadžić to the whole world and his dog, probably before he had even had his cornflakes.

After breakfast I set off with the two siblings for my tour of the city. It took all day and I wish there had been more hours of daylight because there was so much that we weren't able to take in. Belgrade isn't about beautiful architecture. It isn't about museums, churches, or galleries. Sure, you can find all of these in abundance, but you would be doing yourself a disservice if that was what you went there to seek out. Belgrade is about the funny side of everyday life. I'll give you a few examples of what I mean: we walked past a street bookstall where a customer was berating the vendor about something, calling him every name under the sun and explaining in detail what he would like to do to his mother. The vendor just smiled and took it, throwing a few insults back just for good measure. The vendor wasn't little, either. It was all just banter. In Belgrade it is perfectly normal to argue with people you don't know, using X-rated language, and if you happen to be the recipient of such attention you are expected to take it with a pinch of salt and give a bit back. I like that. Forget fake pleasantries. Someone short-changes you or tries to over-charge you, forget all of your, 'Oh, I'm sorry, but there appears to have been a mistake.' That won't do. Why are we always sorry in England, anyway? Down in Serbia, the bloke tries to rip you off, just call him a wanker and tell him you hope he gets a sexually transmitted disease from a dog. Simple. But always make sure to walk away from your acquaintance with a smile of some kind.

We came across a quiet little street with young children playing in the snow, sledding down the road. These kids were so young, so innocent to the world. They only knew about playing. There, on the very same street, was a pub whose name translated into English meant, 'My Mother's C**t.' Only in Serbia would you get that. I asked why a pub would have such a name.

'In Serbia, a typical response to the question, "Where are you going?" is to say, "To my mother's c**t," in the same way as you in England say, "To see a man about a dog." So, if you are going to this pub and your wife asks you where you are going, you can just tell the truth.'

On the wall of the maternity ward someone had spray painted in massive yellow letters the sentence, 'She took my sperm whit out promision.'

The 'artist' had taken the time to think of something funny and ironic, to go out and buy the paint, to creep down to the hospital at night and to spray it on the wall, but hadn't taken the time to check in an English dictionary first if it was spelt correctly or made sense. To me, that makes it funnier than if he had written it without mistakes.

My guided tour of the city came to an end and we returned to the flat early in the evening. I had been told that later on I was going to be given a taste of what Serbs liked to get up to on a Friday night.

The Orthodox religion celebrates Christmas on the 7th of January, meaning that in two days it would be Christmas Eve and also the day that my two hosts would leave Belgrade and head to their family village to spend the holidays with their loved ones; and I would somehow head to Bulgaria. Miroslav offered to buy me a train ticket to Sofia, but I felt that I had taken enough from my new friends already and so declined the offer. Later that evening a friend of the siblings came round to the flat. I was introduced to a quiet guy with scruffy hair who went by the name Mladen. We sat round the table drinking while the topic of conversation was one that I hadn't expected to find on a cold winter's night in Belgrade: Del Boy and

Rodney. Apparently everyone's favourite independent traders had a huge following in Serbia. I soon got asked the million dollar question.

'Kris, can you explain to us.... What's a plonker?'

'I'll tell you later.'

It was time to go out. The walk was long, cold and slippery, but we were all in good spirits as the city of Belgrade seemed to have come to life. All around us, people made their way to bars and pubs. The unmistakeable sound of folk music was faint in the air again, drifting out of grotty little establishments along the river. We spent the new few hours on an improvised pub crawl, gradually getting more and more intoxicated on a heavy combination of local drinks Rakija and Vinjak (a type of schnapps and a Serbian brandy).

As the night was drawing to a close, and we slid along the ice, my eyes were drawn to a statue in the middle of the street of an impressive looking man; an impressive looking man that I felt the need to kiss for a photo. Jasna prepared the camera as I locked lips with the statue of the national hero. Bear in mind that the temperature was -9 degrees.

'Aaam stuuu,' I managed to mumble, without the use of my tongue.

'What did you say?'

'Aaaaam stuuuu!' I moaned.

'You're what?'

'Stuuuuu!'

'Stuck? You're stuck?'

Cue rapturous laughter. I wasn't seeing the funny side. My tongue had super glued itself to the stone and any slight attempt to remove it led to agonising pain. I really don't see why English people have such a reputation for stupidity in cities across the continent. So I had managed to get my tongue stuck to a statue. It happens! The laughter died down a bit once the seriousness of the situation sunk in. There was no way of getting my tongue off of this guy's face without ripping it out of my mouth. I don't want you to think I'm materialistic. I'm not. But over the past 24 years I had become quite attached to my tongue. It had sentimental value. We had been through a lot of firsts together. I didn't want to leave him here in Belgrade, stuck to a statue. Images of myself trying to explain to people in countries I was yet to visit how I had come to lose my tongue filled my head. How would I talk? Kiss? Eat? Lick statues?

As I stood there, face glued to a monument, trying to figure out the answers to these deep questions, Jasna was making herself useful coming up with a plan.

'I have a plan,' she said, confirming this.

She approached me with a look of defiance. I was afraid. Did she really think she could just pull me hard enough and it would come loose?

'Yaaaaaana!' I couldn't even pronounce her name, 'Wayu-doo?'

'Don't worry. Just trust me.'

She cupped her hands around the affected area, made a little mouth piece in between her palms and blew warm breath into the pocket she had created. Ever so slowly I began moving my tongue. It hurt, but there was movement. She continued to blow and I continued to pull. If you found something amusing about that last sentence, grow up! I eased my tongue away from the statue and felt a high I never imagined I would get from removing my mouth from a landmark. The high was short-lived though, as I realised I was bleeding profusely.

'Aaaah! I'm bleeding! My tongue is bleeding!' I screamed.

Sympathy was clearly something my Serbian friends hadn't taken classes in. Laughing at others' misfortune was something they clearly had.

I turned to Mladen and, through the pain, managed to say the words, 'Remember you asked what a plonker was?'

Whilst in the pub I hadn't realised how drunk I, and my companions, had been getting. We were literally staggering through the snow, as my fellow journeymen for the night tried to remember where they lived. Everywhere had closed up for the night and it was time to get to bed; until we stumbled upon a pub with its doors still open. On entering, it was easy to tell what sort of establishment this was. It was there solely to serve the hardcore element of drinkers that wanted to punish their livers for just a little longer before being forced to retire to their homes. A DJ in the corner was literally slumped over his record decks, a strong drink in one hand, a girl's breast in the other; the same girl attempting to polish his tonsils for him using only her tongue as a cloth. All around, boisterous crowds of drunken Serbs shouted at each other over their drinks. It was already 3 in the morning and they weren't going to be open for too much longer so we ordered one final round of Rakijas and then I was treated to one last Vinjak before we were all kicked out by the bar staff. Once back at the flat, Jasna and Miroslav disappeared for the night, while Mladen nipped round to the all night shop for a few litres of beer. The two of us then sat until 7 in the morning drinking at the kitchen table whilst discussing football and women. In that order.

I woke later that morning at about 11:30 with a banging headache. I fumbled around my bag looking for some paracetamol, found what I was after and went back to bed to let it take effect, waking an hour later. Outside it was raining, and the Košava – a special kind of wind apparently unique to Belgrade – was blowing forcefully. I ignored the weather; determined to head out alone and see what the day would bring. It turned out to be the right decision. The first place I headed to was the station to find out the departure times of trains to Sofia for the following day. The woman behind the desk told me there was a train to Bulgaria at 8:40 the next morning.

They don't put granite or salt down on the snowy pavements in Belgrade. The ground becomes an ice rink, and the ice is invisible. As you stand still and look around at the people going about their business you realise that you have slipped into a surreal world where friction no longer exists. People are falling on their arses. The amount of people I saw get seriously hurt in just a couple of hours was in double figures.

Next I made my way to the bus station to see what time coaches to Sofia left, in case I couldn't get on the train and had to try and sneak on to a bus. As I queued at the desk, I got talking to an American, Paul from Texas. He was heading to Ljubljana the next day and was comparing prices between bus and train. I told him what I was doing and the first thing he wanted to know was how it was possible to ride by train. I told him about the stress of trying to blag guards and he asked how much the ticket was. I said I didn't know. I did know really, but I didn't want to make it seem like I was hinting for something, even though I guess I kind of was. He said, 'Then let's go and find out,' and we went to the train station. He turned around from the desk and asked me how old I was, and then he handed me a ticket for the following day saying it was his way of making a donation and that he wanted to be a part of such a ridiculous idea.

'Are you hungry?' he asked next.

'A bit.'

And so we went for a burek. Inside the café I went to take my coat off only to find that it had frozen. My coat had *literally* frozen. How many times in a lifetime does that happen? I was wearing sheets of ice. I told Paul what he should see in Ljubljana, he shook my hand, wished me luck and then we parted company. You gotta love random Americans.

I slept late the following day and missed my early morning train. It didn't matter; it was an open ticket I had, so I could take the night train, which took three hours longer. Miroslav and Jasna left Belgrade in the morning, leaving me to chill out alone in the flat until it was time to leave. An email from Chavdar in Sofia told me he would pick me up from the station there when my train arrived early the next morning.

It was Orthodox Christmas Eve and, as I made my way down to Belgrade station to catch my 9:10pm train, everyone on the streets was in festive mood. People were singing as they made their way to pubs around the city. My train for the night was a grubby, old Yugoslav Railways train from the 1960s. Dirty and dusty it might have been, but that took nothing away from the comfort. I found my own personal compartment; not difficult considering the train was almost empty. Those that had boarded for the journey were all carrying with them sleeping bags and blankets for the night ahead. Not me though. This train was so old that whenever the engine was off, so were the carriage lights. I sat in pitch darkness and waited for the wheels to start rolling.

I wanted to sleep but couldn't, thanks to horror stories I had read on the internet about lone travellers on Balkan night trains being drugged and robbed by gypsies. It didn't help matters when I made my way up to the toilet just before midnight and saw a solitary teenage boy sitting in a suspicious manner in the compartment next to mine. In reality, it made no difference if I were awake or asleep; if someone was going to rob me he was going to rob me.

At about 2am we pulled in to Niš, a small Serbian town I had originally planned to stop off in before I had so easily found a host in Sofia. Outside, small houses were decorated with Christmas lights. A man walked up and down the platform, shovelling snow and whistling. We waited at the station for 20 minutes before finally pulling out. As the engine had been off, so too had the lights, but as we pulled away they failed to come back on. It wasn't the lights that I was worried about but rather the heating which also came on and off with the engine. I was shivering. Whilst sat at the station I had put on every layer of clothing I could grab from my rucksack, but nothing seemed to be providing me any warmth. After a few minutes the feeling of dread hit me. What if I was supposed to have changed trains at Niš and that's why there was no heating or lights on this one. I jumped up out of my compartment and ran down the corridor of the carriage, freaking out when I found that all the other passengers that had been there before were nowhere to be seen. Even the gypsy boy was gone. At the end of the corridor was the door to the next carriage, but it was locked shut. Shit! I was on my way to the depot. I ran to the other end of the carriage and through the door to the next carriage, but again found no passengers. I did, however, pass two ticket inspectors on the way, neither of whom looked at me as if I didn't belong on their train. I walked back to my carriage to check that my stuff was still safe and found the two inspectors waiting for me outside my door. They spoke slowly and in basic Serbian for my benefit, pointing whilst saying, 'Tamo je vruće.'

I understood. They were telling me that the heating was working further up the train. The relief was immense. I found myself an unpopulated compartment and this time managed to get some sleep. I was woken a couple of hours later by the brightness of a torch being shone onto my face through my closed eyelids. I handed the Serbian policeman my passport, he stamped it, handed it back and left me alone. Ten minutes later a Bulgarian copper came in, shone his torch in my face, took my passport, spent two whole minutes staring at my face, another two staring at the picture in the passport, another three staring at my face, before throwing my document back at me and leaving. We sat at the border for what seemed liked aneternity as men searched the train up and down, even underneath. We rolled past the 'Welcome to Bulgaria' sign at 5:51am, or what I thought was 5:51am. I hadn't realised that Bulgaria was an hour ahead of her neighbour.

Just inside Bulgaria we pulled into a station where a load of people got on. I was joined in my compartment by three middle-aged Bulgarians who would spend the rest of the journey to Sofia talking loudly about something I presumed was *The Wombles* and whether or not Uncle Bulgaria was actually a Bulgarian immigrant to Wimbledon. I listened intently. I didn't really. I don't speak Bulgarian. I stared out the window and watched as the bright orange sun rose over the snow-covered fields. It was a beautiful sight.

At 8:10am local time my train pulled into the station and I ticked yet another capital city off of my list.

Welcome to Sofia.

18. Sofia

Capitals left to visit: Amsterdam, Athens, Brussels, Bucharest, Budapest, Helsinki, Lisbon, Luxembourg, Madrid, Paris, Prague, Riga, Tallinn, Vilnius

Days on the road: 70
Distance travelled: 3765 miles
EU capitals visited: 9

BECAUSE I HADN'T known that Bulgaria was an hour in front of Serbia, I had arranged to meet Chavdar at 7am, an hour and ten minutes earlier than it now was. I only hoped that he had not had to rush off anywhere. I walked around the station's main hall looking out for him and hoping that if I didn't recognise him, he would me, but nobody stood out, so I tried calling his mobile. It went straight to voicemail.

Sofia is a dodgy station, full of gypsy youths looking menacing and almost certainly not waiting for any train. There are almost as many gypsies 'working' for the station as there are hanging about in it. Their job is to find foreigners looking confused, ask them what they need help finding (foreigners need help with navigation in the station because literally everything is written in Bulgarian Cyrillic only. I just said navigation in the station. This is turning into a poetry book; and a bloody good one at that. Navigation in the station!), and then after helping the lost foreigner they ask for one Lev; that's about 45 of your English pence.

I spent an hour walking around in circles in the thick snow outside the station, retrying Chavdar's number every few minutes but always finding it switched off. Fortunately, I'd had the foresight to get the number of another Sofia Couchsurfer before leaving Belgrade the night before. Kremena had emailed saying she didn't think she could host me but would be happy to give me a tour of the city if I fancied it. She was now my only hope for the night. I dialled the number and listened as her phone rang and rang without response. At least it was switched on, so I sent her a text explaining my predicament, and waited 20 minutes to read her reply: 'You can stay at my place tonight, but I don't finish work until 6:30 this evening. We can meet then, in front of the city's court. It has two lion statues outside; you will find it.'

I looked at the station's clock. It was 10am. I had eight and a half hours to kill, nowhere to go and I was shivering in the cold. It was going to be a fun day. My bag was starting to weigh heavy on my shoulders, so I walked across to the storage room and begged the old lady behind the desk to let me leave my stuff with her without payment. She looked at me over the rim of her flask full of hot coffee before nodding in the direction of a door to the side of the counter. I pushed it open and chucked my bags inside, before waving her a 'Blagodarya' followed swiftly by a 'Doviždane.' *Thank you and goodbye.*

I picked up a map that someone had dropped on the hall's floor and headed out to explore. I found myself following the main street towards the town centre. My route was lined by shopkeepers shovelling snow from their doorsteps; dirty, black snow that was melting around the city, turning it into a muddied swamp. It was impossible to even cross the road without first having to wade through a mini lake of brown sludge. I hadn't been expecting to find such an under-developed city, especially after being so impressed by Belgrade. Drab, grey apartment blocks grew up from depressingly miserable streets. There were more open-air market stalls than there were proper shops, and even the proper shops most of the time just served the customer through a small window, much like an English petrol station does at night. Everywhere you looked you saw bony stray dogs; packs of them, even in the city centre. The local people hardly seemed to notice. I watched as a small pack chased and barked at a gypsy's horse and cart. The dogs seemed to have picked up the traits of young Roma children: approaching you on the street with sad eyes, begging for something to eat. I saw one dog get given a loaf of bread, after which he ran off. It was news to me that dogs ate bread. Maybe he had a toaster. Stray dogs were just one of many obstacles facing the unfamiliar traveller in Sofia. The pavements were rife with large holes that dropped down to Bob only knows where. My guess was the lair of Splinter and his ninja turtles. Walking from A to B in Sofia required serious concentration and awareness. It made me thankful for the snow, which made the deep soulless pits of darkness stand out. *But how would it be at night*, I wondered? Was it common here for men to leave their wives at home for an evening down the pub, never to return, left to rot in the pit after staggering slightly to the left?

The time to meet Kremena was approaching and I had no idea where the court was. My map was no good, as, quite ridiculously, all street and place names on it had been transliterated in to the Latin script, despite all actual signs being in Cyrillic. The best course of action, I thought, would be to go into a Tourist Information Centre and ask for the court to be circled on my map. The conversation that took place between myself and the girl behind the desk bordered on the farcical.

'You want court?'

'Yes. Court.'

'Bulgarian court?'

'I don't know. Just the court. That is what I have been told. It has two lion statues outside it, apparently.'

'What is lion?'

'Never mind. Can you just show me the court please?' I

asked, handing her my map.

She took it and wrote down the numbers '00359' on it. Then she handed it back to me, saying, 'Here is Bulgarian court.'

'No. That is Bulgarian code. Bulgarian dialling code. I need Bulgarian court.'

'Yes. You ask for Bulgarian court, I give you Bulgarian court.'

'No. Code and court are different words.'

'Yes. Court.'

I saw now that I was going to have an itsy-bitsy problem here. The girl noticed my annoyance.

'I am sorry my English isn't perfect.'

'I just want to find the court,' I said, attempting to mime the actions of a judge, without success.

'I don't know what you want. You should ask someone on the street!'

'But this is Tourist Information. I am a tourist. I need information!'

'You come here, you want court and I give you court. You not happy.'

'I came here, I wanted court and you gave me code. I'm not happy!'

'I'm sorry,' she said.

She wasn't really sorry; I could hear it in her tone. I wasn't ready to give up, so I explained in Slovenian that I wanted to go to the place where the judge worked. She didn't understand, so I tried the Serbian word for 'judge' which I knew from my days playing football (referee and judge are the same word). She understood! Why hadn't I just done that from the start? She drew a circle on my map in black marker pen and I left. I went back to the station to pick up my bags, before making my way to my rendezvous point.

Kremena – after meeting, she insisted I call her Kremi – was stood waiting for me, dressed in a business suit and with a welcoming smile splashed across her face. We were both freezing cold so she said we would save any further talking until we were heading for the warmth of her flat, 45 minutes outside the city centre. We waited 20 minutes in the kerb, trying to hail a taxi, but none stopped for us. So we got onto what the Bulgarians call a 'minibus,' but is actually a Ford Transit with a few seats put into the back. These White Van Men drive around the city at ridiculous speeds, allowing people to hop on or off wherever they choose. If you are waiting to get on one, you just put out your thumb. If you need to jump off, you either tap the driver on the shoulder or you shout at him. There is a set charge of 1.50 Levs (about 65p), and unless you're very lucky – we weren't – you stand for the entire journey, clinging on to the body parts of the people around you, as everyone tries not to get thrown about too much by the roughness of the ride. I liked the system, and was even more impressed when our driver managed to smoke a cigarette, count a wad of money, drink from a can of soft drink and drive his van full of people, all at the same time.

We made it to the flat and I was shown up to the attic where I had my own room for the night. The air in the room was freezing, so much so that I could see my own breath, but the room was clean and tidy. Kremi then took me around the corner from her flat to a home-style restaurant for dinner. By the time we had finished the food in front of us, she had already knocked back six shots of Rakija. I had been warming up with something a little softer: a pint. However, as soon as the plates were taken away I had nowhere left to hide.

'You are in Bulgaria now. We like to relax in the evening with a proper drink,' my host said, whilst catching the attention of the landlady of the place who promptly brought over two more shots of the potent clear liquid.

We sat and talked for the next hour, downing shot after shot after shot. I think the conversation we had was funny, but to tell the truth, I don't remember much after the third glass. Kremi could drink and smoke for her country and, come the end of the night, still seemed to be functioning normally. Meanwhile, on the short walk back to the flat I tripped on a step, walked face first into a glass door, mistook a fur coat for a small dog, and had to swallow some sick that appeared unexpectedly in my mouth. Then we got in and the first thing my host did was pull a couple of glasses out of a cupboard along with a jam jar filled with yet more Rakija.

'Homemade by my parents,' she told me proudly.

'No more for me. I will just have a glass of water, please.'

'Yea right!'

As we sat and drank for another half an hour, my host reminisced about a previous Couchsurfing experience, giving me a real insight into the type of no-nonsense character she was. A Bosnian male Couchsurfer had turned up at her flat, not understanding that the movement is not intended as a dating agency, with a bottle of wine in one hand and a red rose in the other, already half pissed, and had gone straight for the kiss as soon as she'd opened the door. Rather than react with anger, fear or confusion, her response had simply been to tell him to behave himself, and then to drink heavily with him until he passed out on the couch.

Before retiring for the night, Kremi told me that she would like to buy me a train ticket to Bucharest, as she didn't want me to have anything bad happen whilst in her country. I accepted her offer, as I really didn't fancy my chances in Bulgaria.

The following day brought an email from Chavdar explaining that he had lost his phone and had waited at the station for me for three hours before giving up. He hoped I had found somewhere safe. It smelt a lot like male cow excrement, but it didn't matter; in Kremi I had found an amazing host. I emailed six people in Bucharest asking for a place to stay once in Romania and received an almost instant reply from a girl called Adriana saying it would be a pleasure. I was sorted for the next leg of the journey, so I picked up the keys that Kremi had left on the kitchen table before going to work early in the morning and headed out to see if I couldn't accidentally on purpose get lost and find something good about Sofia. I jumped on and off buses until I recognised absolutely nothing from the previous day, and then set about trying to find my way back to the centre of the city unaided. I was glad I did.

Sofia seen through the eyes of a well-rested, well fed and warm traveller is a lot more fascinating a place than it had seemed the day before. Getting out into the suburbs I came across the real ethnic Bulgarians. Every man had stubble, fluffy black hair and a confident and strong expression: the Hristo Stoichkov look. They were a surly bunch, shrugging greetings to each other and refusing to give way when passing each other on narrow pavements. The natives looked more like the peoples of the Caucasian republics than they did typically Slavic. Still, it didn't matter how far away from the city centre I ventured, there was no decline in the amount of stray dogs roaming the streets. Walking down one particularly intimidating road, I stopped in my tracks as I noticed a psychotic dog up ahead, snarling at and showing teeth to anyone who dared stray into his territory. I had to get to the end of the street somehow, I had come too far to turn back and find another route, but I was petrified. What could I do? Then an old lady appeared from behind me, striding purposefully towards the rabid animal. She was going to take him on. Like the real man that I am, I shadowed her the whole way, then as we got to within a couple of metres of the snarling creature I crouched down and hid behind her, putting her between me and a Korean's favourite sandwich filler. The mutt growled, barked and jumped about but the lady was unflinching. She looked at me with pity; I was pathetic in her eyes. I didn't care; I had survived. Later on in the afternoon the dog situation went from out of control to just plain surreal, as I watched a scruffy looking canine stand at a pedestrian crossing where he proceeded to wait for the green man to start flashing before crossing the road safely. Bulgarian dogs are nothing if not observant of the Green Cross Code.

Checking my emails later that evening I was surprised to see that every single Romanian I'd emailed earlier in the day had written back, and every one had offered me a place to stay. Despite all the horror stories I had heard about Romania, from reading the way these people wrote I had a very good feeling about visiting Bucharest.

Kremi and I sat up drinking until the early hours of the morning, and before going to bed she handed me a ticket for the 8:14am train to Bucharest.

I got myself up bright and early at 6:30 and, hungover, jumped into the back of a taxi that Kremi had paid the driver of, to take me to the station. She had also given me a bag full of croissants, some homemade baklava, a bottle of water and a couple of cans of beer. What a host.

At the station, a gypsy with a name badge escorted me to my platform, as I wasn't to know that 'Букурещ' was the destination I should be looking for on the information board. He got a bit angry when I couldn't pay him for his 30 seconds of work, but I guess he figured it bad for business to be seen berating a foreigner, so he soon left me alone. Then I heard something amazing: English over the loudspeaker system.

'The train to Bucharest is delayed by 70 minutes.'

I stood and waited on the platform, passing the time by watching the stray puppies wandering up and down the tracks in search of food. It was sad to see one of the tiny fluff-balls discover a plastic bag with something inside, and rather than trying to get the contents out, just eat the plastic.

My train left at 9:35 and I found myself comfortably sitting alone in a compartment. The journey through the snow-covered landscape was beautiful, especially for the first hour or so after leaving Sofia as we followed a river with snowy mountains staring down on us from all sides, and little valley villages popping up randomly every now and then. The train passed through numerous long tunnels that passed through the base of mountains. After about an hour I got up to go for a wee. The toilet was locked so I waited patiently outside for five minutes before an old lady finally emerged and disappeared back to her seat. I went in and immediately started coughing and retching as I tried to cover my mouth with one hand and my eyes with the other. The toilet had overflowed onto the floor. This in itself wouldn't normally be too shocking, but then let me tell you that these Eastern European train toilets don't usually have any water in. So all of this brown lumpy liquid, with the odd random turd floating around, trying to make a break for it and get to the floor, had all come from the human body. Every last drop of it. The most shocking thing is that the woman before me must have actually used the toilet. How was it possible? Actually, I'd rather not know. I got out quickly, making sure to slam the door shut behind me before any of the overflow could escape into the carriage. I walked up the train to the next available toilet and found the complete opposite. Rather than overflowing, this one was completely empty and bone dry and had even frozen around the sides. But strangely, despite there being no window, there was a thin layer of snow on the floor.

After about two hours, a girl of about the same age as me came into my compartment, asking first in Bulgarian and then in English if I minded her sitting down. Why would I? She was followed shortly by an old Bulgarian man who immediately tried to make conversation with me in his native tongue, without luck. The man got off after an hour, the girl stayed. We both sat, reading in silence. It was clear that both of us would prefer to make some kind of chit-chat to pass the time, but neither of us would be the first to open our mouths.

At one station some people got off with a sleeping baby, and instead of using a pram, they put the infant on a sled and pulled her along the snow. Improvisation. The heating in the compartment didn't have a working lever to turn it down, so after a few hours the temperature was unbearable. I had peeled down to a t-shirt when, still sweating, I asked the girl if she would mind me opening a window.

'Go ahead. It's baking,' she said.

Small flakes of snow blew in and slapped me across the face. They were welcome. At about 5pm we made it to the Romanian border. Still no real conversation had been shared between my companion for this journey and myself. As usual I received suspicious treatment from the border police: torch in face, look at passport, look at my face, look back to passport, look back to my face, look back to passport, flick through pages, wonder why there are so many stamps of Eastern European countries, then radio my details to some unknown place and wait for instructions.

'Where are you going, Mr. Mole?'

'Bucharest.'

'How long will you stay in Romania?'

'Three days.'

There was a pause and I was handed back my passport. A couple of minutes later in walked a new guard. Torch in face, look at passport, look at my face, look back to passport, look back to my face, look back to passport, flick through pages, wonder why there are so many stamps of Eastern European countries, then radio my details to some unknown place and wait for instructions.

'Where are you going, Mr. Mole?'

'Bucharest.'

'How long will you stay in Romania?'

'Three days.'

How do you say déjà vu in Romanian?

As we sat at the border and waited for movement, there was a lot of noise coming from the other carriages: the kind of sound you would hear if you locked a drug addict in a bathroom full of cabinets. It was 5:30pm when we started moving again; the very first ticket inspector of the morning had told me we would be in Bucharest by 5pm. I got up for a walk to the toilet – the snowy one, not the pooey one – and saw that a few of the compartments had been completely turned over by the police. When I retook my seat the girl broke the ice.

'Excuse me, but is it normal for the police to ask so many questions?'

'It is when I'm involved,' I told her.

She laughed and introduced herself in a perfect American accent as Tsetsa, a 24-year-old Bulgarian student from the American University. This was her first time travelling on an international train; she was going to visit American friends in Romania who were flying in from the States just to see her. She was anxious about the delays; we were now running about three hours behind schedule. We passed the time talking about border guards, different customs and funny travel experiences.

After an 11-hour train ride we pulled in to Gara de Nord. It was 8:30pm.

Welcome to Bucharest.

19. Bucharest

Capitals left to visit: Amsterdam, Athens, Brussels, Budapest, Helsinki, Lisbon, Luxembourg, Madrid, Paris, Prague, Riga, Tallinn, Vilnius

Days on the road: 73
Distance travelled: 3989 miles
EU capitals visited: 10

MY HOST FOR the night Adriana had texted me instructions for getting to her place. I needed to take the Metro to Piata Unirii, and I was in luck; I walked with Tsetsa to meet her friends in the station and, as they were also taking the Metro, they said they would buy me a ticket. As I took a seat on the train I looked around at my fellow passengers, so as to get a first impression of Romanians. The only experience I had of them from my past – other than my encounter with Catalina at the AIESEC camp – came during my time working in Italy, where my boss Mario had a zero acceptance policy towards them.

'Kris, this rule is important,' he had told me whilst giving me my initial training, 'if a Romanian walks in and wants a bed for the night, you tell him that we are full. It doesn't matter if we haven't got a single guest in the building, we do not let Romanians in.'

'Okay, Mario. But why?'

'Because they are all thieves. Every last one of them.'

His theory was given more credence in my impressionable mind almost every week when one of our guests would return from the train station crying, and I would have to accompany them to the local police station to act as interpreter as they filed a report about how they had had their wallet snatched out of their hands on the street. The policeman would open up his casebook and the word 'Romania' would be written in the nationality box next to the names of almost everyone arrested in the past week. I didn't trust Romanians. As far as I was concerned, every single one of them was out to either rob me violently or con me gently, but the end result was always going to be the same. No Romanians ever did come and try to book into the hostel, though, so I never actually tested this theory.

As I let my eyes glide over the faces of the locals making their way home from work on this particular evening in Bucharest, something didn't seem right. The people looked decent. They wore nice clothes, had friendly expressions on their faces, and looked anything but threatening. Stranger still, they weren't all playing the accordion. The Romanians on this train all had a distinct look. The girls looked natural and, with their oval faces and large brown eyes, resembled Japanese cartoon characters. The men tended to have short, stylish hair and were clean-cut around the face. They looked respectable and decent. Had I been fed false propaganda all these years? I now felt that it was a distinct possibility.

I made it to my destination and emerged from the subway and up into what I can only describe as an Eastern European replica of Piccadilly Circus. In the middle of everything was the biggest Christmas tree I had ever seen, sat in a little park that also acted as a roundabout for the choc-a-bloc road that circled it and led off in all directions. The tall buildings on all four sides of the roundabout were flashing with bright neon signs telling me to drink Coca Cola or Heineken, to capture my favourite moments on Fuji Film and to let Samsung provide my entertainment. The area was dirty and metropolitan. Gypsy children ran about in the middle of the busy road, cleaning the windscreens of cars stuck in traffic. Gypsy adults wore green coats and shovelled snow off of the streets. It was cold and I wanted to find my way to the warmth of Adriana's flat as quickly as possible.

'Kris!'

I looked across the road and saw, standing outside a cigarette shop, Adriana. She led me through the little door and up the stairs to her flat above the shop. As we walked through the front door into the living room that had been converted into Adriana's bedroom, her flatmate came out of the bathroom and, despite me saying hello and putting my hand out in greeting, walked straight past me as if I weren't there and slammed her bedroom door shut behind her.

'Don't worry about her,' Adriana told me, 'she's like that with everyone. She doesn't like guests, and she really doesn't like Couchsurfers.'

I instantly liked Adriana; she had a strong presence and it drew me in. She was wearing a pair of low-cut jogging bottoms and a tracksuit top unzipped to half way, with a loose fitting t-shirt underneath. Her face was oval, just like every other Romanian girl I had seen so far that day, and she had big brown eyes, just like every other Romanian girl I had seen that day. Her hair was dark and her skin was pale. I stood in the kitchen door and chatted as I watched her prepare dinner.

After we had finished eating the pasta, she stood up, took my plate off into the kitchen and returned with a bottle of Jim Beam. We laid back on the bed, working our way through the whiskey and exchanging Couchsurfing stories and childhood memories in the way that seems to come naturally when lying with a complete stranger, drinking hard spirits straight from the bottle. Before the night was out we polished off the last of the Jim Beam and also half a bottle of Martini. As the clock struck 5, somehow we managed to combine our efforts and pull a mattress out from a cupboard and time was called on our night of bonding.

I woke later that morning at 11, feeling groggy, and was surprised to find Adriana washed and dressed, sitting at her computer studying. Romanians clearly didn't do hangovers. As I pulled myself up she told me that both her flatmates had emailed her from their jobs letting her know that they were fed up with her hosting strangers in the flat. She asked if I minded finding somewhere else to stay. Fortunately, I had a whole list of locals who had offered me a couch, so I emailed the first one who had replied to me after Adriana: Denisa. I called her from Adriana's phone and we arranged to meet after she finished work at around 6:30pm underneath the neon Coca-Cola sign. Adriana went off to university for the day, leaving me alone in the flat to get some more sleep. She returned early, however, also feeling the effects of the previous night, and we spent the afternoon lounging around, listening to music.

Denisa pulled up in her car at 6:45pm and I jumped into the front seat. Full of energy, my new host was 27 years old and worked for a company that provided training courses to companies. I was her first ever Couchsurfer. Denisa's living room doubled up as her bedroom with the couch transforming itself every night into her bed. My place of rest for the night was a camping mat on the floor, with a quilt for warmth.

Early the next morning, just before heading off to work for the day, Denisa came and woke me, looking uncomfortable. I sat up and looked at her, trying to give her the confidence she needed to get the words out.

'I know this is going to sound absurd, but I want to ask you something?' she finally said.

Now I was a bit nervous.

'Okay, ask away.'

'I don't want you to think I don't trust you, but…'

There was a pause.

'What is it, Denisa?'

There was a longer pause, and then she finally hit me with it:

‘Can I take your passport? Just until I get home from work. For security purposes.’

I laughed. I didn’t know what I’d been expecting her to say, but it definitely hadn’t been, ‘Can I have your passport?’

I handed it to her, before awkwardly trying to get a question of my own out.

‘Denisa, can I ask you something?’

‘Sure.’

‘Um, I feel weird asking. I don’t want you to think I don’t trust you. But…’

I paused.

‘What is it? Just tell me.’

‘It’s just, um, well… please don’t sell my valuable British passport to a Romanian.’

The nervous look on her face immediately broke into a broad smile.

‘Fuck off! And go back to sleep.’

She grinned and then was gone for the day.

Back to sleep I went, to be woken at 10:30 to the sound of Kylie and Jason who were singing ‘Especially For You’ at me through the radio alarm clock. Who set that? I caught up on some writing and then headed out to explore Bucharest in the early afternoon. I was colder than I had been at any point so far on the journey, and probably than I had ever been in my life. The street thermometer said it was -10 degrees, but there was a strong wind that made it feel more like -20. I started making my way towards Piata Unirii, the centerpiece of the city as far as I was concerned, and within two minutes of leaving the flat I knew that I should have been wearing gloves, a scarf, a hat, a balaclava and a fur coat; rather than just the jumper and jacket I had on.

As I walked, a thick fog came down and blanketed the city. I couldn’t see more than an arm’s length in front of me and I couldn’t feel my fingers. That’s not exactly true; I could feel them in a way: an excruciating, burning kind of way. I made it to Unirii and set about looking for the famous palace that both Adriana and Denisa had told me so much about. Built in the 1980s at the orders of ex-leader and tyrant Ceaușescu, the Palace of the Parliament (Palatul Parlamentului) was the world's largest civilian administrative building; most expensive administrative building; and heaviest building. It was also, as far as I could see, the most pointless building. Still, I wanted to see the place. The only problem I had was that I didn't have the foggiest – pun intended – idea where to start looking. My hands and ears felt like they had been sprayed with deodorant and set on fire and I couldn't take the risk of standing still and trying to get my bearings for even a moment; I had to keep moving. So, using the biggest Christmas tree in Europe as my focal point, I just walked up and then back down each of the large boulevards that led off of the square. I knew the palace was at the end of one of them. I walked for close to two hours and still somehow managed to completely avoid the building I was searching for, but with the fog as thick as it was I probably walked right through it at least twice without realising. As the fog grew thicker and my hands became more frozen, for the first time that day I had a sensible thought: I was going to go back to the flat. It was so simple and yet so genius. To get back to the warmth of Denisa's home all I had to do was retrace my footsteps. But as I stood in the shadow of the Christmas tree, it suddenly struck me (not the tree!) that every boulevard looked exactly like the next, and I had walked up and down every single one of them throughout the course of the day. I spent the next few hours cold and lost, until shortly before 6 when Denisa called to let me know she had finished work early and wanted to meet me in a restaurant to warm my insides with some soup. I loved the idea but knew it was going to prove harder than it sounded.

'Denisa, there's one problem. I'm a little bit lost,' I owned up.

'Where are you?'

'In front of the National Library.'

'Which National Library? The old one or the new one?'

This question stumped me, as I did not know there were two National Libraries in Bucharest. It had only been 20 seconds since the revelation that there was at least one National Library in the city.

'I don't know.'

'Well, does it look old or does it look new?' she persisted.

I looked across the road and decided that it definitely looked old.

'It's the old one,' I announced, triumphantly.

'Good. Then you are very near the restaurant. It's called Caru cu Bere. If you ask anyone they will point you in the right direction. Wait for me there; I will be about 15 minutes.'

After the call was over she texted me the name of the street, and as she had said that she would be there in 15 minutes and that I should wait for her arrival, I felt pretty confident that I would be there in no time at all. I asked the first guy I came across – an old man carrying a bag of potatoes – and was surprised to find that he didn't think I was as close as Denisa had indicated.

'Go to the university and then ask someone there for more directions,' was what he told me.

I may not have been ready for my Bucharest taxi drivers' knowledge exam, but I did know where the university was and that it would take more than 15 minutes to get to. I spent a minute questioning whether or not this old man was to be trusted. Why had Denisa told me I was near and he had told me I was miles away? Who was telling the truth? Was I really at the old National Library? I decided to trust the man; he had no reason to lie. Neither did Denisa though. This was a dilemma. The last call from Denisa had taken up my final bit of phone credit, so I couldn't call her to ask which one of them was telling me the truth. I also suspected that this would be a bad question to ask, as if it were Denisa who were lying she probably wouldn't admit to it now. And if she were telling the truth, my question might offend her. I had no choice; I made my way to the university, arriving 25 minutes later and asking passers-by for my next set of instructions.

Eventually I found the place and it wasn't what I had been expecting. Caru cu Bere was a huge, grand-looking establishment with revolving doors, a glass front and an elegant hostess standing just inside the door who asked me if I had a reservation. Denisa came out to meet me, and then led me through the themed restaurant to our seat. There were balconies, chandeliers, stained glass windows, frescoes, waitresses in national dress, and traditional music was being played. The place was clearly a tourist trap, there was even a gift shop, but I learnt that the interior had remained unchanged since 1879. When the waitress came to our table and handed me an English menu, Denisa took charge and ordered on my behalf.

After mopping up the last of the juice from our plates, we finished our beers (which were brewed on site) and sat back to watch the show as four dancers came out, two male and two female, and after clearing a space in the centre of the room put on a traditional performance. It was loud, flamboyant and entertaining. After a couple of dances, they would disappear for a few minutes and allow everyone to carry on eating, before returning again to do a couple of new routines. After a while they started picking diners out and encouraging them to join in and learn some of the moves. It was time to leave.

Later, we drove a lap of honour around the palace I told you about earlier, but I still couldn't really see it for the fog. As we stopped at the lights, I was saddened to see young, hungry, toothless children running up to the stopped cars and begging through the windows. The driver of the car in front handed one child a packet of sweets, leaving the kid with the most excited look on his face as he sprinted to the pavement holding his loot tightly against his chest before kneeling down and looking through the bag in the same way a child goes through his Christmas stocking. These children were no older than seven or eight. Further up the road at the next set of traffic lights, their older brothers and sisters wiped your windscreens while you waited, hoping to be rewarded for their efforts. Nobody gave anything, but still they kept wiping.

The next morning was a Saturday and also Denisa's birthday. I was going to experience a celebration, Romanian style. But before any of that, I was going to finally see the city under proper lighting. The sun was shining, the snow was melting and the palace was visible. It was actually quite impressive from the outside. From there we drove up to the Orthodox Cathedral where Denisa followed the lead of everyone else present and lit a candle. Outside the Cathedral in the car park I watched as a small pack of newborn stray puppies played with each other. As I stood, just letting my mind drift, we were approached by a male gypsy in his early twenties who Denisa handed some money to before turning to me and saying, 'I hate that I have to do that.'

'What did you give him money for?' I asked.

'So that he doesn't damage my car. It's how it works here. A gypsy gets a certain patch and then runs a racket on it. You park on his patch and then pay him to protect your car. If you don't pay you will come back and find it scratched. It's disgusting, but it's not worth the bother of not paying.'

Later that evening it was time to party. I had only eaten two bits of toast all day, but I felt ready to hold my own on the drinking front. I had already had a few beers with Adriana in the afternoon as we sat in her flat and chatted (and kissed) for a bit. And now I found myself sat in a lively German-themed pub called Becker Brau, gathered around a table with a group of Denisa's work friends, watching a live band bang out their renditions of hits by Queen, David Bowie, the Rolling Stones et al.

After we'd drunk enough beers to make walking difficult, we left and headed off in taxis to a place called La Comandante, a themed pub dedicated to Che Guevara, situated in a dark little basement and filled to busting point with students wearing combat fatigues and bashing into each other for fun. The drink of choice in here was absinthe. We quickly necked a couple each. Fortunately I wasn't alone in thinking the place was pretty rubbish and so after the shots we left, stepping over a comatose girl who had wet herself on the stairs on the way out. We moved on to a club called Embryo that was apparently the trendiest night spot in the city and one whose interior had been designed to look like the inside of a woman's uterus. And no, I didn't make that up. Denisa told me that the door policy was only to let the best looking people in. Because of this I had to sneak in round the back. The night went on until the early hours and the Romanians made sure that I had a good time.

I received an email from Vanja, letting me know she was going to be in Budapest to meet me and had booked a hotel room for a couple of nights. It wasn't what I had been hoping to find in my inbox. It wasn't that I didn't want to see her, it was simply that she was taking away some of the difficulty yet again. I didn't want to hurt her feelings, though, so I said nothing.

I was pleasantly surprised and touched the next day when Denisa told me she was going to buy me a train ticket to Budapest. I told her that she really needn't, but I also knew that the 13-hour ride would most likely come with severe difficulties without the necessary piece of paper in my hand. She called and reserved the ticket, paying on her credit card, while I washed up the dishes after dinner. I wanted to clean the whole flat, to do anything that would show my appreciation for the gesture. Romania, the country that people had most warned me about and the one that even I had had doubts about journeying into, had given me nothing but happy memories, good friends and a desire to return one day. It's the people that make the place, and for this I loved Bucharest.

I jumped on the back of the bus at 5:45am and stood the whole way, too scared to risk sitting down and falling asleep. Denisa had told me it should take about 10-15 minutes to get to the station, so after 20 I was getting slightly worried I'd missed my stop. When I saw a bus drive past in the opposite direction but with a sign in the window saying 'Gara de Nord', I really started to panic. My only companion on the bus was an old lady who was sat on a chair in front of me, so I looked at her and said 'Gara de Nord?' and gave her a thumbs-up and then a thumbs-down. She smiled and said that I should get off with her. I just read that back and feel that I should rephrase. The old lady did not say that I should get off with her; she said that I should get off of the bus at the same stop as her. I got off with her five minutes later – she loved it – and went into the station to pick up my ticket and then find my train. It wasn't what I had been hoping for. I am a big fan of the old Eastern European trains usually in use on long cross-border journeys throughout the East of the continent. The big, ancient trains with the seats covered in dust, where the compartments are big but often you get a whole one to yourself, meaning you can put your feet up and treat it like a bedroom. Like the train that had taken me from Serbia to Bulgaria. And the one that had taken me from Bulgaria to Romania. Unfortunately, the train that pulled out of Bucharest at 6:30 on this morning was a new one with the standard two seats separated from the facing two seats by a little table. No room for lying down, no room even for putting your feet up. Still, I was tired enough to try. I put my head down on the left seat, curled my body onto the right one, and then let my legs go all the way across the aisle to rest on the seats on the other side of the carriage. It was painful, especially around the waist, but somehow I managed to sleep without disturbance until 11, when I found myself being shaken by a peasant lady talking excitedly at me in

Romanian. She thought that the stop we'd arrived at was mine – why is anyone's guess – and as such felt it her duty to wake me. Denisa had made me a few sandwiches the night before for the trip, but now I was unable to eat them because stupidly I had forgotten to bring any water and my mouth was already too dry to chew food. The air conditioning was doing me no favours. This never would have happened on one of those old, Eastern trains, I thought. I then sat; starving and dehydrating. And exaggerating, clearly.

The journey through Romania was scenic and all snow had been left behind while I slept. The sun was now shining brightly, and as we passed through small village after small village, each one separated by fields inhabited by shepherds and their flocks, I imagined myself leaving the technological world behind and just settling in one of these obscure communities, growing my own food and never having to have contact with the outside world again. What happiness you would surely find in being fully self-sufficient and at one with the earth around you.

Every time our train stopped at a small village platform, I looked out of the window and saw hunched women in headscarves pulling homemade go-carts loaded up with produce on its way to be sold or exchanged for something. As we got further north, we passed through mountains and hills with fairy-tale castles perched on their peaks. A deaf mute made his way through the train, laying on my table a pack of cards, some religious booklets and a lighter. I had no one to play cards with, I couldn't read Romanian and I wasn't smoking. And I had no money. He returned, looking at me sadly whilst packing the things back into his bag. I told him I was sorry. He didn't hear me and he said nothing. Possibly because he was a deaf mute.

The carriage I was in filled up with middle-aged, gossiping Hungarian women in the early afternoon. They sat everywhere, invading the train like a plague of locusts. One particular specimen sat down directly opposite me and immediately set about claiming the entire leg room space with a hostile takeover. I was forced to admit defeat. Then, not content with simply boxing me in to a space the size of a shoebox, she went a step further and tried to make me leave the carriage altogether by torturing me; leaning over to the woman on the other side of the carriage, speaking in a nasal voice that I am sure she modelled on that of Chandler's occasional girlfriend Janice in Friends, the Hungarian dubbed version. My thoughts rapidly progressed from making my own bread and butter in a farmyard cottage, to strangling this woman with her own scarf before stealing her bottle of juice that she was so provocatively sipping in front of me. She knew I was thirsty.

We got to the Hungarian border at 4:45 and the usual fun and games began. The Romanian police didn't make things too difficult, although, to be fair, I was leaving their country and not entering it, so they didn't really give a shit. The train rolled through No Man's Land for a few minutes and then we were at the Hungarian checkpoint. It was a lot more serious an affair than on the Romanian side. A whole army of furry-hat wearing police stormed the train. One of them took my passport and wasn't satisfied with it. He said nothing, he just disappeared off the train, scrutinising my document as he went. I tried to appear carefree, flicking through the book I was reading as if I owned the railway, but the more I tried to look innocent, the more I made myself look guilty and nervous. And the more I felt myself looking guilty and nervous, the harder I tried to look carefree and innocent. I could feel the stares of the gossipy middle aged women burning through me.

'Where is that dark, thirsty looking guy from? I hope they don't let him into the country!' they were saying.

My comprehension of Hungarian is always at its best when I'm dehydrated. The policeman returned and asked me in almost incomprehensible English if I had anything that I shouldn't have in my bags. I answered in the negative, but my word wasn't to be trusted. He told me to open my small rucksack – the big one wasn't with me, I'd put it in a luggage holder a bit further up the train – I opened it up in front of him and, as the women leant in for a better look, the cop put his hand in to have a rummage around and pulled out a pair of dirty boxers that I had taken off earlier that morning. I sniggered. He didn't. He motioned for me to close the bag, before throwing my passport at me and making a hasty exit. I hadn't had a drink for 11 hours. The women around me carried on sipping at their bottles of water, juice, and cola. I tried to imagine the sensation of drinking water, in the hope that I could make my body believe I'd actually had some. It didn't work. My delirium made me surprised that it hadn't worked. It had seemed like such a good idea.

Exactly 14 hours after getting on the train in Bucharest I arrived in Hungary's capital and thirstily ticked another capital off of my list.

Welcome to Budapest.

North Cape
Jan Mayen
(Norway)
NORWEGIAN SEA
Scandinavia
Lapland
SWEDEN
FINLAND
NORWAY
Faroe Islands
(Denmark)
Shetland Islands
(UK)
Orkney Islands
Isle of Lewis
Hebrides
British
Isles
SCOTLAND
UNITED
KINGDOM
IRELAND
DUBLIN
ENGLAND
WALES
LONDON
CELTIC SEA
English Channel
NORTH
SEA
DENMARK
COPENHAGEN
BALTIC SEA
Gulf of Bothnia
Gulf of Finland
Gotland
STOCKHOLM
OSLO
HELSINKI
TALLINN
ESTONIA
LATVIA
RIGA
LITHUANIA
VILNIUS
KALININGRAD
(RUSSIAN FED.)
MINSK
BELARUS
POLAND
WARSAW
NETHERLANDS
AMSTERDAM
BELGIUM
BRUSSELS
GERMANY
BERLIN
Hamburg
Frankfurt
PRAGUE
CZECH.REP.
SLOVAKIA
VIENNA
AUSTRIA
HUNGARY
BUDAPEST
ROMANIA
BUCHAREST
MOLDOVA
KIEV
Carpathians Mts.
FRANCE
PARIS
LUX.
SWITZ.
LIECHT.
Massif
Central
Bay of
Biscay
Pyrenees
Alps
ITALY
ROME
CROATIA
BOSNIA & H
SERBIA
BELGRADE
MONTENEGRO
KOSOVO
ALBANIA
F.Y.R.O.M.
BULGARIA
SOFIA
GREECE
ATHENS
Istanbul
Anatolia
PORTUGAL
LISBON
SPAIN
MADRID
Sierra Morena
Corsica
Sardinia
Sicily
MEDITERRANEAN SEA
Strait of Gibraltar
MOROCCO
RABAT
ALGERIA
ALGIERS
TUNISIA
TUNIS
MALTA
VALLETTA
AEGEAN SEA
Crete
CYPRUS

20. Budapest

Capitals left to visit: Amsterdam, Athens, Brussels, Helsinki, Lisbon, Luxembourg, Madrid, Paris, Prague, Riga, Tallinn, Vilnius

Days on the road: 78
Distance travelled: 4508 miles
EU capitals visited: 11

VANJA WAS WAITING for me on the platform as I weakly lugged my bags off the train. Before even kissing her a greeting, I grabbed at the bottle of water she was holding for me and downed the whole two litres in one. We took the Metro to the centre of the city, where the hotel was located.

After checking in, all I wanted to do was get some sleep, but as is mandatory on any visit to Hungary we went downstairs to the restaurant and ate some traditionally prepared goulash. The atmosphere over dinner was strained. I just couldn't find anything to say, and neither, it seemed, could Vanja, so we sat in silence. I could see a sadness in her eyes, which pained me as I only ever wanted to see her happy, but this was the way things were now. We had grown apart. I had to go my way in life and she had to go hers. After these next couple of days were over, there was every chance that we would never see each other again. Such is life.

She had managed to smuggle a bag of weed across the border, which at least played a part in making the conversation a bit more relaxed once up in the bedroom. We smoked until we passed out.

The following day we took a stroll through the narrow streets and along the Danube. Vanja was in a bad mood and it was rubbing off on me. As we walked, I wasn't paying attention to my surroundings, wasn't taking in the sights of Budapest at all, and was just wishing I was anywhere else. I knew the effort she had gone to to make these few days happen, and I felt like a piece of shit, but I couldn't change the way I felt. There just wasn't a spark between us anymore, and for the very first time I now fully realised it. After a while of walking and saying nothing, I asked her if she was okay.

'What do you care?' she snapped.

At this I finally broke my silence, telling her that I couldn't do this anymore, that she was too much hard work to be around and that she was turning into her mother. Never ever accuse a girl of turning into her mother! She started crying, pulled from her pocket the engagement ring I'd given her three years earlier, threw it at me and walked off into the distance. For the first time ever I didn't go after her to try and make things better. I just sat on a bench with my head in my hands, feeling a mixture of sadness for what she was going through, but also relief that finally she had realised that although we had a past we no longer had a future. Five minutes later she returned to the bench where I was sitting and said, 'Come on, let's go for a beer.'

We walked back to the hotel together and in the room she asked me if I would be happier if she left Budapest later that day and went back to Slovenia without me. My heart was breaking, seeing her in this pain. I wanted her to have a good time. I made the decision to try harder.

'Of course not. We are still friends; we can still have a good time together. You are still like a best friend to me.'

Up until this point we had never really acknowledged out loud the fact that we weren't at least going to try and resurrect our relationship at some point in the future. I think that deep down we both knew the finality of our split, but when speaking we had always left the door open for a reunion in the future when situations were better. But now I had uttered the word 'friend' the truth became clear. She started crying again and asked me if I really meant it. I did. I needed freedom and so did she. At that point I didn't want my family; I didn't want a woman; I didn't want anyone to hold me back or suffocate me. Vanja didn't suffocate me, but still I didn't feel free. And she deserved someone who would put her first and not be at the beck and call of various addictions, habits and impulses. I would never be able to offer that. Over dinner that night there was a new peace between us and I started remembering how I had fallen so deeply in love with her and how hard it had been to get myself to where I wanted to be with her all those years previous. I would always love her; I just wasn't *in love* with her anymore.

The following day we took the train back to Slovenia's capital; Vanja purchased my ticket.

Welcome to Ljubljana. Again.

I promise this is the last time.

21. Ljubljana

I NEEDED TO follow the Pet Shop Boys' advice and go west, but that was all that the 80's synth-pop group had told me. Did they mean for me to trek along the north of Italy, either stopping off in Milan or Turin before making my way up through France? Or was I to make my way to that most mysterious of lands, Liechtenstein? Or perhaps the route they had in mind had me cutting through Italy and making my way along to the Swiss capital of Bern. Saying that, what if I was looking at it all wrong and was actually meant to go up to the Austrian city of Innsbruck and make my way from there. I didn't know, but I was keen to find out the answer as quickly as possible, so I logged on to Couchsurfing and sent requests to two people in each of the above mentioned cities. Wherever the first positive reply came from was where I would head. It was a bit like the draw for the FA Cup quarter final: you knew who was in the bag, you just didn't know which one you were going to have to travel to on a rainy Saturday afternoon. The answer took three days to arrive, and came from a Swiss guy called Hannes. I was going to Bern, a city in a country I had not imagined passing through at all at the beginning of the journey as it wasn't a member state of the European Union. Plus, it's Switzerland; who ever really imagines going there?

On the morning of my departure I met my old mate Steve at the language school and then went up the road to the train station where I allowed him to donate a ticket as far as the city of Brig, just on the Swiss side of the border with Italy. From there I didn't expect too much difficulty navigating my way further into the Alpine country without a ticket or money.

My first train of the day left Ljubljana at 10:35am and took me as far as Venice Mestre in Italy, where I had two and a half hours to kill before my connecting train to Brig pulled in.

'That's nice,' I hear you say, 'There are worse things in life than having to spend a couple of hours in that picturesque, romantic city of Venice.'

Venice proper and Venice Mestre are two completely different animals. Imagine being stuck at Peckham Rye station. Would you go on a sightseeing stroll around the surrounding area and then tell people you had seen London? Mestre is a dirty place where everyone that you come across is either an old alcoholic sitting on a bench, or a Chinese labourer Western Unioning money to family back home.

Once on the afternoon train out of Mestre, I sat comfortably and arrived in Brig at 10pm, along with an Italian man who had fallen asleep and missed his stop at Milan and would have to spend the night at a Swiss railway station. I jumped on the 10:20pm to Bern and when the ticket woman came along I pulled out my pockets and told her that my ticket and money had fallen out somewhere along the way.

'I don't believe you,' she said.

'I don't know what to say to that,' I replied.

'I will have to give you a penalty. This is very bad.'

And with a fine written out to my fake address, I stepped off of the train in Switzerland's capital at 11:30pm, 13 hours after leaving Ljubljana.

Welcome to Bern.

22. Bern

IN FRONT OF the station were a number a different tram stops and an even greater number of wine-drinking alcoholics. I pulled out of my pocket directions to Hannes' home and then asked the only normal looking person in sight – a girl in her late teens carrying a load of books – which stop I needed to pick my tram up from and she explained to me in perfect English. I bunked the number 9 to Breitenrainplatz and, after walking up and down the street a few times asking various kebab shop workers for directions, I found my way to Hannes' home. My host for the night came out to meet me at the door accompanied by his girlfriend, both grinning as we exchanged pleasantries and I was led through to the flat. I was impressed by the style of the place. The main living room wall was printed with a giant pixelated picture of Samuel L Jackson in his *Pulp Fiction* role, while the second wall had a large panoramic ocean scene which hung above the biggest telly I had ever seen. It was bigger than the Brighton Odeon's Screen Number Two. In the corner of the room a minibar was better stocked than Tesco's Wines and Spirits department. The furniture was expensive leather. The whole place was spotless and yet still had that lived-in feel. I stood in awe, wondering how this guy, who had been born in the same year as me, had achieved such a high standard of living for himself; so I asked. Hannes had worked for the same software development company since he was 16, having had his talents spotted in school. He poured three large Bacardi and Cokes and we sat down.

'Do you smoke?' he asked.

'Not cigarettes,' I replied.

'Well I suppose I should roll us a joint.'

Hannes' looked like a surfer: blond fluffy hair, surfer's t-shirt, jeans, a beaded necklace round his neck, and a surfboard under his arm. Not really a surfboard under his arm. But I could picture him with one. I could also picture him wearing sunglasses. Hannes looked like the kind of guy who wore sunglasses a lot. The kind of guy that even if you saw him wearing sunglasses when it wasn't sunny, you would still say, 'That guy looks cool. I wish I could look that cool in sunglasses.' Hannes' girlfriend didn't speak much. She was from Geneva and her mother tongue was French. Hannes was Bern born and raised and spoke Swiss German. They made fun of each other's language. She spoke German as a second language, he spoke no French. We sat, drank and passed around the spliff, and Hannes told me that I would have to leave his place the following afternoon because the two of them were going to Canada for a snowboarding holiday. Yep, he was definitely the kind of guy who would look cool in sunglasses. I had received an email the day before from Christophe, another Couchsurfer in Bern willing to host me, so I decided that I would stay a second night in Switzerland before heading on to Lyon where a guy called Sébastien had let me know he would be able to put me up from the Friday (today was Wednesday). I emailed Christophe before bed asking for directions to his place.

My place of rest for the night was a camping mat on a wooden floor in the spare room. By the time I had said goodnight to the two of them and brushed my teeth it was 2 in the morning and I was so exhausted that the mat looked great. I nodded off immediately, with the thought running through my mind: *I'm in Switzerland. I never in my life thought I would have reason to visit Switzerland. The name Switzerland alone sounds so boring and not worth visiting. I wonder what I will find in the morning in this strange, yodelling, knife-wielding land.*

I was woken with a shock just before 8 by one of the loudest noises ever to pull me from slumber. I can only compare it to the sound a grand piano would make as it tumbled down 100 flights of stairs. It was horrific, and not what I wanted at such an hour of the morning. Worse still, the floor I was on was vibrating. I jumped up to investigate and on lifting the blind and looking out the window I found a bulldozer knocking down the building next door. Every five minutes or so there would be a break and I would quickly drift back to sleep, only to be woken again a few minutes later as the bulldozer got closer and closer to home. In the end I got up and, after drinking a tea with my hosts and finding no reply from Christophe, headed out to see what Switzerland's capital was all about.

I made my way to the main train station and picked up a map from the Tourist Information Centre, asking a girl behind the desk to highlight on it a few things worthy of a visit. I hadn't eaten for close to 20 hours and just then remembered that I still had a little bit of bread and salami left in my bag from the day before, so I took a seat on a bench in Parliament Square, surrounded by small groups of university students eating their lunch. I looked around at the faces of the people around me. Every Swiss girl in this square was a spitting image of Harry Potter. Bernese girls are Swiss female Harry Potters. I imagine that is the first time in history that those seven words have been written in that order. The males of the city were equally Harry Potter-esque. The Swiss were plain; every last one of them… and they seemed content in the knowledge. Not one person wore even slightly interesting or colourful clothing. There seemed to be no life in these people.

I left the square behind and walked around the Old Town, taking in the Houses of Parliament, a palace, the cathedral, and then strolled along the side of the river Aare, tormented the whole time by the sweet, juicy aromas emanating from the shops. Sausages, pastries, cakes and chocolates sat deliciously in every window. All around me, Harry Potters stuffed their faces on the delicious offerings. I had to get away; it was killing me.

The girl in Tourist Information had told me I should take the time to climb up above the city to the famous Rose Garden, from where I would be treated to the best view of Bern. I followed the river to the foot of the path and was just about to begin my ascent when something caught my eye across the road. A group of tourists, mainly Japanese, were leaning over a wall and taking photos of something on the other side. I wondered what could possibly be so interesting that it was just placed over a wall in the middle of the city. I wondered what could possibly be so interesting in Switzerland. I walked up and blended in amongst the crowd and finally fought my way to the front. I peered over the wall and found I was staring down into a small pit. Then I saw it. A bear. A live bear. In the other corner sat another one. Two live bears, peering up hungrily at a load of tourists, in the middle of a city centre. This would never be allowed to happen in the European Union, I told myself. Those crazy Swiss, this is just like them to do something like this. They're mad! And to think I called them dull and boring. The wall wasn't even fenced off, and was only as high as my chest. If this existed in England, the bears would live solely off of human flesh. Can you imagine the Friday nights in A&E?

'So, what seems to be the problem here?' asks the doctor.

'Well, I was just out minding my own business, having a few drinks with my mates in Weatherspoons, when one of them bet me two pints that I wouldn't go over to the pit and stroke the bear. So in I jumped, but then I needed to pee. Something must have woken the bear – I don't know what it was, but it might have been my mates throwing stones at him – and as I was relieving myself up against the wall, the bear ripped both of my legs off. Fortunately, the guard was quickly on hand to tranquillize him. And Gary owes me two pints. Top bants! Wahey!'

I hiked up to the Rose Garden and wished I hadn't. All that was up there was a load more Harry Potters holding hands and looking at flowers. I felt cheated. I wanted to get out of Switzerland and into a country with some sort of life to its people. I checked my emails for free in a hotel and still found no reply from Christophe. It was 3 in the afternoon and I had nowhere to stay, so I decided to go with my gut and just get out of the country. I sent a quick email to Sébastien in Lyon saying that I was going to be arriving a day earlier than planned and asking him to call me if he could help me out in any way. I then checked the train times in the station and saw that there was one leaving for France at 5pm that I could probably make if I hurried. I raced back to the flat and found Hannes just heading out the door.

'Where are you going?' I asked.

'To the station. I can check my luggage in there so I don't have to do it at the airport.'

'Can you wait a minute while I grab my bag? I could use a lift.'

I got back to the station at 3:40pm and then jumped on the 4 o'clock headed for Geneva, close to the French border. As soon as the train started moving I went to the ticket inspector and told him that my girlfriend had our tickets but that the doors of the train had closed before she had jumped on and I now had to meet her at Geneva. My story wasn't believed and I was told to get off at the first stop, a place called Fribourg. At 4:20 I was off, but something was different. I was only 20 minutes from Bern and the station looked pretty much the same as the one I had departed from, but I just felt there was something different.

Wait a minute, where are all the Harry Potters?

The people of Fribourg were French-speaking and good-looking. The girls wore expensive clothes, enchanting perfumes and looked at you with sultry eyes. I liked Switzerland again. When I say 'again' I mean 'for the first time.' Never had the French language sounded so good.

The next train to Geneva left at 4:55 and I was on it. For some reason I hadn't learnt my lesson on the first train and decided to try the exact same method again. It also had the same outcome. I was to get off at the next station, Lausanne. But this time there was one difference; I wasn't going to play by the rules. As we pulled into Lausanne's busy station, I slouched in a chair and pretended to be asleep. I know, outstanding! I proceeded to 'sleep' the rest of the way to Geneva and arrived without hassle at 6:10pm. Just as I was getting off the train I received a call from Sébastien telling me he was out of Lyon on business until the following afternoon but that he would book me into a hostel and get a friend of his to meet me and take care of the payment when I arrived. He gave me the phone number of Alex, and was just giving me directions for where to head from the station when the line went dead. My credit had run out, meaning I could neither make nor receive any more calls. This was bad.

I took a walk around the underground shopping centre at the station while I tried to clear my head and come up with a plan. The whole mall – if you can call it a mall – seemed to be aimed at black youths. I was not in the target demographic, unless I wanted an Afro-Caribbean haircut, a Dr. Dre CD or some 'street' clothing from a shop actually called Black World. Every shop catered to this lifestyle. All along the halls groups loitered around, listening to rap on ghetto blasters or break dancing outside shops. I went back upstairs to the station area. I looked at the information board for trains crossing the border into France and found the platform I needed to go from, but then had a bit of a nasty surprise: there was an official border crossing at the entrance to the platform. To get anywhere near a train heading for France I had to clear customs and passport control. This would have been fine if the police weren't also checking each passenger's train ticket. I stood out of sight and observed the procedure for about 10 minutes, trying to find any sort of weakness that I could exploit, and I noticed that the police weren't checking train tickets nearly as closely as they should have been. People were waving them under their noses and passing through once their passport had been cleared. So I had something that I am sure you are all used to reading about by now: a genius idea. I knelt down and, after rummaging through my bag, found the Ljubljana to Venice train ticket from the day before. I held it in my left hand and walked strongly and with purpose up to the two policemen, handing one of them my passport as I stepped through the metal detector.

'Come back and wait here please,' ordered one of the cops.

'Bollocks,' I mumbled.

'We just need to run some extra checks on your passport,' he said, before leaving me standing with his colleague, holding an invalid ticket and looking more nervous than Diego Maradona awaiting the results of a drug test. A couple of minutes later, he returned.

'Okay, you are fine to go. Thank you, sir.'

He waved me on with a smile. I walked past and then swore again under my breath when just around the corner I walked straight into a French policeman manning another checkpoint. I held out my passport and avoided eye contact but, with an arrogant shrug of the shoulders, he let me know he wasn't interested in wasting his precious time on me. I was waved through to the platform without being checked. As I stood and waited for the 7:17pm to Paris via Lyon, I received a text from Sébastien giving me directions to the hostel and a number to call when I got there. All I had to do now was make it to Lyon and I was set up for the night. It couldn't be too hard, could it? I had made it this far without too much trouble.

At 7:47pm my task looked a little more complicated. I was standing on the platform of a deserted station in the French village of Belleguarde, not far from the Swiss border, after being chucked off of the Paris-bound train. According to the timetable on the wall there was only one more train that evening leaving the station and it went at 8:28pm. If I failed to make it to Lyon on that one, I was in the proverbial *merde*. I hadn't eaten anything other than the bit of stale bread and salami all day, and had hardly eaten the day before either. My stomach was hurting, my head was hurting, I was cold and tired and I again found myself questioning the wisdom behind trying to complete such a stupid challenge.

I jumped on the 8:28 and shared my train carriage with a French woman in her early thirties, dressed all in black, who sat writing what I imagined was dark poetry. Every now and then I would catch her staring at my face and I wondered if I was the subject of her work. I then found myself drifting off into fantasy. I would look up and find her staring into my eyes and I would ask her in French for the time. She would reply in English but with a strong accent, 'Eet ees getteeen late,' to which I would reply, 'Yes. Yes it is.' Then we would both look away at the same time, awkwardly. A few seconds later she would throw her notebook across the carriage, rip her stockings with one powerful swipe and reach across and grab me by the collar, hoisting herself onto my lap and covering my mouth in kisses. I would throw her against the wall, lift her skirt and make hard, passionate love to her up against the window. The ticket inspector would walk in and then immediately turn around and walk out again, saying, 'Pardonez-moi' on the way. The train would slowly grind to a halt and she would light up a cigarette as she made her way to the door and stepped off onto the platform. As the train was pulling away I would retake my seat in the carriage and watch her disappear out of sight, before realising she had forgotten to take her notebook with her. I would pick it up and put it in my inside coat pocket as a souvenir. I never even knew her name.

My dirty mind helped an hour pass quickly and I was now

just two stops from Lyon and still not sure if there was even a ticket inspector on the train. I didn't suppose there was anyone else on the train at all, apart from me and the girl. And then he came. Two minutes before the penultimate stop. I was ordered off of the train at Ambérieu, a place I had never heard of and one that wasn't even marked on my map of France. I was the only person to get off and apart from a cleaning lady I was the only sign of human life in the station. There were no more trains serving the station until 7 the following morning. There was no way of getting to Lyon. The time was 10:30pm but the village was completely deserted; it was a ghost town. My only option for the night was to sleep rough in the grounds of the station, but when I returned to it after a walk around the village, I found all the doors had been locked. I would have to sleep in the car park. I had filled up a bottle of water at Hannes' kitchen, so I wasn't going to die, and the quicker I fell asleep the quicker morning would come and I could be on my way again. I put my bag down as a pillow and stretched myself out on the cold tarmac. I closed my eyes and shivered a bit, and then remembered that Sébastien's friend Alex was expecting me in Lyon and would be sitting up waiting and wondering. I had to let him know that it was okay to go to sleep. So up I got and headed back into the village in search of a phone.

The village was eerily silent and pitch black; there was no light coming from windows. Then I heard the sound of muffled voices coming from somewhere in the distance. I followed my ears and found a tiny bar with a locked door and a sign hanging above it saying, 'Hôtel'. I tapped on the glass. An old husband and wife pulled back the curtain, looked at my face and slowly unlocked the door.

'Chambre, Monsieur?'

'Non. Je n'ai pas d'argent pour une chambre. Je voudrais utiliser le téléphone, s'il vous plaît, parce que j'ai un petit problème,' I replied.

The lady dialled Alex's number from the reception phone and handed me the receiver.

'Alex, you were expecting my call, I'm Kris,' I started.

'Ah, yes. How are you? Where are you?'

I explained my predicament but was surprised to hear that he had never heard of Ambérieu so had no idea how far from Lyon I was. He asked to be put on to the woman, so I handed her the phone. They spoke for a couple of minutes and I managed to follow the conversation enough to know that I was about 50km from Lyon. The lady then handed me back the receiver.

'Okay, Kris. You don't need to worry. I have spoken to the lady and I have booked you into a room that she has there. I will pay by credit card.'

'Alex, no, come on. It's fine, really. I can sleep outside. You don't have to do that!'

'No, don't worry. Sébastien has told me about your trip and this is something I can do. I don't want you sleeping on the street.'

Alex then gave his credit card details to the woman and I was led up the stairs to a small room with a bed, a telly and a toilet in the corner. It looked like something straight out of a 1970's Roman Polanski film. The walls were painted fluorescent yellow, and the doors and all furniture were fluorescent pink.

The lampshade on the bedside table was fluorescent pink with flowers painted on it, not so much a lampshade but more a room brightener. The shower was down the hallway and was shared with the other guests. I decided to leave that until the morning. I just needed to get some kip. I turned the lights off at 11:30pm and was just getting off to sleep when the guests from the adjoining room returned. My room was attached to theirs by a wooden door with a gap underneath, so any noise they made sounded like it was coming from inside my room. They talked loudly for half an hour before getting down to business in bed, as loudly as you would expect from a French pair. After a while I plugged the iPod earphones into my ears and listened to the most appropriate song I could find – 'Duncan' by Paul Simon – allowing myself to sing along:

'Couple in the next room are bound to win a prize; they've been going at it all night long. Well I'm trying to get some sleep, but these motel walls are cheap…'

I woke the next morning to the sound of the couple heading out and slamming their door behind them. It was still pitch black; it must have only been about 6:30. I stretched across to the bedside table and checked the time on my phone. It was 9:00. Those shutters on the window were hardcore. I went back to sleep until 10 when the cleaner started hoovering in the room next door. I was grumpy. I needed food and I needed sleep. Two days of almost constant travelling had taken their toll. I lay there for another half an hour and then got up and rolled up the shutter to reveal a nice, sunny day in the village. Outside my window French people were going about their daily business of being French: carrying baguettes under their arms, shrugging to each other and smoking cigarettes in a cool way.

There was a train leaving for Lyon in an hour's time, so I took a seat in the station's waiting room with a rich old man accompanied by what appeared to be a prostitute. A cheap prostitute. Imagine Dawn French in a miniskirt, knee-high boots, a corset and with her face painted like Coco the Clown, speaking French, and you are pretty close. The train pulled in and was packed to busting point; people were squeezing on and standing in the aisles. There was no way a ticket inspector could make his way through the carriages.

I arrived at Part-Dieu station at 12:25. Happy days.

Welcome to Lyon.

23. Lyon

As I WALKED out onto the street from the station I had no idea whether I was actually in the city proper or out in the suburbs. The station was a large, busy terminus, much like King's Cross in London, full of rushing people in suits, carrying briefcases. After a quick walk around, it became clear that I wasn't in a central part of the city so I jumped on a train to Lyon Perrache, which I hoped might be situated in a more scenic borough. I walked out of the station straight into the middle of a lively fête celebrating local customs, music, food and wine. Men in berets served cheese and bread to smiling old ladies; a middle-aged and suave crooner serenaded female passers-by from up on a stage; people stood around smoking cigarettes and shrugging; and an angry pedestrian kicked the bike of a cyclist who hadn't rung his bell before riding through the middle of the square. I stood for a while, taking in the atmosphere, enjoying being in the middle of such a French scene. I felt like I had strolled onto the set of *Allo Allo*. My bags were starting to weigh heavy in my arms and I didn't want the extra weight slowing me down as I explored more of what the city had to offer, so I found a hotel and dropped them off.

My first impressions of Lyon were positive. Despite being one of France's largest cities, it had somehow managed to keep the feel of a quaint little town. The area around the river was picturesque and the sky was the bluest I had ever stood under at this time of year. I soon forgot my hunger and began feeling good about life in general. People even smiled and said 'Bonjour' as I passed them on the street. Lyon was nice.

After crossing the river, I followed a steep path all the way to the top of Fourvière Hill, turning me out at the site of the ancient Roman Amphitheatre, the Théâtres Romains de Fourvière, which offered the most stunning panoramic view over the whole of Lyon. The Roman theatre, the oldest in France, was built by the order of Augustus in the years 17 to 15 BC, before being expanded during the reign of Hadrian.

This was the place to come if you were local, young and in love. All around me couples sat on the grass, on the theatre's steps or on the wall overlooking the city, sharing ice-cream. Who was I to tell them that ice-cream was not a food for January? From there, I carried on my ascent further still until I came to the highest point possible and found myself standing in the shadow of the Basilica of Notre-Dame; a huge structure built between 1872 and 1896. The basilica, which is dedicated to the Virgin Mary who is said to have saved the city of Lyon from the plague in 1643, actually contains two churches, one on top of the other. The upper sanctuary is very ornate, while the lower is much simpler in design.

The basilica was just as majestic inside as she was from the outside; the only thing slightly spoiling the serenity was a loud vending machine churning out souvenir medals for two euros a pop. The Church is a business like any other, though; just another racket. I wondered whether this encouraged the Japanese tourists to carry on flashing away with their cameras, despite the local French worshippers paying their respects in the aisles. From there, I walked back down to the city towards a large square I had seen from the top, which had as its centrepiece a huge Ferris wheel. Place Bellecour, at 62,000m², is the largest clear square in Europe. In the middle of it, next to the Ferris wheel, stood a statue of King Louis XIV mounted on a horse. This was clearly the city's main meeting place and I had to carefully navigate my way in and out of small children on scooters, parents pushing prams, and long haired teenage boys on skateboards. In front of the statue, black youths practiced their hip-hop dance moves, watched all the time by their less confident white friends.

As I stood, still enjoying my surroundings but wondering whether Sébastien was ever going to get in touch, my phone vibrated into action. My mum had put some credit on it earlier in the day, so I was able to take a call. Sébastien told me to meet him at Croix-Rousse Metro station at 7pm. I only had an hour. I made it at 6:40 with 20 minutes to spare. Sébastien arrived dead on 7, listening to music through a large retro pair of headphones. He introduced himself and I was surprised by how well he spoke English. It turned out he had lived in Chester for two years and had been in a long-term relationship with a Scottish girl. This association with a Scot had, thankfully, not affected his use of the English language too detrimentally.

Sébastien's flat was like a barn conversion, up in the loft of a house. You had to duck in places so as not to knock your head on the wooden beams holding up the roof. The inside walls were brick slabs, just as they were on the outside. There was no plasterboard, no wallpaper and no paint. It was rustic, and I liked it. The first thing my host did when we walked through the door was make a call to a local pizza place to place an order for collection, and then we headed out to pick up dinner and a few cans of super-strength lager. It was a Friday night and Sébastien wanted to let off some steam. After we'd worked our way through the cans and the food, he pulled a bottle of expensive champagne from the fridge and said that he had been given it by his bosses as a reward for some good work he had done, and felt that now was as good a time as any to drink it. I quickly washed and we headed back out the door, champagne in hand, and worked our way to the bottom of the bottle as we walked into town. The rest of the night is a blur, but I can just about remember being in at least three different clubs throughout the course of the session, one that was located inside a boat moored at the side of the river, in which we tried unsuccessfully to impress the local womenfolk. I also have a vague memory of the two of us partaking in a pull-ups competition on some scaffolding.

I woke the following afternoon on a settee in the living room with the headache to beat all headaches. Sébastien was still asleep in his room, where he stayed for the rest of the day. That evening, still carrying my monumental headache, he gave me a tour of the city's massive park that also housed the zoo, before taking me to an Australian pub, Ayers Rock, where there was a free barbecue taking place to celebrate Australia day. The owners of the place had really made the effort and the whole interior of the pub had been turned into a beach. There was sand on the floor, surfing on the TV screens, Victoria Bitter being served in cans, and drunken Aussies in shorts falling all over the place and calling each other wankers. I hoped that a couple of cans of VB and a few free hot dogs would be just the cure for my headache, but surprisingly it had the opposite effect. Once the food was all gone we headed over to an Irish pub, Wallace's, for fish and chips. The dinner was filling, my host was taking good care of me, and I already felt like he was an old friend. Unfortunately I feel I let the side down a bit, because despite Sébastien being up for another heavy night of drinking, I was by now feeling so ill that after meeting his friend Alex for a couple more beers, I had to ask that we call it a night, but not before thanking Alex for what he had done for me the previous night. I was in bed by half past midnight and slept right through to late the next morning.

The following evening I sent out a few couch requests to people in both Montpellier and Marseille, asking anyone with an available place for me to send a text message to my phone. Both cities could be used as a stopping off point on my way to Spain, and I would only choose which one to head to once I received a reply from either city. Sébastien was going away on a business trip at 7 the following morning so I would have to be up and out by then too.

My new friend and I parted company with a handshake and

a promise to keep in touch. Sébastien handed me a little bag that he had filled with sandwiches, a packet of biscuits and a bottle of water. He also gave me a Metro ticket that I could use to get to Hot Shots Part Deux; I mean Lyon Part-Dieu station. I still hadn't received any news from potential hosts, so I had no idea where I was going to go. I decided to attempt to head south to Valence, by which time hopefully I would have received a text and would then get to either Montpellier or Marseille from there.

As I stood inside Lyon's station a curious thing happened that could only happen in France. From nowhere, a floppy-haired man wrapped in a flamboyant scarf walked up to me and asked if I had any spare lip balm that he could use. What the fuck? That's a bit much even for a Frenchman.

I jumped on the 9:07am Lyon-Nice express, hoping to make it as far as the first stop of Avignon without too much stress. As I had a whole day and no real plans I decided to break my journey down into lots of little stops, resting and rethinking my plan at each break. The ticket man, a young guy who spoke good English, came along pretty soon after departing. I told him that my girlfriend had told me to meet her on the train as she had our tickets to Nice, and that I had just gone to buy a bottle of water before it left; I'd missed the train that she was on and now had arranged to meet her at Avignon where she would get on this same train for the rest of the journey. He said, 'No problem,' smiled, and left me alone. I got off at Avignon at 10:15. The weather was hot. T-shirt hot. In January! I didn't feel like rushing, as I still had nowhere to go, so I sat in the sun for an hour eating a sandwich. I asked a girl working behind a ticket desk how I could get to Montpellier and she told me that I would have to take a train from Avignon Central, which was far from where we were now, an outpost TGV (high-speed rail) station outside the city. I decided that rather than take that option I would jump on another TGV train and get to

Marseille, where I fancied my chances of finding a place for the night. I jumped on the 11:49 to Marseille and jumped off at the first stop of D'aix-en-Provence. No ticket inspector had come along but I still felt more comfortable breaking my journey into two 20-minute legs. It was psychological. The area outside the station looked exactly the same as it had in Avignon, surrounded by the dry mountains of Provence, with an abundance of green trees and brown land at their feet. I got on the very last carriage of the 12:22 to Marseille and arrived in the city stress-free at 12:35. Outside the station a Mediterranean metropolis awaited me. People loitered about in t-shirts, shorts and sunglasses. It was hard to imagine that only a week earlier I had been knee deep in snow and wearing a coat that had frozen while I walked. I set about trying to find a hotel that would let me use their Internet and look after my bags for me, when I received a text from a girl in Montpellier.

The Law of Sod.

Marie was offering me a place to sleep for the night. So I retraced my steps all the way back to Avignon, arriving at 2:16pm. From Avignon's TGV station I had to somehow get into the city proper to catch my train to Montpellier. The bus cost just over a Euro, which was pittance, but it was pittance that I didn't have. Working in the ticket office was a young girl who looked bored, so I decided to try a bit of the old charm. I gave her a sob story about losing my wallet and needing to get to my French grandma in the city. I want to say that it was because she found me adorable, but the reality was more likely that she found me pathetic, but with a, 'This isn't normal procedure, you know?' she handed me a free ticket. I thanked her and asked her name.

'Aurelie,' she said, blushing.

'Merci, Aurelie.'

I would have winked but I don't know how to. When I try, I look like I've just suffered a stroke.

Avignon town centre was beautiful, with a large Roman wall running through the centre of it. Sadly, I had no time to really take in the town that many years ago used to be home to the popes. I hopped on the 3:25 to Montpellier and was pleased to see that I only had to survive four stops. The guard came along just after the first, though, and told me to get off at the second, which was Nimes, before leaving me alone. Just before we got to Nimes I 'fell asleep,' keeping my head down low so as not to be noticed from further up the train. My plan worked, I wasn't disturbed again, and I arrived in my target destination at 4:30pm.

Welcome to Montpellier.

24. Montpellier

After a long day of travelling I had finally made it to a place where I knew I had a bed for the night. The Southern French sun was still shining brightly and warmly. I was quite excited to be in a city that had held a place in the back of my mind for the past 16 years, ever since as a seven-year old I'd watched the 1991 European Cup Winners Cup quarter final between Manchester United and Montpellier on the telly. I had cheered for the French team that night, and the image of the Montpellier kit of blue and white shirts and bright orange shorts, being worn that night by Colombian legend Carlos Valderrama among others, had forever stayed with me. Whenever I thought of France as a young boy I thought of the city that I actually knew nothing about. Whenever checking foreign football results and league tables I had always looked out for Montpellier, even through the difficult years they struggled in the lower leagues. I certainly never expected to end up in the city.

I left the train station and found a truly beautiful little town. The streets were as clean as anywhere I had seen before. In front of the station, trams ran off in all directions as people in designer sunglasses dodged between them. The only shops on view were those selling the fashions of the top designers and all the locals seemed to have been on a mad shopping spree shortly before my arrival, as everyone was dressed and presented immaculately. I knew I wasn't in Montpellier just to people-watch and enjoy the sun, so I headed across the street and into a picturesque little park where designer mums played with their designer children and designer dog owners walked their designer dogs and picked up their designer dog poo, placing it in designer carrier bags before depositing it into designer rubbish bins. I felt a bit out of place, but only until I found the part of the park frequented by the down-and-outs. There I could blend in. I took a seat on a bench and sent a text to Marie telling her where I was. She didn't take long in arriving. Marie was a tall girl with dark flowing hair and a Gallic face. The first thing she asked after greeting me was if I spoke French.

'Un peu,' I replied.

In school I was taught that 'un peu' meant 'a little' but clearly I had been taught wrong. What it really meant was, 'yes, I am fluent.' I know this because for the whole half-hour duration of the bus journey back to Marie's flat, my host spoke to me in nothing but her native tongue. This was frustrating, because it was obvious that she understood my language a lot better than I understood hers. As we walked in through the door of her flat I was starving and hoped she would soon offer me something to eat. Instead I was offered something better: an opportunity.

'I suppose you are tired. If you like, you can stay here and get some sleep, but I must go out now to help feed the homeless. It is something that I do every week. You are welcome to join me if you wish,' Marie told me in French, breaking it down slowly for me to understand.

Of course I wished to join in and help out. I knew only too well what it was like to be cold and hungry without a place to sleep but I was doing it purely through choice and could always give up my challenge and go home at any point if I so wished. These people that Marie helped out were genuinely needy and had nowhere else to turn. Throughout the journey up to this point I had wanted to give something back, to help people in the same way that so many had helped me, and now the chance had presented itself. I was stinking, tired and starving but just had enough time to change my clothes before we were back out the door. Back on the bus and with Marie still yapping away in French, I asked her if she had ever been to England. Her answer surprised me.

'No I have never been to England and I never will. I hate the English people. I hate the English language. I hate the English weather. I hate the English food. I hate everything about England.'

She didn't seem to be joking, either. How could you hate so many things about a place you had never seen with your own eyes?

We got off the bus and walked the rest of the distance to the warehouse where everything for the night was to be set up, and as we walked Marie went one step further in describing her level of hatred for Angleterre. She decided to play the Jacque Chirac card, telling me how much she missed him and how he was the only one who truly stood up for France and all things French against the Anglo-Saxons. She really used the term Anglo-Saxons. I told her that ever since Chirac had stood up and walked out of a European trade conference in disgust simply because a Frenchman had addressed the delegates in English, I had found him ridiculous.

'No, no, it is good that he did that,' Marie replied. 'Because the French language is becoming less and less important; foreigners don't learn our language any more. We must save it. Anglo-Saxons are taking over the whole world and France must do something to protect herself.'

I was confused as to why this girl, who hated the English and everything about them so much, had invited an Englishman into her home to spend the night. I figured she probably didn't mean everything she said and that she just enjoyed a wind-up and was entertaining herself. I had been guilty of the same crime many times in the past.

We arrived at the big warehouse in the industrial estate and I was introduced to two men and three women, all of whom looked like the close-to-retirement workers you find sat on checkouts in Tesco. I was immediately put to work putting biscuits and sweets into little plastic bags before tying them shut. I wanted so much to help myself to a couple of Digestives but suspected it wouldn't look too good if I got caught. Marie told everyone that I spoke French, but after a couple of minutes when they realised just how bad my grasp on their language was, I became quite unpopular. They just grunted random sounds at me from time to time, pointing with their eyebrows at whatever task needed doing. I was feeling pissed off and wished I hadn't come along. The French were treating me like a dog, and not their own family pet dog. I was the neighbour's dog that crapped in their front garden. At 7pm we finished loading all of the stuff into the back of the large van and drove off to a car park in the centre of the city where the local poor and homeless were waiting for us. For two hours we handed out cups of soup, sweets, biscuits, hot chocolate, coffee, bread, cake, books, socks, and even the occasional sleeping bag. My job was to pour the coffee and ask each person the question, 'Voulez-vous du sucre?'

Most of the people were so friendly and grateful; a lot of them even thanked me in English after hearing my giveaway accent. There were single mums who brought their little boys and girls along; kids in rags who probably had no food at home. They happily took the biscuits and thanked us politely. I felt for them as I remembered back to my childhood and the times when we had no money for food; when my sister and I used to ask why we only had a slice of bread and margarine to take to school when our friends had crisps, chocolate bars, biscuits and cartons of juice; wondering why instead of taking a drink in we had to take an empty cup to get water from the tap. I looked at the mums and felt a pang of guilt for ever asking my parents why we didn't have what they would have so loved to be able to provide for their children. Had we been ungrateful? No. Just children with children's questions.

I was finding it hard by now to concentrate on anything the people were saying to me as I was feeling faint from hunger myself. The acid in my stomach was burning its way up my throat. As the evening wore on I could sense that my French co-workers were warming to me. I was getting a lot of smiles from the old ladies and thumbs-ups from the men. They had seen that I wasn't just there to make myself feel good; I was prepared to work hard. We finished serving at 9, said goodbye to the not-so-hungry hungry and headed back to the warehouse to wash everything up. It took a long time but when it was all done we sat around a small table as a group to a meal of quiche, French bread and pâté. As I stuffed the food down my neck, Marie filled everybody in on what I was doing and why I was in Montpellier. They were amazed. I fielded their questions in a mixture of French and English and gained some respect. All of a sudden the English guy who had been getting in the way earlier on was now the most popular person at the table. As I was wiping my plate clean with the last piece of bread, I was asked where I was heading after Montpellier and how I planned on getting there. I told them that I needed to get to Spain, probably Barcelona, but didn't know yet how.

Then the latest generous offer was put in front of me. In two days' time, on Wednesday morning, one of the ladies, Marie-Amelie, would be driving to Spain to do some shopping and would be more than happy for me to come along for the ride. I'd had a nice meal, met some nice people, helped some people a lot more needy than myself and had sorted my path out of France. All in all it had been a pretty decent evening.

It was coming up to midnight when we walked through the door of the flat. Marie told me that she would be leaving early in the morning for university but would leave me a key and a map of the city so that I could get out and do my own thing during the day. I told her that I would really prefer it if she started speaking English to me and she said, 'No problem.'

My bed for the night was the settee in the living room, but after the day I'd had it felt as though I were staying in the Honeymoon suite of the Ritz, minus the beautiful new wife. As soon as I got my head down I was off and away into dreamland.

I woke fairly early the next morning. When I say I woke what I mean is I was woken, by the loud play session going on in the school playground that Marie's living room overlooked.

The sun wasn't shining as it had been the day before and it was overcast and windy outside. This didn't mean that the locals left their sunglasses at home or even in their bags though. The streets of Montpellier are really quite exquisite. The 19th Century buildings are built of old Mediterranean style brickwork with delicate balconies hanging off of the sides. The roads and pavements are paved with sexy little slabs that give the effect of a pedestrianised shopping centre. The women were expensively dressed; it was all Gucci and Armani. I smiled as a woman of about 35 came out of a building in front of me, threw her scarf behind her neck in dramatic fashion, pulled her dark glasses down over her eyes and strode briskly off into the distance leaving in her wake the strongest aroma of perfume you are ever likely to smell. She couldn't be any more French if she tried.

About a year earlier, whilst on a journey through Bosnia with Vanja, we had met a girl from Barcelona in the hostel we were staying at who told us, 'If ever you find yourself in my home city, send me an email and I will give you a place to stay.' Vanja had built up a better relationship with her than I had, so I emailed her and asked if she would contact the girl and find out if the offer still stood.

Marie came to meet me at the free internet centre and with her she brought a friend with long dark hair and brown eyes. She was from Morocco, studying in Montpellier, but her real wish was to get to England as she had a real love of everything English, including the people. As I talked to Amira about my home country, the look of disgust grew ever stronger on Marie's face to the point where she eventually said to her friend, 'Why don't you just leave France and go and study in your wonderful little England, then?'

The two girls took me on a tour through the Moroccan district of the city where we stopped off in a little Sheesha café for a sweet Moroccan tea and a smoke. Afterwards, we strolled through the city's tourist spots, passing the impressive 17th Century cathedral, Cathédrale Saint-Pierre de Montpellier, chatting the whole time as I now had an ally; someone who didn't hold a grudge against me because of where I had been born. Amira agreed when I said that the French were prone to being a bit rude and arrogant, that French food wasn't filling and was overpriced, and that the language wasn't as beautiful as native speakers would have you believe. Obviously I was saying these things to get a rise out of Marie, and not expressing my true feelings. Well, apart from the bit about French food. On the other hand, she was happy living in France and felt she owed the country a debt for allowing her to come there to further her studies. I was sad to say goodbye to Amira later that evening, I had enjoyed her company and her wit.

That evening Marie showed me some of the photo albums she had filled on her travels. She had been to places that were high on my own wish list, countries like Belarus and Ukraine. She had actually travelled around Europe quite a bit and I started to find her a lot more interesting a person. Underneath her fervent nationalistic views was a real traveller, open to new cultures and experiences. I understood now that she was playing a character purely for entertainment purposes.

Woken early again the following morning by the bouncing of basketballs and the whistling of teachers, I was thankful for this natural alternative to an alarm clock, as I had to get ready to move out of Montpellier. After showering and packing my bags, Marie walked me to the place where I was to meet Marie-Amelie; the same car park where we had fed the homeless. The weather was perfect again, and when we met my chauffeur for the day at 10:15 she was standing outside her little red Renault in a pair of designer sunglasses. I said goodbye to Marie, knowing I would never meet her again, stuffed my bags into the boot of the car and strapped myself into the passenger seat. The first challenge of the day was actually getting out of the city as all of Montpellier's taxi drivers were on strike and blocking the city's main exits. As well as that, the local radio DJ told us that the hospitals' doctors were threatening strike action for the near future. The previous evening before bed I had had yet another debate with Marie, this time about how there was always someone on strike in France and how you could never make plans in advance because you never knew who was going to be disrupting your day with their demands. Marie disagreed, obviously, and told me that it was a good thing that people went on strike because if they didn't they would never get better conditions, money, or benefits. Here was proof that the next generation of French worker was going to be no different from the current. But let it be said here, I am all for striking if the reason is just. It is just that too often in France it is not.

The drive to Spain was gorgeous. We went through vineyards, past chateaux, through the Pyrenees, and alongside row after row of green fields with little buildings flying the Catalan flag. It was exactly midday as we crossed over the border. Marie-Amelie didn't feel comfortable just dropping me off in the middle of nowhere so we drove for an extra half hour into the country until we found a small town with a train station, Figueres. It was 12:50 when I kissed my driver on both cheeks and waved goodbye.

I walked into the station and found that the next train to Barcelona left at 2:02pm. I sat down, feeling too dizzy to stay on my feet any longer. As I sat, taking in my surroundings, I heard what would become my saviour: an English couple. An upper-middle class pair; the man was asking the station worker for train timetables for Barcelona. If anybody was going to help me it was these two, and I certainly needed help. I followed them as they left the train station and entered the car park.

'Hello,' I said, happily.

'Hello,' the woman replied, smiling.

I knelt down and pulled the newspaper from my backpack. The newspaper I was carrying around with me was no longer a *Shoreham Herald* – that had slowly died a death – but was now an *Argus*, Brighton's city rag, which my dad had posted out to me after they'd covered my story in a spread. I explained my situation and stressed how hungry I was. Could they be so kind as to buy me a loaf of bread? They turned out to be so friendly and generous I was once again left completely humbled.

'Can we also buy you a train ticket to Barcelona?' the man asked.

We headed back into the station where I was handed a ticket for the next train to my target city. Then, rather than buy me some bread, they took me to a little café where I was told to order whatever I wanted from the menu. I went for a turkey escalope with chips and a can of Coke. They each drank a cup of tea. Peter and Mary were from Salisbury and had just bought a holiday home in Figueres.

Peter was an amateur pilot who regularly flew from Shoreham airport, a five minute drive from my home back in England. They explained that when their son was 16 he had gone off to a kibbutz in Israel but after six weeks had decided it wasn't for him, so left and went travelling around Egypt… With no money in his pocket. The people he met along the way were kind and generous and helped him to survive, and now his parents had the opportunity to help another young lad who found himself in a similar situation; they were more than happy to offer what they could. After a little while they had to leave, but not before paying the bill and also handing me a wrapped kebab to take on my journey. I thanked them profusely and then sadly said farewell. It had been such a short encounter but another one that had touched my heart.

I took the 2:02 train to Barcelona and was disappointed that not one ticket inspector was on board; the one time I actually had a ticket to be checked. Half way through the journey I got a text message from Gina, the girl we had met in Bosnia, telling me that she wasn't in Barcelona but that she had arranged for a friend of hers to host me. She gave me a phone number but no name and told me to text it to say when I was arriving. I did so, and got a reply telling me where to go once in Barcelona. I was to make my way to the Picasso museum for 8pm before giving a quick call to tell him or her that I had arrived.

My train rolled in to the station at 3:50pm.

Welcome to Barcelona.

North Cape
Jan Mayen
(Norway)
NORWEGIAN SEA
Scandinavia
Lapland
SWEDEN
FINLAND
Gulf of Bothnia
NORWAY
Faroe Islands
(Denmark)
Shetland Islands
(UK)
OSLO
STOCKHOLM
HELSINKI
Gulf of Finland
ESTONIA
LATVIA
LITHUANIA
Gotland
BALTIC SEA
SCOTLAND
NORTH
SEA
DENMARK
COPENHAGEN
British
Isles
UNITED
KINGDOM
IRELAND
DUBLIN
ENGLAND
LONDON
NETHERLANDS
BELGIUM
POLAND
BELARUS
WARSAW
MINSK
BERLIN
GERMANY
CELTIC SEA
English Channel
PARIS
FRANCE
CZECH.REP.
SLOVAKIA
AUSTRIA
HUNGARY
ROMANIA
MOLDOVA
Carpathian Mts.
KIEV
Bay of
Biscay
Massif
Central
Pyrenees
SLOVENIA
CROATIA
BOSNIA & H
SERBIA
BELGRADE
BUCHAREST
BULGARIA
SOFIA
ITALY
ROME
Corsica
Sardinia
MONTENEGRO
KOSOVO
ALBANIA
F.Y.R.O.M.
PORTUGAL
LISBON
SPAIN
MADRID
Barcelona
Sierra Morena
MEDITERRANEAN SEA
Sicily
GREECE
ATHENS
Peloponnesus
Anatolia
AEGEAN SEA
Crete
MOROCCO
RABAT
ALGIERS
ALGERIA
TUNIS
TUNISIA
VALLETTA

25. Barcelona

I PICKED UP a map from the Tourist Information Centre inside the station and set about trying to find my rendezvous point for later that evening but didn't get close to locating it before I was distracted by something a little more attention grabbing. According to the piece of paper in front of me, I was just a few streets away from arguably the most famous football stadium in the world: The Camp Nou. Some 25 minutes later I had lugged my bags up and down little side streets and through a residential estate, and was stood looking up at the instantly recognisable stadium. I walked around it once and then strolled through the main gates and into the complex. I stood and watched a group of Japanese tourists get led into the stadium for the start of a guided tour, and decided that I too wanted to see inside. Once again the *Argus* was dragged from my bag, as I made my way into the Members Office where I asked the young lady behind the desk if she spoke any English. She did. Well, a little.

'OK. Well, I am actually here in Barcelona because I'm currently in the middle of a project that I am working on for the BBC,' I told her. 'Basically, I am on a challenge to get to every capital city in the EU without so much as a penny in my pocket. In the process, we are making a programme about the kindness of people in different countries. If I could get a few pictures of myself inside the stadium it would really help with publicity at home and would be great later on for the TV.'

Bear in mind that for someone making a programme for the Beeb, I was quite conspicuously lacking one tiny ingredient: a camera crew. But this minor detail didn't seem to arouse any suspicion in my Catalan friend as she bought my story 100 per cent.

'I am really sorry that I cannot help you because I don't have the, how you say in English? The power? Yes, the power! But if you go to the press office, somebody will talk to you. They will be happy to meet the BBC.'

I made my way across to the press office and was asked by security if I was a member of the foreign press.

'Of course I am. Why else would I be here?'

'Come back in 45 minutes, at 6 o'clock. Press cards will be issued then,' I was told.

'Oh, but…'

'Not now. Come back at 6,' I was told again, a little more strongly this time.

I did as I was told and buggered off, spending the time sitting on a bench, watching the mass of fans from all over the planet coming and going with their cameras, cheesy grins and plastic shopping bags from the megastore. I returned to the press office dead on 6 and put myself in the middle of the throng of reporters. All seemed to be on first name terms with the business suit wearing woman handing out the passes and after a minute or two all those who had stood around me had now disappeared into the stadium, leaving me standing there like the puppy in the rescue centre that nobody wanted to take home. I looked at the woman and put my hand out hopefully.

'My press pass, please?'

She said nothing.

'BBC,' I heard myself saying.

She looked at me, before smiling and turning to walk away into the stadium.

'Wait!' I had just one shot and I had to make it count. 'Do you speak English?'

'No.'

That was not the answer I hoped to hear; however, Catalan has a lot of similarities to Italian.

'Capisce Italiano?'

'Si.'

I explained that I was working for the BBC and had only just arrived in the city – hence the luggage – and that I had been told by my employers to seek out the club's press officer on arrival to arrange with him the details of my stay at the club. Amazingly, her previously sceptical eyes now turned to something more closely resembling credence. How was nobody finding it strange that the BBC would send a scruffy man wearing a tracksuit and carrying all his worldly belongings in a combination that consisted of a rucksack and some brown paper shopping bags, to talk to one of the most prestigious football clubs in the world about the television programme he was filming, amazingly without the technology of even a camera phone? The woman asked if I would mind waiting for a couple of minutes while she went to find the press officer.

As I stood outside the main doors I became aware of movement behind me. I turned around to see all the Japanese running to the carpark entrance taking photos through vehicle windows and screaming excitedly. The players were arriving. The woman in the suit returned a few minutes later accompanied by a smartly dressed, smooth looking guy in his thirties. He greeted me in English and shook my hand strongly, introducing himself as Fernando. I quickly put the copy of the *Argus* into his hands and began once again my BBC story. I finished with a little touch of brilliance, even if I do say so myself.

'In every big city I have been to so far on this journey, I have visited the main football club and they have got involved with my project. It really helps with picking up sponsors back in England, as everybody at home loves football. I just hoped that you could help me with publicity.'

'Really? Which other clubs have you visited?'

'Both Milan clubs, Marseille, Hertha Berlin were really helpful, Roma and now here.'

'I see. I really wish that I had known in advance that you

were coming; I could have arranged something special for you. You know, tonight the players are training in the stadium for tomorrow's cup match against Villareal. It will be difficult to persuade any of them to meet with you this evening.'

I hadn't even thought of meeting the players; but he said it as if it were normal procedure. I now had my heart set on the Great Euro Freebie Challenge picking up the backing of a world famous footballer.

'Yes, I understand that,' I said, 'but they are all good guys. I'm sure they would be happy to help, if you just explained the situation to them.'

'Why don't you come inside with me now? I can take you up into the stands and you can have your photo taken.'

Before I had time to realise what was going on, I was led through some doors, up a flight of stairs and out into the press box, where I found myself looking down onto the pitch and around at the huge stands. After taking a couple of photos I turned round to see Fernando was keen to escort me back out of the stadium.

'So, shall I wait around until after training's finished for you to have a word with the players?' I asked.

'I can't say for sure. They will be in the dressing room getting ready soon. I will go and speak to them and show them the newspaper story. Maybe one of the English-speaking players will meet you. It's not a promise; it's just a maybe. Come back in an hour and a half and ask for me.'

It was 6.20pm and I knew that if I was to meet any famous footballers then I wouldn't make it to the Picasso museum for 8 o'clock as arranged. I texted my mystery host to say I was running late and then killed time until 7:50pm when I went again to the main entrance and asked for Fernando. The security guard spoke to someone on the radio and then told me to follow him. He took my bags from me and put them behind a desk in the main hall and then led me down a flight of stairs and along a corridor to a room that looked familiar. Where had I seen this room before? I put the pieces together in my head – the journalists and microphones were a bit of a clue – and realised that I was stood in the pressroom where they interviewed the players and manager before and after matches. There was obviously a press conference due to start and the journalists seemed impatient and bored. At the front of the room a woman was recording a live feed for Barcelona TV. All of a sudden the place became silent and every photographer and journalist in the room took his or her seat. I looked around, saw that I was the only person standing, and so took a seat in the front row as I wondered which star was about to come out to meet the press. There was a tap on my shoulder. I looked around to see Fernando staring down at me.

'I have spoken to the players and Eidur Gudjohnsen has agreed to come and meet you and have his photo taken for your website. The players are showering at the moment, so he will come out when he's ready. But you will have to come with me because you are not allowed to be in here for the press conference.'

My immediate reaction was one of disappointment. Not because I was going to meet the Icelandic footballer, but because I wasn't going to experience a press conference. Fernando led me out the door at the side and to a big room that also looked familiar. I was in the post-match interview area: the big wall with all the advertisements printed on to it that the players stand in front of to mumble clichés at us.

'Okay, wait here and Eidur will be out to meet you shortly. I have to go and sort some things out. Don't go back into the press conference room,' Fernando instructed me.

As he walked away I played back in my head what he had just said: 'I have to go and sort some things out. Definitely go back into the press conference room. I won't be here to stop you. Do it. Do it now.'

As soon as he disappeared up the stairs I nipped back into the conference room, just in time to see the team's manager, Frank Rijkaard, taking his seat at the front. I stood at the back and quickly took a couple of photos as I tried to understand what he was saying.

Then Frank Rijkaard looked at me. Frank Rijkaard looked at me, and then looked around the room as if searching for someone. He made eye contact with a heavily built guy in the other corner of the room and then glanced back at me. Before I knew it, I was being escorted back out through the door by the over-sized man from the corner of the room. Frank Rijkaard's first impression of me clearly hadn't been a good one.

'You stay here!' said the ogre.

'Okay.'

I wasn't going to argue with this particular gentleman. Just to make sure that I didn't go back on my word, he went to the trouble of shutting both doors. I spent the next 20 minutes just standing in front of the wall, conducting imaginary interviews with myself. My fantasy time was cut short by someone entering the room talking on a mobile phone. I turned around to find Xavi, all 5'6' of him, standing beside me having a chat to someone. He glanced at me with a look that said, 'Who the fuck are you?' and I nodded a greeting his way. He finished his conversation and left me alone once again.

After another 20 minutes Gudjohnsen still hadn't turned up to meet me. I should have interrupted Xavi and told him to tell his mate that I was waiting. The press conference room started emptying of journalists. Nobody was watching me so I quietly opened the door through which Xavi had disappeared and saw in front of me the door to the home team's dressing room. The air smelt of shower gel and deodorant. It reminded that no matter how big and famous these footballers were, they weren't really any different from me and my mates. Whether you are playing in front of 100,000 people and the watching world on the telly or on a rain soaked mud bath in front of one man and his dog, the post-match ritual is still pretty much the same. These were just the best players in the school team who didn't let other distractions, such as girls, drinking and drugs, stop them from realising their dreams. There is nothing superhuman about them, they are just very good at what they do and are fortunate to get paid for doing something that most of us would do for free. I closed the door and went back to where I had been told to wait. I waited a long time. Soon it was 9 o'clock and nobody had come to fetch me. The journalists had all gone home and I was starting to lose my patience with Eidur Gudjohnsen.

I had a host waiting for me; a host that I hadn't yet met and who was probably growing just as impatient if not more so than I was. I sent a text to him or her saying that I had been held up and wouldn't make it to the Picasso Museum until at least 10. He or she replied angrily, saying that he or she had to be up for work early in the morning and didn't like being messed around, especially by a stranger. Which is fair enough.

'I am going to turn off my phone at 11:30 when I go to bed. If you are not here by then, you will just have to find somewhere else to stay,' read the text.

Our relationship hadn't got off to the best of starts and I blamed Eidur Gudjohnsen.

More time passed; I had clearly been forgotten. I popped my head back into the Press Conference room just to confirm that I was definitely the last man standing and then went back to the door to the players' area and quietly opened it and peered down the corridor. The smell of shower gel had cleared and all sounds of life had been silenced. I was all alone in the depths of The Camp Nou. The corridor that I had been led down earlier in the evening was beckoning me. Halfway along it were the stairs that led back up to the main reception area, but beyond the stairs there was a mystery that needed exploring. So, past the stairs I crept, all the time looking around for authority figures. A few seconds later I was standing in the players' tunnel looking out onto the pitch. I walked down it as I hummed the Champions' League music. I strolled past the subs bench and out into the centre circle. I knew that I only had a minimal amount of time before I was discovered and ejected from the stadium, so I ran up to the goal and curled an imaginary ball into the top corner from just outside the box, before jumping up and swinging on the crossbar in celebration. I sat on both benches. The pitch was like a bowls lawn. I was on borrowed time and wanted as much of the behind-the-scenes experience as I could get. I wanted to have a look in the players' dressing room. I walked back down the tunnel and took a right turn at the end as the players would have done after the match. I could see the dressing room; the door was open.

'Hey!' A loud, deep voice broke the silence.

A large African man in a security uniform stepped in front of me with an angry look on his face. He grabbed me by the collar and dragged me up a flight of stairs.

'Wait! You don't understand. I was told to wait here by Fernando. I am supposed to be interviewing Gudjohnsen.'

'No. Nobody should be here. Come on!'

'My bags are still inside. Fernando put them behind the desk. Will you listen to me?'

The guard led me to a hut full of other security guards outside the stadium and let me explain to them. I told them the whole story and that as I had got bored waiting I thought it would be cool to see the pitch. The boss of this small group made a phone call and then told his boys that I was telling the truth.

'All the players went home a long time ago. There is no Gudjohnsen here now. I will take you to get your bags and you should come back tomorrow afternoon to speak to Fernando.'

'Great,' I said with a sigh.

I was taken to collect my stuff and then escorted out through the main gates and dumped onto the street. At least before waving me goodbye and closing the gates behind me, the guard was kind enough to point on my map to where I needed to catch my train.

The walk from the stadium to the Metro station was pornographic. I was obviously in the city's red light district, as the street was lined on both sides with girls of all races, sizes and ages advertising their merchandise. It was coming up for 11pm and I had just received a final warning text message from my host.

'I don't care what your excuse is; you should be here by now. I am turning my phone off in half an hour and going to bed. If you get to the Picasso Museum before then, call me.'

I was in another race against time. I found the Metro station. To get to the Picasso Museum I had to take the train to one station before changing lines for my final destination of Jaume

1. As we pulled into my changing station, I made my way to the door. I then stood and watched through the glass as my station disappeared and my train took me on to the next stop on the line. Unlike on the Tube in London, Rome or anywhere else I had ever been, the doors of the Metro trains in Barcelona didn't open automatically at every station; they had to be opened manually. Someone's really got to tell me these things in advance! So I went to the next station, managed to get the doors open, crossed the platform, went back a stop, changed line and made it to where I had to be. It was 11:20pm when I walked up the stairs and out onto the street but I couldn't see any Picasso Museum. I began to panic. I had ten minutes before my host's phone would be switched off and I would be out on the streets for the night. The only person around was a homeless old man sitting beside a fountain smoking the dog-end of a cigarette I had watched him pick up off the pavement. I felt uncomfortable asking him for directions without having something to offer him in return, but what could I do? He smiled a toothless smile and with his gloved finger pointed to where I had to go. It was a few streets away; narrow little pedestrian-only streets. I raced through the tiny passageways and there it stood in front of me; the big, metal door on the old stone building. I looked at the time on my phone and saw it was 11:29pm. I didn't have time to type out a complete text message so I rapidly tapped in the words: 'Museo Picasso. Here,' and sent it off to my host, hoping that he or she hadn't yet turned off the phone. I stood in nervous silence for the next couple of minutes; my host had clearly lost patience and given up on me. After a while I began to accept the fact that nobody was coming to meet me. How could I have even expected it to all be alright? I mean, I had been exchanging text messages with someone I didn't know and who had only heard about me through a quick text message from a friend. He or she could have been on a wind-up all day, or if they had indeed

intended to host me they had long ago given up the ghost and forgotten all about it by now. Either way, I was homeless. I walked around the little streets, checking if there was perhaps another entrance to the museum and I had just gone to the wrong one. No luck. I pulled my phone out of my pocket again and saw that it was 11:45pm. I sighed and put it away. As I did so, it vibrated. I read the text: 'Wait there. I will arrive in two minutes.'

Carlos was 26 years old, thin in build, wore sandals and had a thick, black beard to go with his scruffy dark hair. He looked like my long lost brother. He greeted me in a completely relaxed way and I wondered what I had been so worried about. His flat was just a minute's walk down a small alley and he led me through the wooden door and mock courtyard and up the stairs to his home. The flat was large and tidy.

'I live with three women,' he grinned. 'That's why it is so clean. If you are hungry, there is some couscous left in the pot from earlier.'

We sat down at the large table that was the centrepiece of the room and he asked if I smoked weed.

'I wouldn't say no.'

And just like that I had a joint in my hand and was trying to explain to this guy how it was that I found myself in Barcelona. He knew nothing of and cared little about football so my stories from the day were wasted on him, but he responded well to the whole idea of my challenge. He told me of the eight years he had spent living in London, squatting in various properties and working as a street cleaner. He laughed as he shared memories of life in England. I laughed too, mainly at the way he used Cockney expressions but still had the strongest of Spanish accents. 'I lived with this mental geezer,' 'It was proper rough,' and my personal favourite, 'It's all daily bread, innit.'

For all the worry he had caused me with the text messages, Carlos was actually the most laidback person I had ever come across in my life. He wore brightly coloured clothes, was a vegan and smoked spliffs like others smoked cigarettes. We sat up for an hour talking. He worked as a street fundraiser for the charity Doctors Without Borders, approaching strangers armed with only a clipboard and pen for 15 hours a week over three days. The rest of his time he spent 'getting high, man.' At different points during the hour, his three flatmates came in through the front door and disappeared into their bedrooms, giving me a quick handshake and hello before doing so. Not one of them felt the need to ask who I was and what I was doing in their flat. If Carlos had an unshaven foreigner in the living room past midnight, it was nothing to be curious about; there was no need to doubt his judgement. I responded well to this relaxed atmosphere and felt immediately comfortable. 2am came and it was time to try and get some sleep. Carlos told me that he would wake me at 8 and that I would leave the flat at the same time as him. He fetched a mattress from his room, put it down on the living room floor for me and disappeared to bed.

I was woken to the chant of, 'Hey man, wake up. Wake up!'

I looked up to see Carlos standing above me, his hair sticking up all over the place and a joint hanging from the side of his mouth. I jumped up and put myself under the shower before sitting with my host and sharing a little herbal smoke. At 9 I left the flat with him and we headed our separate ways. I had been hoping all morning that he would give me a piece of bread or something for the day but no such offer was forthcoming. I did, however, get handed something in a little plastic bag.

'Take this, in case you need some in the afternoon.'

The little bag contained some weed, some tobacco and some rolling papers. Under what circumstances would I possibly need this later in the afternoon? I might want it later in the afternoon; but need?

I set off in the direction of the beach. The day was beautiful and the water of the port glistened under the bright sun, sending sparks of light reflecting off of the rollerblades of the fit and healthy. The waterside area looked more like television depictions of Los Angeles than anywhere I had ever seen in Europe: joggers, skaters, dog-walkers, coffee-drinkers, mobile-talkers; all hiding their early morning eyes behind designer shades. I saw no point returning to the Camp Nou, so I spent most of the day hungrily walking the streets of the city.

I arrived back at the flat in the afternoon to find Carlos sitting in the same seat that he had occupied the night before, smoking joints just as he had done the night before.

He offered me some cold boiled potatoes and green beans that he'd cooked up earlier, along with some chop sticks.

'A fork maybe?'

'Ah, sorry, man. I forgot that you are not me. I only use chop sticks when I eat, I don't like Western cutlery. I will find you a fork.'

How do you forget that someone isn't you?

As he fumbled around in the kitchen looking for some decent cutlery, I wolfed down everything in front of me using my hands. Carlos returned to the living room, laughed the kind of laugh that only stoners do, and then took my plate out to the sink. He returned, rolled another joint and passed it my way. The next hour was spent in silence as we chain-smoked spliffs. A little later on I met Celia, one of the girls I had briefly shaken hands with the night before. She spoke with a strong voice, had a slim build, long, dark brown hair and wore bright red lipstick, an 'I love NY' t-shirt and a pair of tight jeans.

'Are you hungry?' she asked, after I had told her about the nature of my trip.

'Getting there.'

'Well, you won't be tonight. I'm having a party in the flat with a load of people from my work. There will be plenty of food, and you are invited as my special guest.'

The evening came and Carlos disappeared to his yoga class. The people started arriving: well-dressed women and effeminate men with silk scarves wrapped around their necks and sparkly bits on their t-shirts.

'Celia, I forgot to ask. What is it that you do?'

'I work in the fashion industry as a stylist. So does everyone else at this party.'

I hovered around for a bit, stuffing my face and sharing joints with Celia. She asked me where I was heading after Barcelona and I told her that I was trying to find a way of getting to Madrid.

'Don't worry. One of my best friends lives there. I will give him a call and let him know you are coming. He will host you.'

The party slowly ground to a halt and at 2:00am I found myself sitting alone on the settee surveying the damage. The other two flatmates then appeared from a bedroom and invited me to the pub with them. I was too stoned to be able to move, so was forced to decline the offer. I dozed for about an hour until I was disturbed by Carlos walking in the door at 3am. In his trademark impossible-not-to-warm-to way he asked simply, 'Shall I roll a spliff?'

'A quick one before bed wouldn't hurt.'

We smoked continuously until 5:30, the last couple of hours also spent with the two girls who had returned from the pub.

The following afternoon I accompanied Carlos in walking a friend of his' dog over the beach. The sun was shining again and we decided to sit on the sand with a couple of cans of beer while the dog swam around excitedly in the sea. Sitting a few yards from us were two girls with whom we seemed to share a mutual interest. They were looking over at us, we were looking over at them, and the question was being posed: 'Do you think we should go and join them?' to which the answer was a resounding 'Yes!'

So, confidently we got up and walked over, encouraged by their smiles as we made our approach. Marta and Magda were two Polish brunettes in their early twenties who had just moved to Barcelona a few days previously to start work as English teachers. We made a bit of small talk and then they asked if we could recommend any good pubs for them to go to that night. Carlos was just about to give them a list when I interrupted him.

'Why don't we meet up tonight and hang out together?'

It was agreed that we would give them a call at about 8 to arrange a meet. Back at the flat we sat and smoked a load more weed with Celia while some friends of Carlos worked in the kitchen preparing a cannabis butter that would be used the next day in the making of a cake. Meanwhile, we sent a text to the Poles telling them we would meet them at 9.

At 9:10 we were still sat in the same seats that we had been in for hours when I suddenly got the feeling that there was something we were supposed to be doing, but for the life of me couldn't remember what. It was like that scene in *Home Alone* where the mum is sitting on the plane going through the mental checklist and suddenly yells, 'Keviiiiiiiiiiin!'

'The Polish girls!'

Another text was sent, apologising for our tardiness and re-scheduling the meet for 9:45 in front of the Hard Rock Cafe. We arrived at the meeting point and were pleasantly surprised to see that our companions for the evening had gone to considerable effort: make-up, perfume, tight jeans, knee-high boots and expensive looking coats. Kissing the girls on both cheeks in greeting, we felt a little underdressed. We made ourselves comfortable at a table in the corner of an Irish pub and picked up the small talk from where we'd left off on the beach. As the girls paid a visit to the toilets, Carlos and I called a quick conference. Who was going to pair up with whom? Marta was prettier but Magda seemed more enthusiastic.

Carlos chose the latter. Before the girls returned, we switched seats so as to be sat next to our newly designated partners. There were a couple of knowing glances between the two of them on arrival; they knew the drill. Sharing the pub with us was a hen party from England.

'Poor girl,' said Marta, in reference to the bride-to-be.

'Marta is just confused because she knows her boyfriend is going to propose soon and she isn't ready,' replied Magda with a laugh.

Boyfriend? That's why she seems so unattainable and hard to talk to. Carlos and I looked at each other as we read each other's minds; we were resigned to defeat and were trying to think of a way to lose the girls and get back to the flat. The Poles were equally keen to part company with us, as Marta said, 'We should really be getting home. We don't want to miss our last train.'

It wasn't yet midnight, so the excuse was a poor one as the Metro stayed open until 2am. This was embarrassing.

'Okay, well it was nice meeting you. We'll be off,' I said, standing up to leave.

'Oh. Don't you want to come back to our place? We can buy some alcohol from a shop on the way and chat over a few drinks. Only if you want to, of course,' Magda then said.

Again Carlos and I exchanged glances, but this time the look was one of disbelief. They didn't want to get rid of us; they wanted to spend the night with us. Or Magda wanted to spend the night with Carlos and needed Marta to keep me entertained with idle chit-chat. I cursed my luck at being stuck with the sensible one who had a boyfriend. Carlos was grinning from cheek to cheek.

We picked up a couple of six-packs on the way to the girls' flat which was situated right next to the famous church, Sagrada Familia. It was a tiny little place that had a hole in the outside wall where a fan had once been, and there was no functioning heating. We sat down at the small table in the kitchen and worked our way through the beers and a load more weed; not the girls, they didn't smoke. The hours ticked away but things weren't going to plan. Part A had been implemented just fine. We were engaged in separate conversations, so that rather than chatting as a group of four, we were each engaged solely with the girl we intended to pull. Well, he intended to pull. I was simply a wing man. Part B, though, the actual pulling part, was becoming more and more distant the longer the night went on. When it got to 5:30am and no one had so much as kissed anyone else, we were about ready to throw in the towel.

'I'm going to bed; it's too late for me,' Magda said.

She had had enough. She stood up and made her way to the bathroom. I looked at Carlos to see if he had any plan to save the night. He did! Bravely and heroically he lost any ounce of self-doubt he might have been harbouring, cleared his throat and said, 'Shall I come with you?'

Both Marta and I pretended not to hear.

'No, I don't think so. There's not enough room for the two of us to sleep in my little bed. Goodnight.'

And just like that she was gone, leaving Carlos sitting in a state of semi-shock as the humiliation set in. At this point I knew the game was up. I also knew that I couldn't look at Carlos because if I did, I would laugh. I stared down at the ground, trying to think sombre thoughts. Nobody was talking, nobody was looking at anyone else; everybody was replaying over and over in their heads what had just taken place. I looked around. I saw Marta looking down at her feet, I saw my reflection in the window, and I saw a bearded hippy sitting in the corner looking crushed. I laughed. I laughed until it hurt; not directly from laughing, but from the hefty kick under the table that Marta administered. Carlos finished his beer, ran his fingers through his beard and stood up.

'I guess I'll be leaving, then. I'm tired,' he muttered.

'Isn't it best if you wait until the trains are running again, rather than walking all that way? If you are sleepy, you can go and lie down in my bed for a while. Kris and I won't disturb you.'

Marta wasn't ready to let the night end.

I was confused. Magda, the single one, had gone to bed. Marta, the one with the boyfriend who was about to propose, wanted me to stay. This wasn't how I had envisioned the night ending up. I now felt that if Carlos were to leave, it would be the right thing to do for me to go with him: a) to show solidarity with a fallen comrade, and b) because I didn't know the way back on my own and didn't have a key either.

But I didn't want to leave yet.

'Just have a lie down, mate. You will feel better for it later,' I told him.

He immediately understood the situation and didn't want to ruin my chances so he allowed Marta to lead him to her bedroom. Marta and I then picked up the pace and began the age-old dance – not literally a dance – I like to call the Mutual Appreciation Waltz. I looked into her eyes, she looked into mine, she rubbed my leg with her foot, I rubbed hers with mine, all the time gradually moving our faces closer together as we spoke. I was still afraid to make a move, though, not least of all as a result of the slaughtering I had seen Carlos take just a little while before.

'You have a beautiful face,' she said, running her fingers down my cheek.

I had to reply with something profound.

'Thanks.'

Half an hour after leaving us, Carlos returned to the kitchen with his hair even messier than usual, complaining that it was too cold in Marta's room. He joined us at the table, rolled a spliff, smoked it, and then said he really had to be leaving. It was after 6 and I knew I was close now to the finish line. Marta looked at me.

'Will you stay?' she asked.

'Mate, I will see you back at the flat later on. I think I am just going to kip down here, I'm too tired to walk anywhere now,' I told Carlos.

He smiled knowingly and left. As soon as the door was shut, I reached out to touch Marta's face, moved closer and we kissed. It had only taken 9 hours. All talking now ceased as we moved to the bedroom. Marta had the softest skin I'd ever felt. Soon we had reached the part where my hand was struggling to unbutton her jeans without ruining the flow. As I did so, Marta reached down, took my hand and moved it away from that part of her body.

'We can't,' she said. 'I want you to stay. But we just can't do that, not now anyway.'

Time of the month. Of course. I didn't see that there was much point in me hanging around any longer.

'That's pretty bad luck that of all the times in the month we could have met, it had to be at the wrong time. Well, let's just try to fall asleep. Or I could just go back and sleep at the flat,' I said, through the agonising pain of aching balls.

'What? You think that we can't do it because of that? No, it's not that. Do you promise not to be disgusted?'

I didn't like the sound of this. My head filled with images of genital warts. Then a penis popped into my mind. No, she didn't have a penis; I would have felt it already. Genital warts, though. Eurgh!

'Okay, I won't be disgusted,' I lied.

A kind of sick curiosity came over me.

'It's just that I wasn't expecting to end up in bed with anyone during my time here in Barcelona. So I haven't shaved my legs for a little while. It's horrible. I'm so sorry. I will shave them later today and we can have a good night tonight. I feel so ashamed. Do you understand?'

I laughed my relief.

'I don't care about a bit of hair. Have you seen mine?'

'I wouldn't feel comfortable. Plus, I don't have any condoms. Do you?'

I did, but not with me; they were back in my bag at Carlos' flat. If I was going to see this through to completion, I was going to have to return later on and spend another night with her. It's not that I was against the idea of spending time with Marta; it was just that I knew there was soon to be a big cake made of Cannabis sitting in Carlos' kitchen. I wanted to have my cake and eat it too.

I stayed awake with Marta for a couple more hours, kissing and rolling around. I was sure that she would soon cave in and let me get her naked, but she turned out to be more stubborn than that. What I did get was an even more excruciating ache in my nuts. I don't recommend to anyone reading this ever sustaining an erection for five hours straight. Pun intended. At one point I put my hand up Marta's jean leg to find out just how hairy she had let herself get. The answer: Not very hairy! It was a tiny bit of stubble, less than was on my face, hardly even noticeable. At 11am there was a lull in our playful games and I managed to close my eyes for long enough to fall asleep. It only lasted an hour, as I awoke to find a still turned-on Polish girl straddling my aching area and kissing me wetly on the lips. A further hour of agony ensued as we got back down to rolling around, kissing and cuddling. The problem was that I now physically needed to, um, how can I put it? Empty myself. It wasn't a lust thing, it was physically necessary to take away the severe pain I was in.

'I have to go,' I said. 'I'll go back to the flat, have a shower and pick up some protection. In that time, you can shower, shave your legs and do whatever else you need to do.'

'I will come with you. I have to get a present for Magda, it's her birthday today. I'll go to the shop while you're in the flat, and then meet you at the Metro station and we'll come back together.'

What would usually have been a five-minute walk to the local station took a good 20 minutes as I was forced to crawl rather than walk. I cried like a baby as I attempted the steep stairs down to the Metro. Marta, rather annoyingly, found the whole scene hilarious. We got to Jaume I Metro station and arranged to meet there again an hour later. I crawled down the road to the flat and found Carlos in the kitchen making the cake. I wasn't sure what sort of mood he would be in, but I should have known that he was never anything but relaxed, happy and blissfully stoned. He laughed as he said, 'What the fuck happened, man? How many hours did I waste sitting in that freezing cold kitchen? And then the bedroom. Man, it was the coldest room I've ever been in. I thought there was a ghost in there with me.'

I laughed so much at this that my balls felt like they would explode. This was no time for joking around; I had pressing matters to take care of. A half-hour long cold shower did the trick. I took care of my needs. Feeling invigorated, I picked up a few Jonnies and made my way back to meet Marta. Back at her flat, an angry-looking Magda was standing in the kitchen as we walked in. I offered a quick hello, got a curt one back and then was left standing in the corner as the two girls went into another room to have a little Slavic argument. I left them to it and started boiling some water to cook up the spaghetti that Marta had bought on the way over. As I sat down to eat, the argument moved into the kitchen. It was pretty heated and I didn't want to make things worse by saying anything. Also, I was pretty hungry and didn't want to have my plate of food taken from me and thrown at the wall by a rage-filled Pole. I wasn't able to stay out of the firing line for long, though.

'We are arguing about you,' Magda informed me.

'Why? There's plenty of me to go around. I can come to your room after I've finished with Marta if you like.'

I felt that humour might break the atmosphere a bit.

'Wow, you are so modest!' she said, but at least she was laughing as she disappeared to her room.

The Krissy Magic had calmed yet another confrontational situation. Why I have yet to be invited to the Middle East to sort things out for them over there, I really do not know.

'Apparently, I am a bad person for cheating on the boyfriend that I don't love anymore,' Marta filled me in. 'Later on this evening I have to go to a Polish Cultural Evening with her to make up for our falling out. It is her birthday, after all.'

'That sounds fair,' I said.

This was the best news I could have hoped for. It meant that I wouldn't have to hang around late into the evening, and could instead go and enjoy some of the cake.

'Oh. I thought you would at least try and persuade me to stay here with you,' she then said, with a look of disappointment on her face.

I will never learn.

'No, no. I'm not a selfish bastard. You need to be with your best friend. I completely understand. It's her birthday!'

I finished my spaghetti and was taken by the hand and led to the bedroom. Until this point I had forgotten how tired I was, but as soon as I lay down on the bed I was suddenly overpowered by heavy eyelids. Marta disappeared to the bathroom and I fell asleep. She returned 20 minutes later and resorted to her tried and tested method of waking me: wet kisses to the lips. I opened my eyes, pulled her off of me and into the space by my side, and went back to sleep. The relief I had given myself earlier in the shower probably hadn't been as perfect a preparation as I'd thought it would be at the time. I'd lost my mojo, baby, yea! I woke a few hours later at 7:30pm after she put the radio on; loud. It wasn't very subtle but I didn't care as I was now battle-ready. Once again I will spare you the details, but let's just say I got the job done. Twice. I know what you're thinking: 'Twice? What a stud!'

And you would be right.

I stood up and searched the floor for my discarded clothes.

'There's no need for that,' Marta piped up. 'Magda left about an hour ago. We are alone for the evening.'

This wasn't good. I was in that post-fun period where all I wanted was some personal space and time to reflect. I put forward my argument that she really needed to go and find Magda at the Polish evening as their friendship depended on it. I didn't want to be the reason they fell out.

'No, it's okay, really. I want to spend the night with you,' she said.

This was getting serious.

'Go and spend the evening with Magda. I'll leave now and come back later tonight.'

'No. It's too late now. Don't you want to be with me?'

'Of course I do!'

I faked a 'don't be silly' smile and slid myself up to her naked body. I tried to relax but something was stopping me. I didn't want to be kissed, cuddled or even touched. I wondered what fun I was missing back at the flat. The cake! I jumped back up and started dressing.

'I feel bad about Carlos and his flatmates. I should really spend some time with them. I don't want them to think I am just treating their place like a hotel. I will sit down and eat dinner with them, then come back in a couple of hours.'

'Are you sure this isn't just an excuse for you to leave?'

'Of course it isn't. Why would I want to leave? I feel great with you.'

I kissed her one last time and closed the bedroom door behind me. I know this was a bastard move, but come on; after a football match you don't hang around watching the groundsman water the pitch, do you? Entertainment over: go home.

I made it back to Carlos' place at about 9:30. The cake was

just being put into the oven to bake, so I had another long shower. It was midnight when the finished article was cut into slices and handed out to the five of us who had been waiting so patiently for such a long time. It was worth the wait; it was gorgeous. As soon as I had finished my slice I was ready for a lie down. I'm not sure if this had anything to do with the ingredients or if I was just dead on my feet from the previous 36 hours. Either way, I disappeared into Carlos' room and threw myself down onto my mattress. I awoke four hours later and got up to go to the toilet. What I failed to think about was the potential scenario I would find in the living room. I also forgot to put any clothes on, making my way from the bedroom in nothing more than a white vest and a pair of boxers. Sleepily, I pushed open the door to the living room and in a zombified state made my way towards the bathroom. I was stopped in my tracks by the sight of four hippies, all sat round a settee, all with bright red eyes, doubled over, pissing themselves laughing at the sight of me in my underwear. I looked at them and then down at myself and I wondered who the more ridiculous sight really was; me, a half asleep hairy man in a vest and pants; or four fully-grown men, sat up 'til 4 in the morning, giggling like a gaggle of schoolgirls. I reasoned it was probably me. I went to the toilet, did the walk of shame back to the bedroom, then got back down onto the mattress where I waited a good few minutes for the laughter to die down in the other room and for it to be peaceful again. Stoners; what can you do?

The next few days in Barcelona were pretty uneventful. I did the touristy walks, took the photos, hung out in the flat with the guys and went to a party in a nightclub at which Celia was DJ-ing. When it was time for me to leave, I did so with a newly acquired fondness for Catalonia's principal city; it was a place in which I could quite happily have spent more time. Still, I had to be moving on, and as Celia had arranged my accommodation in Spain's capital, I had no valid excuse to prolong my stay. Celia walked me to one of the cities train stations shortly before 2 in the afternoon.

An interesting aspect of train travel in Spain is that since the terrorist bombing of a passenger train in Madrid in 2004 you are not allowed to enter the platform of any of the main stations without first having your entire luggage x-rayed, just like at the airport. I hadn't been aware of this little detail and so found myself standing impatiently in the queue, knowing that my train was leaving in just a few minutes. I really didn't want to miss it and spend another two hours in Barcelona, as it decreased my chances of making it to Madrid at all that day. I got through with a couple of minutes to spare and Celia accompanied me to platform number 9. Assembled at the front of the platform were a group of railway employees, sat at a table, checking the ticket of every passenger before allowing him or her to pass on to the train. Celia was quick off the mark and immediately started explaining to them in Spanish that I was a friend and that I'd had my wallet stolen the previous night out on Las Ramblas, the main tourist street in the city centre. My parents were ex-pats living down in the south of the country and were going to drive by car all the way to Madrid to meet me at the station and to pay for my ticket on arrival as they would be arriving in the city at about the same time as me. These people were nobody's fools, however, and told Celia that I would have to go to the police inside the station to have them call my parents to confirm my story. I watched as a man in a hat, further down the platform, put his whistle to his lips and sent my train on its way without me. I gave up the ghost and trudged back to the terminal where I parted ways with Celia as she had to get to work. I was now left without a friend and interpreter.

As I sat on the station's bench with my head in my hands, I became aware of some movement. I watched intently as the ticket inspectors from the platform carried their little table through a Staff Only door, leaving the platform unguarded. *So, they only take up their positions shortly before the train is due to depart, do they?* I rubbed my hands together, did an evil little cackle and uttered the word: 'Eeeeeeeeexcellent.' All I had to do was walk all the way to the very end of the platform, out of sight of the terminal, and hide behind one of the station's support pillars for a couple of hours. And so that's what I did. It wasn't the most comfortable couple of hours, standing leant against a piece of metal, constantly aware that if any bit of myself or my belongings were to stick out from the sides it would lead to me getting chucked off of the premises at the very least, or having to answer to the local constabulary as a probable worst-case scenario. Fortunately, I have the hiding skills of a really good hider.

Author's Notes: I really tried to come up with something a bit better there than 'really good hider'. I wanted to use an example, you know, of a really good hider. But none of my efforts pleased me as much as 'really good hider'. It just seemed funnier, although my comedic judgement has often left much to be desired, so just in case I got it wrong I have added a few alternate endings, like you get in the 'extras' part of a DVD.

Alternate ending Numero Uno: I have the hiding skills of Salman Rushdie.

Alternate ending Numero Dos: I have the hiding skills of Wally.

Alternate ending Numero Tres: I have the hiding skills of Elvis. He's not really dead, you know?

And finally, alternate ending Numero Cuatro: I have the hiding skills of Anne Frank.

I am aware that that last one was borderline risky. But I will bet a fiver with any of you that you weren't expecting to see it in the list. *

** That last statement is not legally binding.*

A few minutes before 4pm I spied my train approaching through the haze of heat that was in the air. As it got nearer, I patted myself on the back for a job well done; I had outsmarted the authorities. Why did they even bother? They couldn't beat me. I was clever. I had hidden at the end of platform 9 for almost two hours and evaded all monitors, but now I could enjoy the fruit of my labour and how sweet it was going to taste; for there was my train, sitting invitingly… on platform number 6.

Shit! How did this happen? My plan was fool proof. Not to worry, this can still be saved. Think sharpish. I was far enough down the platform to be able to nip across the tracks without being spotted as long as I moved quickly and stealth-like. Or at least just quickly. I crouched down and then took off, sprinting across tracks 9, 8 and 7 before jumping up onto the beautiful number 6. Then horror set in as I realised that everyone sitting in the end carriage of my train had just watched me audition for a part in the remake of *The Great Escape*. Surely someone would stitch me up. I wasn't going to hang around to find out. I walked briskly up the platform right past that end carriage of witnesses, nodding my greeting to a few of them on the way as if I did this sort of thing every day, and clambered up the steps and into the next carriage along. I wiped my brow of sweat and stood waiting for a guard to come and escort me off of the train and out of the station. He took his time. Then the beeping sounded and the automatic doors closed and locked shut. The guard wasn't coming and the train was moving. I was on my way to Madrid.

At 4:12 we pulled into the next station, Barcelona Sants, and I noticed something very interesting through the window: To get to the train, passengers had to pass through the same kind of walkway that takes you from the terminal of an airport on to the plane. Just like at the airport, there was a lady standing at the end of that walkway checking every single ticket before letting anyone through. If this was happening at every station we stopped at, I thought to myself, then surely there would be no need to employ anyone to walk up and down the train checking tickets; what would be the point? We sat at that station for 18 minutes, although it seemed more like 18 hours as I was continuously expecting someone to come and grab me by the scruff of the neck, especially after I was kicked out of the seat I was sitting in by a well-dressed lady who had reserved it. I got up and found an empty one to put my bum on, but made sure not to get too comfortable just in case someone had booked that one, too. My nerves weren't done any favours by a man in a large trench coat and a Gomez Adams moustache who spent the entire 18 minutes pacing up and down my carriage. *Fucking sit down and relax, you're making me tense!* At 4:30 we finally pulled out of the station and I sat back in my chair. This train wasn't like any train I had been on before; it had the look and feel of the interior of an aeroplane, and not a crappy Ryanair one, either. I'm talking British Airways. A glamorous stewardess even made her way up the carriage handing out free newspapers, packets of dried fruit, cartons of freshly squeezed orange juice and headphones that could be stuck into the back of the seat in front for listening to the radio. At the front of the carriage there was a TV mounted high on the wall that played a DVD that could also be listened to through the headphones.

Just before 5 the unthinkable happened: I was dropping off to sleep when there was a tap on my shoulder. I looked up to see an inspector frowning at me, asking to see my ticket. I was just about to start explaining about my parents waiting for me in Madrid when he cut me short by signalling for me to stand up and follow him. I did so without question; I knew my time was up. He led me through the carriage and into the next one – a less luxurious one – took me to an empty seat and then pointed for me to sit down. I did as I was told, even if I did think it strange that he was going to bollock me right there in front of all the other passengers. Then he muttered something that included the word 'Primera' and left me alone. As he passed through the door and out of sight, I took a look around my new surroundings to try and work out what had just happened. The people around me didn't look anywhere near as classy as they had in the other carriage. They looked more like Ryanair passengers. And why wasn't there a telly up on the wall? And where was the pretty girl handing out freebies? And what had the inspector been waffling on about? Primera? Aha … I had only been sitting in First Class. What a stroke of luck. I hadn't got into trouble for not having a ticket; I'd just got into trouble for not having a First Class ticket. My feeling of joy quickly turned to one of offence as I questioned why I had been singled out for special treatment. No one else around me had been asked to show a ticket. What made me look any less likely to be travelling First Class than anyone else? I could have been travelling first class! I consoled myself with a packet of dried apricots that I had managed to smuggle out with me and plugged my free earphones into the seat in front. At least there was still radio in this class. My fellow Cattle Classers eyed me enviously as I savoured the little bag of nutritious goodness. I had experienced how the other half lived for almost an hour back there; these guys hadn't. Probably ever. And they probably never would, either.

The journey towards Spain's capital took us first Southward along the country's eastern coastline. The blue water of the Mediterranean glistened to my left as it washed in and out onto the golden beach. At 6 we arrived at our next station, Lleida Pirineus. No inspector came along. At 6:55 we arrived at the next stop, Zaragoza. No inspector came along. I knew now that I was only two stops away from making it to Madrid. I closed my eyes and flicked through the three available radio stations; one that played Spanish pop, one that played classical music and one that played kind of native South American stuff with wind pipes and strange chanting, I guessed from Peru or Bolivia. It was definitely my station of choice and I quickly became a fan. I had been listening to it for about an hour, drifting in and out of sleep, questioning again the logic behind this ridiculous and stupid challenge I found myself on, thinking about all my vices that I could be indulging in if I were back at home with my mates – the poker, the drinking, the betting, the drugs – when something strange happened. And this really did happen, I didn't just dream it. At least, I don't think I did. The indigenous music faded out and was replaced by the English lyrics of Bob Dylan:

'I'm a rambler, I'm a gambler, I'm a long way from home. And if you don't like me, just leave me alone.'

The song had been put on for me; there was no doubt about it! I looked around at my fellow passengers to see if anyone had noticed that the music had changed so dramatically, but everyone looked normal and content. I wondered if this was because the song hadn't come through their headphones and was indeed something supernatural, or if it was just the case that no one else on the carriage had chosen radio station number 3. I decided the latter was more likely. I was still trying to work out what was going on, when just like that Dylan's voice disappeared and was replaced by the original pan-pipe selection. I spent the rest of the journey to Madrid feeling invigorated and to this day I can't explain why.

At 8:25pm we pulled into the penultimate stop, Guadalajara. Not the Mexican city; that would have been supernatural. A quick look at my atlas told me I was now almost in Madrid. At 8:55pm my train stopped for the last time and I ticked another capital off of my list.

Stood up by Eidur Gudjohnsen; who does he think he is?!

Welcome to Madrid.

26. Madrid

Capitals left to visit: Amsterdam, Athens, Brussels, Helsinki, Lisbon, Luxembourg, Paris, Prague, Riga, Tallinn, Vilnius

Days on the road: 95
Distance travelled: 6297 miles
EU capitals visited: 12

I FOUND DIEGO's flat directly opposite the station and was just about to press the buzzer to the four-storey building when a strange looking man with long brown hair and a handlebar moustache, carrying a brown paper bag filled with cans of beer, stopped me in my tracks.

'Kris?'

'Diego?'

'Ah, hola amigo. I am glad you made it safely.'

And then he hugged me tightly. He hadn't confirmed that he was indeed Diego, and just like in Warsaw I wondered whether I'd bumped into a mystic.

'I am Diego, welcome to my home,' he said, opening the door.

I was a bit disappointed then that he wasn't a mystic. My trip around Europe had yet to produce an encounter with a mystic of any kind, not least the kind with a handlebar moustache. Diego's flat was on the third floor and opened into a long, unlit corridor. I was ushered into a chair at the small kitchen table and a bottle of Russian beer was poured into a glass and passed my way. Diego sat opposite, opened a beer for himself and began rolling a spliff.

'I smoke too much hash,' he began explaining, 'but it isn't a big problem, because I work from home. So I have no boss to fire me for sleeping through the afternoon.'

He laughed. I laughed too, out of politeness. I couldn't work my host out. To go with his long hair and handlebar moustache, he wore a World War 2 Russian Army coat.

'I bought this coat yesterday,' he told me, as if in the psychic knowledge that I would be writing about his clothing style at some point in the future, 'but I want to change these.'

He pointed to the buttons; each one carrying the Soviet Star.

'This is just as fascist a symbol as the swastika. But I do like the coat.'

Diego was an eccentric. He worked as a freelance artist for some of Spain's largest publications, mostly of the satirical kind. He worked to strict deadlines, slept late in the mornings and then worked late into the night, and produced everything from a couple of computers in his bedroom. Now in his late twenties, he had met and befriended Celia at university. He passed me the lit spliff just as a new face joined us in the kitchen. Alex was in his mid-thirties and was Diego's flatmate. Smartly dressed and clean cut, he had a job in the city. The three of us sat around the table late into the night, smoking and discussing some of life's important issues; such as Monty Python. Both of my new Spanish friends were big fans of the legendary British comedy troupe and to prove it they acted out a few of their favourite scenes in the kitchen. I then suggested it was as good a time as any to take a group photo.

'Wait here, I have to get something,' Diego said, as he stood up and walked out of the kitchen. When I say 'walked' I don't mean in the conventional sense.

'Welcome to the Ministry of Silly Walks,' he said, laughing, as he recreated his favourite Monty Python sketch of all time. He returned a couple of minutes later, still in Silly Walk mode, clutching three different World War 2 military hats.

My bedroom was at the far end of the corridor and was occupied by a cat. I am allergic to cats and also, embarrassingly, quite afraid of them. Cats can smell my fear; a fear that I can't smell because my nose is blocked up due to the allergies.

'Ah yes, I forgot to tell you, the cat thinks of this bedroom as her own,' Alex explained. 'You don't mind her being in here, do you?'

'I'm allergic, but if there's nowhere else for her to go then I'll just have to put up with it,' I said, hoping that there was somewhere else for her to go.

'No problem. Just put her outside the door when you are ready to sleep. She will go to the kitchen balcony.'

I prepared myself for slumber and then knelt down to gently pick the cat up from under the bed and gently put her outside the door. The cat had other ideas. The cat was unfamiliar with the word 'gently.' She hissed and swiped at me, catching my arm with a sharp claw. This cat could definitely smell my fear.

'Here pussy, pussy, pussy,' I said, gently.

The cat swiped at me again. She didn't speak English, and I didn't know the Spanish for 'pussy.' I wrapped a towel around each arm and went in again. This time not as gently. There was a screech, another swipe and lightning fast movement as the cat ran from under the bed to inside an open wardrobe. With her back to the wall and staring out at me from inside the wardrobe the cat was laying down a challenge. A challenge that I was not up for. So I resorted to grovelling.

'Come on, cat. Please. Just leave. You can have your room back in a couple of days. Look, I'm already sneezing and my eyes are red raw and itching.'

I sneezed and rubbed my eyes to emphasise my point. The cat only grinned, like her great-great-uncle from Cheshire had done many times in the past.

'Cat, seriously, this isn't funny. I need to get some sleep. Get out!'

And then a tense stand-off ensued, with neither one of us blinking; apart from when I was sneezing, but that was involuntary. Try sneezing without blinking; it can't be done. Unless you have no eyelids. Ten minutes later I had psyched myself up enough for a fight. I swooped. The cat jumped through my arms and returned to her original territory under the bed. I was losing. I lifted up the bed. The cat returned to the wardrobe. I retreated to the kitchen to rethink my strategy, tripping up along the way over the cat's bowl of food. The light bulb above my head switched on. Metaphorically. And then physically, as I switched on the kitchen light to pick up a small handful of biscuits from the bowl on the floor. I returned to the bedroom a confident man. The cat could now smell more than just my fear; she could smell biscuits, and the expression on her face changed to one of interest.

'What's in it for me?' she asked.

'Fetch!'

I threw the biscuits through the door and into the corridor. And then shut the door behind the cat. I had won. And after half an hour of constant scratching on the woodwork, the cat gave up the ghost and went away. I punched the air in triumph and went to sleep.

I checked the time on my phone, it was 9am and I had slept well. The flat was silent, meaning I could squeeze in a couple more hours kip, but first I needed a wee. I got up and turned the handle of the door. Nothing happened. I tried it again. Still nothing happened. The door was broken. I banged on it. Nobody came to my rescue. Then I remembered Diego proudly telling me how he was able to sleep late every morning. And Alex would already have left for work. I called Diego's mobile. He didn't answer. Desperate times called for desperate measures, so I dug deep into my bag and found the bottle of water that I had filled up in Barcelona. I emptied it off of the balcony – just missing the heads of the people below my window waiting for the bus – and then did what I needed to do before going back to sleep. I woke again at midday and this time Diego answered his mobile and came to let me out.

'All of the doors in this flat are dodgy,' he told me, laughing. 'Look,' he then said, leading me into his bedroom where he pulled a pot from under his bed. 'For when I can't get out of my room and I need to pee.'

Diego was a man who thought like me. Still, I didn't mention what I had done.

I received an email from Diana, a Romanian girl living in Lisbon who had read about me in the Romanian newspaper *La Cotidianul* after they had written a story about the positive words I had written about their country on my blog. She left her phone number and told me that she would like to meet me and treat me to dinner once I arrived in Portugal's capital. At the same time, I received a new donation on my sponsorship page from a guy called Radu, who signed it off with the words: 'Just another friend in Romania'. I loved the Romanians. Great people. I also loved the Spaniards. Even more so when Diego and Alex offered to buy me a train ticket to the town of Caceres in the far west of the country, close to the border with Portugal. They suggested it would be wise to bed down there for a night before attempting to make it to Lisbon, so as to break up a long journey. I quickly found a Couchsurfer willing to host me in Caceres. Things were looking good, for the next couple of days at least.

The train journey west took just under four hours and I arrived at 11pm.

Welcome to Caceres.

27. Caceres

MY ARRANGED HOST Marina was stood waiting for me on the platform, next to a short bloke with designer stubble and wearing sunglasses. Yes, I did say it was 11pm. Marina looked to be in her early-to-mid-thirties, had olive skin, brown eyes and looked like Penelope Cruz. I kissed her on both cheeks before turning to shake the hand of the man. My hand was ignored, though, as he grabbed me round the shoulders and planted a wet one on each cheek. I'm not big on that sort of thing, but this was a continental man and I was on the continent. When in Rome. Or Caceres.

I followed the two of them out of the station and into a parked car, as they told me that we were going for something to eat and a few beers. Listening to the sunglasses-wearing man speaking, I was surprised to hear his accent wasn't as Spanish as Marina's. Instead, it was exactly as Spanish as Bob Geldof's. The man who preferred to kiss me in greeting rather than shake my hand was 100 per cent Irish. Derek had been living in Spain for the past 15 years, working as a painter. Not the Michelangelo kind, but rather the Handy Andy kind. He decorated people's houses. We parked the car in the centre and walked the cobblestones of the medieval town to a small family-run restaurant. The place was empty but for a couple sitting quietly in the corner and, as we entered, a fat man in a suit rose from a chair at the back and came to greet us, kissing Marina, shaking Derek's hand and then welcoming me in English to his establishment. Why did this man get a handshake from Derek while I got a couple of kisses? After making ourselves comfortable at a table, three beers were ordered along with a plate of cheese. Five minutes later my glass was empty. Thirty seconds later I had another full one in front of me. We quickly demolished the cheese and then Derek told me that for dinner we would be having a local speciality, although I wasn't told what it was to be. The couple in the corner left and we were now alone in the place, ordering dinner just past midnight. The waiter brought over the plate and I couldn't help but salivate when I set my eyes on the food in front of me: some kind of juicy looking meat in a thick gravy, surrounded by roast potatoes and crusty bread. I was also given a third beer, replacing my empty glass. I asked Marina what the meat was but was told to try it first. Without waiting for a second invitation I grabbed a chunk of it and put it onto my plate. It was mostly bone.

'Just bite off the flesh where you see it,' Marina instructed me.

The flavour was strong and not one I recognised. It was definitely something that I would eat again though.

'It's bull's tail. Good, isn't it?'

Marina looked proud of her local offering. She had every reason to be. The three of us then feasted on the meat, mopping up every last drop of gravy with the bread. The waiter came and took away the empty plates, before standing impatiently with his colleagues at the bar watching us, wanting us to leave to let them close up for the night. Their wish was our command.

Caceres is jaw-droppingly beautiful. People have been living in the town since about 25,000 BC and every generation has left its mark. The first city walls, built by the Romans in the 3rd or 4th century, are still visible around the old town, including a gateway, the Arco del Cristo. My two hosts filled the silence of the walk with random bits of information about the town.

'There are four main areas of the city: the historic quarter, the Jewish quarter, the modern centre and the outskirts,' explained Derek.

'Caceres was occupied by the Romans, the Arabs, and the Visigoths. We also had an important Jewish community but

Queen Isabella and Ferdinand of Aragon expelled them in 1492. We have a fascinating history here,' continued Marina, proudly.

I tried to digest the information I was being fed whilst taking in the sights around me that included a castle, a palace, some ancient churches and fortifications. It was a perfect evening for a stroll, with temperatures up around 12 degrees Celsius and not a breeze in the air. We came to a large disco pub, found a large cushioned settee inside, made ourselves comfy with a few more beers and got to chatting. Both of my new friends, I found out, were 39 years old. Neither of them looked it. The conversation between Derek and I centred on how neither of us missed one bit the drunken fight culture of Friday and Saturday nights in Ireland and England. As Derek spoke, I noticed he had a couple of annoying traits. He repeated himself, retelling stories over and over again, leaving a space of about three minutes between each telling. The story of his mate Superfly, an American from Detroit who came over every summer for the WOMAD festival and always pulled the hottest women; the story of his brother Brian, an Arsenal fan from Dublin; the story of another American friend who came to Caceres a few years before for a party, met and fell in love with a local girl and then married her in Vegas. All stories that were enjoyable the first time, bearable the second, and cringe-worthy the seventh. Still, being the polite guest that I am, I reacted to each retelling as if I were hearing it for the first time. Derek's second little annoying habit was to say, 'this, that, and the other,' in his thick Dublin accent, at the end of the every sentence.

'So, my brother Brian's an Arsenal fan. He lives in Dublin; this, that and the other. Superfly will be coming over again in a couple of months for a bit of partying; this, that and the other. Can you believe that guy got married in Vegas? Now they're settled down, you know, this, that and the other.'

Despite all of this, I would be doing him a disservice if I didn't make clear that he was a loveable character.

We got back to the flat at about 3:15 in the morning, as Marina reckoned she hadn't drunk that much and was more than capable of driving us safely. The flat was that of a well-off resident: two floors, comfortable yet not over-the-top, leather settees, a large screen telly, huge speakers mounted on the walls, and a big space in the middle of the room. I lounged back into one of the seats as Marina stood up to make her way to the kitchen.

'One last beer each?' she asked.

'No, not for me, thanks. I'll just have a glass of water, please,' replied Derek.

'What? Seriously?' asked Marina, surprised.

'Yea, I've had enough for tonight. Thanks anyway.'

'Oh, okay.'

She made her way to the kitchen to get me a beer and Derek a glass of water.

'Marina, how fucking long have you known me? When have I ever taken a water instead of a beer?'

Derek was cracking up with laughter. It was infectious. Tears began streaming down cheeks as we giggled. It was all the funnier because of how convincing an act it had been. It made me seriously question if the repeating of stories was also just Derek entertaining himself, seeing how long I could go before I cracked. Marina went up to bed, leaving me to listen to some more of Derek's stories. The story of his mate Superfly, an American from Detroit who came over every summer for the WOMAD festival and always pulled the hottest women; the story of his brother Brian, an Arsenal fan from Dublin; the story of another American friend who came to Caceres a few years before for a party, met and fell in love with a local girl and then married her in Vegas. This, that and the other.

Just before calling it a night, I decided to probe a bit and find out what the situation was with my two hosts. Were they more than just friends? Derek explained that they were an ex-couple who had managed to keep a close relationship. He didn't live there in the flat but had his own place just down the road. Still, after showing me to my room, he disappeared into her bedroom for the night. Lucky so and so. This, that and the other.

I woke the next day at midday to find an empty flat. I showered and then found a note on the kitchen table telling me that the two of them had gone to paint the walls in Marina's office. The balcony doors were open and the bright sun shone in. Standing out on the balcony I noticed the block had its own swimming pool. On the next balcony along, a shirtless old man tended to his plants and vegetables. In February! I grabbed a pair of sunglasses from deep within my rucksack and headed out to explore my surroundings. In a pair of shorts and a t-shirt. In February! The main street outside the building was lined with palm trees. Just down the road was the town's bull fighting arena. Behind that was a path so long that the end couldn't be seen, leading away from the road and civilization and into a mystery. Curiosity compelled me to follow it, and after 15 minutes of walking I found myself in a beautifully peaceful countryside setting. In the middle of the nothingness sat a delicate, little old church; the kind you would see on an early 20th century watercolour postcard. Carrying on the walk beyond the church I came to open fields home to grazing sheep and relaxing horses, where an old peasant dozed against a pile of hay, flat cap down over his eyes. As I lay on the grass, enjoying the sun, I received a text from Marina, which read: 'There's a train to Lisbon leaving tonight at 3am. Shall we book it for you?'

I didn't know what to make of this. I didn't like the idea of leaving at such an hour. Surely there were morning trains running the following day. But clearly my hosts didn't want to put me up for another night. Had I done something to offend them? I was confused. I contemplated replying, letting them know that I would rather wait until the next day, but then changed my mind at the last moment. If they wanted me to leave, then fair enough, especially if they were going to be kind enough to buy me a ticket out of there. I didn't want to take liberties.

'If you are sure you don't mind, yes please. I appreciate it greatly,' I sent back.

She replied, letting me know the two of them would be home for lunch between 2:30 and 3 and would like to eat with me. I retraced my steps back along the seemingly infinite path and then headed down towards the centre of the town. Beautiful women sitting out on bar terraces, enjoying drinks in the sunshine with short men, lined the narrow streets. Old ladies walked around in pairs, smiling and talking. A little boy played football with his dad in a small square. Street market-stall vendors weighed bags of mushrooms and oranges before handing them to their customers with a smile. Despite the heat, the majority of the locals wore coats. If this was cold for them, I didn't want to be stuck here midsummer.

I got back to the flat at 3pm and was told to help myself to a cold beer from the fridge before joining the two of them out on the balcony. Derek told me that the information they had given me about the 3am train had turned out to be false. There were railway works being done and no Portugal-bound trains were passing through Caceres. This, that and the other. There was, however, a bus leaving the border town of Badajoz bound for Lisbon at 2am.

'It's about an hour away, but we will drive you there and buy your ticket for you; this, that and the other,' Derek told me.

Marina then explained that her sister was paying her a previously unplanned visit from Madrid later that evening, hence there not being a bedroom available for me. They felt bad about leaving me in the predicament, so wanted to do everything they could to help me get to Lisbon. All talk of travel then ceased as we tucked into a gorgeously roasted chicken, rosemary coated potatoes, and more cold beer. What a beautiful summer's afternoon. In February!

Looking down at the empty plates in front of us, I realised that I hadn't arranged anywhere to stay in Portugal's capital. It was already 4:30 in the afternoon and Marina wanted to leave at 6:30 to be back in Caceres by 9 for the arrival of her sister. I sent quick emails to Diana the Romanian and also Caterina, a Couchsurfer in the city that had said she might be able to put me up, informing them both of my very early arrival and asking either of them to send me a text if able to accommodate me at such short notice. I packed up my belongings before leaving, but decided it would be wise to leave my winter coat behind as spring was clearly now upon us. I hadn't worn it since Slovenia, and carrying it around was only adding to the strain on my back.

We climbed into the car, ready to leave, when Derek suddenly jumped out again and ran back into the house saying he had forgotten something important. He returned a couple of minutes later with two bottles of beer, proclaiming, 'I get travel sick if I'm not drinking beer; this, that and the other.'

It was dead on 7 in the evening when we pulled out of the driveway and off towards the border town of Badajoz. The drive was stunning, as the most beautiful sunset I had ever witnessed materialised up ahead, turning the horizon the same shade of pink as a flamingo. As I let the majesty of the scenery around me sink in, I listened to Derek's stories about his mate Superfly who could get any woman; his mate from America who came to Caceres and married a local woman; his brother in Dublin the Arsenal fan; and this, that and the other. He also took the time to explain how he never drank water, only beer, and how he couldn't eat fruit because it made him feel sick, even though he loved it.

'I can eat it cooked,' he explained, 'just not raw. And if I do eat some, I need a beer to settle my stomach.'

I now seriously believed that Derek was on a permanent wind-up. Everything he said was hilarious. We got to Badajoz bus station at 8:30pm. Derek and Marina bought my ticket before rushing back to Caceres, leaving me with five and a half hours to kill before my bus departed. I still hadn't heard from either Diana or Caterina, so I sent them both text messages telling them that I would be arriving at 4:30am. My credit was running low, so I hoped that any reply wouldn't require further communication. Caterina was first to get back to me, telling me that she was going out for the night and wouldn't be able to wake up early to meet me and she wouldn't be out as late as 4:30 either. She would write back if she thought of a solution. I then got a call from Diana saying that her boyfriend would come to pick me up from Lisbon's bus station to take me back to theirs. I relaxed.

Badajoz bus station is a lonely place at night: a large hall with a few benches in the middle, surrounded by various ticket offices and shops all with their shutters down. About 10 or 15 migrant workers from South America sat around eating fruit, waiting for the 12:30am to Madrid. After it departed I was left with a scary looking Peruvian man who could have been in his 20's or his 50's – his short muscled body and withered face giving no indication – pacing up and down for hours on end, dropping to the floor every ten minutes or so to do 50 push-ups. I made a conscious effort not to stare too much at that guy. The bus station wasn't just lonely at night, it was also cold. I began to wonder if leaving my coat behind had been such a wise decision.

The final hour and a half of waiting was spent alone but for a security guard strolling around the hall whistling and farting loudly; each fart triggering childish sniggers from within me. 2am finally came and I handed my ticket to the driver: the all-whistling, all-farting security guard. I hoped the bus had air conditioning.

I was one of about four or five people on the darkened coach. I plugged my earphones into the socket in the chair in front and let the local radio send me to sleep. I woke at 3:30 as we pulled into a large bus station and everyone around me got off. I still had an hour until we reached Lisbon, so I closed my eyes and tried to dose back off. After a couple of minutes of not moving I opened my eyes to see if there was a problem. The driver was out of his seat and was walking up the aisle putting rubbish into a bag and farting loudly. I sniggered. He looked at me, growled something, farted and pointed to the door for me to get off.

'Lisboa?' I asked, puzzled.

'Si,' he said, before farting.

I sniggered again.

I wasn't convinced he was telling the truth, but had no choice other than to disembark. I found myself in a huge forecourt inhabited by gangs of youths stalking the area menacingly. Now I was sure I wasn't in Lisbon. Sleepily, I dragged my knuckles out of the station to the street, where a large clock on top of a building told me it was 2:30am.

How can it only be 2:30? I left Badajoz at 2, and that was definitely an hour and a half ago. And I'm not supposed to get to Lisbon until 4:30. What's going on?

Then I remembered that Portugal was in the same time zone as England; an hour behind the rest of continental Europe. The ticket saleswoman in Badajoz had, when telling Marina the arrival time, got her time difference calculations wrong. I was definitely in Lisbon; the large Casino Lisboa in front of the bus station gave that away. But I was two hours earlier than I had told my hosts to expect me. I ticked another capital off of my list and sat down on a cold wall.

Welcome to Lisbon.

North Cape
Jan Mayen
(Norway)
NORWEGIAN SEA
Scandinavia
Lapland
SWEDEN
FINLAND
NORWAY
Faroe Islands
(Denmark)
Shetland Islands
(UK)
Galdhopiggen
OSLO
STOCKHOLM
HELSINKI
TALLINN
ESTONIA
LATVIA
RIGA
SCOTLAND
NORTH
SEA
DENMARK
COPENHAGEN
British
Isles
UNITED
KINGDOM
IRELAND
DUBLIN
LITHUANIA
BALTIC SEA
BELARUS
MINSK
POLAND
WARSAW
NETHERLANDS
AMSTERDAM
BERLIN
GERMANY
ENGLAND
LONDON
CELTIC SEA
English Channel
BELGIUM
PARIS
PRAGUE
CZECH.REP.
SLOVAKIA
KIEV
FRANCE
VIENNA
AUSTRIA
BUDAPEST
HUNGARY
MOLDOVA
ROMANIA
Carpathian Mts.
SWITZ.
Massif
Central
Bay of
Biscay
CROATIA
BOSNIA & H
SERBIA
BUCHAREST
BULGARIA
SOFIA
ITALY
ROME
Pyrenees
MADRID
PORTUGAL
SPAIN
Sierra Morena
Corsica
Sardinia
MEDITERRANEAN SEA
ALGIERS
TUNIS
TUNISIA
ALGERIA
MOROCCO
RABAT
Casablanca
ALBANIA
GREECE
ATHENS
Peloponnesus
Anatolia
Strait of Gibraltar

28. Lisbon

Capitals left to visit: Amsterdam, Athens, Brussels, Helsinki, Luxembourg, Paris, Prague, Riga, Tallinn, Vilnius

Days on the road: 101
Distance travelled: 6685 miles
EU capitals visited: 13

I SENT A text to Diana letting her know I had arrived early and that her boyfriend would find me standing outside the large Vodafone building. It was freezing, a lot colder than it had been in Spain. I fished a jumper from the bottom of my backpack, put it on and then read Diana's reply letting me know that her boyfriend would be there to meet me at 5. I had over two hours to wait.

It was a Saturday night and had obviously been a heavy one in Portugal's capital, as the streets were filled with drunk, young girls, and their not-so-drunk boyfriends, who were always a lot older and holding the keys to their cars. Hypothermia was starting to set in, so I spent the next hour walking around the block repetitively.

Diana's boyfriend Ovidiu arrived at 5:15 and introduced himself. He was Romanian and looked like the long lost twin of Eric from *That 70's Show*. The city's Metro was closed for the night and wouldn't open again until 6:30, so we took the time to get to know each other. Ovidiu was the same age as me, came from Transylvania and had been the president of his university's branch of AIESEC. Those guys again. He was in Lisbon because his girlfriend Diana was serving an AIESEC apprenticeship in the city. I told him about my previous encounters with the organisation and he asked me what I made of the whole thing. I was honest, and was surprised to find him in agreement with my view that to the outsider it felt very much like a strange sect.

The journey to my hosts' flat took an hour and a half and comprised two separate Metro rides plus a stint on a bus. It was 8 when we arrived in the area of the city that the two Romanians called home and the sun had come up. Whilst in Spain, I had heard people talk about the vertically challenged Portuguese, but had assumed the stories had been exaggerated. Now I realised that it had been gospel. Nobody on the bus, on the Metro or on the street was taller than five foot. Walking the streets of Lisbon is like wandering around in a mystical land inhabited solely by hobbits. As we strolled the final part of the journey to the flat, I looked up in both disbelief and horror, as I saw something that I can only compare to video footage of the September 11th attacks on New York. A commercial jet plane flying so low that I was sure it had been hijacked and was on its way to an office meeting.

'You will soon get used to that,' Ovidiu said, noticing the stunned expression on my face.

The plane just missed the top of the buildings and carried on with its descent.

'The city centre of Lisbon is right on the flight path to the airport. We are in one of the only places in the world where the main international airport is slap bang in the middle of a capital city,' he continued.

The flat was silent and dark as we entered and, fortunately, Ovidiu was as keen as I was to get a few hours kip before undertaking any Sunday chores. I was shown to my own bedroom, as the previous tenant had moved out only a few days earlier, and shut the door behind me, not to be seen again until the afternoon. I woke to find Diana making brunch in the kitchen. Just like her other half, she was friendly, easy to talk to and made me feel at ease. I was disappointed when the couple informed me that someone was moving into the empty room the following day and that they wouldn't be able to put me up for a full night. Fortunately, Caterina let me know by text message that she was free to host and would meet me later that night at 11 in front of a famous statue. Before then I had plenty of time for a home cooked meal with my two new Romanian friends plus a guided tour of the harbour area of the city and a portion of the local delicacy, Pastéis de Belém, which is basically a custard tart with a fancy name.

Ovidiu and Diana accompanied me to my designated meeting point and stood and waited with me for my new host to show. At 11:10pm Caterina hadn't arrived, but I was told not to worry as it was Portuguese tradition to turn up fashionably late for everything. It was quarter to midnight when some doubt was finally cast on this explanation for Caterina's tardiness. After calling her number from Diana's phone and receiving no reply, the situation was starting to look a little worrying. We waited another 15 minutes before I finally received a text from my host-to-be telling me that something had come up and that she wouldn't be able to meet me after all.

'It's okay, you can stay at our place tonight. The room is still free until tomorrow. It will give you a chance to meet our flatmates,' Diana told me.

As we made our way back to the flat, I was filled in on the two other young people that shared the premises. Anthony was French but with a Portuguese dad, and had taken himself from Paris to Lisbon with the sole intention of working in restaurants and learning the language of his father. Saumya was Indian. He was in Lisbon serving an AIESEC apprenticeship, but the real reason he had come to the city, according to the Romanians, was, 'To discover women and lose his virginity. He is obsessed with the idea, although he's had no real life experience at all. He has been here eight months already, but only manages to scare girls.'

I was looking forward to meeting him and I didn't have to wait too long. As we walked through the door the two flatmates were standing in the hallway brushing their teeth. After the initial introductions, the usual questions were posed, before Saumya asked how I spelt my name. I told him, and on hearing that I use a K to spell Kris he said, 'Oh, like the Indian Superman, Krissh.'

'Yes, just like the Indian Superman, Krissh,' I nodded.

I had never heard of the Indian Superman, Krissh.

'I have the DVD in my room. I've watched it 25 times since I arrived in Portugal and another 45 times while still in India. I love it. Do you want to watch it with me tonight?'

I could hear Ovidiu and Diana trying and failing to hold back laughter in the kitchen, from where they could hear the conversation.

'Thanks for the offer, but it's been a long 24 hours,' I told him. 'I really need to get some sleep.'

'Okay, I understand. Maybe tomorrow then. Will you be here tomorrow evening? I would like to cook you some traditional food from my country.'

'That sounds lovely; thank you. Right, I really should be getting to bed now. Goodnight,' I said, edging towards the bedroom door.

'Wait. Do you have any condoms?'

Saumya's question wasn't what I had been expecting. It was, however, just the sort of question Diana and Ovidiu had been waiting for, as they now entered the room grinning.

'Um, I've got a couple. Why do you ask?' I feared his response.

'I just thought that on a trip like yours, you must sometimes find sex, right?'

'Define "find."'

'You know what I mean. Anyway, I have some spare ones, so I can give you some to take with you,' he told me, showing no sign that he was joking.

'OK... Thanks. Goodnight.'

I locked the bedroom door behind me.

The following morning I woke to an empty flat. On the floor outside my door was a box of condoms, with just two left inside, and a note from Saumya reading: 'These are for you. Also, please feel free to take the bananas and yogurt that are in the fridge if you get hungry.'

On checking my emails for the day I found one from Jason, my ex-football teammate, laying down a challenge. He wrote: 'Your mission, should you choose to accept it, is to swim in the freezing cold Atlantic, stark naked but for a handkerchief on your head. The swim must be photographed or filmed to provide evidence. If you succeed, I will make a new donation to Cancer Research UK.'

Jason had clearly forgotten that I had done a large part of my growing up in Brighton, a cold seaside resort. I could count on one hand the number of nights out between the ages of 15 and 20 that *hadn't* concluded with an early-hours dip in the English Channel. This was no challenge. This was recreation. Ovidiu arrived back at the flat soon after and together we headed out to catch the local train to the beach. Neither of my hosts owned a handkerchief – they weren't my nan, after all – instead, Ovidiu provided me with a substitute: a traditional Romanian hat called a clop, which sits on the crown of your head. We concluded that this would look sufficiently funny on top of a naked, hairy man.

The seaside resort town of Cascais took half an hour to get to by train. The beach was sandy, the sea was calm and the air temperature was, unlike in Spain, very cold. Skegness cold. Nobody was on the beach, but people, mostly pensioners, were walking up and down the promenade, wrapped up in thick coats and scarves, appropriately. Accompanied by designated cameraman Ovidiu, I made my way down on to the beach, where I took off all layers of clothing, applied the clop to the top of my head and waded out to sea, where I performed a couple of minutes of front crawl, much to the disapproval of the local populace, who stood open-mouthed, shaking their heads. Once I felt we had enough evidence, I hastily dried off with a towel, got dressed and made a quick escape before the local constabulary had time to turn up and nick me for public indecency. I can confirm that the Portuguese piece of Atlantic in February is warmer than the English Channel in mid-August. Just about. Jason kept his promise and made his donation later that evening after seeing the video and photos posted on the blog.

Diana and Saumya were both at the flat when we returned.

'Did you get the condoms?' Saumya asked immediately.

'Yes, thanks. But what happened to the other four from the box?'

'I wanted to see what a condom actually looked like.'

'You don't have them in India?'

'Yes, we do. But I'm a virgin, so I had never seen one before.'

'Right, fair enough. Then what happened to the other three?'

'I used them.'

'Used them? I thought you said you were a virgin.'

'I am. But my friend taught me how to masturbate with them using yogurt.'

At this, Diana and Ovidiu both doubled up laughing. It wasn't as funny for me, however, as I remembered what I had eaten for breakfast: the bottom half of the pot of yogurt Saumya had left in the fridge.

After enjoying an evening meal of curried vegetables together, it was time to leave. Ovidiu and Diana had arranged for a Spanish friend of theirs, Alberto, to put me up for the remainder of my time in Portugal's capital. We entered Alberto's flat in complete darkness. The electricity had gone out and my new host was fumbling around in the kitchen trying to find a set of candles. The flat made me think of the line in the song 'Hotel California':

There were voices in the corridor; I thought I heard them say...

It was just one long, dark corridor, with doors along both sides. Ovidiu had a look at the circuit board and soon restored light, revealing Alberto to be a smart, well-dressed man in his early thirties who looked more American than Spanish. He was stockily built, clean-cut and not your typical dark haired, hairy Spaniard. He spoke perfect English and worked at the Spanish Embassy. After showing me where I would be sleeping – in a small bedroom at the end of the mile-long corridor – we all sat down to enjoy a couple of cold beers. Just like with the two Romanians, I felt immediately comfortable and at ease with Alberto. He too had been a member of AIESEC and he also agreed that the organisation was a little bit weird.

It soon got late and Alberto had to be up early for work the following morning, so he handed me a set of keys and said goodnight as I left the flat with the Romanians to go for a drink in the city. On the way to the pub, as we ascended a flight of stairs and emerged from the Metro station out onto the street, we bumped into two Romanian girls, Roxana and Alina, both friends of Ovidiu and Diana, making their way home for the evening. Diana introduced me but both had already heard about my journey and had been reading my blog. They quickly decided that rather than go home, they would now like to join us for a couple more drinks. Both girls were the same age as me. I was taken to a trendy jazz bar, where I was told by my two new female friends to sit in the middle of them on the comfortable bench at the back. I obliged, quite happily. We drank and chatted until closing time, just after 2 in the morning, when I took the bus back to my new home accompanied by Roxana, who was getting off at the same stop.

My bedroom was freezing. I could see my own breath. And I didn't have a pillow. I just lay, my head resting on a jumper and my body shivering. The flat was empty when I woke in the early afternoon. I was getting used to this. On the kitchen table Alberto had left a note telling me he wouldn't be home until the evening, along with a travel card that I could use on the city's Metro and buses. I made my way to a large park on top of a hill overlooking the sea and sat down to enjoy the sunshine and do a bit of hobbit watching.

Sitting in the park, feeling bored, I received a text from Alina, one of the Romanians I'd met the previous night, asking if I felt like hanging out with her. I told her where I was and that she was more than welcome to join me, which she did half an hour later.

'Let me take you to dinner this evening,' she offered, as we greeted each other.

'Okay.'

So that evening we walked through the narrow streets above the city, close to the castle, where local eateries served up locally caught fish and Portuguese wine. Along the way, as we chatted, my escort for the evening was getting friendlier and friendlier, almost holding my hand. I wished I fancied her. But I didn't. We took our seats at a small table in a romantic little restaurant, where we were brought a plate of whole sardines – eyes included – along with crusty bread, new potatoes and a bottle of white wine. In all my years I've never been a wine drinker, and as I poured out two glasses I told Alina as much.

'Yes, I know.'

'Oh, did I tell you already last night?' I wondered.

'Nope. You just filled both of our glasses up to the rim. It's not beer!'

The food was amazing, but it didn't help to ease my discomfort at the way the evening was going.

'I was talking to a friend about you today,' Alina said, as I put away my last potato. 'I told her how good looking you are.'

I gulped.

She continued, 'And she said, "Really? He doesn't look that great in the photos on his blog." So I told her that in the flesh you are perfect.'

What could I say to that? And what was wrong with her friend's eyes? I mean, really, "he doesn't look that great in the photos!" Leave it out!

'You know, you are what I would consider to be the perfect man: beautiful looking, funny and intelligent.'

'Stop it,' I said.

I meant it, too. I was not comfortable with these compliments.

Still she continued, 'I really admire English men. English men are the real men of Europe. I love how English men are manly enough to not feel the need to be prettier than their girlfriends. Not like Italian men, they're like gays.'

I laughed at this, glad that the conversation had switched to ethnic generalisations rather than specifics relating to me.

'But I imagine it is almost impossible for you to find any woman better looking than you,' she concluded.

I had smiled too soon. Don't get me wrong, ordinarily I would have loved the way this conversation was going. If it were taking place with someone to whom I could return some of the compliments. Or even with someone that I just really felt like having sex with. But with Alina, I couldn't and I didn't. As nice a girl as she was, and as easy as she was making it for me, I just didn't feel the twinge in my pants. A part of me hoped I would change my mind after more alcohol, which was just as well, because after paying the bill my admirer told me that our night together was far from over. We were going drinking. About four hours later it was kicking out time in the Irish pub we had been sat in since 10pm. I had put away four whiskeys and three pints, but still wasn't quite feeling up to anything intimate. Alina, realising this, then suggested we carry on.

Reluctantly, I agreed. I didn't want to be rude, especially after all the food and drink I had been so generously treated to. And as I have already told you, Alina was good company.

'I know a little after-hours place,' she said, as we entered the night air.

The 'after-hours' place she took me to turned out to be nothing more than a beach hut down a side alley in which an old man served up paper cups of beer for 1 euro a pop. He soon shut up shop too, but rather than head for home I was then taken to a dark and dirty little bar, in which loud techno music banged out of the speakers and cabbages hung from the ceiling, full of drunk American students falling over each other. Two beers later, I was too pissed to be able to stand up straight, but not pissed enough to feel like pulling Alina. Oh well, nobody can accuse me of lack of effort. Together, we walked to the city's main bus depot from where we would each catch different buses home.

I was well taken care of over the next few days as between them Alberto, Ovidiu and Diana made sure I never went without a meal, while they also called around people they knew in other cities, trying to plot my route towards Paris for me. Eventually, Alberto found a friend in the city of Porto who would give me a bed as I journeyed north. He also emailed friends and family of his in Spain asking if anyone there would be willing to host me if I passed their way. I liked Alberto; he was one of life's nice guys.

It was a sunny afternoon when, feeling bored, I set off in search of Benfica's stadium, Estádio da Luz (Stadium of Light). With the help of Alberto's travel card I made it to the stadium, admired the statue of Eusebio and then walked around the outside of the complex, just like I had done in Barcelona, taking in the place, imagining the atmosphere on derby day: Benfica against Sporting Lisbon. There was one minor difference to detail when compared to Barcelona's Camp Nou, however. At the Camp Nou, nobody had failed to properly shut one of the gates. I had heard about the laziness of Portuguese workers and now I apparently had the proof. I stood for a moment, checking around me for witnesses, then when the coast was clear slipped through the slightly ajar gate and up the steep set of stairs inside, at the top of which I found myself standing all alone in the top tier of the stadium in the curve behind one of the goals. I then set about trying to find a way down to the lower tier and out onto the pitch, but every door leading down was locked, and so I made my way back outside.

I pencilled in the date for leaving Lisbon for two days' time. Alberto let his friend in Porto know to expect me, and I also sent out a few couch requests to locals in the Spanish town of Valladolid, just in case I was able to make it as far as there. From either of those two towns I would aim for either of the Basque towns of San Sebastian or Pamplona, both close to the border with France. From there I would look to get through France and up to Paris, either in one day or splitting it over two, stopping off for a night in Bordeaux.

'We are having a party tonight,' Alberto told me, happily. 'A Spanish dinner party. You will enjoy it.'

Dinner turned out to be a feast, as 15 Spaniards joined us in the flat, all seated around a table fit for a Royal banquet. The table was filled with tomato and tuna salads, different types of fish, gnocchi, chicken, tortilla chips, bread, sausages, salamis, different cheeses; a ridiculous amount of food. But the seating arrangement was like a primary school disco: all the boys sitting down one side, all the girls down the other. How old were we? Six? And no one had been brave enough to cross into enemy territory. The men talked football; I don't know what the girls talked about, I wasn't on their side of the table. After a few glasses of Port I crossed the divide and made conversation with a girl. Isabel was intelligent and bubbly, and had lived in London for a while, working as a journalist. Noticing the cockerel on the Spurs jacket I was wearing, she told me, 'Ah, it is just like the Portuguese symbol. The little cock is very typical in Portugal.'

Classic!

The party soon wound down and everyone left, but not before Isabel asked for my number and told me that she would like to show me around Lisbon before I exited the city.

A couple of days later came my penultimate in Lisbon. I packed my stuff and headed out to meet Isabel early in the afternoon. She had called me to see if I was free and fancied spending the day with her, and of course I had said yes. I took with me a couple of books that I had borrowed from Diego, as Isabel was from Madrid and often made the trip back home, so would be able to return them to him the next time she was in Spain's capital.

Isabel was the same bubbly, fun person when we met in the city centre that she had been the night I'd first become acquainted with her. Together we walked the streets, stopping off occasionally in little cafés for a cup of tea or a slice of cake. After my tour of the central part of the city was over, I was taken to a part of town called Alfama.

Alfama is a village within a city. No cars are allowed to enter and the streets are narrow. People sit out on their doorsteps, drinking beer and talking to the neighbours. Old ladies lean out of the windows of every building, just watching the world go by. People hang their washing out to dry on wire lines strung across their doorways. Pet budgies hang in cages in front of houses. Fresh oranges grow on trees in the street. Children play with brooms, mimicking their mothers. Some of the passages are so narrow that you must pass through them in single file. The area is served by little shops that open out onto the street; staffed by an elderly man or woman sat lonely waiting for a customer. They sell only the most basic of goods, and to enter or exit the premises you must always step over a sleeping dog in the doorway. Alfama was one of the most alluring neighbourhoods I had come across on my travels. But it was a paradox. For as quaint and pretty as it seemed, you only had to look at the inhabitants to realise that Alfama was the Portuguese equivalent of a rough and deprived council estate back in England. The people were unwashed and uneducated. The streets were lined with drunks; young and old. One old woman crouched behind a bush to piss and no one batted an eyelid; it was clearly the norm here. Every young teenage girl pushed her young child along in a pram. The tone of voice used to communicate between residents was aggressive and threatening. Tourists – in this case, me – were watched with menacing eyes. Alfama was like the dressing room of the Jeremy Kyle show; the Portuguese version. Isabel told me that she would love to be able to live in Alfama, for the character and the fact that it was completely pedestrianised, but would never take the step because the area after dark became a no-go zone.

'It's just too dangerous,' she explained, 'which is really a shame, because the buildings and streets are so beautiful.'

Darkness soon fell and it was time to call an end to my tour. I thanked Isabel for the day and also for being happy to return Diego's books to him when she next returned to Madrid.

'It's no problem at all. In fact, I am going to Madrid tomorrow for a job interview, so I will be able to give them to him then. But why don't you come with me? I'm going with a friend of mine, but we have space in the car for one more.'

I had arranged to spend the following night with Alberto's friends in Porto, but had been told that they were only going to be in town for one night. If I returned to Madrid, I would be halfway to France and, assuming Diego still had a spare room, would have time to sit down properly and plot my next bit of travel, sending emails and arranging things in advance. It made sense. A quick call to my moustachioed friend in the Spanish capital confirmed that there was a place for me there, so my decision was a no-brainer. I was going back to Madrid.

Shortly before 10 the next morning I handed Alberto the keys to his flat and thanked him for all that he had done to make my stay in Lisbon a comfortable one. We then hugged in manly fashion and I walked down the stairs and out onto the street, feeling a twinge of sadness that I was leaving my new found friends behind, in this city that I had already come to call home. I didn't want to travel north-easterly towards colder climes.

The sun was shining over the Iberian Peninsula as we loaded up the car. Isabel's male friend drove, Isabel sat in the front passenger seat and I made myself comfortable in the back. Since arriving in Portugal I hadn't been sleeping well, perhaps getting four hours a night if I was lucky. I couldn't put my finger on what it was that had kept me awake. There had been a cold draft in the room, but I didn't think that had made such a difference. The walls also creaked a lot at night; it was an old building after all. As I left Portugal that morning, I was feeling run down and exhausted. At least I knew I would get a proper sleep in Madrid. I also hoped to get one in the car, so I put my feet up and closed my eyes, before Isabel turned round and asked, 'How have you been sleeping in that flat?'

'I haven't,' I told her.

'Hmmm. Which room were you in? The little one at the end of the corridor?'

'Yep.'

'That's the ghost's room, you know?' she told me, as matter-of-factly as you like.

She went on to explain that two friends of hers had slept in the same room on different occasions and had both told afterwards of feeling cold breathing on their faces, banging and scratching noises on the walls and the feeling that they weren't alone in the room. I laughed it off, not bothering to mention the draft I had felt or the creaks I had heard. But was I glad she had told me this now that I had left and not on the night of the party. I can tell you sincerely that there is no way I would have gone anywhere near a room referred to as 'the ghost's room.' No way at all! And I don't even believe in ghosts!

We arrived in the outskirts of Madrid shortly after 6 in the evening, where I was dropped at a local train station to catch my ride into the city centre. Isabel handed me the €1.80 ticket and waited with me on the platform. As my train pulled in and we hugged each other goodbye, I felt a warmth of friendship from Isabel that is hard to explain. My time in Portugal had been made too easy for me, thanks to the amazing generosity and all-round niceness of my new Romanian and Spanish friends. And in this case they really were friends; people that I would stay in touch with and see again in the future.

Welcome back to Madrid.

29. Madrid

THE FAMILIARITY OF Madrid's Atocha train station was comforting. I crossed the busy road in front of the concourse, rang the bell and waited to be buzzed up. Alex opened the door to the flat, eating a sandwich, while Diego slowly emerged from the darkness of his bedroom with a joint between his lips. It was like I had never been away.

'Hola amigo,' he said, before hugging me and patting me on the back.

Luis, a friend of Diego's, turned up shortly after and joined us as we saw the night in sitting at the kitchen table chain-smoking hash and discussing politics and revolution. Luis was lanky, wore a black hoody, had long unkempt hair and a dark beard. He had a lot to say about the mistreatment the British had dished out whilst setting up and then maintaining the empire. He didn't, however, seem to have an opinion on the Spanish colonisation of almost the entire continent of South America. Luis was a provocateur; his sole aim to set off a reaction in me. He was out of luck; I was exhausted. I bid them goodnight and headed off to my bedroom, where I despatched the cat in double quick time before drifting off into the land of nod.

A couple of nights later, and with Alex out of Madrid visiting family, Diego and I were again joined in the kitchen by Luis, but this time it was only for a warm-up session of weed and Russian beer before going out to sample Madrid's nightlife. The small bar we went to was so full that it was standing room only. So we stood. Naturally. The clientele mostly looked like Luis. The ceiling was low, the lighting was off and the barmaids had numerous piercings. And the beers were small. And mostly foam. But rather than complain, I went toe to toe with the two hombres as Luis laid down the gauntlet.

'You English,' he slurred. 'You English all think that you are so tough and that you can drink so much more than anybody else. But you are wrong. The Spanish can drink you hooligans under the table.'

As he spoke, he swayed from side to side and struggled to focus on my face. His arms flew about wildly, almost hitting people as they passed us en-route to the toilet at the back, and he had to prop himself up by leaning against the back wall. He was on his third beer since arriving at the place. His third tiny, foamy beer. His argument didn't hold much weight. Neither did his glass. A table soon cleared and we sat down, while Diego asked one of the waitresses to bring us some food. We worked our way through plate after plate of tapas. There was a cold tomato and garlic soup (gazpacho), crusty bread with salmon and creamed cheese, pickled mushrooms and different cold meats. As we ate, a part of me wondered if there was any substance to Luis' claims regarding the Spanish ability to drink heavily. Maybe he was right. Maybe the Spanish were really just suntanned Irish. A few hours (and a few more beers) later, my question was answered, as I stood in the street outside the bar, the only one of the group of three not completely and utterly wankered. While Diego stood in the middle of the road with his trousers round his ankles, urinating against the wind and shouting, 'Look at my tiny willy! It's so tiny!' Luis had decided it would be a good idea to try and lift me up above his head. Then, after realising I was heavier – or that he was weaker – than first imagined, he dropped to his knees and bit me on the calf. Actually bit me.

I planned to make it from Madrid to Paris in a day; a mere 1270km (790 miles) by road. If I left early enough in the morning and managed to reach the border by around 1pm, I should have no problem train hopping to France's capital before nightfall, as long as I used the TGVs. The hardest part would be actually getting out of Madrid, as it was near impossible to get anywhere near the trains without holding a valid ticket, and hitchhiking was illegal under Spanish law. I decided that I would undertake the challenge the following day, Monday.

Monday came but brought with it sickness. I was struck down with a sore throat, stomach cramps, a headache too powerful for Nurofen to take care of, nausea and tightness in the chest. A 790-mile jaunt was out of the question. I was going to have to break down the journey north a bit, so sent an email to a Couchsurfer in Bilbao requesting a place to put my feet up for a night. John replied quickly, letting me know he would be out of town until Thursday but would be more than happy to host me after that. I would probably need a few days to recover from my ailments anyway, so told him to expect me Thursday night. Wednesday came and I still had no idea how I would make it to Bilbao. I heard a female voice coming from Diego's room.

'Kris, come through. I would like you to meet someone,' Diego called out.

I entered his room and was introduced to Emma, Diego's sister, who was only in the city for a couple of days visiting a trade fair related to her work, but who lived in … Bilbao. She would be making her way back to the northern city the following day. Fate had intervened once again to see to it that my life was uncomplicated. I could just bum a lift with her.

'I am sorry Kris, but I didn't come here by car,' Emma told me, in response to my suggestion of the lift. 'I am going back by bus. But, if somehow you manage to make it to Bilbao before the weekend, I am driving to the French border on Saturday morning and could give you a lift if you are around.'

I had to find a way to Bilbao. Emma called all of her colleagues asking if anyone had space in a car for the drive north, but nobody did.

I decided that rather than attempt to make it all the way from Bilbao to Paris in the same day, it would be wiser to stop off for a night in Bordeaux. I had to find a place to stay once there, so logged into Couchsurfing to see who was about. One of the locals there, a 25-year old woman, had the following statement written at the top of her profile page:

'Bonjour (hello!), I have my boyfriend and I don't want boys come for relationship, please. Thanks!'

I found this strange, mostly because I had never seen anything like it on Couchsurfing before. I mean, it went without saying. I needed a place to sleep, not a person to sleep with. I emailed her anyway, and in my message made a light-hearted comment along the lines of: '… and don't worry, I'm definitely not looking for a relationship.'

A few hours later I received her reply. The message read exactly as: *'Hi Kris, I sink this not a problem for come in my home, I give you my number:* ** ** ** **. *Call me for, tell me when you need my couch. I just to be clear, I have my boy friend, and I juste want to be friend… It's ok for you, no probleme for comme in my home. See you soon, maybe. Bye.'*

Firstly, the fact that she wrote in a French accent is priceless. Secondly, she really wasn't attractive enough for this kind of insistence to ever be necessary. She seemed crazy. I emailed her back and told her I would call when I arrived in Bordeaux, hoping in the meantime to find someone else.

Friday morning came and saw me up with the cockerels. I hadn't found any easy way of getting out of the city, so was going to have to attempt the usual blag. The first train of the day from Madrid to Bilbao departed from Atocha Station at 8am. I was there at 7:30, but after twice getting caught by the female security guard attempting to pass the wrong way through the exit gates to get to the platform, I had to give up the ghost. As I have mentioned before, the reason for the strict security in Spanish railway stations was the multiple bombings that had taken place at this very station four years earlier. I did not want to be putting security to the test. What's more, the biggest threat to Spain, according to the authorities, was the Basque separatist group ETA, who mainly hit targets in Madrid. Bilbao is in the Basque Country. Therefore, people travelling from Madrid to Bilbao were viewed with more suspicion than people travelling from Madrid to, say, Valencia. Dotted around Atocha Station were 'Wanted' posters displaying the mug shots of known ETA terrorists. Every single one of them looked like me! I did not want to be shot through the head before having my body paraded on Spanish national television to the sounds of victory music. My nan would not like that. The next train to Bilbao wasn't due to depart until 3:50pm, so I sat down on a bench to think things through. The only other option for getting out of the capital was to hitchhike; a means of travel I had been reliably informed was forbidden under Spanish law.

'It is not only the law that will make it difficult,' Diego had explained, 'it is also Spanish people; they are very suspicious of anybody wanting a free ride. Spanish drivers are not usually in charitable mood.'

I went back to the flat to fill up a bottle of water, waking Diego to let me back in. I told him of my efforts and my misfortune. He laughed. Then he said that neither he nor Alex nor even his sister wanted me to hitchhike. They would pull together and buy me a bus ticket. He called the company and booked me the last available seat of the day, on the 5pm Basque Express. I don't think it was actually called the Basque Express; I gave it that title myself to make it sound romantic. Like the Orient Express. Or the Gatwick Express. Well, like the Orient Express.

The seat next to mine on the bus journey to Bilbao was taken by an attractive older woman. Not that old. 35 maybe. We exchanged smiles and glances and I gave her a chewing gum. Not because her breath smelt; just because I'm a nice person.

After four and a half hours she broke the silence and began talking to me. Her face was so friendly and nice, her smile beautiful, her eyes beaming.

'I have no idea what you are saying, but I am sure it is something profound,' I told her, before adding, 'no hablo español.' I then pulled that face that says: 'I don't know!' – the one where you sort of scrunch up your nose and produce a broad closed-mouthed smile. Then she pulled the same face back and we laughed together. Our bus pulled into the bus station and we exchanged one final look before heading off to continue our lives without one another for company.

It was 9:45pm.

Welcome to Bilbao.

30. Bilbao

DURING THE BUS ride I had received a text message from my host for the night, John, letting me know he would be a bit late arriving at the bus station to pick me up, so I followed his instructions and stood patiently at the top of the stairs to the Metro. It was a Friday night and all around me groups of teenagers loitered, stinking of perfume and cologne and carrying plastic bags filled with clinking glass bottles and cans of beer. A lot of the men I saw were wearing a type of hat I had not seen before; like an oversized French beret. The city, from where I was standing, looked quaint. The architecture reminded me of Bern, and the whole city looked clean and well kept.

John finally turned up at 10:30pm. He was tall and stocky with gaps between his teeth, blond messy hair and was wearing a blues hat. The hat soon made sense once he told me he was from St. Louis and was a musician. He had ended up in Bilbao after visiting the city a couple of times whilst completing an apprenticeship on a radio station in Stuttgart, Germany. He had fallen in love with the city and, after his apprenticeship was up, had moved here hoping to make a go of it. Four months later things were going well; he was enjoying his new life as an English teacher.

The walk back to John's flat took a good hour, and I use the term 'good' lightly. Not only was it painful under the weight of my backpack, it was also painful having to listen to John's one-man comedy show; a show that consisted for the first 30 minutes of one-liner N-word jokes, followed swiftly by 30 minutes of jokes about disabled people and dead babies. Most of them were so offensive that I couldn't even bring myself to laugh politely. Looking back, I'm disappointed in myself for not stopping him, but at the time I figured it would only complicate things. We got back to the flat and my host immediately set about chopping up a load of potatoes before telling me he had to go to the nearest Metro station to pick up another Couchsurfer that was staying the night, a Peruvian guy.

'While I'm gone, can you chop up these onions and carrots and put them in the water with the potatoes?' he asked me before leaving.

I did as I was told. John then returned with Samuel: the tallest, blondest, most Germanic-looking guy I'd ever seen, and not the brown-skinned, short Peruvian I had been expecting. Samuel spoke perfect American English; something he had picked up during five years spent studying at an American university. His grandparents had been German immigrants to Peru. I imagined (quietly to myself, of course) that they had been wanted war criminals. We sat and smoked a strong spliff before working our way through the huge pot of soup that John had prepared. Then we smoked another one, which quickly led to me pulling a whitey, burning up, sweating profusely and feeling as sick as a dog. I didn't want to say anything, as the other two were handling their weed just fine, so I disappeared into the bathroom where I took off all my clothes and hung my head out the window for about 20 minutes. Fortunately, my two smoking companions were stoned enough to not notice my absence, and on my return not a word was uttered. Time flew and when I saw that it was already 1:45am I was ready to sleep, not just because I was still too stoned to move, but also because Emma had sent me a text telling me that we were to leave Bilbao the following morning at 10. John had other ideas though, and I soon found myself walking around the streets of Bilbao looking for an open-air Pelota court. Pelota is a traditional Basque sport, much like Squash but played with the hands. We eventually found a place and then Samuel and

I sat and listened as John played us some tunes on his guitar. Another spliff was rolled.

It was 6:00am when we got back to the flat. Before going off to his room, John gave me a Metro ticket that I could use later in the morning to get to my arranged meeting point with Emma.

'Just let yourself out in the morning, man. Don't worry about waking either of us to say goodbye!' were his last words to me.

I immediately fell asleep in a sleeping bag on the living room floor. I slept until 9:00, before going and picking up my lift with Emma. We drove for two hours to Irun, a town on the French border, where my driver dropped me off in a petrol station before leaving me to make my own way into France and on to Bordeaux.

Irun was a complete circus. The whole town resembled a huge bazaar. As far as the eye could see street vendors were selling boxes of counterfeit cigarettes, bottles of bootleg alcohol, fake designer sunglasses, fake designer perfumes, fake designer clothes and anything else that could be bootlegged. All around, French shopping tourists went from stall to stall picking up bargains. I felt claustrophobic and needed to get out, so I walked until I came to the bridge that crosses the river that acts as a natural border between Spain and France, the Bidasoa.

On the other side of the bridge I found myself in the French town of Hendaye, although on both sides of the river all street signs were written in the Basque language. The weather was cloudy and the atmosphere grey and humid. I walked for half an hour, asking directions along the way, until I found myself at the town's train station. It was 12:30 and the next train to Bordeaux departed at 1:27pm. I sat in the waiting room feeling hungry, tired and a bit dizzy. Emma had given me a small baguette at the petrol station but it hadn't really hit the spot. Five minutes before my train was due to leave, some unexpected guests paid me a visit. I looked up to see three French policemen staring down at me. The leader of the group asked to see my passport. I gave it to him and he asked me in English which train I was taking. I told him that I was waiting for a friend to arrive from Bordeaux. They took my passport and walked outside the station with it, leaving me to watch them from a distance as they scrutinised every page, holding it up to the light and radioing through my details to someone in an office somewhere. It was the familiar routine. I must have been given the all clear because they soon came back, handed me my passport and said 'Merci,' before exiting the station. My train had already left without me. The next one leaving for Bordeaux was the TGV to Paris, departing at 2:11pm. I sat and waited patiently again until it pulled into the station but as I went to board I found my path blocked by inspectors checking the tickets of every passenger at the entrance to the platform. A quick look around revealed that there was an opening in a fence further up the platform, past the inspectors, that led out onto the station's car park. I hastily exited the station through the main entrance, before nipping through the car park and through the gap in the fence, and was feeling smug when I took a seat in the end carriage of the train. Unfortunately, one of my fellow passengers had seen my little stunt from his window seat and stitched me up to one of the guards who came and frog-marched me off of the train and out of the station. Before he had made it back to the train, I was already on a seat in a different carriage after repeating my shortcut just with a lot more haste. Just as I took a seat, the doors locked behind me and we were on our way.

I sat nervously in my seat until we got to our first stop of St. Jean de Luz Ciboure at 2:26pm. I stood up and waited in the corridor in case someone had pre-booked the seat I was sitting in, but they hadn't. Fifteen minutes later we were in the Atlantic seaside resort of Biarritz and I went through the same procedure but still no one took my seat. Twelve minutes later and we were at the last stop before Bordeaux, Bayonne. Again nobody sat in my place, and still no ticket inspector had walked through the carriage. Although Bordeaux was the next scheduled stop, there was an hour and forty minutes to go before we got there. It was going to be a nervous stage of the journey. Then I saw them. The three policemen that had questioned me at the station were patrolling the train. What would they do if they found that I had stowed away, especially after telling them I was just waiting for a friend? I didn't want to find out. I spent the remainder of the journey hiding behind a newspaper that someone had left on the seat next to me, dropping it down from my face only occasionally to stare in amazement at the old couple opposite me that sat sharing a flask of strong coffee with their grandson. The kid wasn't a day over three years old and yet he consumed his grown-up beverage like a seasoned high-ranking city executive.

It was only as we started approaching Bordeaux that I remembered that I hadn't arranged a place to stay. There was always the weird woman who wasn't looking for a relationship, but I hadn't been in contact with her recently and she had no idea I was coming today. *Maybe I will call her when I arrive,* I thought. My stomach hurt from hunger and my eyes were closing from tiredness. I didn't like the situation I found myself in. I liked it even less when just before pulling into the station the heavens opened and the rain fell in monsoon fashion. Still, I couldn't really complain, I had at least made it to another city, the half-way point on my way to Paris.

Welcome to Bordeaux.

31. Bordeaux

THE STATION CLOCK said 16:27 as I walked down the platform looking for the exit. The sky was grey, it was still raining, and the atmosphere was miserable. For a minute I thought I was in England. I had been optimistic in the belief that someone would have offered me a place to sleep in the city by the time I arrived but no one had come through for me.

I tried calling the girl who wasn't looking for a relationship. She didn't answer. I walked around the dirty streets for half an hour, trying her number again every five minutes or so. Still no answer. I headed back to the train station. It was still early enough in the evening for me to try to get to Paris before the trains stopped running. It would at least mean passing the time travelling instead of sitting and watching a station clock. It would also mean that come the following morning, rather than having to go through the stress of bunking trains after a night of sleeping rough, I would have all day to try to find a Parisian host. There was a high chance that I wouldn't make it all the way to Paris and would end up instead in a small town or village, much as I had done trying to get to Lyon earlier on in the journey, and this time there wouldn't be an Alex to come to my rescue. But hey, that's life. As I sat on the bench watching the festival of human emotion that is on show in every main terminus anywhere on the planet, my attention became focused on a young Chinese guy struggling with the ticket machine. Noticing me watching him, he walked up and asked if I could help him as he couldn't understand the French instructions the machine was arrogantly dishing out. It turned out that the ticket he wanted, an open-ended return to Biarritz, had to be purchased from the ticket office in person. I accompanied him to the room. The queue was long and, as he seemed to speak quite good English – at least it was better than his French – I took the opportunity to explain my situation to him in the hope that he might be able to return the favour in some way.

'Let me show you something while we are waiting,' I said, as I got down on to my knees and struggled to pull the now half-demolished copy of the *Argus* from the bottom of my bag.

My Chinese friend was visibly wary of this western stranger, smiling nervously and looking around for an escape route as he waited to see what I had in the bag. He breathed a sigh of relief when he saw that my weapon was made of paper and had a photo of me on it, taking it from my hands to read it in detail.

'Wow, this is really something amazing and funny,' he said, as he handed me back the paper.

I acted as interpreter for him as he bought his ticket and then as we were saying our goodbyes I took the opportunity to ask if he could provide me with a loaf of bread to get me through the night. It was embarrassing but I was desperate. I was then made to feel smaller than an ant when he refused my request, telling me, 'I am sorry, but I cannot buy you anything.'

'Okay, thank you for your time. I'm sorry to have bothered you.'

'The reason I cannot buy you anything is because it would not be enough. Please, allow me to prepare you a proper meal at my home,' he then said.

Ah, the Chinese and their love of suspense. I hadn't been expecting that. There was no way I was going to refuse such a kind and selfless offer. Maybe, just maybe, things were taking a turn for the better on this most grey and miserable of French days.

My new friend lived in an apartment block close to the station and, as we walked down the long corridor from the lift to his room, I didn't see a single non-Chinese face. The whole block, he explained, was inhabited by rich Chinese students who had been sent by their parents to get an expensive education in Europe. As I dropped my backpack down onto the floor in the corner of his room I realised I didn't even know my new friend's name. So I asked. Baijian was 24 years old – the same age as me – and was completing his post-graduate studies in IT. There was an open-door policy in force on his floor and every couple of minutes a different Chinese student stuck his head in to say hello to my host. Each time this happened Baijian would take the time to explain to the person in Chinese the story of how this English guy ended up in his block, and then would switch to English to introduce me. Every single person I met spoke decent enough English and every single one of them expressed their awe at what I was doing. The words 'brave' and 'crazy' were used liberally. I had taken on almost instant hero status amongst the Chinese. The Chinese have always loved me, though. I'm massive over there.

As Baijian set about cooking dinner, I was invited into the bedroom opposite my host's to use another guy's laptop and to watch telly. If I was thirsty, I was poured a drink. If I was tired, I was told to put my feet up on the bed. After feeling so exhausted, hungry and dejected just an hour earlier, I couldn't quite take in all that had happened to change my predicament. I was being treated like royalty and it didn't sit right. Dinner, despite taking me an hour to eat as I struggled to get to grips with the chop sticks, was delicious. I wasn't so hot on desert, though. Chopped banana and pear covered in mayonnaise. The less said about that, the better. Fortunately it was custom for us to eat from the same bowl, and Baijian loved this strange mix, so all I had to do was pretend to eat very slowly whilst watching him demolish the lot. As evening drew in I started wondering how much longer Baijian would put up with me before the time came for me to go back to the train station, probably for the night, as I didn't expect there to be any more trains leaving for Paris. His room was so tiny and cramped that I felt I was intruding on his personal space a bit too much, so I stood up and thanked him for everything, before heading for the door. As I did so, a young girl – someone that Baijian later told me was his ex-girlfriend – came into the room dragging a mattress behind her. While I had been on the internet in his friend's room earlier, Baijian had paid a visit to every single student on the floor asking if anyone had any extra bedding.

'You will stay here tonight,' he told me. 'You can't sleep in the train station; it is too cold and dangerous. Please, you are my guest. We will wake early tomorrow and go to the station together, as I am going with my friends to Biarritz.'

Once more I was lost for words at another random act of kindness shown me by a complete stranger. How had this happened? I had helped him understand a bit of French in the station and had ended up with a full stomach and a warm place to sleep. The final piece of the jigsaw was put into place that evening as I received an email from a girl in Paris, Hélène, letting me know she could host me the following night.

Throughout the night Baijian behaved like a young teenager on a school camping trip; he just would not stop talking. Each time I got five minutes of silence and thought he had dropped off to sleep, he would from nowhere ask another question about my journey or my life back in England and I would answer him. I didn't have the heart to tell him to go to sleep. He was too nice a guy. We parted company at the train station early the following morning, but not before he handed me a couple of salami sandwiches he had taken the time to prepare for me while I showered. What a genuinely lovely human being.

The first train heading to Paris departed at 10:27 and took me with it. It was packed full of students on a school trip, something I immediately saw as an advantage. If I sat myself right in the middle of them perhaps the ticket inspector wouldn't fancy having to walk through the carriage and would just leave it be. I couldn't get a proper seat but managed to bag one of the little pull-down ones that you find in the corridor next to the toilet. There was a small group of French lads at the table opposite me, playing cards, watching a film on a laptop and generally being annoying in a teenage way.

At 11:25 the train stopped for the first time at a place called Angouleme. It had been a very nervous hour, the ticket inspector had walked past me three times, but each time I had managed to appear calm and relaxed and he'd just kept on going.

Every time a train makes a stop at a French railway station it is mandatory for every man, woman and child to jump up out of their seats and get on to the platform to try and squeeze in a crafty smoke before having to sit down again for the journey to continue. And when I say every man, woman, and child, I really do mean every man, woman, and child. I actually saw on more than one occasion in France an adult ask an infant if he could bum a cigarette, and each time the child obliged.

At 12:16 we arrived at our next stop, Poitiers, the halfway point between Bordeaux and Paris. As my fellow passengers quickly smoked their fags, a new inspector got on the train at the door closest me and set about checking tickets. I reasoned with myself that I had been extremely lucky to make it as far as I had without being checked and rather than wait where I was like a sitting duck I jumped off to have a little break. The station's information board told me that a break was out of the question though as there was another train departing in a few minutes from platform 6. I took my seat on the 12:20 to Paris. At least, the board said it was the 12:20 to Paris. In fact it was delayed for an agonisingly long twelve minutes, during which time every French man, woman, and child tried to break the Guinness world record for number of fags smoked in a twelve minute period. We had only been moving for two minutes when the ticket guard made a beeline for me.

'Comprendez-vous Anglais?' I asked him.

'Non.'

I didn't like it, but I had to resort to explaining my made-up situation in bad French, telling the old story about the girlfriend being on the other train.

'Vous êtes Anglais?' he asked.

'Oui,' I replied.

He took my passport and began explaining how serious a situation this was. He became increasingly angry as he spoke, not appreciating me remaining blasé to the situation. He called the police from his mobile phone and then explained to me that there would be an English-speaking constable waiting for me on the platform in Paris to arrest me and take me to the local nick.

'D'accord. Ce n'est pas un problème pour moi,' I said with a shrug the French would be proud of.

I was quite enjoying annoying him because I could see in his eyes that he just plain hated the English. I had seen it immediately after I'd answered his question as to whether or not I was Anglais. Eventually he just snapped, veins popping out of his head as he cursed loudly about the 'fucking English.' He kept mentioning prison and even went so far as to put his wrists together in a handcuffed position. I yawned. I am positive that he wanted to slap my face as he threw my passport back at me and handed me a fine made out to my fake address before walking away mumbling Gallic obscenities under his breath. Inside I was jubilant. I wasn't going to be kicked off the train in some remote town and would be in Paris in a couple of hours' time.

Arriving at Paris Montparnasse station a couple of minutes after 2 in the afternoon I boldly strode off of the train, expecting to be met on the platform by Mr.Veiny Head and a member of the gendarmerie, only to see the above-mentioned ticket inspector strolling down the platform towards an office. He had been bluffing. So with no one waiting to nick me I wandered into the station's lobby where I stood and took in my surroundings. I ticked another capital off of my list.

Welcome to Paris.

32. Paris

Capitals left to visit: Amsterdam, Athens, Brussels, Helsinki, Luxembourg, Prague, Riga, Tallinn, Vilnius

Days on the road: 123
Distance travelled: 7897 miles
EU capitals visited: 14

THE ELECTRONIC GATES to the Metro system weren't working – most probably on strike – so I was able to make it to Place Cliche, the station closest to Hélène's flat, without hassle. She hadn't given me the address though, so I gave her a call to navigate me in to base. Hélène spoke perfect English, without that silly accent that can make even the simplest conversation incomprehensible, and she also sounded reassuringly pleasant. She gave me some directions and told me she would see me in about three minutes. Half an hour later, and after numerous phone calls, I found her home. I climbed the stairs to the third floor flat. Hélène opened the door smiling. She had long brown hair, blue eyes, smooth complexion and a sweet smile. The mandatory scarf was tossed carelessly around the neck. The flat itself was unmistakably Gallic, with black and white film posters dotted around the walls; a wooden creaky floor; French windows (obviously); a bed and settee next to each other against the wall; and a small piano in the corner. We sat at the kitchen table for a quick chat, in which I discovered that my host was a 21-year old medical student in her fourth year of 10. The flat belonged to her nan, so she didn't have to pay any rent, but she only earned 100

Euros a month studying to be a doctor, so her parents helped out with bills and living costs. She lived alone but told me that two more girls would be there that night, both Couchsurfers; one German, the other French.

Hélène had a good sense of humour, and was baiting me for being English as soon as I was in the door. To be fair, it was a two-way thing. I asked her how many Frenchmen were needed to protect Paris from foreign invasion.

'I don't know.'

'Don't worry, you are not alone,' I smiled. 'Nobody knows, as no Frenchman has ever attempted it.'

Hélène laughed, before saying something about terrible food. I pretended not to hear and asked if I could use the shower.

'Of course. But you better take a cloth in there to wipe away the cobwebs first, because I'm French, so I never wash.'

I liked my host already.

I jumped onto Hélène's laptop to check my emails and was disappointed to read that Roberta, an American girl living in Paris, wouldn't be able to host me the following evening as I had hoped. Hélène was leaving Paris to go and stay with her own parents in Montpellier early the following morning, so it looked as if I would only be spending the one night in France's capital before trying to get to Luxembourg. *Luxembourg, who the fuck goes to Luxembourg?*

The German Couchsurfer Julia arrived back at the flat after spending the day at the Louvre, where she had apparently contracted verbal diarrhoea. On and on and on she went about her day, describing every piece of art she had seen, what she had eaten for lunch, what number bus she had taken, and how many times she had been to the toilet; both for number ones and number twos. She didn't really go that far, that would be disgusting. I could see how bored Hélène was becoming, and she threw me a look that said, 'Help!'

Sympathetically, I threw her one back that said, 'Nah!'

before leaving them to it as I went to shower. I returned 25 minutes later to find that Julia was still going, only by now her monologue had somehow got on to how the biggest problem facing Germany was the amount of Turks living in the country.

'Turkey should never be allowed to join the European Union,' she declared, 'as they are all so uncivilised and can't even separate religion from government. They are all criminals, too.'

Julia was entertaining enough already, but I got the urge to take the fun up a notch.

'My parents are both Turkish. In fact, I suppose that means that I am Turkish too, even if I was born in London.'

Julia's face turned a deep shade of red. I quickly threw Hélène a glance, letting her in on the game.

'I can understand some of your prejudices,' I said, 'but I really do find it offensive that all of us Turks are painted with the same bigoted brush. And also I wish to point out that in Turkey we have a very secular government. We have even banned the veil.'

Hélène struggled to keep a straight face as Julia started retracting some of her statements.

'Well, I don't mean *all* Turks are like that.'

But before she could dig herself out of the hole she now found herself in, Hélène dropped bombshell number two.

'My grandma is Turkish too. I have been to Istanbul many times and can tell you that the Turks there are nothing like how you describe them.'

What? Where had this come from? Hélène's performance was so convincing that I couldn't tell for sure that she was making it up. How did Julia feel now? All of a sudden her views changed completely. Turks were fantastic people, the salt of the earth, and it was just the ones living in Germany that were slightly undesirable only because they chose not to assimilate. Hélène and I made a formidable duo. I soon noticed that my partner in crime had performed a very subtle disappearing act and I was now alone with only an embarrassed German for company. It was starting to get dark outside and I wanted to see some of the area before it got too late, so I said *auf wiedersehen* and headed out the door.

Hélène lived in a predominantly Muslim neghbourhood, in the 9th arrondissement of the city, in which the headscarf was uniform. Julia must have loved it. The smell of Sheesha filled the air, and old Moroccan and Algerian men sat outside cafés drinking thick, gooey coffee and devouring sweets. I walked for close to an hour only to discover that, apart from an impressive old church – Église de la Sainte-Trinité – the area offered nothing but tobacco shops, cafés and Sheesha bars. And a couple of Chinese prodigies playing the fastest game of table tennis I had ever witnessed, in a park barely lit by streetlights.

Hélène made dinner – crepes with maple syrup that had been left by a Canadian Couchsurfer – and we sat down to eat, joined by the third guest of the night, Marie, a 20-year old in Paris for 24 hours to see an exhibition for her study class. I was still feeling playful from the earlier interaction with Julia.

'Can I ask a question? It's just something that has always bugged me, and now that I'm seated with some French people, I feel that you might be able to clear it up for me.'

Hélène threw me a look that suggested she knew where this was going, but Marie was yet to be introduced to the game and said, 'Please, ask away.'

'Okay. I was just wondering why France was treated as one of the victorious nations after the Second World War, when really they were exactly the same as Poland. You surrendered, let Germany occupy you and then waited for other countries to go and win the war on your behalf.'

A look of shock overcame both French girls' faces, even Hélène. I knew this would hit a nerve as I had heard many a Frenchman in the past describing De Gaulle as a brave hero and

France as a real powerhouse of the era. I also knew how wound up us Brits get when an American makes a similar comment about how we would be speaking German now if it weren't for them. As the two of them sat there, still too surprised to answer my question, the hilarity was raised to epic proportions when Julia decided to join in.

'Yea. Why did France have any say over what happened to my country after the war? After all, we defeated France. Easily!'

'Yes! That's right! Germany *did* defeat France. So please can you explain.'

Marie stared me in the eye and said, 'Never say these things to a French person in the street. He would be most offended and angered by these lies.'

It was at this point that I realised I probably couldn't take it any further without getting stabbed with a butter knife, so I left the French alone, switching my attentions instead to the German in the room.

'And Julia, please explain something to me. I know that in Germany you have a law against holocaust denial; all symbols of the Nazis have been outlawed; the book *Mein Kampf* has been banned and you are not even allowed to sing that catchy little number 'Deutschland Deutschland Uber Alles' in public anymore. I would argue that Germany today is actually no different from Germany under the Nazis, as the freedoms and liberties of its citizens are being taken away. Surely the banning of such things only acts to glamorise them to a mindless minority, making them much more attractive. What is it that Germans are so afraid might happen?'

I was good at this game. When it comes to speaking absolute total bollocks, you won't find a more talented individual. In fact, a few years back I took part in and won an episode of *Mastermind* on BBC2, in which my specialist subject was Bollocks. No, that's bollocks too. Julia's response to my baiting was an absolute peach, much better than anything I could have made up for your entertainment here. She simply said, 'Those are the rules, and we, as Germans, just do as we are told. We don't question, we only obey.'

To which I replied, 'Now where have we heard that excuse before?' leaving both Hélène and Marie with tears of laughter streaming down their faces, as Julia caught on to what I was doing and broke into a smile herself. She then, for reasons unbeknown to the rest of us at the table, reiterated her belief that all non-German speaking Turks should be forced to learn the language or be sent back to Turkey.

'Turkey? Is that where you are sending your undesirables these days?'

The French girls laughed. The German girl knew she was in checkmate. The Englishman knew there was nowhere further that he could take things without causing real offence, and that was the last thing he wanted to do. It was all just good old-fashioned inter-European banter. And let's not forget, I've held a great love and admiration for our friends from the continent since I was a very small boy.

Although I would be leaving Hélène's flat early the next morning, I discovered that I wouldn't be leaving Paris so soon. Hélène had called her sister, another Marie, who also lived in the city, and asked if she would put me up for an extra night or two. Hélène let me know the good news of Marie's response after dinner. Julia had to be up and out of the flat at 4:30am to catch a train back to Germany the following morning, while the remaining three of us would be leaving before 7:30; so, shortly before midnight, the mattresses were laid down next to each other on the floor, the girls were changed into their bed clothes, the lights were turned off, the candles were lit, the Barry White Greatest Hits LP was put on nice and low and everyone's needs were taken care of simultaneously in a perfect demonstration of inter-European cooperation. I opened my eyes a few seconds later to find that I had drifted off whilst brushing my teeth and none of those events had actually taken place. I went back into the living room, where the mattresses really were laid down next to each other, the girls really were changed into their bedclothes and the lights really were turned off. But there was no Barry White, the Walrus of Love.

'Good night, bonne nuit, gute nacht. Oh, and Julia?'

'Yes?'

'I'm not really Turkish.'

I still didn't know if Hélène's nan was.

After moving across the city to Marie's place I received a couple of emails. The first was from Roberta, the American, inviting me to a walk around the city. The second was from Jason proposing his latest sponsorship challenge. He wrote: 'Your mission, should you choose to accept it, is to be photographed in front of the Eiffel Tower wearing a beret, a stripy jumper, a string of onions around your neck, a newspaper or baguette under your arm and a silly French expression on your face. Should you complete this mission, I will make a new donation.'

Roberta had left a number for me to call, so I did and we arranged to meet in the afternoon. I told Jason I would try but couldn't make any promises as it was a pretty tough challenge he'd laid down. I met Roberta in front of the Metro station and she led the way.

'Where are we going?' I asked.

'To my favourite place in Paris: the graveyard.'

The cemetery was massive, more like a town within a city. It even had street names, and before entering we had to purchase a map so as to be able to find our way out at the end. Roberta was in search of her holy grail: the grave of Oscar Wilde. She had never been able to find it in three previous visits. I was keener to see the resting place of the Doors' frontman Jim Morrison. Locating Morrison's grave wasn't too difficult, and once in front of it Roberta pulled a couple of sandwiches from her bag and handed me one.

'Here. I wanted you to try one of these.'

'Thanks. What is it?'

'A Fluffernutter.'

'A what?'

'A Fluffernutter. It's peanut butter and fluff. It's good.'

Fluff? It was something that could only sound good to an American. I took it anyway. The first bite was a taste sensation, its deliciousness blowing me away.

'It's the unofficial Sandwich of New England,' Roberta told me, as I shoved the rest of it whole into my mouth.

'Cool. What's the official Sandwich of New England?'

'There isn't one.'

'Makes sense.'

(Fluff, by the way, is spreadable marshmallow.)

As we walked through the dead bodies, talking, I found out a bit of Roberta's unusual story. She told me that her girlfriend back in the States was a 23-year old post-op transsexual. A straight man who underwent an operation to become a lesbian.

The weather had taken a turn for the worse as Roberta and I went our separate ways and I headed for the Eiffel Tower, hoping to be able to borrow the props needed for the photo once there. It was the Eiffel Tower, what chance was there that I wouldn't find a beret-wearing Frenchman with a string of onions around his neck? Exactly. It was in the bag. The onion bag.

As I emerged from the Metro into the shadow of the tower the wind was gale force and it was sleeting heavily. The area surrounding the tower was deserted but for a few Dutch students on a school trip, and not one of them had so much as a beret, let alone a stripy jumper. They were wearing clogs though. But Jason hadn't mentioned anything about clogs. I didn't think they would secure me the donation. Which is just as well because they weren't really wearing them. I made it up. For no reason whatsoever. I was soaking wet and shivering so had to throw in the towel and head back to the warmth of the flat, jumping the ticket barrier en-route and receiving a pretty strong electric shock whilst doing so, which almost blew me back to England. Note to self: touching an electric device with wet hands is ill advised.

Whilst out I had received three emails from Couchsurfers in Luxembourg, Brussels and Amsterdam, all letting me know that I had a place to stay in each of their cities over the coming days. I was a bit worried about the host in Luxembourg, a creepy looking Frenchman, but there had been nobody else in the tiny country to try my luck with so he would have to do. I was set to leave France the following day.

I left Marie's flat at 3 in the afternoon and took the Metro across the city to Gare de L'est, where I hoped to jump on the 4:09pm train to Luxembourg. I very much liked the fact that the gates on Paris' Metro system were rarely manned or functional. Unfortunately the same could not be said of the overground railway. I didn't get anywhere near the 4:09pm as guards stood at the entrance to the platform checking all tickets, whilst a colleague stood in the middle of the platform making sure no one snuck across from anywhere else. The next train wasn't due until 5:39pm. I waited for it to come in, and again failed at getting myself on it. At 6:10pm I found a train was leaving shortly to the city of Nancy. Nancy was a 30-minute ride by fast train from Paris and was on the way to Luxembourg. There was no ticket control to get past to board this one. Once moving, the ticket woman came and saw me, telling me she would return to write me out a fine once she had checked the rest of the train. She never returned and I made it to Nancy at 7:40pm. From there I took the 8.20pm to Metz, arriving at 9. That one was easy, as I told the young female inspector that I had got on the wrong train and that my friend was on the other train with my ticket, and that he would make his way to Metz to come and get me. She laughed at my predicament and said simply, 'No problem,' no doubt thinking, 'This prat needs all the help he can get.'

Metz was freezing. I waited on the platform half an hour and at 9:30 got on the cross-border train to Luxembourg. The inspector came along but was obvious at the end of a busy day and couldn't be bothered to write a fine for me as soon as it became clear that I didn't have a French address. So with a shrug he just let it go. I ticked another capital off of my list.

Welcome to Luxembourg. I bet you've never been there.

33. Luxembourg

Capitals left to visit: Amsterdam, Athens, Brussels, Helsinki, Prague, Riga, Tallinn, Vilnius

Days on the road: 126
Distance travelled: 8125 miles
EU capitals visited: 15

THE ELECTRONIC INFORMATION board in the station let me know that the temperature was minus one degree. I wished I could turn back the clock to my time in Spain and *not* leave my coat there. I sent Tristan, my host, a text telling him I had arrived and asking how to get to his place. He replied with an address and instructions on how to get there by bus. It wasn't due to leave the station until 10:45pm so I took a stroll around the block to try and keep warm and ended up standing outside an Italian take-away for 20 minutes watching the Champions League match through the window. I was shivering, my teeth were chattering and my chest felt as if it were being sat on by Pavarotti. My bus finally pulled up and everyone but me got on at the front and showed a ticket to the driver, but I slid on through the back door and quickly slumped down in a seat. I found the house, rang the bell and waited. The light in the hallway went on and I watched through the tinted glass door as a shadow moved down the stairs inside. The door was opened by an effeminate Frenchman. Tristan was weird. And I don't mean the funny kind of weird; I mean the kind of weird you see sitting in the park at 3am wearing a trench coat. I felt uncomfortable in his presence.

'Come in,' he said, ushering me up the stairs as he shut and locked the door, 'you look freezing.'

Tristan didn't walk, he minced. I was led up through to the kitchen where he made me a cup of tea before we proceeded on to the living room to sit down and get to know each other a bit. As I told him about my day's adventures I noticed that he wasn't looking at me in the way a person normally looks at you when you are having a chat. Instead he gazed at me in much the same way I would a Shakira video on MTV; a look that would make any man (or woman) uncomfortable. I decided to try a bit harder to relax and ignore it, in the hope that I would soon be asleep and not have to worry about this potential pest. My plan got a bit more difficult though when out of the corner of my eye I caught sight of the repetitive motion his hand was performing inside his pocket. It was the very first time in my life that I had, knowingly at least, had a conversation with a man while he pleasured himself. I wasn't 100 per cent sure whether he was doing it deliberately to be provocative or if he didn't even realise that I had noticed. Either way, I was not best pleased. I was giving serious consideration to standing up, picking up my bags and leaving. Then I remembered that it was below freezing outside, I hadn't eaten and I had nowhere else to go. I didn't even have a coat. I was going to have to put up with it. After all, it was just a man masturbating in my direction; what was so weird about that? I needed to get him up out of his seat and doing something productive.

'Do you know what the worst part of this trip is? It's the hunger and the time I have to go without any food,' I said, as subtle as a Millwall fan in a mosque.

'Ah, I forgot. You must be hungry now. Are you?'

'Quite. Yes.'

'Let's go to the kitchen and see what we can find then.'

From the cupboard he pulled out a box of spaghetti and a jar of pasta sauce and asked if it would suffice. Just the sight of it was enough to have my mouth watering and my legs getting shaky with excitement. As soon as the food was cooked and put onto the plates we went back into the living room to eat. Tristan enjoyed the sight of another man stuffing his face, as the whole time I was shovelling the food into my gob he was staring at me with a dirty little smile on his lips. I made sure not to catch his eye, just focusing straight ahead at the telly where *Life on Mars* was showing on BBC Prime. He continued to talk to me, mostly utter nonsense, and continued to gaze at me whilst speaking this utter nonsense, but at least his hands stayed out of his pockets. He told me there were five people that shared the house but that mostly they stayed in their rooms and didn't socialise with one another and that he rarely knew how many people were in the house with him at any one time. I couldn't think why his housemates would avoid his company. Eventually he decided to call it a night, but not before showing his frustration as I refused to give in to his advances.

'Right,' he said in a huff, throwing his arms down, 'I'm going up to bed now. If you want me, you know where to find me, it's the bedroom to the left at the top of the stairs. I'll leave my door open for half an hour.'

'I'm quite sure I won't be needing anything. Good night.'

'Listen, in the morning I leave for work at about 9:30 but I guess you will be up and out before then to see the sights of the city. It would be nice if you are around though, we could go for breakfast together.'

I nodded. I had spent the day being kicked off of trains; almost frozen to death at a Luxembourg bus stop; and to finish I had been masturbated over. I was knackered and the last thing I wanted to do was get up at the crack of dawn to stroll around in the ice-cold air taking photos of statues. Wait, I tell a lie. That wasn't the *last* thing I wanted to do… that would be to have breakfast with this guy. He left the room and as I heard his footsteps go up the stairs I felt safe.

I made a bed out of the settee, shut the living room door and put my bag in front of it so that I would hear if he tried to come in during the night. I woke at around 11 the next morning in a completely silent house. Tristan was at work. The sun was shining through the window; it was a cold and clear day. I got on to the computer to make sure that my bed in Brussels hadn't cancelled and, as I sat there typing, a weird little bearded man in a dressing gown scurried down the stairs and into the bathroom, giving me a shocked 'hello' along the way. Then he scurried back up the stairs like a small rodent. *What a strange household,* I thought to myself.

I had a quick shower, stuffed my clothes into my backpack and went to see if there was any food in the kitchen cupboards. I wanted to get out of the house and out of the country as quickly as possible. I'd had a quick look around the city centre the night before and hadn't seen anything that had made me want to return to the scene in daylight. Perhaps I am doing Luxembourg an injustice when I tell you this; I don't know. In the kitchen I found nothing more than a tin of peach slices and some stale bread. I ate the peaches there and then and took the out-of-date bread in my bag for later. I left the house and walked for almost an hour to the station. The local population seemed young and relaxed. I mostly saw students standing around in small groups eating pastries and chatting in a carefree manner. How I wished for a pastry. The next train out of the country was leaving at 1:25pm and was already boarding. After the previous day's difficulties I decided that it might be a better option to try and speak to the conductor beforehand rather than jump on and then get chucked off again 10 minutes down the track. I found the man I needed to speak to and asked if he spoke English. He didn't. So in a mix of French and some Basic English I proceeded to explain my challenge and asked if there was any chance that he would let me ride without a ticket to Brussels. He told me he was only going to be on the train for about 20 minutes, just as far as the next station, but that he was happy for me to ride as far as there and then I would have to speak to his replacement to see if he felt the same way. Twenty minutes into the journey I watched the original guard get off and I stayed in my seat at the end of the train. I was left alone for another 45 minutes until the new inspector came up the train doing his rounds. I asked if he spoke English.

'Yes, I do,' came the smiling reply.

'Ah good. The previous inspector, the one with the beard…' I started but was interrupted.

'Oh yes, don't worry, he already spoke with me. It's fine, you can go to Brussels.'

I was travelling to Belgium, stress-free.

Looking out of the train window for the rest of the journey was like being on a tour of the set of *Saving Private Ryan*. Village after village of cobblestoned, terraced houses; each village separated by open green fields and small industrial towns. I pictured the house-to-house fighting of the second World War and couldn't think of a more stereotypical scene for this than what I was now seeing. Then, just as I drifted more into my imagination, I was snapped back to the present as a stray bullet shot straight through my window, just brushing past my ear at lightning speed, and nestled itself in the beehive haircut of a lady sitting across the carriage from me who barely reacted other than to utter a muffled, 'Sacre bleu.'

Thinking back, I may have imagined that bit too.

It was 4:30pm when I got off the train.

Welcome to Brussels.

34. Brussels

Capitals left to visit: Amsterdam, Athens, Helsinki, Prague, Riga, Tallinn, Vilnius

Days on the road: 127
Distance travelled: 8262 miles
EU capitals visited: 16

I RECEIVED A text on my phone from my host Leen instructing me to make my way to the city's opera house, as she was working in a gallery just around the corner from there and would come to meet me. As I made my way through the tiny little lanes, the smell of chocolate and waffles was enough to have me floating rather than walking. I could actually taste the stuff, such was the overpowering aroma filling the air. Everyone around me was speaking English. Not native tongue English but foreign-on-foreign English. Brussels was a place where people from all corners of the continent came together for one reason or another, and these people had chosen English over French as their lingo of choice. Jacque Chirac, I do hope you are reading this. Imagine Jacque Chirac reading this!

Having never visited Brussels before, the image built up in my mind over the years was one of an ugly, grey city, full to breaking point with parliamentary buildings, bureaucratic centres, law courts and more parliamentary buildings. What else would you expect of the political capital of the EU? But what I actually found was a quaint city of charming little sweet and pastry shops, jewellers and fashionable boutiques. The people came across as friendlier than average but it was a genuine friendliness rather than the fake kind you so often find in other tourist centres.

I found my way to the Opera House at Place de Monnaie, sent a text to Leen, then sat down to wait on a bench in the middle of the small square for her arrival. All around the perimeter of the square loitered small groups of young teenagers, staring at me and giggling, forcing me to realise just how much of an out-of-towner I looked. I could easily have passed for a vagrant: army trousers, a dirty tracksuit top, a beard similar to the one that the lead character in the film *The Pianist* grew whilst in hiding, a look of hunger and tiredness in the eyes and a rucksack on my back. I was starting to feel pretty self-conscious and wished Leen would speed up her rescue operation. Finally she arrived and quickly whisked me off down the street and in through a door to a busy photo exhibition where people stood around, talking in a pretentious fashion about pretentious issues. I assumed the topics were pretentious; my Flemish isn't what it once was. Leen had a camera the size of baby hung from a strap around her neck. Her look was what I would describe as kooky. She had short hair with random long streaks, an elaborate scarf around her neck and an all-round air of non-compliance. She explained to me that the photo exhibition was just a sideshow to the main event that was a book launch of some work written by a professor at the Flemish language university. Most of the people here were from the above-mentioned educational institute, and the professor was a very popular man. Leen's job title for the afternoon was Official Photographer. She introduced me to a friend, Jan, and then left us talking as she went around the room snapping shots of people's faces. Jan was the same age as me although he had a serious air about him that made him come across as someone much older, or at least wiser. He had shortly cropped hair and a trimmed, tidy beard. His job for the afternoon was to sell books, but all he seemed to be doing was enjoying the free alcohol. As soon as I spotted the free wine my instinct immediately told me there must also be free food knocking about somewhere. I scanned the room and, sure enough, there on a table in the middle sat bowls full of crisps. I didn't want to come across as a freeloader or liberty taker so waited patiently for Jan to make the first move then followed him to the prize. There was also a free supply of Coke. The American symbol of capitalism kind; not the Colombian powder kind. That would have been a proper book launch.

Jan was a film student. He readily admitted that he was a pretty bad maker of films but that in time and with plenty of hard work he hoped and expected to become great. We got on well and spent the next couple of hours talking randomly in between speeches that were being made up on the stage. My stomach was wrapped up with hunger pain. I was making a valiant attempt to fill the gap with crisps, but there weren't too many left on the table, and there are only so many crisps you can eat when you are in need of something real, something hot.

Just before 7pm it was finally time to leave the building. I found myself a member of a group of eight people stood in the open air outside the main door. One of the group, a loud guy in his late forties with an earring, started speaking to me in Flemish. He was obviously joking about something but I had no idea what.

'Je ne comprends pas,' I said, shrugging my shoulders and looking at him blankly.

At this he started laughing and speaking French to me whilst frisking my bag and jacket. As the confused look on my face turned to a nervous smile, Jan translated for me.

'He says, "you don't speak Flemish and yet you are here at a Flemish function. Where have you hidden the bomb?"'

Everybody gave a little laugh but the joke was wasted on me.

'Let's eat!' said Jan.

They were the words I had been longing to hear.

Everyone in the group spoke perfect English and, apart from the comedian and his portly wife, were all in their early twenties. As a group we made our way through the narrow streets towards a Lebanese restaurant that all assured me was the best in Brussels. Everyone talked, laughed and joked amongst themselves while I tagged along at the back, feeling like a hanger-on who didn't belong. I had hardly shared two words with Leen and wondered if she regretted inviting me to stay. Loneliness had reared its ugly head. My self-confidence was at an all-time low and I wanted nothing more than to be picked up by the hand of a giant and dropped back down on the south coast of England. I had had enough of the continent. Then, after the Lebanese waiter had led us all to a large table in the basement of the restaurant, everything changed. Leen introduced me properly to each member of the group and told them why I was in Belgium, instantaneously transforming me from complete outsider into centre of attention. The questions flew at me from all directions and my feelings of awkwardness vanished. I belonged. Such was the kindness of the group that each person decided to put some money towards my food and a beer, meaning that I wouldn't go hungry, and nor would Leen have to sub me. Yet again I had been humbled. As we ate, I found myself in conversation with the old comedian, who expressed surprise at finding out I was English.

'I thought you were an Arab! You don't look English at all. I was sure you were a Muslim fundamentalist,' he said.

Now I understood the bomb joke. It still wasn't funny.

After dinner, the group took me to a place called Dolle Mol, which I was told was something of a rarity in Brussels: a Flemish bar. The reason it was a rarity was that almost all Brussels natives were French-speaking. The place was a classic dive: small, dark and smoky with the walls painted a moody red. The first thing that took my attention on entering was a Goth, completely passed out, lying face down on his table. At the table next to the

Goth sat two older, long-haired drunks, laughing and shouting boisterously at everyone else in the bar. In another corner, a group of French speakers sat drinking wine. What were they doing here, I wondered? This dirty, dark little bar had character. As the evening wore on the barman asked everyone for quiet as he introduced a man who was to give a poetry reading in Flemish, except all of the pieces were classic French works of humour that he had translated himself. The audience around me roared their approval and howled with laughter. I couldn't understand a word, obviously, but just being surrounded by the collective joy made me laugh with everyone else. This was another one of those moments that made all the struggling of the journey worthwhile. Another cultural experience that I never would have been gifted had I not set out on this voyage of discovery. If I ever return to Brussels I shall definitely seek out that little Flemish watering hole.

Before crashing out on the bottom bunk in Leen's tiny bedsit later that night, I was introduced to a Dutch girl who lived down the hallway and shared the communal bathroom. Chermaine worked for a student online magazine called *Indy Media* and felt that my story would make a great feature, so we arranged a little photo shoot and interview to be had over breakfast the following morning before I left for Amsterdam.

Getting myself up at 7:30 proved to be completely worth the effort, as I stuffed my cheeks full of fresh ham, cheese and hot bread. We got through the interview, I smiled for a few snaps and then Chermaine accompanied me to the city's main train station as Leen had to rush off early for a lecture.

'I have another question for you,' Chermaine said, as we walked the streets together. 'If you were allowed to stop your challenge for five minutes and spend a couple of euros, what would you buy?'

'Definitely a Mars Bar and a can of Dr. Pepper. My body's been craving sugar lately,' I told her honestly.

'Wait here,' she said, leaving me standing outside a newspaper shop, before returning and handing me the two things I had wished for. I welled up a bit at the gesture as I hugged my new friend and thanked her. I've said it before and I will say it again: people are pretty cool. Have a bit more faith in your fellow human being; there's a lot more good out there than bad.

As we continued the walk to the station, Chermaine told me that her mum had twice been struck down with cancer and had twice beaten it. She thanked me for what I was doing to raise awareness of the charity and I thanked her for further inspiring and motivating me to complete the challenge. I needed moments like this. We embraced one final time on the platform and then I climbed aboard the 10:24 to Amsterdam. I had wanted to speak to the ticket inspector before boarding but hadn't been able to find him. I made my way directly through the carriages and walked into him just as the train was pulling out of the station. He was a middle-aged man with a bald head and an earring. He spoke English. He wasn't the same middle-aged, bald headed, earring wearing, English speaking man that I had met the night before, though. I know that's what you were thinking. I explained to him my challenge, showed him the newspaper and asked if I could stay on the train to Amsterdam. He told me that he only had authority once we arrived inside the Netherlands and then pointed to his Belgian counterpart, a woman who was standing in the next carriage, and said that she was in charge as long as we were still in Belgium. I told her my story and that the Dutch guy had said he had no problem with me travelling through the Netherlands for free, which he confirmed with a nod. She read the newspaper article and with an enthusiastic smile said that of course I could ride the train. I arrived at my destination at 1:10pm, ticking another capital city off of the list.

Welcome to Amsterdam.

35. Amsterdam

Capitals left to visit: Athens, Helsinki, Prague, Riga, Tallinn, Vilnius

Days on the road: 128
Distance travelled: 8392 miles
EU capitals visited: 17

STEPHEN'S FLAT WAS in an area of the city called Jordaan, which he had told me was within walking distance of the station. It was raining heavily and I didn't want to be walking around aimlessly, so I asked a bored-looking policeman for directions.

'You will be better off taking a tram,' he told me.

I had just watched a tram leave, and seen that you needed a ticket to get on it.

'Can you just give me directions for walking, please?'

He laughed. I didn't take this as a promising sign.

'It'll take more than half an hour, you know? Are you sure you don't want to take a tram?'

'Quite sure. Thanks.'

The officer pointed me in the right direction and sent me on my way. The rain was coming down heavier and heavier by the minute and I started wishing for a coat. Everyone that passed me on the busy streets was English. Northern English. It was more like being in Leeds than the image I'd had in my head of a cool, relaxed Amsterdam. After about 15 minutes of walking I came across a Tourist Information centre and popped inside to check that I was still on the right path. The girl behind the desk was young and bubbly. She had no idea where the street that I was looking for was, but she wasn't going to let this stand in the way of sending me away happy. And so, with a steely determination, she took a map, took it to a desk, spread it out in front of her and set about scanning the entire piece of paper until she came up with a result.

'Aha! Here it is. I knew I would find it!' she exclaimed after a couple of minutes, picking up the map and bringing it over to where I was standing.

And then there was silence.

'So… where is it?'

There was more silence as the colour in the girl's face turned darker.

'I'm sorry. I've completely forgotten already.'

This girl is useful, I thought to myself.

She picked up the map and a minute later re-found the spot, but this time had to admit that she hadn't actually found the street, only the area it was in.

'When you arrive in the area, just ask a passer-by for more precise directions,' she told me. 'But you need to change your pronunciation. It's not pronounced Jordan like the country, it's pronounced Yor-Darn.'

She couldn't let me have a map because they sold for 2 Euros. Still, I left with a smile on my face.

About an hour later and after following numerous inaccurate directions from local residents, most of whom I'm sure were stoned, I finally found myself stood outside Stephen's building, right next to the water on one of the city's many canals. I pressed the buzzer and then walked up the steepest and narrowest of staircases. Stephen met me out on the landing and invited me in. I was immediately struck by how spaced out my host seemed. I no longer thought the other residents I'd met had been stoned; not compared to Stephen anyway. His pupils were dilated, more like he was on MDMA than weed.

He was wearing a pair of yoga bottoms and what at first glance appeared to be a cycling jersey. I couldn't see a bike.

'Come, sit down. Let's have a tea.'

Stephen spoke with a calming Irish lilt, and was in his late twenties. As he boiled the water I took in my surroundings. The tiny bedsit contained no furniture; just cushions on the floor all the way round the walls. There were no electric lights; only candles. There was no electricity in the flat at all, just a gas cooker on which he could boil the water for tea. There was a mattress in the corner of the room, where I guessed he slept, and a large mirror up against a wall facing the mattress.

'The reason for the big mirror is that I meditate into it for four hours a day. I was just meditating when you arrived,' Stephen told me.

His voice was soft and yet authoritative. It contained an eeriness. I was slightly unnerved.

'So, what brings you to Amsterdam? Are you a student or do you work?' I asked.

'Neither,' came the calm reply.

'Well, what do you do then?'

'I moved to Amsterdam to expand my consciousness through meditation and the consumption of hard drugs.'

What do you say to that? Seriously…

Stephen went on to explain that he had arrived in Amsterdam four months previously after saving up his money for a few years at home in Ireland. He planned to spend a year in the Dutch capital before moving on to India. He then shook me somewhat by staring deep into my eyes and proclaiming, 'I will show you things that will open your eyes. I will show you deep into your own pain. It will be hard to deal with but will be beneficial to you in the long run.'

He then turned away from me, staring himself face-on in the large mirror, as he said, 'Put your belongings in the corner over there, next to the belongings of the other Couchsurfer I have staying here. She is out exploring the city. Now you must go out and explore, too. Come back between 6 and 7 this evening for dinner. After dinner I will show you the many faces of my past incarnations.'

I was staying with a guy whose mind had been so frazzled by drugs that I wasn't sure he wouldn't act on voices in his head and offer me up as a sacrifice to some strange deity. I left the flat. I had to explore the city. I had been told. I headed back in the direction from which I had come, towards the city centre. Canals ran up and down the city almost in grid format, crossing paths at every crossroads, meaning that each street I walked down looked identical to the last. The city seemed to be no more than a network of bridges and barges. The most noticeable aspect of Amsterdam was the abundance of coffee shops. When I say coffee shops, you should know I don't mean coffee shops in the English sense of the word. These were no Starbucks. And let's be honest, who really wants another Starbucks? Who wants any Starbucks at all, come to think of it? Almost every other shopfront belonged to one of these café's, each one blowing out onto the street the most delicious aromas of different types of cannabis. Never in my life had I strolled through a city that seemed so at peace with itself. Everyone that passed me was so laid back, so relaxed, so friendly. I carried on walking, smiling and not thinking about the uncomfortable atmosphere that awaited me back at Stephen's flat. Then my surroundings changed. The people around me weren't laid back and friendly anymore; they were pissed up and dressed as super heroes. They spoke in Northern accents and had their names printed on their shirts. Gary, Baz, Mikey, Dave. They carried half-full pint glasses in their hands and pretended to push each other into the canals. The coffee shops had been replaced by sex stores, erotic cinemas, live sex performances, pornographic peep shows and novelty condom shops. The Englishmen popped in and out of each one casually. I crossed a canal, looking to escape earshot of the roving stags, rounded a corner, looked up and saw my first one. I had heard about them before, of course. I had read about them, too. Standing behind a glass window stood an almost naked girl. Standing behind lots of windows stood lots of almost naked girls. Almost naked girls that blew kisses at me and waved their arms for me to join them on their side of the glass. One opened her window and lent out as I passed.

'Hey, sexy. Come and spend some time with me. Only 50 euros for suck and fuck.'

I walked on, though I couldn't help but take a look at each new girl that I passed. The thing that struck me most was the natural beauty of them. I couldn't understand how they came to be living the lives that they now were. Surely girls that looked like that could do alright for themselves without having to sell their bodies. Maybe I was being naïve. Maybe the life wasn't that bad. Maybe the money was that good. Maybe they just loved sex with old, fat blokes from Yorkshire and this was the only way they could get it. Or maybe they had been tricked and forced into it, trafficked into the Netherlands by ruthless criminals. I needed to get away, the thought of what the girls in front of me might have been through depressed me greatly.

I crossed a couple more canals until all signs of depravation had vanished, and then climbed down a ladder to the entrance of an uninhabited houseboat, where I sat and cleared my mind. Amsterdam was a strange place and I wasn't sure if I liked or hated it. It didn't seem real.

I got back to the flat before 7 and found Stephen serving up a chicken curry and rice. The American Couchsurfer Elizabeth hadn't come back yet so Stephen and I ate together and then followed it up with a spliff. After we'd smoked he asked me if I was ready.

'Ready for what?'

'Ready to see. Ready to have your eyes opened.'

I nodded. I wondered if my host could tell that I was mocking him in my head. I sat down in front of him, face to face as instructed, and told myself that I would humour him for a couple of minutes just to confirm to myself that he really was talking bollocks and that too many drugs will mess you up. Then it began. It wasn't what I had been expecting. Face after face after face morphed itself onto Stephen's own, flicking through like a slide show. Some had beards, some had stubble, some had long hair, some had short hair, some smiled, while others scowled. I looked away, blinked and then looked back. It was still happening. I had to break eye contact.

'I'm sorry, I have to stop,' I told him.

'That's fine. I told you I would show you something. I knew you didn't believe me. I know you were mocking me inside. But now you see.'

I didn't know then and I don't know now how to explain what happened that evening in Amsterdam, and I am not going to guess. All I know is that I saw something that I'd never seen before.

'Let's go to the pub,' Stephen then said, standing up. The experience was never mentioned again.

The next day was a Saturday and once again Stephen kicked me out of the flat in the early afternoon.

'I need time alone. You need time alone. Go now and explore some more. Meet me at Dam Square at 5; there is something I want you to see.'

I spent the afternoon sitting in a park, watching a dad play football with his young son and remembering my own youth, when every Sunday afternoon my dad had taken me to a large field close to our house to practice my free-kicks, volleys and chest control. That was all before alcoholism had really taken control of my dad's life. I wiped away tears sat at that park bench in Amsterdam until a large smile was brought to my face by a piece of profound graffiti written in permanent marker on the bench behind my back. It said simply: 'I like reading'. That was it. I smiled because I like reading too. Then I took a book out of my bag and began to read. I read for hours that afternoon.

I arrived in Dam Square, Amsterdam's main meeting place, dead on 5 and found Stephen standing in the middle of a large group of young people each holding a cardboard sign. Closer inspection revealed that the signs were advertising free hugs.

'Kris, I'm glad you made it. This is what I wanted you to see. Every so often we get together here and offer strangers free hugs. Hugs make people feel good. Take a sign; get involved.'

Stephen smiled as he handed me a piece of cardboard and a black marker pen.

'No, thanks. I think I'll just watch. I'm not much of a hugs guy.'

'Suit yourself.'

I stood far enough away from the crowd that I wouldn't be grabbed randomly by a hugger and watched in amazement as people young, old, male and female stopped to hug the volunteers before carrying on with their daily chores. I couldn't believe what I was witnessing. There was no self-consciousness, no embarrassment; just hugs.

In amongst the group of volunteers, one girl stood out above the rest. It wasn't just her looks that captivated me; there was something different about her; something warm; something positive. She laughed, smiled, danced, sang and interacted with people, and I noticed that everyone that came into contact with her went away with a big smile splashed across their face.

'That girl's different,' I told Stephen.

'Yep, I think we would all do her,' he said with a wry smile.

That wasn't what I had meant.

He told me that we had been invited to a party later that evening and instructed me to invite anyone else I felt worthy. He then walked away and started a conversation with the girl that I was now curious about. I didn't catch the beginning of their chat but I did overhear her telling him that the last thing she wanted was a boyfriend. I moved closer.

'So really you just want to fuck a lot of guys without any commitment?' Stephen then asked her.

And I thought the Irish were meant to have charm. She didn't like the question, replying, 'No. No fucking for me. Every guy I meet wants and tries to fuck me. I know I can have who I want, but I don't need to sleep around to boost my ego.'

I liked the way she handled herself; the self-confidence, the attitude. The conversation ended and Stephen moved away. She was now stood in front of me and offered me a hug, which I accepted. She smiled and put her arms around me, and then we got talking. Jalila was 19 years old and from Brazil, but lived and studied in Riga, Latvia.

'I'm going to be in Riga quite soon,' I told her, 'maybe I'll see you there.'

'Yea, maybe,' she said, unenthusiastically.

She had heard it all before.

'But let me warn you in advance; I have no intention of letting you fuck me, so please don't even allow that thought to pop into your mind,' I told her in a serious tone.

'Okay, then we should swap numbers. When you arrive in Latvia, give me a call.'

We exchanged details and then talked a bit more. She had only arrived in Amsterdam that morning but had lost her group of friends whilst walking around the city and couldn't reach any of them by phone; she also had no idea where the hostel was that she was booked into, and so had nowhere to sleep for the night. She had stumbled upon the Free Hugs meeting by chance and stayed because she felt good around like-minded people. I asked Stephen if it was alright to invite her to the party and if she could spend the night at his if she needed to.

'Of course you can ask her, but I'm telling you, there is no way a girl as special as that is going to say yes.'

'Yea she will.'

And so she did.

The Hugs session finished at 6:30pm and we were invited back to the home of a Frenchman for the party. We all began walking in the same direction, first in a couple of large groups, and then as the groups became smaller and more numerous I found myself walking with only Jalila for company. I was carrying her suitcase, which was slightly heavier than Ricky Gervais in his prime, but I didn't let on. My hands were freezing in the cold air so she took off one of her gloves and put it on me, and with her ungloved hand she took my ungloved hand and we linked fingers. We walked for 45 minutes and managed to lose the rest of the group. And then from nowhere the Frenchman came out of a block of flats right in front of where we stood, saw us and said, 'Ah good, you made it.'

Inside the small flat about seven or eight hipsters sat around the living room floor on cushions talking. Everyone was from a different country but all conversation was in English. I wished it wasn't, as I had never been so bored in my life. Radical politics, the concept of world peace and hardcore Marxism were all being discussed, but unfortunately by unimaginative people just repeating soundbites or quotes they'd read in books; as we picked small pieces of bread off of plates in the middle. Jalila sat next to me and put her hands in my lap. They were cold, so I took them in mine and held them until they were warm.

I was getting bored and hungry. The bread wasn't hitting the spot, and I hadn't eaten anything else all day. Stephen read my mind, coming over as he did to ask, 'Shall we just eat a bit more bread and then fuck off?'

I told Jalila the plan and she liked it, saying that she would come with us. Back at the flat a few more of Stephen's friends joined us, and together we sat in the candlelight and passed around a bong containing a strong strain of the hallucinogenic, Salvia. Only, no one thought to tell me that that was what we were smoking; I just assumed it was some weird-smelling weed. Nobody was talking; nobody needed to. Slowly I slipped into a trance. This was the first time I had ever tried this drug and I very much liked its effects. I drifted away from reality; the only thing I was aware of was my own slow breathing. I looked around at the people I was with and started to trip, as I watched their spirits come out of their bodies before smiling at me and getting back in. I was aware of the smiles on everyone's faces as we let ourselves disappear into our own personal journeys. Jalila came into my arms, still not saying a word, and we just held each other, gently stroking each other's skin, until we fell asleep for the night, wrapped up as one. I hadn't kissed her; I hadn't tried to sleep with her. I didn't want to. This felt like something more gratifying. We had shared a moment.

Just before dropping off, I had promised her that I would wake with her at 6:30 in the morning to see her to the airport and carry her suitcase for her. Her flight back to Riga departed at 9:20. Her alarm woke me first at 6:15. I shook her until she opened her eyes and told her it was time to get up.

'What's the time?'

'Quarter past six.'

'Not yet. A few more minutes.'

I was too tired to argue, so went back to sleep. At 6.30 the alarm went again.

'Jalila, come on. We have to get up now; you're going to miss your flight.'

Again she just opened her eyes, mumbled something and went back to sleep. I didn't have the strength to do anything about it. It was dark, cold and cosy.

'Shit! Shit! Shit! It's 7:30! I'll miss my flight! I have to go! Why didn't you wake me?'

I awoke to Jalila's panic. I hurriedly pulled on a pair of jeans and followed her down the stairs, dragging her heavy suitcase and freezing my balls off. It was pissing down with rain. We hailed a taxi and made it to the airport just as they were closing her gate. We hugged and she disappeared. I bunked the train back to the city and returned to the flat to find Stephen still fast asleep. I climbed back under my own blanket and was just about to drift off again when my peace was interrupted by the words, 'Don't go back to sleep. You need to go out and explore.'

'But it's raining outside. And I'm knackered. Can't I just...'

'You need to go out. We both need alone time.'

I sighed; and out I went. To McDonalds. Where I sat at a table with an empty paper cup, pretending that I had bought a drink. I sat there all day, watching tourists and listening for the hundredth time on the journey to the complete works of Cat Stevens on the iPod. Without that man, my jaunt across the continent would have been a lot less bearable.

I was ready to leave Amsterdam; it had drained me. Fortunately I had the perfect place to go to next: Dresden. I know what you're thinking: *'Dresden, the perfect place?'* Probably not to most people. Probably not to anyone, actually. But to me it was just what I needed, for it was the home town of Stefanie, the person that had been with me on that fateful night back in Brighton when the idea of travelling around Europe without any money had reared its head for the very first time. Stefanie was just the person I wanted to see. I needed the familiarity, the warmth, the laughter. I needed to be myself around someone. Dresden was a long way off though, right in the east of Germany. Getting there would be a mission.

I slept long and comfortably that night. After a hearty bowl of muesli and a hot shower I left Stephen's flat just after 10, making my way to Amsterdam station through the driving wind and sleet. The first train heading for Germany would be the 12:34 to Frankfurt. I waited patiently with a book and then had a decision to make as I watched my train pulling in to the platform and saw that the inspector was in an intimidating German uniform rather than a friendly Dutch one. Should I jump on and try to hide from him for as long as possible, or should I seek him out and try to appeal to his good nature? I decided I couldn't handle the stress that came with playing the stowaway. If I came up against a brick wall then I would simply wait for the 2 o'clock to Berlin and jump on it. But I wanted to at least try my luck first. As luck would have it, the inspector turned out to be a legend.

'Sure, you can travel on my train. As far as you like!' he said.

At first I assumed that he was being sarcastic, but then when I realised he wasn't I thanked him and jumped aboard.

My train arrived at Frankfurt at 4:30pm and I quickly found out that the next train heading eastwards departed at 5:20pm. I went outside for some air, found it was still raining heavily, saw a sign pointing people in the direction of an Indian restaurant called Gaylord, laughed and then went back inside.

The Dresden train came in and I took the same approach that had worked so well in Amsterdam. It didn't work. The guard told me to go away. I didn't bother arguing and I watched as the train left without me. The next Dresden-bound train wasn't due to leave until 7:20pm and wouldn't arrive in the East German city until past midnight. I jumped on at the back as it was sitting at the platform; there was no way I was going to try and get fancy by speaking to anyone first. This way, if the inspector turned out to be another mean-spirited character I would at least make it part way to Dresden before being kicked off. The train set off and I made myself comfortable until the inspector finally came to me. It was a woman, and seemed to have evil running through her veins. I could see it in her eyes before she even uttered her first words. She neither spoke nor understood a word of English and, as I tried my hardest to explain myself in German, she just hurled abuse down onto me in her native tongue, peering at me over the top of her glasses in a Margaret Thatcher kind of way. She was definitely a Tory, and I have a serious dislike of Tories. The German Maggie Thatcher then started getting other passengers involved, speaking to them about me and encouraging them to shake their heads and point their fingers in my direction. Not content with giving me a ticking off, she wanted to well and truly humiliate me. And then, just as we were approaching the station at which I was to be thrown off, she started explaining to a girl waiting by the doors what a low-life piece of scum I was. The girl looked at me with sympathy. I could take no more. I snapped.

'Why are you speaking to her and not to me? What business is it of hers? Why do you think she cares what you have to say about me? Do you not know you look like a more evil version of Margaret Thatcher and that no one cares what you have to say?'

Maggie just smirked and continued making comments in German. My secondary school German lessons meant that I could make out some of what she was saying: 'He comes here to Germany and doesn't even speak German! Doesn't even speak German!'

'I know why you won't speak to me directly. It is because you are a bint. Do you understand the word bint? It isn't nice when someone abuses you in a language that you don't understand, is it?' I told her.

And as she grabbed me by the scruff of the neck and physically threw me out on to the platform, I bid her farewell with a final, 'Auf wiedersehen, bint.'

Welcome to…

Wait…

Where the hell am I?

36. Fulda

AFTER READING THIS far into the book you surely know me well enough to realise that this was out of character. This was the first time I had resorted to name-calling on the trip and I hoped it would also be the last. Usually I wouldn't get myself so worked up and stressed, especially not if it was directed at someone doing their job, but this particular person was taking joy from talking down to me and she knew full well that if I got kicked off the train I was going to have to spend the night out in the cold. And she looked like a Tory. I think that was what tipped me over the edge. Fair enough, I knew the risks; but then don't take joy in kicking me off. Her face just triggered an angry reaction in me. Let me put it a bit more into context. I had eaten nothing but a bowl of muesli all day; it was 8 in the evening and there were no more trains going my way; it was icy cold outside and I was now stranded in a small town that I had never even heard of before called Fulda. Yes. Fulda. The station's sign told me where I was. Fulda! To sum up: I was feeling pretty rubbish and I took a little bit of consolation from being able to vent a bit at the person who was intent on making my day worse.

As I walked down the platform, counting to ten in my head and breathing deep breaths, I tried to look at my options. I didn't have many. The only thing I could do other than freeze to death throughout the night in the station was to try to find a motorway to hitchhike along. The chances of finding a car going to Dresden at this time of evening – and one that would be willing to pick me up – were pretty remote. I felt demoralised. But it wasn't to last more than a minute, as the girl who had been forced to listen to the ticket guard's rant about me came up and asked in English if I was fine in Fulda or if I needed any help finding my way. I told her my story.

After I had finished speaking, the girl's boyfriend came onto the platform and eyed me suspiciously. Fair enough; after all, I was a foreign guy chatting to his girlfriend in a train station after dark. She explained things to him before we walked together to check the information board. Taking another train was out of the question because there was only one more to Dresden and it didn't leave until after midnight. We were still 4 hours away from my target city and if I got kicked off of the late train I would be in a dire situation. I was close to collapsing from tiredness, hunger and stress, and really didn't fancy spending the night standing on a motorway holding up a piece of cardboard with the word 'Dresden' written on it. The boyfriend made a call while I stood next to him, not understanding German but kind of guessing that he was trying to sort something out for me.

'My boyfriend has just phoned our flatmate and it is not a problem for you to sleep in the living room tonight,' said the girl whose name I was soon to discover was Andrea.

Just like in Bordeaux I had been saved by a stranger who I had met in a train station. She had approached me without really knowing why, had spoken to me for less than five minutes, and now, along with her boyfriend, had made me such a generous offer of hospitality that I felt humbled. I squeezed into the back of their little car for the drive to their flat. Andrea even popped into a kebab house to sort us out some dinner. My mood had gone from one of despair to one of contentment in a matter of minutes, thanks once again to a couple of kind-hearted strangers. The three of us sat at the table eating the kebabs and I got to know my unplanned hosts a bit. Andrea worked as a social worker with young, vulnerable people. The boyfriend, Benni, taught physics and maths at a local comprehensive school. They were a young couple, 27 and 30, and had been together for many years already. After eating, it was time for my lesson in local studies. The town we were in, Fulda, was strange as far as German cities went because it was predominantly Catholic. Centuries ago, when the reformations had taken place across so many parts of Europe, Fulda managed to keep her Catholic identity thanks to the huge number of monks living in the city at the time. The tradition has lived on right up to the present, and today's Fulda is home to a beautiful and grand cathedral, which was pointed out to me as we passed it.

My bed for the night was going to be a mattress on the living room floor. Benni had to be up for work at 6:45 the next morning and was going to drop me off at the train station on his way; so I needed to get some rest. I took a shower and then climbed under the blanket before midnight. I woke up early after sleeping better than I had for a long while and headed out the door with Benni and a banana in my hand; he had given it to me. It was freezing outside and there was a covering of ice on the ground, making it slippery. I thanked my new friend for everything he and his girlfriend had done for me over the past 11 hours and gave him a firm handshake before wishing him a good day at work.

I paced up and down the platform, trying to keep warm as I waited for the 7:15 train, which I got on and then got kicked off of before I'd even had a chance to take a seat, as the ticket inspector booted me onto the platform of the first station we stopped at; a place so pointless I didn't even take note of its name. It was 7:40 and there wasn't another train leaving for Dresden until 9:37. I spent two hours shivering in the waiting room. The 9:37 finally pulled in and I jumped through the electric doors and found a seat. This time I wasn't going to bother explaining my true situation. Instead I was going to go back to the trusted technique of fibbing.

'Somebody stole my wallet when I was asleep last night. I

really need to get to Dresden, otherwise I am stuck in this little place. My friends in Dresden will come and pay for my ticket when we get there. Please let me get there!' I pleaded with the conductor.

'Your friend will be able to come and see me on the train in Dresden?' she asked.

'Yes.'

'Okay, it's no problem. I am sorry about your bad luck.'

Another nice German in a uniform.

I arrived just after 1pm and by then the friendly inspector had forgotten all about me.

Welcome to Dresden.

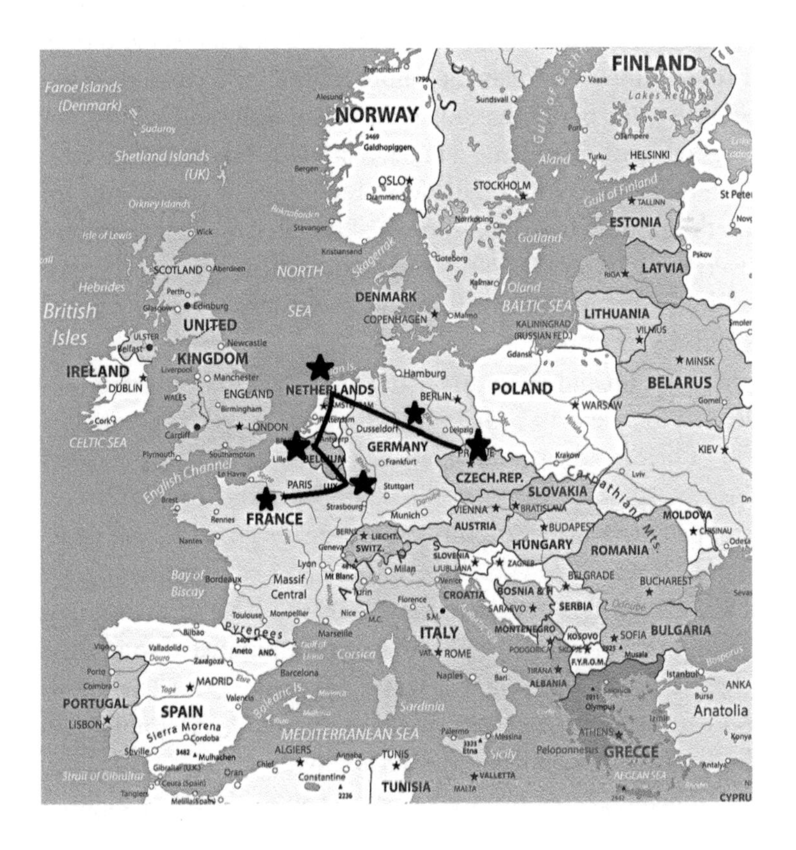

37. Dresden

THE FIRST THING that struck me about Dresden as I walked through the pedestrianised streets away from the train station on this Tuesday morning, dodging trams as I kept my eyes open for a hotel, was the cleanliness and tidiness of the city. The second thing was that the city seemed so new. Then I remembered: the bombing. I don't mean I remembered the bombing, I wasn't there, I mean that I … never mind.

Between the dates of 13th and 15th February 1945, the allies pummelled Dresden over four air raids in which 1,300 heavy bombers dropped more than 3,900 tons of high-explosive bombs and incendiary devices. The resulting firestorm destroyed 25 square miles of the city centre. It has since been argued that Dresden was a cultural landmark of little or no military significance, and that the attacks were indiscriminate area bombing and not proportionate for the military gains achieved. Because those in authority hadn't expected Dresden to ever be targeted in such a way, there were very few air raid shelters in the city. The largest one, underneath the main train station, was housing 6,000 refugees at the time. As a result, most people took shelter in their cellars, but one of the air raid precautions the city had taken was to remove the thick cellar walls between rows of buildings and replace them with thin partitions that could be knocked through in an emergency. The idea was that, as one building collapsed or filled with smoke, those using the basement as a shelter could knock the walls down and run into adjoining buildings. With the city on fire everywhere, those fleeing from one burning cellar simply ran into another, resulting in thousands of bodies being found piled up in houses at the end of city blocks. A Dresden police report written shortly after the attacks reported that the old town and the inner eastern suburbs had been engulfed in a single fire that had destroyed almost 12,000 homes. The same report said that the raids had destroyed 24 banks, 640 shops, 64 warehouses, two market halls, 31 large hotels, 26 pubs, 63 administrative buildings, three theatres, 18 cinemas, 11 churches, six chapels, five other cultural buildings, 19 hospitals, 39 schools, five consulates, the zoo, the waterworks, the railways, and 19 ships and barges. According to an official German report, issued on 22nd March 1945, the number of dead recovered by that date was 20,204 – including 6,865 who were cremated on the Altmarkt square – and the total number of deaths was expected to be about 25,000. The number of people registered with the authorities as missing was 35,000; around 10,000 of those were later found to be alive.

In a nutshell, Dresden was completely obliterated.

The rebuilding of the city began shortly after the war and continued right up until after the German reunification in 1989, with great effort being made to rebuild some of Dresden's former landmarks, such as the Frauenkirche church, the Semperoper (the Saxony state opera house), and the Zwinger Palace. In 1956 Dresden entered a twin-town relationship with Coventry, another city to have suffered some of the worst air attacks of the war, at the hands of the Luftwaffe during 1940 and 1941, during which over 1,200 civilians were killed and the city's cathedral destroyed.

It was a sunny day and while the Germans were walking around wrapped up in thick coats and scarves, I was comfortably warm in just a t-shirt and an unzipped, light tracksuit top. I found a hotel and was permitted to make a quick call from reception to Stefanie, who told me she would meet me in ten minutes next to the fountain in the little square outside. I sat and waited, thinking with a smile about that warm October's night on Brighton beach when a drunken chat with the girl I was about to see again had given birth to the idea of the epic life-changing journey I now found myself on. I never for a minute imagined back then that I would be sitting under the Dresden sun a few months later waiting for my friend to turn up and give me a place to sleep. Stefanie arrived and on seeing me produced a grin that I knew so well.

'Welcome to Dresden!'

She laughed as she led me off to grab a slice of pizza before we took the tram back to the room she rented in the university-owned block of student accommodation. The type of block was very familiar by now, and the suburb it sat in was very Eastern looking: just big grey building after big grey building. Stefanie lived on the 11th floor of 15. Each floor was split into sub-compartments of three bedrooms, with each floor sharing one large communal kitchen and each sub-compartment sharing a bathroom. Stefanie's room was like that of a 13-year old girl's – hold on! I know this not because I regularly frequent young girls' bedrooms, but because at the time of my stay in Dresden I had a sister in her early teens – everything was pink, including the paint, and the walls were covered in posters of Robbie Williams and Jude Law. There were even glow in the dark moon and star stickers on the ceiling. My bed was a mattress on the floor. Over the next couple of days I was introduced to and spent time with Stefanie's best friend, Marlin, a brunette. There seemed to be an instant spark between the two of us and I wondered if anything would come of it.

The more I sat with Marlin, the more I fancied her. Her long black hair glistened, her deep brown eyes looked straight into my soul, and she didn't wear any make-up; there was no need. Her body was perfectly shaped, curvy in all the right places, and she displayed it through a tight-fitting jumper and jeans. She was shy around me and had the softest German accent; nothing like the guttural one I was used to hearing on her compatriots. I would catch her eye every now and then and hold her glance. While she was on a visit to the bathroom, I decided to let Stefanie know that I quite liked her friend, and to find out if it would have a happy ending.

'I knew this would happen. I just knew it!'

She sounded angry.

'But I have to tell you that nothing will happen between the two of you, simply because of our history. She knows everything that happened between us, obviously; she's my best friend! What did you think? That girls don't talk? Anyway, she knows how I feel about everything. But, if it makes you feel any better, I am sure that something would have happened if it wasn't for our past. But you have to admit, you would be a bit of a bastard if you even thought about trying to get with my best friend.'

'The thought never even crossed my mind, Stefanie! I was only saying that I think she's a nice girl.'

And that was the end of that idea. Sadly. I went to bed that night frustrated.

The weekend arrived and it was time for me to leave Germany and make my way to the next capital city on my list, Prague. I had been feeling nervous about the journey there for the past couple of days. My nerves were heightened by the fact I'd left it until quite late in the day to leave the city. The train I planned to take departed Dresden at 5:20pm and was the penultimate one of the day, meaning that I could easily find myself stuck overnight in a village on the border. I did have a little plan up my sleeve though. I got Stefanie to write a small note in German explaining that during the night I had lost or had stolen my wallet and passport and now desperately needed to get to the British Embassy in Prague, which was already expecting me because my hotel in Dresden had phoned ahead on my behalf.

I took my seat in an empty compartment and was soon joined by a Canadian backpacker in his early twenties called Dean and an Australian Michael Barrymore lookalike in his forties who went by the name Tony. The German ticket inspector came around almost immediately and gave me no problems after reading the note. He even showed some sympathy. Conversation then began between us three English speakers all cooped together in a small compartment, as we watched the fairy-tale castles passing us by outside the window. When I say conversation began, I feel I should be a bit more accurate. A monologue began, while Dean and I sat looking at each other, wondering if the third guy in the compartment could get any more outrageous. Tony knew about one thing and one thing only: prostitutes.

'You know, in the Philippines they really do love you long time,' he told us in all seriousness. 'I try to get to Asia at least once a month, just because the hookers in Australia are too expensive and don't give you any real loving.'

'Do you ever sleep with girls that aren't prostitutes?' Dean asked.

'Rarely. Why would I want to meet a woman in a bar and buy her drinks all night, especially in Australia where the women have a bad attitude and are feminist, when I can pay 20 Australian dollars for a woman who will love me long time?'

He had by now said 'love you/me long time' twice already, and not in a joking way.

'So, what brings you to Europe?'

'Ah, you know what it's like. A mate of mine is in a band here and he just sent me an email and asked if I fancied coming over to see him. I asked him what the prostitutes were like and he said "cheap and beautiful", so I bought a ticket.'

Tony then told a story that he seemed especially proud of that involved him turning up at a famous brothel in Sydney with a painting he had done and was trying to sell. The Madam told him that she would love the picture to hang in the waiting room but that she didn't really have the money to buy it, but could offer him a couple of hours with some of the girls as payment. Obviously Tony agreed.

'But I still made her hand over some cash for the frame.'

Somewhere inside the Czech Republic, a young, female ticket inspector entered our compartment. She spoke no English but could understand German, so I handed her the note. It angered her.

'This is problem,' she fumed, before slamming the compartment door shut and disappearing up the train.

I spent the rest of the journey waiting for her to come back and punish me in some way, but it never happened. I feel that Tony's stories were punishment enough. It was dead on 7:30pm when we arrived into Central Station. I shook hands with each of my travel companions and wished them luck on their journeys. I then went into the nearest toilet to wash my hands of any diseases I may have been passed by Tony.

Welcome to Prague.

38. Prague

Capitals left to visit: Athens, Helsinki, Riga, Tallinn, Vilnius

Days on the road: 138
Distance travelled: 9022 miles
EU capitals visited: 18

I NAVIGATED MY way through the large terminal and out into the open. This wasn't a place you would send your kids to play in after dark. The area in front of the station consisted of a small patch of grass, some trees and benches. Drunks paced up and down alongside dodgy looking characters with their hoods up, while skinny drug addicts sat around in small groups rolling cigarettes out of dog ends. I cut through the area and crossed the main road opposite before striding through the revolving doors of the 5-star hotel on the corner of the street. The receptionist had no problem letting me use their phone to call Florin, who told me he would be along to meet me outside the station in half an hour. I thanked the receptionist and strolled back to the area that I refuse to call a park, to sit and wait. I had been sitting on the bench, watching the degenerates pacing up and down for less than a minute, when I had my first contact with one of them. A hooded character with a scar on his left cheek leant over me as he asked for a cigarette. I told him in Slovenian that I didn't smoke, assuming that the phrase would be similar enough to Czech for him to understand. It was. Czech for 'I don't smoke' is 'Nekouřím,' Slovene is 'Ne kadim.'

Less than a minute later another one of these gentlemen made a beeline for me. A man in the later years of middle age, wearing a dirty green jacket and sporting a tramp beard, again asked me if I could spare a fag. I replied in the same way as to the first but instead of my new friend just accepting my answer and turning away he decided to start a chat. He asked me in his language where I was from, and rather than risk taking the conversation further by opening him up to questions like, 'How come you can understand a Slavic language?' I told him I was from Slovenia.

'Ah, Slovinsko,' he said, before proceeding to explain to me in what I now knew was Slovakian that he was from Bratislava and that us Slovenes and Slovaks were blood brothers with much more in common than with the corrupt, power-hungry Czechs. His words, not mine. I smiled and agreed and after a couple of minutes he wished me luck and left me alone, no doubt after realising that I was telling the truth when I said I didn't have anything for him to smoke. During the course of the next fifteen minutes three more of these characters came and asked me for either smokes or money. Then Florin sent me a text telling me to take the tram and get off three stops down the line at a place called Lipansko, where he said he would meet me outside the flower shop. He told me that I would recognise him because he'd be holding a white rose between his teeth. He didn't. It took me a little while to find the right tram but eventually I got to where I needed to be and was greeted by my contact in the city; a 24-year old Romanian working in the Czech capital as an apprentice for a multinational recruitment agency. Florin was tall, clean-shaven and serious looking with shortly cropped, gelled dark hair. Standing with him were three others: Adrian, a stockily built guy with a cheeky face; Andreea, Adrian's blonde girlfriend; and Florin's other half, whose name I didn't catch.

It was Florin's birthday and he informed me that a few of

his friends were gathered in a restaurant just down the road to celebrate the occasion and that I was warmly invited by all to join them. They led the way and I followed, finding myself in a small dining establishment, taking my seat at a large table at the back full of Romanians. A quick head count revealed there to be fifteen. I found myself sat next to Adrian, who it turned out was a very knowledgeable football man. We spent the rest of the evening there discussing the beautiful game and downing pints of deliciously smooth Czech beer that kept appearing in front of me to replace the empties, courtesy of my new Romanian friends. Florin even got me a ridiculously large cheeseburger and chips when the time came for everyone to order their food. I hadn't asked for it, he had just assumed I was hungry after the day I'd had and unselfishly made sure that I wasn't sat without nourishment while everyone around me tucked in. Again I found myself asking the question: how is it that I continually got so lucky in meeting such friendly, generous and genuinely great people? Again I ask: How is it that Romanians have managed to get themselves such a bad reputation abroad? If I ever get the opportunity to promote Romania and in particular the people of the country in any way, I will not hesitate, starting here with this book. Stop believing everything you read in the papers and see on the telly regarding the rather unsavoury side of Romanian exports – the minority – and just keep an open mind. Of course there are good and bad wherever you go on the planet, but (and I used to be as guilty as the next man) there are too many who jump to the conclusion, thanks mainly to the media, that everyone that comes out of Romania is genetically incapable of human decency. It is simply not true. Romanians are lovely people.

Okay, rant over, back to the story.

As our time in the restaurant was drawing to an end I still had no idea where I was going to be spending the night. Before arriving in Prague Florin had told me that there was no room at his place but that he would try to sort something out. It was already past 11pm and nobody had updated me on the situation and I felt too embarrassed to ask, for fear of putting anyone in an awkward position. Fortunately, Florin hadn't forgotten about his strange guest and as we waited for the waitress to bring over another round of beers he leant over the table and told me that he had checked out a hostel earlier in the day that accepted late check-ins and that he would take me there later and pay for a bed for me. Before I had time to thank him though, Adrian turned round and said that he and Andreea would feel much more comfortable if I spent the night at their flat. They lived with a Polish guy who didn't allow guests, but he was away on business until the following afternoon, so as long as I was out of the house before midday it wouldn't be an issue. I felt at ease in the company of both Adrian and Andreea and was pleased to have been made the offer.

'The only thing I'm not sure what to do with,' Adrian said, 'is your bags. Because after we leave here we are all heading off to a club for the night. We might have to go back to the flat and drop off your stuff, but it's quite a long way and will cut into our night.'

As he said this, a girl sitting further up the table joined the conversation, saying, 'We're going back to the flat after we leave here, we are too tired to go out tonight. We can take Kris' stuff and he can get it in the morning.'

I glanced at her and her boyfriend and quickly decided that they could be trusted with all my belongings. To have come to any other conclusion would have been pretty hypocritical after the rant I just put you through regarding Romanians, wouldn't it?

At 11:30pm we were all politely kicked out of the restaurant and in a drunken rabble spilled out onto the streets. The group separated, with half going off to bed. We arrived at the Infinity nightclub and someone paid for me to get in.

Once inside the door and down the stairs to the main room the first thing you noticed was that the place was filled with glamourous young Czech women and foreign (foreign as in not Czech) middle-aged, letchy, fat men, who spoke loudly to the girls in broken English.

We made our way across the packed dance floor to the one available table at the back. For the next couple of hours vodka was poured down my neck as we stood around chatting. I was tired. I had all but used up my energy for the night and was starting to shut down when across the floor I spied something a little bit naughty. Two girls, both perfect 10s, were sitting at a table in the corner of the room literally warming up for an orgasm. Each girl's hands were being used to gently squeeze the fleshier parts of the other's torso, and their tongues were in each other's mouths. Skirts were being edged upwards. Had anyone noticed? I looked around and was surprised to see that they were attracting little to no attention at all. It was a direct result of the vodka that led me to do what I did next. Before I tell you this story, allow me to apologise in advance. I strutted across the dance floor and up to the table where the two girls were sat; waiting a few moments for them to break in kissing each other and notice someone standing over them.

'Girls, do you speak English?'

'Of course.'

'OK, well, I'm not going to waste your time or mine with any bullshit. Here's the deal. You two look like you are going to be enjoying yourselves in the bedroom tonight. Only, I can't help thinking that you would have that little bit more fun if a man were involved. I don't mean just any old man. I mean me; a man who is willing to let you do anything you want. A plaything for your lesbian games, if you will. I repeat, I will do anything with you girls.'

This wasn't me! I wasn't that guy! Where was this coming from? As I finished my piece I gulped as the realisation that it might have actually worked dawned on me. The two girls smiled before turning to each other and speaking in Czech. They were nodding. I was in! I was going to lose my threesome virginity. The more dominant of the two looked at me, smiled again and then said those words I longed to hear:

'Okay, why not? One night only. It will be fun.'

They started getting up out of their seats. I felt like a Jehovah's Witness who had just been invited into someone's living room for a nice cup of tea, some biscuits and a chat. I had never been this far before. What did I do now?

'Let's go,' said the same girl. 'Which hotel are you booked into? And have you got any coke?'

These questions did not fall into my evil master plan. I could hardly turn around and say, 'Well, actually, it's not so much a hotel as someone's flat. We just have to wait for my new friends over there to decide it's time to go home, then they will show us to the spare room. As long as we are quiet throughout the night, there will be no problems. And I almost forgot; we all have to be out by midday tomorrow so as not to get my friends in trouble with their Polish flatmate. So, sit down and have another drink and I will call you when it's time to go. And in the meantime I'll check out the Coke situation, but you might have to settle for Pepsi. Is that alright?'

Instead, I said something that sounded cool in my head at the time but on reflection is one of the most pathetic things I have ever uttered.

'Actually, I thought we would go back to your place instead as I'm sure you've got all the toys and everything you need there. My hotel room doesn't have any of that stuff, and besides, I'm not allowed to bring guests back after midnight.'

Not allowed to bring guests back after midnight? How had that sounded believable and cool in my head? Fair enough if I was taking them back to my nan's house; but a hotel… a hotel!

'Right. Goodnight then.'

Both girls sat back down, looked at each other and laughed. It was time for me to leave.

I slept comfortably on an inflatable mattress through the early hours of the morning and then dragged myself up and into the kitchen at 11. Adrian was in the shower, so Andreea made me a hearty breakfast of eggs and salami.

After cleaning up, Adrian and I headed round to Florin's flat that he shared with the couple that had wandered off with my bags the night before. Lunch was had in one of Prague's more interesting establishments. Krčma u Parašutistů (the Parachutists' Tavern), is located next to the Russian Orthodox Church where the assassins of Reinhardt Heydrich hid after carrying out his execution in 1942. At the time, Heydrich had been one of the most powerful and feared men in the Third Reich. I'll be honest, I didn't know the man personally, I wasn't yet born, but by all accounts he wasn't the sort of bloke you would want round for dinner and a glass of wine. Although he did have a few cute little nicknames that do make you wonder: The Butcher of Prague; the Blond Beast; and the Hangman Heydrich. They don't sound too bad, do they? In 1941 Heydrich had become the 'protector' of Bohemia and Moravia (the part of Czechoslovakia that had been incorporated into the Reich a couple of years earlier), and ever since his swearing-in, the Czechoslovak government in exile in London had been plotting to have him assassinated. Heydrich, convinced that his brutal crushing of any Czech resistance had been successful, was starting to lord it a bit, even driving around the city in an open-topped green Mercedes without so much as an armed escort for protection; a show of confidence in his intimidation of the resistance and successful pacification of the population. Fool! On the 27th May 1942, two Czech parachutists, Jan Kubiš and Jozef Gabčík, who had been trained in England, attacked as his car slowed down to take a sharp turn. Firstly, Gabčík took aim at Heydrich with a sub-machine gun. A sub-machine gun that failed to fire. Now, I don't know about you, but if I tried to kill someone with the nickname The Butcher of Prague and my gun failed to go off, I would more than likely chuck the weapon at his head in a bid to confuse him before running off screaming. But fortunately for Czechoslovakia, as I have already mentioned, I hadn't been born yet and so the responsibility wasn't left to me. As Gabčík stood there, Heydrich ordered his driver to stop the car so that he could personally take on the two attackers. Kubiš reacted quickly and threw a converted anti-tank mine at the rear of the car, which exploded, wounding Heydrich and also Kubiš himself. But as the smoke cleared, Heydrich emerged from the wreckage with his gun still in his hand and gave chase after Kubiš, attempting to return fire. I know, mental, right? He's the fucking Terminator. He ran for half a block, became weak from shock, and so sent his driver on foot to continue the chase. In the ensuing firefight Gabčík shot the driver in the leg and escaped. At the time, Heydrich didn't appear to be seriously wounded. He'd only been blown-up by an anti-tank mine, after all. He was taken to the hospital for a check-up anyway, where it was discovered he'd suffered a severe injury to the left side of his body with major damage to his diaphragm, spleen and lung as well as a broken rib. He slipped into a coma and died ten days later. The two assassins initially hid with two Prague families but later took up refuge in the crypt of the Karel Boromejsky Church. The Gestapo couldn't find them until a member of the Czech resistance gave up their hiding place for the reward of one million reichsmarks. The Germans, despite the best efforts of 700 Nazi soldiers, were unable to take the parachutists alive, and after a two-hour gun battle Kubiš died of his wounds while Gabčík shot himself after fending off SS attacks, attempts at smoking him out and even fire engines being brought in to flood the crypt.

The Parachutists' Tavern was a shrine to the Free Czech Army during the Nazi occupation of their country. The walls were adorned with photographs and maps from the period, along with written stories so that you could get a feel for what happened there. Sitting around the tables were men who I assumed were ex-military. They had the look, at least: eye patches, canes, smartly pressed green trousers. The food was excellent and I was again spoilt by the group who sorted me out with a huge piece of roast chicken and as many beers as I could handle. Florin and Adrian felt that a few more beers were in order though, so after a guided tour through the touristy centre of the city that included a walk over the famous Charles Bridge, we sat ourselves outside a bar in the Old Town where we were greeted by the waiter in about 47 different languages.

I had been to Prague once before to play in a European football tournament. We had driven in a minibus from Slovenia to play against teams from the Czech Republic, Hungary, and Croatia. We finished bottom of the standings; the sole reason being that we arrived on the Friday evening and had to play early on the Saturday morning. As we checked in to the hotel and found our rooms, the outrageous instruction from our manager was: 'Boys, I don't mind you going out for a couple of quiet ones tonight, but nothing silly and I want you all in bed by 1.' The next morning I think there were about three members of our team who had actually been to bed at all.

Earlier that morning, Florin had been busy. He had walked from his flat to a nearby youth hostel and had booked me in for the night and paid the rate. He had also been to the train station and bought a ticket for the following morning that would get me as far as a town in the east of the country called Bohumín, on the border with Poland.

'Adrian and I put our money together for this. We figured that half the problem tomorrow would be getting through the Czech Republic, so at least now that part won't cause you any difficulty. Once you are at the border you will have to work your magic to get the rest of the way,' Florin explained.

I was completely taken aback; I hadn't expected any gesture like this. 'Mulţumesc,' I thanked them in Romanian, something I had learnt earlier on the trip and had been waiting to use.

After collecting my stuff from Florin's flat I checked into the hostel. I was hoping that it would be a night of mixing with the other guests in the common room and making friends. That was how I remembered hostel life. I was, then, disappointed to find myself sat alone on an armchair for the evening as little cliquey groups around me chatted loudly about their travels. I had a hot shower before taking myself up to the 14-bed dorm earlier than anyone else in the hostel and getting under the covers. Going to bed early turned out to be a completely pointless exercise as I didn't manage to get a wink of sleep the whole night. If it wasn't the drunks coming in and out the door, whispering more loudly to each other than if they had just decided to talk in normal voices, then it was the constant snoring of a German guy on the other side of the room. And if it wasn't the snoring of the German then it was the French bloke on the bunk above me who, if I didn't know better, I would have said was an epileptic. Non-stop fidgeting made the whole frame of the bed shake as I stared upwards at the mattress pushing its way through the wooden planks almost to the point of touching my nose.

As loudly as possible I got myself up at 7 and banged as many things as I could whilst taking my bag from the locker and stuffing my clothes into it. I coughed loudly and I played with the ring tone on my phone. The room's inhabitants were so comatose, though, that my efforts were in vain. I was the only one in the canteen area for breakfast, which was exactly what I wanted because it meant that I could fill my bag with slices of bread and cheesy triangles undetected. Florin turned up at 7:30 and helped himself to a hearty feast before we took the tram to the train station. I thanked him for all he had done and we parted with a handshake, then I jumped onto the 8:06 to Bohumín just seconds before it departed. I found myself a compartment with two sleeping girls in and just got my head down myself. I got to Bohumín at around half past 12, and ten minutes later was on the fast train to Warsaw. As soon as the wheels were rolling I left my compartment and went to find the conductor. She was young and gentle, and I immediately knew getting round her was going to be easy.

'I'm really embarrassed but I really need your help,' I started. 'I just got off of the train from Prague and found that my ticket and wallet were missing from my coat pocket. I left the coat hanging in the compartment on the train while I went to the toilet for a couple of minutes and someone obviously came in and took everything. The only thing I can think to do now is to make my way to the British Embassy in Warsaw to get some help. Can you please allow me to stay on the train?'

The girl was compassionate.

'I am so sorry. I feel so bad for you. I have to get off the train at the next stop once we've crossed into Polish territory, but I will speak to the Poles that replace me and let them know the situation. I really hope that it turns out okay for you.'

'Thank you. You just made my day a whole lot better.'

Once we'd crossed into Poland and started moving again I got myself up out of my seat and again went to seek out the conductor. I found a couple of them sitting in a private compartment and knocked on their window before entering.

'Sorry, but do either of you speak English?' I asked.

Not one of them did. This didn't look too promising. I fell back onto Slovene and began explaining the same story about the wallet and ticket. They understood and cut me short by finishing my sentence for me because they had already been told the story by the Czech girl. The guards sympathised with my plight and told me to sit down and not to worry. Four comfortable hours later I arrived at Central Station for the second time on this epic journey.

Welcome back to Warsaw.

39. Warsaw

WARSAW WAS DIFFERENT to how I remembered her. The Warsaw that lived on in my mind was dark, gloomy, bleak and depressing. She gave you wet feet, cold ears and an all over dampness. She made legs and eyelids feel heavy. She needed Prozac. But that had been during the dark days of November. Warsaw in March was bright, sunny, warm and optimistic about the future. She danced through the fields, collecting berries to be used as ingredients in a fruity punch she would be making later on. Warsaw in March whistled and sang. She was an altogether different host to her winter alter ego. I hadn't arranged a place to stay in Poland's capital and none of my old acquaintances in the city even knew I was in town, but I wasn't flustered. The sun and the mood of the people walking around the city acted to enhance my good feeling. I still had Hollywood actor Sean Penn's number in my phone. If anyone would be able to help me out, it would be Hollywood actor Sean Penn. Borrowing the phone at a hotel reception desk I rang my old friend and was told to make my way to Jon's flat – the same one I had stayed at last time around – in a couple of hours.

I made my way to the bar that had been my first stopping off point in Warsaw four months earlier, to see if Max was still around. He was, and we spent the next couple of hours drinking tea and catching up. As we chatted and laughed, the weather outside gradually transformed back to how I remembered it, and by the time I was ready to make my way to Jon's place it was dark, cold and raining. At least it wasn't snowing. And surely the clouds would soon pass and I would get to enjoy a little bit more Polish springtime before moving on upwards into the Baltics.

The flat was as I had left it. Almost. Nick and Paul the Canadian brothers had moved back to their homeland and had rented their room out to a Polish couple, but Jon still occupied the largest of the rooms and still used it as a communal gathering place for watching films and smoking weed. Kim the German vegan had moved out, to be replaced by Emma, Jon's new Swedish girlfriend that he had met outside a nightclub on a short visit home to England and had immediately invited to come and live with him.

'So, you are the famous Kris. I've heard all about your diarrhoea,' were the first words Emma spoke as we met for the first time.

I woke the following morning to a shock. Snow. Lots and lots of snow. More snow, in fact, than had been here when I'd left back in November. You couldn't see out the window; the whole world was just a haze of white. But how could it be so? Yesterday, when I'd arrived in the city, girls had been tanning under the sun's rays, showing off shapely bodies and roller-skating. Now, the city looked like Siberia. I guess. I've never been to Siberia. Venturing out for some sightseeing was out of the question but it didn't matter, for just a couple of days earlier a Canadian friend of Jon's had purchased a poker chip set and the small group of ex-pats had all been reading the rules of the game and were determined to put their new found knowledge to good use in a home game that they hoped would become a regular occurrence. To a degenerate gambler and long-term card player like myself this would have been a dream situation – a table-load of beginners willing to put money in the middle – but for obvious reasons I was unable to partake in any gambling. Instead I played the role of dealer and got to watch first-hand the debacle as the group of rookies took their first steps on what could easily become a life-wasting path to addiction.

'Does a straight beat a flush?' 'How many cards do I need to make a straight?' and my personal favourite, 'Are aces high or low?' were all questions that indicated none of the players had any real feel for the game. The evening dragged on and the first couple of mini-tournaments had been played, when my constant jibes of 'I wish I could play against players like you back at home, I would never have to work again,' finally had an effect.

'We're not as bad as you think. You probably wouldn't even win,' they told me.

Jon went a little bit further.

'I have a proposition for you. You can play in the next game. We will all put our money in as usual, and you will put your shoelaces into the middle. If you do the unthinkable and win the tournament, we will go to the train station in the morning and buy you a ticket to Vilnius out of the winnings. However, if one of us wins, you are not allowed to replace your shoelaces at all while you are in Poland, meaning that you will have to hitchhike to Lithuania with your shoes falling off of your feet. And on top of that, you will be the slave of the winner for 24 hours. Are you in?'

I took one look at each of them and knew that I would have no problems taking it down.

'I'm in.'

'Oh baby, this is going to be the ultimate humiliation. No shoelaces! In the snow! Brilliant!' Jon cackled.

The cards were shuffled and dealt and my laces were thrown into the middle of the table on top of the pile of prize money. The game started and I put all of my focus into blocking out the relentless remarks about how foolish I would look and how cold my feet would be. I was under pressure, pressure that I hadn't taken into account when agreeing to take the bet. But I am Kris Mole, degenerate gambler extraordinaire. I don't turn down bets. Ever. Besides, I had played more hands of poker than all of these guys put together had had hot dinners, cold dinners, breakfasts, baths, showers and holidays. I couldn't lose, could I?

The poker went exactly as expected, and before too long I found myself in a heads-up battle with Hollywood actor Sean Penn for the prize, while the rest of the group gathered round to cheer on their last hope. I had taken each one of them out single-handedly up until that point. Once they realised I only had to take a look at their face to know exactly what cards they were holding, they as good as just handed their chips over without too much of a struggle. Hollywood actor Sean Penn put up a bit more of a fight than his friends, but before long I was re-lacing my shoes and looking forward to our visit to the station the following day.

The snow continued to fall and the temperature continued to drop. And my coat continued to sun it in Spain. I arranged places to sleep in Vilnius and also later on in Riga through

Couchsurfing, and the word from the people in those places was that the further north I went, the colder and more extreme the weather was going to get.

'It will be a laugh,' I told them defiantly.

The train ticket was bought and handed over to me. I would be out of Poland's capital and on my way to Lithuania at 7:20 on the Saturday morning, arriving in Vilnius 11 hours later.

Saturday came and I was up and out of the flat shortly before 6:30am, despite sitting up until after 4 drinking vodka shots with my hosts. Feeling groggy, I encountered no problems reaching the main train station by tram. The streets of Warsaw were already bustling with people making their way to work, school, university or the park bench for a day of analysing the world over a bottle of vodka. Inside the station, rough alcoholics were escorted off of the premises by police after being caught attempting to steal from the small convenience stores dotted around the complex. The mist of breath lingered in the freezing air. My train pulled away from the platform dead on 7:20 and, feeling confident clutching my ticket, I took one of the last empty seats on board, in a small compartment filled with a mix of young and old. If the timetable I'd picked up at Warsaw's station was correct then I would be sat in this same seat for the next seven hours, before having to change at the small Polish town of Sestokai, close to the Lithuanian border. From there, it would be a simple ride on to Vilnius. The day was going to be a smooth one; I could feel it. My compartment stayed full for the next few hours, before everyone jumped off at the busy station of Bialystock, leaving me a nice little bit of room to put my feet up and attempt to squeeze a nap in. My train was due to arrive in Sestokai at 2:40pm, so I set my alarm for 2:30 and went to sleep. I was woken a short while later by an old man in a green overall with a rubbish bag in his hand, shaking me gently. I checked the time on my phone; it was only 12:30. We were sat at a station but nobody was on the platform outside my window. The man was speaking Polish at me. I told him I didn't understand.

'Sestokai?' he asked.

'Tak. Sestokai.'

Tak means yes, in case you were wondering. The man laughed. Polish humour was lost on me, so I looked at him blankly. He then pointed towards the back of the train and said, 'Sestokai,' once again. I guessed that the train was going to split and I needed to be in the back end to carry on my journey. So I stood up, picked up my belongings and left him to carry on emptying the rubbish bin in the compartment. I walked quickly down the corridor to the small door and then my heart sank. On the other side of the door was only daylight. The rest of the train – the rest of the train that had definitely been there earlier – wasn't there anymore. By now it was cruising through the forest on its way to Sestokai. I, meanwhile, was stranded at an empty station somewhere in Northern Poland. The day was not going smoothly. I jumped off of the train and onto the platform and read the name on the station's sign. I was in that famous old place, Suwałki. Famous only to people from Suwałki. Still, there was no need to panic, as I would just wait for the next train to come in and split, and I would make sure that I got on the back end of it. The station was unmanned, apart from one old boy with a bushy moustache sitting in an office reading a newspaper. He spoke not a word of English, so switching to my hybrid Slavic language I managed to get him to understand my question, 'What time does the next train to Sestokai depart?'

The answer was bad; the answer was 'jutro'.

'Tomorrow? That can't be true! I have to get to Lithuania today!'

The man then came out of his office and walked through the station's exit, motioning for me to follow. I was being ejected. We got out on to the street and he continued walking up the road, still beckoning for me to walk with him. The station's thermometer said it was minus one outside. I thought of my thick, winter coat, lying there in Spain. Together the man and I walked for ten minutes until we found ourselves on the side of a busy dual carriageway. A large part of the vehicles passing us had Lithuanian plates. The man then stood in the side of the road with his thumb out. He was hitchhiking on my behalf. Or maybe he needed to go to Vilnius, too. I didn't know. Either way, he wasn't a very good hitchhiker. Cars and lorries flew past, not even glancing at the man in a railway uniform and his bearded, under-dressed companion. After a demoralising ten minutes, the man shook my hand and headed back in the direction of the station. I couldn't knock his efforts in helping me; he had gone far beyond the call of duty just by bringing me to this point. I continued where my helper had left off, standing in the kerb with outstretched thumb. I would be picked up and taken to Lithuania soon enough, I knew it. Half an hour later and I wasn't so sure. Drivers honked their horns and laughed as they passed me by. I was a source of entertainment. I decided that I probably wasn't in the best spot, so I picked up my things and set off walking in the same direction that the traffic was heading. Some 20 minutes later I saw up ahead a bus station. My luck was back in. I waited patiently in the queue and eventually got to the information desk and asked the woman behind it if she spoke English.

'No,' she replied in English, before calling for the guy in the queue behind me to make his way up. I had been dismissed before I'd even had a chance at communicating properly with her. I stood and waited until the man had bought his ticket and then made sure I got back in the woman's face before she called the next passenger up.

'Vilnius?' I managed to ask.

'No,' she replied, as she called the next queuing passenger up.

What the fuck?

'Am I invisible?' I wondered aloud.

I waited until the next passenger had bought his ticket and then jumped right back in.

'When is the next bus to Vilnius?'

This time she just laughed, before calling up the next customer. I was just about to slam my hand down on her desk and demand a complaints form when I heard a voice say, 'Maybe I can help you.'

I turned to my left, where a skinny girl in a black hooded jumper stood smiling. She looked like a heroin user.

'I hate the people in these shitty little towns,' she told me. 'They are so rude to anybody that can't speak Polish.'

'It's fair enough, I suppose. I don't imagine a non-English speaking Pole would get much assistance at a bus station in Scunthorpe either.'

'What is Scunthorpe?'

'Never mind.'

Anja was a student at Warsaw University and was on her way home to the countryside to visit family for the Easter break. I told her what had happened on the train, but rather than laugh she showed sympathy, saying, 'It's just like the Poles to not come and tell you that you were in the wrong part of the train. No wonder we have such a bad name in other countries.'

Anja was a self-hating Pole. A self-hating Pole is like a self-hating Jew, but is allowed to work on Saturdays. She took me to the other side of the bus station to a different information desk, where she did the talking and then gave me the bad news.

'There are no buses to Vilnius today or tomorrow because of the Easter Holiday. The best advice I can give is to try and make your way somehow to the Lithuanian border which is about 30 kilometres away, and then once inside Lithuania you might be able to find a national bus or train heading to the capital.'

I thanked her for her help and left the station, heading back to the motorway to re-start my hitchhiking efforts. Half an hour of being mocked by Polish and Lithuanian drivers alike later, my hands were too cold to feel and morale was at an all-time low. I told you this day wasn't going to run smoothly. Why had I sat up drinking all night? Why hadn't I rested ahead of this most challenging of days? Why is corn on the cob called corn on the cob but apple on the core is just called an apple?

If there was a train station, there had to be a town. So I set off in search of it, hoping to stumble upon an idea whilst warming my body parts through brisk walking. On a quiet road I found myself standing outside the local police station. In need of advice, I walked in through the main doors and then waited ten minutes in the lobby while the officer on duty tried to find an English-speaking colleague to come and hear why I was in their building. I explained my predicament and waited for the good instructions that I was sure to receive.

'There is a homeless centre close to here,' the officer explained. 'You can sleep there tonight. I will take you in the van.'

'Is it safe?'

There was a pause, before he asked, 'Have you got anything valuable?'

'Not really.'

'Then you should be okay. The tramps will go through your bags when you are sleeping, but if there's nothing worth taking then you shouldn't be robbed.'

He grinned. This was funny to him. Again the Polish sense of humour left a lot to be desired. I didn't like the idea of being a foreigner in a hostel for the homeless, but I didn't see any other options. I would at least have a roof over my head, and as long as I kept my eyes open all night then I should still be in possession of my belongings the following morning, when I would rise at dawn and return to the train station and explain why I had to use a day-old ticket to get to Vilnius. The officer then asked for my details, so I handed him my passport and watched as he tapped them into his computer and then called ahead to the centre to book me in for the night.

'Wait outside for me. I will go and get the van and pick you up in ten minutes.'

I did as I was told, but as I stood out in the cold my mind filled with doubt over the wisdom of the plan. It was 2:30 in the afternoon and I didn't want to spend the rest of the day lying on a bunk bed before I had at least tried a bit harder to get out of Suwałki. My decision was then made for me when the copper pulled up in his van and told me that he had called the railway company and been told that there were no trains going my way the following day either, due to the holiday period.

'Great. Listen, I appreciate your help, but there is no way that I am going to spend two nights in the homeless centre. The other 'guests' will have the Englishman for breakfast, lunch and dinner. I am going to have to somehow get back to Warsaw and assess my options from there,' I told him.

'Do you want me to take you back to the train and bus stations to look at your options here, then?'

'Yes please.'

I jumped into the van and we drove to the bus station. Rather curiously, he left me locked in the back while he went in to speak to the information desk. I looked every bit the criminal, as Polish eyes stared at me through the reinforced glass, all wondering what act of terrorism I had been prevented from committing. Plod returned after a couple of minutes, smiling.

'No buses to Warsaw today or tomorrow. No buses to Lithuania today or tomorrow. Do you want to try the train station?'

Why is he smiling?

'Yes. Let's go,' I said, resigned to the next piece of bad news. Again I sat locked in as he went inside and made his enquiries. Again he returned smiling, which I knew meant only one thing.

'The next train to Warsaw isn't until tomorrow. Shall I take you to the homeless centre now?'

'Nope. Can you take me to a good spot for hitchhiking out of this town, towards Lithuania? I have to give it a proper go.'

And so he did.

'This is where you want to be,' he told me, as he dropped me off at a small bus shelter at the side of the road. 'Just try to wave down a truck.'

We shook hands, he wished me good luck and I thanked him.

The cold air smacked me in the face as I came out of the wagon. I felt a right plum as I stood there in front of that bus stop, freezing my nuts off and being derided by every local that walked past. The drivers were equally cruel, and in the space of an hour at least 50 Lithuanian cars and lorries sped by with not one so much as slowing down. I looked up to the skies, wondering what my next move was. I felt like dropping to my knees and lying in the cold; I didn't feel I could go on anymore. Too many things had gone wrong. I was shot to pieces. It's hard to put into words the feeling of despair I was experiencing in that little town where nobody spoke English, where I had no food, and where I was likely to freeze to death if I didn't find a solution to my problem soon. I was going to have to return to the police station and then spend the night with the homeless in the centre; providing they would still have me after I'd snubbed their offer earlier in the day. I felt the end of the game might be nigh. I was ready to quit. I ran everything through my head. What would people's reaction be if I gave up now and went home? Would I be ridiculed in the press? Would I hate myself for not seeing it through to the end? Would the people that had sponsored me feel let down? Would I bring shame to my family? Did I really care? Surely none of these situations would leave me feeling worse than I did at this particular moment in time. Saying that though, what could I actually do? How could I quit? How would I get home if I did decide to call it a day? I was in the middle of nowhere. And then just like that something in me changed, as I found myself saying, 'Hang on a minute. How many times has something come along when you needed it most? Didn't you say that you would sooner die in the cold than give up and go home a quitter? Start thinking positively again and you will get yourself out of the shit!' And so I did. It was hard to switch the mentality back to a positive way of looking at things, but I managed to do it, firstly by laughing at the fact that for the previous few days I had been happily thinking about the stress-free trip I was going to have to the Baltics with a train ticket in my hand, and how it had all gone wrong. I should have expected this. Here I was, still in the same day that I'd left Warsaw without a care in the world, now stuck in the stickiest situation of the journey so far. I had to laugh. No sooner had I started feeling positive again than a car pulled over and the driver asked if I wanted a lift as far as the border, where he was going to pick up his daughter. I was in the passenger seat with my seatbelt on before he'd even finished the question. As I jumped out of the car at the frontier, the previously grey sky vanished and was replaced by a sunny outlook that took the chill out of the air. If the scene had been in a film, there would have been that 'aaaaaaaaaah' sound that accompanies religious miracles and moments of enlightenment.

I walked across the border from Poland into Lithuania, showing my passport to a Lithuanian guard on the way. I carried on walking along the side of the road, keeping my thumb outstretched at all times in the hope of a lorry driver fancying some company. But none did, and so I just kept on going. My atlas told me that I was about 105 miles (170km) from Vilnius.

'105 miles? Is that all you got? I will walk your 105 miles! You will never beat me!' I shouted loudly in defiance.

Nobody heard me. Just as well, as I might have felt embarrassed. The border road was a quiet one, surrounded on either side by fields. Each Lithuanian lorry driver that passed me felt the need to laugh out the window. In my life I had never met a Lithuanian, and so these drivers weren't doing much to implant a good first impression of their people in my mind. It was fair to say that I was no great lover of the Lithuanian tribe. As I carried on my defiant march towards Vilnius I had to stop and wait politely as a lorry driver stood by the side of his parked vehicle, blocking my path, relieving himself onto a small patch of grass. I waited patiently for him to finish, have three shakes and then zip up his flies, before I asked him where he was heading. He told me in German that he had to wait there for an hour, as ruled by his taco. I pointed to my wrist to indicate an hour and asked, 'Und?'

'Und Kaunas,' he answered.

Brilliant! If I could get to Lithuania's second biggest city, my chances of making it to Vilnius would be greatly increased. And if they weren't, I could surely find shelter for the night.

'Ich komme mit du,' I said in incorrect German, pointing at myself.

'Okay,' he said.

My day had just taken a turn for the better. I knew it would come. I never doubted things; remember I told you that I knew all along that things would go smoothly.

'Danke schön!' I thanked him, punching the air triumphantly.

In an hour's time I would be on my way to Kaunas.

I sat in the kerb playing with my phone as my driver-to-be sat in his cab smoking a cigarette and reading a porno magazine. In front of his lorry sat another one and I met the driver of it when he came to ask me to move from the kerb so that he could reverse to get out. As I was getting to my feet, my driver called out to him and asked him something in Lithuanian. The two of them stood and had a little chat, before I was called over to join them. The new driver then asked me where I wanted to go, to which I replied, 'Kaunas.'

'Okay,' he said, and pointed for me to jump in the front of his vehicle. So I did, and off we set. Conversation didn't exactly flow, as my driver spoke not a word of English, and his German was only marginally better than mine; which is terrible. Our chat resembled a Year-8 Deutsch oral exam. And I failed that. But I did manage to understand that he wasn't driving exactly to Kaunas but would be passing close by.

I told him that this wasn't a problem, as I would try to get to Vilnius from wherever he dropped me.

'Vilnius? Ich gehe nach Vilnius,' he declared with a smile.

I could have kissed him. I resisted. After everything I had gone through in the day, I was now definitely on my way to Vilnius.

My driver's name was Alek and he was employed by a Lithuanian company to make deliveries to Germany, Poland, Belgium and Holland. He worked 17 days of the month and earned 1000 Euros for his efforts; not a bad wage for a Lithuanian, especially when you add on the extra 400 or so that he made on the side by stealing the petrol that the company paid for by sucking it out of the tank through a tube and then selling it on to other drivers he met in lay-bys. Just to make sure I believed him, he showed me a large plastic container full of his loot. He was clearly proud of his work. As the sun came down on the horizon Alek lent me his phone to ring my host in Vilnius, Cori, to let her know that I was on my way.

Worryingly, there was no answer, so I sent a quick text instead. Half an hour later I tried calling again and this time got a response. Not from an American girl called Cori though, but rather a Lithuanian whose name I didn't catch, who spoke no English and so asked me in German, 'Ist das Kris?'

What? Who the hell was this and how did he know my name? Then I remembered that I had written it in the text I sent earlier and this was no psychic Lithuanian I was talking to. As we approached Vilnius I was worried. After all I had gone through to make it to the city, it now looked like I would be without a place to sleep as the number I had for Cori was the wrong one. Alek was also worried and asked if I needed to stay at his place with his family. The offer was warm and humbled me, but I declined it, even though it broke one of my rules, as I felt that if I could find a place to check my email, I would find that I had just copied down Cori's number incorrectly. I also felt that Alek's family would want some quality time with him, seeing as how he was returning from a 17-day shift. After a three-hour drive Alek dropped me off in front of Vilnius train station, where we exchanged a surprisingly emotional farewell. We shook hands and then he drove off, beeping his horn and waving until he was out of sight. During the three hours of broken German we had bonded, and I was overcome with gratitude to my driver for seeing that I made it to Lithuania's capital in one piece.

I ticked another capital off of my list.

Welcome to Vilnius.

40. Vilnius

Capitals left to visit: Athens, Helsinki, Riga, Tallinn

Days on the road: 145
Distance travelled: 9734 miles
EU capitals visited: 19

So, I was in Vilnius, but that was only half the job done. I still didn't have any place to go, but I was sure that my luck would soon change. I dodged speeding cars as I ran across the busy roundabout in front of the station and into a hotel, where I politely asked the girl behind the desk if I could use the net for a couple of minutes. No problem. Logging into my email, I found that I had been dialling the wrong number all evening, but I now had the right one and also Cori's address. The receptionist showed me on a map how to get there, and 20 minutes later I was walking into the flat of a surprised Cori who had given up hope of me making it.

'You look like you could use a cup of tea,' she said, before obliging.

Cori was an American student, studying Slavic languages and linguistics at Vilnius University. It was the exact same subject that I had looked into studying myself (and still hoped to do one day in the future). She had an English boyfriend, hence the immediate cup of tea. The tea was followed by a hot bowl of soup, the first thing I'd eaten all day. After freshening up a bit, I was taken to a lively little bar in the centre of the city, where Cori introduced me to some of her friends and I was given copious amounts of beer, before staggering back to the flat where I crashed out immediately on the sofa-bed in the living room. It had been a long day.

The following afternoon my host gave me a guided tour of the city, reading information to me from a guidebook as we walked for about three hours first through sunshine, then rain, then sleet, and finally heavy snow. The weather didn't matter; I fell in love with the city. It reminded me of Ljubljana, with the Baroque architecture, the pedestrianised streets of the old town, the market stalls, and the weather. Vilnius also has a sense of humour, as was shown to me when we visited a part of the city known as the Republic of Užupio (Užupio Respublika) that in 1991 declared itself independent from the rest of Lithuania. Of course it wasn't a serious declaration; it was just a piss-take of the situation of the time when so many Eastern European republics were declaring independence from their former oppressors. The place has its own constitution, signs welcoming you to the republic, and even ministers. If you go there on the 1st of April – Užupio's Independence Day – you can get your passport stamped. Užupio, which literally means 'beyond the river', has its constitution written on a wall inside the republic and can be read in a number of languages. I chose English. There are 41 points to this constitution, which I will share with you now:

- Everyone has the right to live by the River Vilnelė, while the River Vilnelė has the right to flow by everyone.
- Everyone has the right to hot water, heating in winter and a tiled roof.
- Everyone has the right to die, but it is not an obligation.
- Everyone has the right to make mistakes.
- Everyone has the right to individuality.
- Everyone has the right to love.
- Everyone has the right to be not loved, but not necessarily.

- Everyone has the right not to be distinguished and famous.
- Everyone has the right to be idle.
- Everyone has the right to love and take care of a cat.
- Everyone has the right to look after a dog until one or the other dies.
- A dog has the right to be a dog.
- A cat is not obliged to love its master, but it must help him in hardness.
- Sometimes man has the right to be unaware of his duties.
- Everyone has the right to be in doubt, but this is not a duty.
- Everyone has the right to be happy.
- Everyone has the right to be unhappy.
- Everyone has the right to be silent.
- Everyone has the right to have faith.
- No one has the right to violence.
- Everyone has the right to realize his negligibility and magnificence.
- Everyone has the right to encroach upon eternity.
- Everyone has the right to understand.
- Everyone has the right to understand nothing.
- Everyone has the right to be of various nationalities.
- Everyone has the right to celebrate or not to celebrate his birthday.
- Everyone shall remember his name.
- Everyone may share what he possesses.
- No one can share what he or she does not possess.
- Everyone has the right to have brothers, sisters and parents.
- Everyone is capable of independence.
- Everyone is responsible for his or her freedom.
- Everyone has the right to cry.
- Everyone has the right to be misunderstood.
- No one has a right to make another person guilty.
- Everyone has the right to be personal.
- Everyone has the right to have no rights.

- Everyone has the right not to be afraid.
- Do not defeat.
- Do not fight back.
- Do not surrender.

It was as we were leaving the Old Town and Užupio that the rain started to fall heavily. Our next port of call was the Soviet-worshipping Green Bridge (Zaliasis Tiltas). On each of the four corners of this bridge that crosses the Neris River stood a sculpture of two people standing strongly. Cori explained to me that the four Communist couples represented agriculture, industry, peace, and youth. She also said that according to the guidebook she was reading from, these were the only Communist monuments left in the city centre. Apparently, the locals liked them too much to have them removed. Next up was a visit to the TV Tower, Vilnius' tallest structure. Standing at 326.5m and built in 1980, it is taller than the Eiffel Tower and, during the fight for independence at the start of the 90s, became a focus of Soviet aggression. On 13th January 1991 Soviet tanks encircled and assaulted the tower, killing 14 unarmed civilians and injuring hundreds more. There is now a small museum on the ground floor to remind Lithuanians of the period. There's also a restaurant and observation platform at a height of 190m that slowly rotates, but without money I was unable to get up there for the panoramic view of the city, not that I would have been able to see very far through the thick, grey clouds. From there I was taken back towards the Old Town where Cori told me I was going to be shown an egg. To be honest, I didn't really know what to expect from this, so I went with it and soon found myself looking up at a huge statue of an egg sitting in a nest in the middle of a little square. According to the guidebook, the egg had sat on a nest of real twigs in Užupio's main square, until it 'hatched' the angel of Užupio in 2002 and had to be moved. And staying in the area of Užupio, I will take this opportunity to tell you about Lithuania's favourite son, for whom there is both a statue and a wall mural inside the independent republic's walls. American jazz musician Frank Zappa; the only man who gets to be a country's 'favourite son' despite not actually having any links to that country. In fact, Zappa, who died in Los Angeles in 1993, never even set foot in Lithuania. Try arguing that point to the Lithuanians, though; they love him. The statue of Zappa, known more for his moustaches than any musical ability, was unveiled in 1992, and shows Frank from the neck up, his head balancing on top of a tall metal pole like the trophy of some indigenous head-hunters.

That evening I accompanied my host to a dinner party at the residence of an obviously very wealthy couple, some friends of Cori's. All of the guests worked in the film and theatre industry and the whole affair was a bit too lovey for me to feel comfortable in. There wasn't any beer, only wine. I spent the evening sat in the corner, eavesdropping on some of the most stuck-up conversation imaginable. At one point I stood filling my plate with mini sausages as I listened to an English upper middle class toff with floppy Hugh Grant hair who I had spoken to only briefly a few minutes earlier, explaining to a Lithuanian friend that the very worst thing about England was the working class folk. As soon as the words had left his lips he turned around, noticed me standing behind him, turned red, and said, 'Oh, hello again,' as he tried to work out whether I had heard or not. Staying in character, I replied, 'You alright, son? Blinding little do, this, innit? Free grub, an'all. Fill ya boots, 'Arry!' before turning around and walking back to my little corner of the room. Later on I was privy to another one of his little chats, this time in which he explained how special he was as an Englishman who could speak not one but two foreign languages: French and Italian.

'I guess I'm what you could call a linguist,' he smugly declared.

I didn't bother telling him that that isn't what linguist means. Instead I snorted back laughter as the Lithuanian he was talking to asked him how long he had been living in Vilnius.

'Four years,' he replied.

'Oh, and you don't speak Lithuanian?'

Brilliant.

The weekend soon came to an end and I needed to be getting out of Vilnius and continuing my journey towards the ever nearing finish line. However, my plans for hitchhiking out of the city that day were put on hold when Cori told me she'd arranged a Couchsurfing get together in a pub later that evening with some people who wanted to meet me, so I decided to put my exodus on hold until first thing the following morning.

The meet started in an Irish pub at 8pm. Joining Cori and I were three girls from the Couchsurfing community, Ieva, Ruta and Ozge, plus two of Cori's friends. I sat drinking beer, vaguely listening to some of the girls' conversations about such fascinating aspects of life as why there's always so much toilet paper in the ladies' toilets in pubs and clubs; how African men are really sexy; and why you should never eat a big dinner before going out for the night because you will just look fat. After about an hour of this riveting stuff, we headed on to a place called Woo. Not quite a bar, not quite a club, but something in between. There was a dance floor in the middle of the room but nobody was on it as everyone sat around the outside at little tables talking loudly over the music. Cori and her friends decided to call it a night pretty early on but the three Couchsurfers asked if I would stay and, as I was by now quite enjoying their company, I obliged. Cori gave me a key and told me to have a good night. Ruta was 18 years old and in the final year of high school. She was already a seasoned traveller, and despite living with her parents also regularly hosted Couchsurfers. She also knew how to drink. Ieva was about the same age as me, had long blonde hair and came across as a fulltime party girl. Before the music was even turned up she was beckoning me to get up and dance with her. I declined; I wasn't yet nearly intoxicated enough. Ruta's best friend Ozge was a Turkish Erasmus student in her early twenties. We sat and drank until the place did turn into what you would call a proper nightclub. The tables and chairs were cleared away by staff, the house music was turned up to full volume and people started pouring in from outside. Ieva headed home in the early hours, leaving me to continue the festivities with the two remaining girls until just after 4 in the morning when staff began emptying the place for the night. What we hadn't known all the time we were down inside the club was that outside it had been snowing relentlessly, and there was now already an ankle-high layer of fluffy white stuff on the ground, being added to by the second. I said goodbye to the girls, before staggering about for 45 minutes until I eventually stumbled by accident upon Cori's flat, by which time I was up to my knees in snow.

Hitchhiking out of the city later that day was off the cards, as due to the meteorological conditions no cars were braving the roads. But the forecast for the following day was one of clear skies, so I waited. In the meantime a friend of Cori's called to let me know of a spot on the outskirts of the city from where it was supposedly very easy to get picked up by passing drivers.

'You couldn't have picked a better day for hitchhiking,' Cori said, the following morning, pointing out the window to the bright sun and melting snow. At 12:30 we left the flat together under the falling flakes of snow being blown off of the rooftops by the wind that was becoming increasingly stronger.

'Are you sure this snow is coming from the roofs?' I asked, as we made our way through the streets of the Old Town. 'Only, the flakes are pretty big and the flow is constant. It's not snowing again, is it?'

'No it's definitely second hand snow. Oh, wait.'

I took the trolley bus to its final stop and then walked for another 20 minutes until I found the spot at the motorway's entrance that Cori's friend had told me about. My feet were already soaking and I had slipped to the ground twice in the slush. At least I knew I was in the right place, as I spotted a 40-year old scruff standing with his thumb out. I pulled out my homemade sign with the letters LV written on in big, bold capitals and stood a bit further up the road than the original hitchhiker, taking my place in the queue. It was 2:05 in the afternoon. Neither me nor the scruffy man were having any luck and after 20 minutes of standing in the freezing cold, getting buried under snow and being splashed with brown water by every lorry that sped past, my competitor gave up and left the scene. I wasn't alone for long. Five minutes later, walking up the road towards me, I spotted a little peroxide blonde. I knew she would be trouble. The first thing she did to piss me off was take up her spot about five metres behind me, in effect jumping the queue of one that already existed. The second thing she did, which I knew would happen but didn't infuriate me any less, was get picked up by a lorry driver after standing at the side of the road for less than a minute. That part I could understand. What I found rather distasteful though, was that both she and the driver felt the need to laugh at me as they drove off. A laugh that said, 'Do you really expect to get picked up looking like a drowned rat? A drowned, male rat.' I smiled back, not wanting to let them get to me in case it affected the image I was trying to project to other drivers of a cold, wet, but still smiling happy-go-lucky foreign guy just trying to get to Latvia. At 2:40 another lorry sped past me, splashing my white jacket in mud and getting some in my eyes. As I rubbed them to try and regain sight, a little car pulled over. I looked inside to the driver who was speaking on his mobile and he indicated for me to chuck my bags in the back. He was a huge, scary-looking bear of a man and I wondered if he would take me into the woods and cut me up, but curiosity got the better of me, so I did as I was told and got into the front seat and waited for him to finish his conversation. The guy was about 45 years old and looked such a beast that I didn't imagine for a second that he'd speak any English. He said something to me in Lithuanian, then in Russian, then in Polish, and all three times I said, 'Ne razumen' which means 'I don't understand' in a whole host of Slavic languages.

'English?' he asked next.

'Yes.'

'Ah, no problem. I speak English.'

I was surprised, but pleasantly. He asked what I was doing in Lithuania and I explained the story. He told me that he was only going 60km up the motorway but that at least it would get me out of the snow for a bit and maybe I'd find it easier to get picked up from there. We spoke throughout the drive. His name was Tomas and he lived in a small town in the country and worked in Vilnius in the building trade as some kind of boss. The Tony Soprano kind, I imagined. He had worked in Norway for a few years and that's where he had learnt English, and he was married with one son. He had also spent many years in the Soviet navy, but was 100 per cent Lithuanian and proud of it (his words). Along the way we stopped into a motorway service station where he bought me a cup of tea and some pâté and cucumber on bread, saying that I needed to have food inside me if I was going be standing in the cold for a while. I was grateful to have been picked up by such a nice bloke. Over the tea he spoke about how he was looking forward to getting home because he was going to make lunch with his wife. He told me how even though he worked long hours in the city, and she was a busy estate agent, they still always tried to find the time to make lunch together. It was touching. As we drove the last 20 minutes before he would have to let me out, the snow got ridiculous. We couldn't see through the windscreen at points. When he dropped me off, he got out of the car and went to the boot where he pulled out a pair of gloves for me to wear – not the especially warm kind, but rather the builders' kind for gripping stuff, but still better than nothing at all – as well as putting into my hands a packet of cigarettes, a lighter and a bottle of Latvian brandy.

'This will keep you warm,' he said.

I didn't know what to say, other than 'thanks!'

He wished me luck and drove off to his house. What an absolute legend of a man.

It was now 3:45pm and I got my sign out again and started trying to get another lift. The snow was still falling. I looked like I had turned up to audition for a part as the lead character in a stage production of Raymond Briggs' *The Snowman*. Remember I said about Lithuania having a sense of humour? Well let me give you another example of this razor-sharp wit. Lorry-driving comedians had a little joke they would play that involved putting on their indicator lights and then pulling over to the side of the road, waiting for me a few yards ahead, watching me pick up my bags and struggle through the blizzard to get to them, before driving off laughing just as I was reaching out to open the passenger door. It happened four times. Four fucking times! I reasoned that they were actually doing me a kind service by demonstrating a little Lithuanian cultural game; one that I otherwise would never have known of. It was a local studies lesson. To show my appreciation I returned the favour to each one, teaching them the British gesture performed with the repetitive movement of the wrist. Cultural exchange … it's what travelling's all about.

At precisely 4:45pm I had one of those inspirational (by inspirational, I mean stupid) moments and found myself saying out loud, 'Fuck it. Riga's only 200km away. I'll walk it!'

So I picked up my bags and started trekking along the side of the motorway, keeping my thumb out on the off chance that someone might pull over and pick me up. Like that was going to happen. But after 45 minutes of walking, it did. The 21-year old driver of the small car told me he was going about 50km further on to a place called Panevezys. It was a start. The motorway was never-ending, and 25 minutes after being picked up I was dropped off at the side of the same road that had come all the way from Vilnius and I carried on the walk. It was becoming dangerous, as every time a lorry went past, the speed of it combined with the wind and almost blew me off my feet and into the path of the stream of vehicles coming from behind me. The blizzard was relentless; the most extreme experienced on the journey. Undeterred, I continued to walk for another hour, repeating over and over, 'I won't stop until I get to Riga. I won't stop until I get to Riga.' And at 7:10pm the car that I had been waiting for finally pulled up behind me. I could feel it was going to be the one to take me to Riga without even needing to turn around. It was my time.

'Hey!' the voice shouted, and I span around with a sparkle in my eyes.

'Oh, for fuck's sake.'

It wasn't my lift. It was the Lithuanian police. The driver was already out of the car, while his partner sat in the warmth of the passenger seat.

'Passport, please.'

I handed it over and the officer passed it through the window to the other guy to run a check over the radio. He then got out of the car, I assumed to arrest me for trespassing on the motorway. I assumed wrong, as he turned out to be the friendliest policeman probably anywhere on the planet.

'Do you have a reflective coat?' he asked. 'It's almost impossible to see you in these conditions. You could get killed.'

'I don't have any sort of coat, let alone a reflective one.'

He went round to the boot of the car and pulled out some reflective strips, the kind that cyclists wrap around their arms, and tied them to my backpack for me. The two of them then wished me the best of luck and jumped back into the car.

'Wait!' I shouted. 'Are you driving that way?'

'Yes.'

'Take me with you.'

'Okay, we'll take you a bit further but then we'll have to turn around.'

We drove at speed for 20 minutes before I was put back out to face the elements.

'There is a petrol station a little bit further up the road,' the policeman told me. 'It is a refuelling point for drivers going to Latvia. You might have more luck if you talk to drivers there.'

I thanked them and carried on through the blizzard, finding the garage at 7:40. It didn't look as promising as the coppers had made it sound; just a tiny little building with no customers. The sign at its entrance told me it was 145km to Riga. I reckoned I could make it in about 30 hours of walking. *That's not too bad*, I thought.

But first I was going to wait for a bit under the roof to see if anyone turned up. The first few cars that came in either had no space for me or weren't going my way, but just as I was about to give up, a white transit van pulled in, driven by a middle aged guy with no passenger. He walked past me and into the shop, so I called out and asked him where he was going.

'Close to Riga.'

'Perfect. Can I come with you, please? I'm freezing,' I pleaded.

'Sorry,' he replied, shaking his head.

I could tell that his knowledge of English was rudimentary, so I looked at his plates and saw he was from Poland.

'Proszę!' I said.

He told me to wait, and then went in to buy cigarettes before going to the toilet. He returned to his van and was just getting in when I decided the time was right to play my trump card.

Out came the bottle of brandy.

'This is for you if you take me to Riga,' I said, holding out the bottle.

All of a sudden a smile broke out on his face.

'Okay,' he said, and opened the passenger door for me to get in.

If there's one thing you can rely on with Poles it's that they will do anything for a drink. We weren't able to speak much, as his English was appalling and my Polish was worse, but I managed to understand that my chaperone drove all over Europe delivering building materials, and that he often drove in England. He also sometimes delivered Polish contract workers to the plants there. He wasn't going to Riga but would be passing fairly close by and would stop just outside the city for me to get out. Around two hours later at 9:50pm he dropped me off...

Nowhere near Riga.

I was in the middle of a forest. An unlit forest. I couldn't really complain, he had brought me a long way and at least I was in the right country now. But still, how was I going to navigate my way to Latvia's capital from here? It was pitch black.

A few minutes before getting out of the car I had seen a sign indicating that Riga was 17km away. Annoyingly, I couldn't remember in which direction the sign had been pointing, and there was no way of finding it now. I walked around for about an hour, up and down different motorway turn-offs, in complete darkness – I couldn't even read the roadside signs unless a car went past and put its headlights on it – trying to find anything that would point me in the right direction. This was dangerous and I was pretty sure I was going to get hit by a car. I eventually found the turn-off for Riga though, and set off walking down this tiny little slip road that took me from one main motorway to another. You would think that at least one car would see this guy walking around in the blizzard, struggling with heavy bags, looking lost, and at least pull over to ask if he knew where he was going. You would be wrong. I think I scared people, more than anything else. I walked and walked until up in the distance I spotted a motorway service station. It became my holy grail. I battled through the wind and snow to reach it. My body was hurting from carrying the bags, I had cramp in my right leg from the effort needed to walk through thick snow, I was soaked through, there was a pond of water in each of my shoes, I had eaten just a few slices of bread and pâté all day, and I was exhausted and demoralised. I made it to the petrol station and staggered up to the first parked car I saw, as two guys roughly the same age as me pumped air into one of the tyres.

'Do you speak English?' I asked.

'Yep.'

'Are you going to Riga?'

'Yep.'

'Can I please jump in?'

'Sure! Why not?'

And after all the struggles of the day, I was getting a lift into Latvia's capital. Renars and Janez were two Latvians returning to Riga after a day of snowboarding in the mountains. They asked what I was doing in the country and, after hearing my story, Renars went into the shop and returned with a hot cup of tea and a tuna sandwich for me. These boys were my saviours. They asked where I was staying and I told them that I didn't know exactly but that I had the number of a Couchsurfer there. Janez called the number from his phone and after a brief conversation told me that they lived just around the corner from the part of the city I was going to, and would be able to drop me off at the door. Everything had fallen into place.

We got to the flat at around 11:30pm. After 11 hours of hell, I ticked another capital city off of my list. Thank fuck for that.

Welcome to Riga.

41. Riga

Capitals left to visit: Athens, Helsinki, Tallinn

Days on the road: 149
Distance travelled: 9917 miles
EU capitals visited: 20

LIVA AND HER boyfriend Paulis were stood waiting in the snow in front of the Soviet-style block as I jumped out of the car and hugged my chauffeur and his mate. I was feeling superhuman after getting through what had been by far the hardest day of the 149 since leaving England. There was no way now that anything would stand in my way and stop me completing the journey.

Liva was stunning. Blonde hair, blue eyes, fit body, and a smile that could stop a war. I couldn't take my eyes off her. Sitting down in their living room to more hot tea, I learned that this young couple both studied at the local university; Liva reading history, Paulis philosophy. There is a lyric in a song by Essex-based musical duo Scroobius Pip Vs Dan le Sac that reads, "Don't use poetry to get into girls' pants, use it to get into their heads," which I am pretty sure sums up perfectly how Paulis found himself sharing a home and a bed with Liva, only substituting poetry for philosophy. He had to be a fascinating and complex guy. Or it could have had something to do with their shared passion in life: snowboarding. Whatever it was, I didn't really care. I wanted peace, quiet, darkness and sleep. After a long, hot shower I was granted three of the four, but went the whole night deprived of what I craved more than anything else, sleep, as I lay in agony; every single muscle in my body aching excruciatingly.

The duration of the next day was spent sitting in a skateboard shop in the city centre, hanging out with Paulis in his place of work. The small basement shop, that Paulis manned alone, shared the building with an equally tiny record shop, manned solely by a German who shared the same job description as Paulis. It read like this:

As an employee you will:

1. Sit in front of a laptop watching Bill Hicks on YouTube all day.
2. Pause the video clips three or four times during the day to assist a customer who will eventually walk away without buying anything.
3. Eat sandwiches.
4. Play poker, but not for money, for forfeits. (An example of a forfeit: going out onto the street and telling the first man that passes that you think he has nice hair).
5. Chain-smoke cigarettes.
6. Make a snowman to guard the door (weather permitting).
7. Go home at the end of the day safe in the knowledge that you have done absolutely nothing to earn the money you will be paid at the end of the month.

Nice work if you can get it.

The journey from the flat to the shop earlier that morning had taken 30 minutes in the back of a minibus, packed full of locals seated along ethnic lines. Passengers on the left side of the vehicle conversed in Latvian, passengers on the right in Russian. I had never seen anything like this in all of my European travels, but Paulis explained that it was standard for

Riga. Apparently the break-up of the Soviet Union back at the start of the 1990s had left Riga with a large ethnic Russian population that had never fully seen eye to eye with their ethnic Latvian cohabiters.

'Everything is split here,' he told me, as I listened, fascinated. 'Russians deal with Russians, Latvians deal with Latvians. They have their own neighbourhoods, their own schools, their own shops, their own churches, their own alphabet, their own representatives in parliament, and they only really mix with themselves. It is the same for us Latvians. It is not that we don't like each other; it's more that we don't trust each other. Most of them (the ethnic Russians) don't even know the Latvian language. Everywhere you go in the city, you will see this divide.'

I knew from my own personal experience of spending three years in Slovenia's capital that the break-up of some of the ex-Communist countries had left large numbers of people living amongst people that spoke a different language and had a different culture, but still it surprised me to see these two groups of people sharing a small city but living such segregated lives. Sure, there were plenty of jokes, petty insults and minor tensions between Slovenes and their southern guests, but a casual visitor to the city wouldn't pick up on it. Everyone worked together, went to school together, drank together and lived together. So my immediate thought when hearing about the situation in Riga was, why is it different here to Slovenia? Then I remembered: Slovenia, during her time as a Yugoslav Republic, was a mostly willing member of a federation, whereas Latvia was technically occupied by a foreign force. The Russians had suppressed Latvian culture, the Latvian language and the Latvian people. According to recent data, Riga's population is made up of just 42.3 per cent ethnic Latvians, 41.7 per cent ethnic Russians, with 16 per cent other ethnicities. That's almost the same amount of Russians as Latvians living in Latvia's capital city. During my teenage years spent meeting foreigners in Brighton, I became good friends with a girl that I still keep in touch with today, Olga. Olga was born and raised in Riga and, as far as I was concerned, was a Latvian. I knew no different. We used to write letters and text each other, and then one day she told me that she had just started seeing a new boyfriend.

'Great! Is he Latvian?' I asked, innocently.

'No! No way! I would never go out with a Latvian boy! I don't like Latvians. He is Russian, of course!'

I didn't understand, so asked, 'But you're Latvian. How can you dislike your own people?'

'I am not Latvian. I am Russian. A proud Russian. Yes, I was born here and have lived here my whole life, but I am definitely not Latvian.'

What did I know?

As the day drew to a close, Paulis asked a difficult favour of me. He planned to go straight from work to a skateboard ramp with a group of mates but had forgotten to bring his board with him in the morning. Could I go back to the flat and pick it up for him while he sat out the final hour in the shop? I had paid no attention whatsoever that morning to the route we'd taken on the minibus, but I did clearly remember that Paulis had had to pay the driver for the two of us. How would I find my way back to the flat? And how would I get there without handling any money?

'Don't worry about that. There is also a regular bus that goes to our suburb, and it will be so busy that you won't have to buy a ticket. Just jump on the back like everyone else,' Paulis reassured me, before writing down instructions and pushing me out the door.

Making my way to the bus stop proved to be the most difficult part of the challenge. Not because it was hard to find but because the thick snow that lay on the rooftops was melting quickly under the sun, sending monumental chunks of solid ice and compact snow tumbling to the streets below. Most of the city's shops had put traffic cones outside their buildings, diverting people into the road – presumably because being hit by a bus rather than an ice bomb was seen as the lesser of two evils – but when, just a few feet in front of me, a ball the size of a grown man came crashing down and smashed through the windscreen of a parked car, I wondered how many lives the cones were really going to save.

I made it safely to the bus-stop and squeezed through the back doors, taking my place right in the middle of the bus, not wanting to be accused of favouring the company of either of the two ethnic groups. Paulis had been right; the bus was packed to busting point as people made their ways home from work. There was no way that a ticket inspector could get on and manoeuvre through the throng of people, but yet I witnessed a strange procedure taking place, proving that no matter what the Latvians may say of the Russians, and the Russians may say of the Latvians; both groups are nothing if not honest. Passengers at the back of the bus, who hadn't yet bought a ticket, were passing their money forward, watching it move from hand to hand until it eventually reached the driver, before a ticket was passed hand to hand all the way back to the man or woman at the back. Everyone bought a ticket this way, and not once was there any confusion as to where the money had come from or whom the ticket was for. This would never happen in England. Even now, the train stations that have not yet had ticket gates fitted are the busiest of all because people would rather get off and walk the extra mile for the sake of a free journey. Fare dodging is a sport where I grew up.

I made it back to the block of flats and was joined in the lift by a young, bearded Pakistani dressed in traditional robes, who got out on the same floor as me. We were going into the same flat. Sohail was the 25-year old flatmate that hadn't been at home the previous night. I introduced myself to the medical student from Lahore, and then we chatted in the kitchen.

'That's amazing!' he said on hearing about my journey. 'Please, let me make you some dinner. Do you like curry?'

And just like that, Paulis was going to have to wait a while for his skateboard. Sohail called him to explain and he didn't complain. The vegetable curry with rice and spicy potatoes was delicious and we sat down together at the kitchen table to enjoy it, talking throughout, mostly about religion. Sohail was a Muslim fundamentalist and at one point during the meal had to leave the room for a couple of minutes to kneel on the prayer mat in his room. I waited respectfully before carrying on eating on his return. At first I made the mistake of believing that our two way conversation was just a simple exchanging of views to pass the time at the dinner table, but after a couple of minutes it became apparent that I had read the situation incorrectly. Sohail wasn't simply telling me what it was like to be a Muslim; he was trying to convert me. Just to be sure, I asked him straight out if this was the case.

'Yes, you are right. It is my duty as a good Muslim to educate infidels and help them to see the truth. You must see the error of your ways and join Islam.'

The food was so good and I hadn't yet finished half of it, so I decided against arguing in case my plate was taken from me. Instead I just listened with interest to the preacher, finding great entertainment in one particular belief expressed.

'You shouldn't drink alcohol. You see, alcohol is very bad. Very, very bad. Because it is impossible for a drunk man to differentiate between his wife and his sister. If you drink, you may accidentally sleep with your sister.'

'This is terrible! I drink. And I have two sisters!' I told him.

'Then you know the dangers of which I speak, don't you?'

'Yes, I do. Luckily, though, I don't have a wife.'

It wasn't my intention to offend my host, but I did want to demonstrate that no conversion was going to take place on this particular evening. I mean, come on! How can someone really believe that?

After dinner, I sat in Sohail's bedroom watching the full collection of sermons on DVD by a Saudi Arabian cleric 'scientifically proving' that every word written in the Qu'ran was the word of God. I couldn't argue with such evidence, could I? I went to bed. I awoke the following morning to not one but two pieces of good news. The first was an email from a Swiss businessman living in Estonia, Oliver, who had seen the message I'd left on the Couchsurfing Tallinn forum and had come forward with the offer of a place to sleep once in Estonia's capital city. The second piece of good news was even greater. A Riga native, Elina, had been following my adventures through the blog and wanted to help me out.

'I am a big fan of your blog. If you would accept, I would like to buy you a bus ticket to get you safely from Riga to Tallinn,' she wrote.

I was gobsmacked, and immediately replied to thank her and to arrange a meet. After the ordeal I'd gone through in getting from Vilnius to Riga, I had feared the worst again for the upcoming journey north. Now though, it was going to be plain sailing.

Before moving on I wanted to properly see the city of Riga, so out I headed with the usual plan of just wandering around and getting lost. In Lithuania, people I had spoken to had all said the same thing: 'The Baltic countries get more beautiful the further north you travel. Tallinn is more beautiful than Riga, Riga more beautiful than Vilnius.' After spending time in Riga I disagreed. There is nothing wrong with Latvia's capital, it is a beautiful city, but not nearly as quaint and pretty as Vilnius. Nowhere was this more evident than when comparing the two cities' Old Towns. Riga just didn't cut the mustard. My day-long stroll took in the Russian Cathedral, the city centre, a trip along the banks of the Daugava River and also off into housing estates and residential areas. I wanted to see the real life of Riga, and what I found was further confirmation about the ethnic split in the city. There were streets where only Russians dared walk and streets where only Latvians dared walk. That's how I imagined it anyway. In all likelihood it had nothing to do with dare. After all, I was neither Latvian nor Russian and I trod everywhere. I am a crazy bastard though.

Shortly after returning to the flat, my phone rang. It was Jalila, the Brazilian girl I'd met in Amsterdam. She had seen on Facebook that I was in Riga and wanted to know if I was up for meeting her later that evening for a stroll. I had completely forgotten she lived in Latvia, and was excited at the thought of seeing her again. In a race against time, I washed, brushed my teeth, sprayed all over with deodorant – I believe this is known as a French shower – and jumped on the back of a bus to meet her in front of the Russian church at 8. We embraced, kissed and then walked the dark streets together. Not saying much. Everything that had seemed so natural and perfect in Amsterdam was a distant memory, leaving us like two complete strangers, both freezing cold and with very few words to share. It was always going to be hard to match Amsterdam, but this was like pulling teeth. I walked her to her bus, saw her on her way and made my way back to the flat, feeling a sense of loss. The moments we had shared in Amsterdam had been facilitated by the drugs, and in the cold night of day we were just two strangers.

It was Saturday and it was time to leave Latvia. Liva and Paulis were away for a weekend of snowboarding, so I spent the day sleeping in a park until just after 5 when I had to meet Elina outside an Irish pub in the Old Town. She was 23 years old and a self-confessed travel addict, with a strong Scandinavian facial structure and she wore a broad smile. The first thing she did on meeting me was hand me a ticket to Tallinn. We drank some tea together in a pub and then walked to the city's bus station, where I stood and guarded her bike while she went in to the building to double check departure times. We swapped email addresses, wished each other luck and then she waved me off as my coach pulled out of the station at 6:30pm.

Before arriving in Riga I had never met a Latvian before, unless you count Olga the Russian. So on leaving the city, every Latvian I had ever met had been introduced into my life in the past few days, and every single one of them had been amazing. Renars and Janez warmed my heart with their kindness, Liva and Paulis made me feel at home in their flat, and Elina went way beyond the call of duty in offering me not just a ticket, but the whole act of coming to meet me, treating me to a drink and then waving me on my way. I will return to Latvia one day.

The ride to Tallinn was peaceful and uneventful – exactly as I hoped it would be – and I arrived in Estonia's capital four hours later at 10:30pm, ticking yet another capital off of my list.

Only two more to go before I can return home.

Welcome to Tallinn.

42. Tallinn

Capitals left to visit: Athens, Helsinki

Days on the road: 153
Distance travelled: 10,110 miles
EU capitals visited: 21

Oliver arrived to pick me up shortly after 11pm, accompanied by a pale, thin woman in her early thirties who introduced herself as Kristina. Oliver was in his mid-thirties, stockily built, clean shaven with short brown hair and wore a sports jumper with jeans. Despite the casual outfit, he didn't look comfortable. There was something forced about it, as if he longed to be in a suit. Before getting into the car I was subjected to the longest handshake and gaze I had ever experienced with another man; now it was my turn to look uncomfortable. Oliver spoke slowly and quietly, as if off his tits on valium. So did Kristina. And when conversing, they would pause for moments at a time just to stare into my eyes or into nowhere.

They asked me the usual questions: How has your journey been? Are you tired? How many more cities have you got to visit? Have you ever sacrificed a kitten to the gods? And then we were driving towards Oliver's flat. As we walked up the stairs of the building, Kristina swore. Well, she did if the words 'uh oh!' count as a curse. I am just trying to make her a bit more interesting, for the sake of the story.

'The beans,' she said, almost inaudibly.

Was this code for something exciting? We entered the flat

and Oliver ran to the kitchen. I stood in the doorway and watched as he opened the window, took the batteries out of the smoke alarm and flapped around the air with a tea towel. A few minutes later and we might have been entering a blaze. The blackened beans were stuck to the bottom of the pan, with only a few on top that had lived to tell the tale. Beans was not code for something more exciting. Beans was code for beans.

'These ones will be fine to eat,' said Oliver, scraping bits from the pan onto three plates. I said nothing.

We sat around the dining-room table as Kristina served up beautifully rare steak and rice to go along with the barely edible Brazilian beans. Three cold beers were also poured.

Oliver had been living in Estonia for four years. He was originally from Zurich but had moved to Tallinn for a short-term work project and ended up staying after falling in love with the country (and probably a person, too). He had set up his own computer software company and was doing very well by the looks of things. The flat was Scandinavian in style: open-plan, with wooden beams in the middle of the room, a large fireplace in the corner, and a sauna in the bathroom. I couldn't work out what the relationship was between Oliver and Kristina. They sat closely together and spoke gently to each other, but there was very little in the way of touchy-feely. I also had the feeling that Kristina wanted to seduce me. I know what you're thinking: 'Kris, you think every woman wants to seduce you. You are the most deluded person I have ever come across.' And I take your point on board; but listen, this time it was different. She really did want me naked. She gazed deeply into my eyes, touched my arm with her hand every time she spoke to me and had a constant loved-up smile on her face. I chose against acting on this blatant come-on for two main reasons. The first being I still wasn't sure if she had something going on with Oliver. The second was that she weirded me out. They both did. If I was going to assume that Kristina wanted to bed me by the way she interacted with me, then I was probably going to have to make the same assumption of Oliver. And that really wasn't an avenue I was willing to explore.

I started to suspect that I had been lured into the house of a couple of swingers and that I was going to be the night's entertainment. I shifted uneasily in my chair. I was relieved when the conversation and gazing was put on hold, as Oliver got up to put on some tunes.

'This is traditional Brazilian music,' he said. 'I love everything from Brazil. This dinner was also a Brazilian recipe.'

I wondered how well the burnt offering would go down in Rio. Conversation soon moved on to hobbies. I mentioned that I enjoyed a little game of poker every now and then and was surprised to see their eyes brighten with fascination.

'I've never gambled,' said Oliver.

'Me neither,' Kristina chipped in, 'it all sounds so risky.'

'Are you good? I mean, can you win money when you play?' Oliver asked, looking like a man with a plan.

'Well, I know how to play.'

I didn't want to get myself into anything.

'How tired are you? Do you feel like going out?'

I looked at the clock on the wall and saw it was almost 1am. I was knackered and would happily have gone to bed, but now that another option had been posed, I knew I had to stick to the philosophy of never say no; especially if it involved gambling, which I had a sneaky feeling it did.

'Okay.'

The casino was just a five minute walk down the road from the flat. Inside, Norwegians and Russians walked around in small groups, carrying plastic chips and drinks. The Russians wore suits and drank vodka; the Norwegians were in jeans and t-shirts and drank whatever they could carry.

'I am going to buy you into the poker game over there,' Oliver said, pointing to a table in the corner. 'Are you familiar with the currency exchange rate for the kroon?'

'What's a kroon?'

'Perfect. I'm not going to tell you how much you are playing with. Just play your game and count them as tokens, not as money, then at the end I will tell you how much you have won me. We might be able to buy you a ticket to Finland out of the winnings.'

I sat down at the table of Norwegians with 3000 kroons. Three hours later it was gone. I had played a shocker and had lost the lot. I stood up, thanked my opponents for the game and went to find my backer. The two of them were propping up the bar, drinking cocktails.

'How much did you win?'

'Not a lot.'

'Something is better than nothing.'

'Then I won something worse than something.'

'Huh?'

'Huh?'

'You lost me, Kris.'

'I lost your money, Oliver.'

There was silence. In retrospect, I realise that my attempt at riddling probably made the moment more awkward, but either way this was never going to be pretty. I still had no idea if I had just lost £10, £100 or £1000. Eventually he spoke.

'Oh well, it's my fault. I should have known not to put money into gambling.'

'Yes you should!' I shouted.

I didn't really. I bowed my head. Oliver looked at me deeply. Kristina looked at me deeply. Oliver looked at Kristina deeply. Kristina looked at Oliver deeply. I looked at the floor deeply and prayed it wasn't orgy time.

The walk back to the flat was tense. Oliver had the look of a man who had just lost money. Ah wait, yea… Kristina had the look of someone frustrated by lack of sexual activity. I had the look of a tramp. I was relieved when we got to the entrance to Oliver's building and Kristina said her goodbyes. She lived just across the street. I didn't think Oliver would be up for an orgy now that she had left. My assumption was correct, as he showed me to my bedroom and then disappeared, closing the door behind him. My room was decorated with racing car wallpaper and had a pile of toys in the corner. Oliver told me the next day over brunch that it was where his young son slept when he stayed over. His boy's mum was Estonian. Now it made a little more sense why he was so attached to Tallinn.

I was pretty tired after only getting about four hours sleep, but was keen to see the city. It was a Sunday but Oliver still had to go into the office to get some work done, so he walked me towards the city centre on his way. Tallinn's Old Town was beautiful that day: pristine white buildings with bright red roofs, a large cobblestone square, and restaurant terraces laced with people enjoying the sunshine despite the icy air. It was grandeur yet understated; busy yet peaceful; historic yet modern. I truly felt that I had saved the best of Eastern Europe's Old Town's for last. There was only one thing that wasn't perfect about Tallinn: the people. Watching the natives go about their business, it dawned on me that there was nothing strange about Oliver or Kristina. No, they were perfectly normal Tallinn residents. Everyone went through the same motions: slow walking, slow speaking, and probably slow thinking. Walking around Tallinn was like taking a tour of the set of Shaun of the Dead during filming.

I climbed the hill to the Alexander Nevsky Cathedral, a huge Orthodox church, and witnessed the strangest ritual I have ever seen in a Christian place of worship. In a packed out main hall, the congregation all stood together facing the front of the church. A voice then belted out of the loudspeaker system in that tone and style you only tend to hear in religious establishments; half speaking, half singing. I couldn't make out the language, but took an educated guess that it was Russian. The voice would pause for a minute during which the whole congregation would in sync perform the cross – spectacles, testicles, wallet, watch – and then drop to their knees, bow their heads and kiss the floor, before standing up again to listen to the next instruction from the voice. Another pause would follow, the ritual would be repeated, and then the voice would start again. The act went on forever. It resembled images I had seen of Jews at the Wailing Wall, or Muslims praying to Mecca. The head of every single woman was covered by a scarf. When the ritual was finally over, everybody involved walked around the inside of the church kissing crosses and pictures of religious beings. Outside the church, one man – the hardcore element – continued the ritual on his own for a good fifteen minutes. Cross, kneel, kiss the floor; cross, kneel, kiss the floor; cross, kneel, kiss the floor. He was so good at it he didn't even need the voice telling him what to do. The man was a pro.

That evening Oliver told me that he was going to buy me a ferry ticket to Helsinki. I was overjoyed and grateful for this unexpected show of kindness and gave myself a private bollocking for the assumptions I had made about him luring me into his house for something sordid. A quick check of my emails before bed found four messages in my inbox from different people in Helsinki all willing to host me once I arrived in Finland. I could smell the end of the journey now, even if I still knew that getting from Finland to Greece for the final capital could take weeks.

The day had come for me to leave Estonia and continue my journey over water to Finland. It was a bright, sunny day and I was feeling good. Before leaving the flat around lunchtime to go and meet Oliver close to the ferry terminal to sort out my ticket, I read an email from a follower of my blog, Steve from Alaska, offering a suggestion that had never crossed my mind. He wrote, 'Why don't you email some local businesses in Brighton, like restaurants and bars, asking if any of them would be prepared to sponsor you on the final leg of the journey by donating an air ticket from Helsinki to Athens. They will get a mention on your blog and you'll also give them a plug when the newspapers and radio stations interview you. It's very cheap advertising for them.'

One establishment immediately sprang to mind: Donatello's, a well-respected local Italian restaurant. I hastily wrote a few lines and emailed them, before meeting Oliver and driving down to the ferry terminal at midday with the intention of getting me on the cruise ferry, the Galaxy, departing at 1:30pm. Oliver queued for the ticket, before handing it to me and telling me it was the least he could do to help me on my way. He then popped in to the terminal's shop, returning with a parting gift for me of a four-pack of premium lager. Once again totally indebted to somebody who only a couple of days previously had been a complete stranger, I bid him farewell and boarded the ferry at 1.

As a kid I had once taken the Newhaven-Dieppe ferry for a day-trip to France, but it hadn't prepared me for what I now found myself on. The ferry that day had been a tiny little piece of scrap metal with a deck and a sitting room in which to pass the four hours. The Galaxy, on the other hand, was nine decks high and had a number of discos, pubs, restaurants, swimming pools and shops. Every shop was packed to busting point with wrinkly old Finns stocking up on cheap alcohol. I was on the Scandinavian version of the Booze Cruise. As we pulled out of the dock I watched the seagulls hovering close to the water in the hope that the boat's engine might churn up some fish for dinner. The sounds, the smells, the view; it was all so close to home. I would be back in Brighton soon and I couldn't wait. I spent the first hour of the journey walking around on the deck, hoping to find some young lady with whom to pass some time with a little chat. I soon realised, though, that I was the only passenger under the age of 65 on the whole boat. Inside, a ballroom dancing club, The Starlight Palace, was in full swing as the blue rinse brigade sipped Martinis and boogied the day away on the dance floor. It didn't matter one little bit that it was only 2:30 in the afternoon. Not as crowded was the Moonlight Dance Bar, an almost exact replica of the Starlight. I guessed it was for overspill if the Starlight got too busy or too rowdy. Those pensioners are a nightmare to control at times. The alcohol shops did a booming trade throughout the duration of the journey as people queued up and down the aisles to get their purchases through the checkout. My stomach hurt from hunger as pensioners walked around me eating crackers and salmon.

Three hours and fifteen minutes after leaving Tallinn, my ferry pulled up to the dock in Finland and I ticked the penultimate capital city off of my list. And I opened a can of beer.

Welcome to Helsinki.

North Cape
Jan Mayen
(Norway)
NORWEGIAN SEA
Scandinavia
Lapland
Lake Inari
Kiruna
Kebnekaise
Tromsø
Hammerfest
Vardø
Vadsø
Luleå
Oulu
Lake Oulu
SWEDEN
FINLAND
Umeå
Vaasa
Gulf of Bothnia
Lakes
Trondheimsfjorden
Trondheim
Ålesund
NORWAY
Galdhopiggen
Sundsvall
Tampere
Turku
HELSINKI
Aland
Faroe Islands
(Denmark)
Suduroy
Shetland Islands
(UK)
Bergen
OSLO
Drammen
STOCKHOLM
Gulf of Finland
ESTONIA
St Peter
Orkney Islands
Stavanger
Norrköping
Gotland
Isle of Lewis
Wick
Kristiansand
Göteborg
LATVIA
Pskov
SCOTLAND
Aberdeen
NORTH
SEA
Skagerrak
Kalmar
Öland
Hebrides
Perth
Glasgow
Edinburgh
British
Isles
UNITED
KINGDOM
DENMARK
COPENHAGEN
Malmö
BALTIC SEA
LITHUANIA
KALININGRAD
(RUSSIAN FED.)
ULSTER
Belfast
Newcastle
Gdansk
MINSK
IRELAND
DUBLIN
Liverpool
Manchester
Frisian Is.
Hamburg
BELARUS
WALES
ENGLAND
Birmingham
NETHERLANDS
AMSTERDAM
Rotterdam
BERLIN
POLAND
WARSAW
Gomel
Cork
Cardiff
LONDON
Dusseldorf
Leipzig
CELTIC SEA
BRUSSELS
Antwerp
GERMANY
PRAGUE
Krakow
KIEV
Plymouth
Southampton
Lille
BELGIUM
Frankfurt
English Channel
Le Havre
CZECH.REP.
Lviv
Carpathians Mts.
PARIS
LUX.
Stuttgart
SLOVAKIA
Brest
Strasbourg
Munich
VIENNA
BRATISLAVA
MOLDOVA
Rennes
FRANCE
AUSTRIA
BUDAPEST
CHISINAU
Odesa
BERN
LIECHT.
Nantes
Geneva
SWITZ.
SLOVENIA
HUNGARY
ROMANIA
Lyon
Milan
LJUBLJANA
ZAGREB
Bay of
Biscay
Bordeaux
Massif
Central
Mt Blanc
Venice
BELGRADE
BUCHAREST
Turin
Florence
CROATIA
BOSNIA & H
SARAJEVO
SERBIA
Toulouse
Montpellier
Nice
M.C.
S.M.
Pyrenees
Marseille
ITALY
MONTENEGRO
KOSOVO
SOFIA
BULGARIA
Bilbao
Vigo
Valladolid
Douro
Zaragoza
Aneto
AND.
Corsica
VAT.
ROME
PODGORICA
SKOPJE
Musala
F.Y.R.O.M.
Istanbul
Bosporus
Porto
Coimbra
Barcelona
Naples
Bari
TIRANA
ALBANIA
Tage
MADRID
Ebre
ANKARA
PORTUGAL
Valencia
Balearic Is.
Menorca
Mallorca
Ibiza
Sardinia
Olympus
Bursa
Anatolia
LISBON
SPAIN
Sierra Morena
Córdoba
Izmir
MEDITERRANEAN SEA
Palermo
Messina
ATHENS
Konya
Seville
Mulhacen
ALGIERS
Annaba
TUNIS
Etna
Sicily
Peloponnesus
GRECCE
Antalya
Strait of Gibraltar
Gibraltar (U.K.)
Ceuta (Spain)
Oran
Chlef
Constantine
VALLETTA
AEGEAN SEA
Rhodes
Tangiers
Melilla (Spain)
Tlemcen
TUNISIA
MALTA
Sfax
Crete
CYPRUS
RABAT
Fes
ALGERIA
Gabes
MEDITERRANEAN SEA
Casablanca
MOROCCO

44. Helsinki

Capitals left to visit: Athens

Days on the road: 156
Distance travelled: 10,164 miles
EU capitals visited: 22

I WALKED INTO the terminal and saw a strange trainspotter-type hovering around as if waiting for someone. He was wearing a blue rucksack, an anorak, had the body of a 12-year old boy, and walked hunched over. He looked about 40 years old, was no taller than my shoulder and had less meat on him than a bowl of Mulligatawny soup.

'Miko?' I asked.

'Yes. Hello, Kris.'

My host was timid and had a strong, song-like accent. He spoke extremely slowly, elongating every syllable, and seemed afraid of his own shadow.

'It is a long walk to my flat. But I like walking, so it will be nice,' he enthused, as we walked out of the arrivals hall and into the winter sun.

The hour-long walk was taken up by discussion about hiking through fields and forests and how much pleasure could be found in such treks. It was a monologue. Miko informed me that he would only be able to put me up for two nights, as he was going to the Lake District in England for a couple of weeks.

'Nice. What are you going there for?'

'Oh, just walking. I will wake up every morning and then walk until it gets dark.'

Miko's flat was dull and without colour. There was a telly sitting in the corner, which he informed me didn't work as he refused to pay for the upgrade to digital and would rather go without TV just out of principle. He also had a VCR plugged into the back with a rack full of recorded-off-the-telly films from the 80s sat next to it.

'If you need to check the internet you can do it in my room, I just have to put the password in for you first. While you do that, I'll start making some dinner,' he said, whilst washing some dishes.

Sitting down in front of Miko's computer I made a little discovery – albeit not an altogether surprising one – about my quietly spoken host. Miko was a porn fiend. The browser's autosuggest offered a whole host of previously visited specialised sites. More interesting than that was an email sitting in my inbox. Sue, the manageress of Donatello's Restaurant in Brighton, had written to me asking if my request for sponsorship was an April Fools' joke – it was the first of April, obviously – and to let me know that if it wasn't and my journey was for real, that her restaurant would be more than happy to book me a flight to Athens for the following Monday. I immediately tapped out a reply, explaining that it wasn't a joke and that I really had been stupid enough to put myself through five months of torment and was now just one capital city from home. I had chosen to write to Donatello's because I knew it was a family-run business that placed a lot of pride in their support for the local community – they had even been shirt sponsors of Brighton and Hove Albion FC for a few years, and at a time when no one else was willing to put a penny into the club – and I figured that they must have read about me in the *Argus* already and would enjoy some of the publicity that would come from sponsoring me. Still, when I'd sent the email I hadn't truly expected anything more than a polite explanation as to why they couldn't use their budget to sponsor every Tom, Dick and Harry who took himself off with the aim of performing some ridiculous stunt. I was now completely stunned.

That evening Miko took me on a guided tour of the city, which included the story of why the statue of the naked lady down at the waterfront had her buttocks pointing towards Town Hall. Apparently it was a protest move by the sculptor who had been outraged by the outrage caused by having a depiction of nudity in the city. Outraged by the outrage; imagine that. As well as a protest arse, the city is also home to not one but two impressive cathedrals; one belonging to the Lutheran Church, the other Russian Orthodox.

Back at the flat and just before going to bed, Miko made us both a late night snack: bright orange fish eggs spread on toast. A poor man's caviar, if you will. Taking into consideration that I am repulsed by the sight, texture and taste of rich man's caviar, I kind of knew what to expect from this luminous variation. The first bite did nothing to change my opinion. The stuff was awful and reminded me of the frogspawn we used to fish out of the school pond when I was little. I gagged as it went down my throat but, not one to be rude, I figured the best way of dealing with the situation was to swallow it as quickly as possible, chasing it down with a glass of water. I executed the plan perfectly and it was all gone before Miko had even taken a second bite of his. Unfortunately, Miko wasn't as perceptive as he was generous and, seeing my empty plate, quickly spread another slice and handed it to me saying, 'I'm glad you like it so much. We are very proud of it in Finland.'

This time I ate slowly, wondering if my host possessed a cleaning product strong enough to remove bright orange vomit stains from a white carpet. My place of rest for the night was a foldout camper bed set up in the living room next to the telly and the audio cassette tape player. That's right, not only did Miko watch his films on VCR, he listened to his music on tape. There was something kind of retro-cool about it. I somehow resisted the temptation to watch *Terminator II*, and was asleep before midnight, much earlier than I had been getting my head down in Estonia. This was just as well, as Miko was up and loud at 5:45 the following morning. I listened to him make and eat porridge, shower, shave his face with an electric razor, wash the dishes and generally just make as much noise as possible.

'Kris, if you need to use the internet while I'm out,' he told me just before going to work, 'I have set up a new account on there for you, one that doesn't need a password.'

As soon as he had closed the door behind him at 6:50am I jumped up and out of bed, too full of energy and excitement at the thought of finishing my journey and getting home, where I would once again be able to pay for things that I wanted instead of having to sponge everything off of everyone. I checked my emails and found that Sue had already booked the flight to Athens. There was also an awaiting message from a Greek Couchsurfer called Voula who would not only host me in Athens but also pick me up from the airport when I arrived. Life was good. Pulling back the curtains I found a beautiful, sunny day. I used it to visit the uninhabited sea fortress of Suomenlinna, using the monthly pass that Miko had left for me on the kitchen table to board the ferry. Suomenlinna (or Sveaborg if you're a Swedish-speaking Finn), a UNESCO World Heritage site, is built over six islands and served in the past as a defence post against foreign invasion from the seas. The building of the fortress was started in 1748 when Finland was still part of the Swedish Kingdom. At the time Russia was becoming a threat, and Sweden set about fortifying the Russian frontier and establishing a naval base at Helsinki as a counter to the Russians' base at Kronstadt, located near the head of the Gulf of Finland. These days, Suomenlinna is a visitors' attraction rather than a military base, having been turned over to civilian administration in 1973. The presence of the military on the island has been drastically scaled down in recent decades. The Suomenlinna garrison houses Finland's Naval Academy, but that's about it. Suomenlinna also still flies the war flag, the swallow-tailed state flag of Finland. I didn't find a lot to do on the island apart from looking out to sea over the top of rusted old cannons. I sat down on the grass next to one of them and awoke almost two hours later.

The following afternoon I said goodbye to Miko and wished him well on his journey through the Lake District, before meeting my new host, 24-year old Christopher, at a Metro station in the centre of the city. Christopher was an American and had walked straight out of 1984 film *Revenge of the Nerds*. With his goofy teeth, heavily greased hair with side parting, glasses thicker than Coke bottles and jacket with his surname stitched into the left breast, I wondered if he had lost a bet. He then explained to me what he did and I realised that this really was his everyday style. My new host was a linguistics student who specialised in the endangered languages of the tribes of the ex-Soviet Union. He spoke 17 languages fluently, including Russian, Bulgarian, Romanian, Finnish and French. Despite this obvious gift for languages, he was lacking in the communication department and seemed to possess very few social skills, if any at all. I was pretty sure I was dealing with a genius savant; a real-life Rain Man. Christopher lived in an immigrant suburb, one in which he appeared to be the only white inhabitant. As we walked through the corridor and up the stairs to his flat, past the abandoned mattress and the broken radio in the hallway, I asked him more about his studies.

'Well, the course I am on only attracts nerds and weirdos, for some reason. I'm the only normal person in the class,' he told me in all seriousness.

I nodded. There to greet me as we walked through the door into the flat was a 19-year old girl standing naked but for a small towel wrapped around her torso. She had dyed jet-black hair, giant hoop earrings and a large chest with small tummy, big hips and what I believe they call on the street a bubble butt. I wondered how on Earth Christopher had got this girl into his flat. He threw her a look of contempt and walked straight through to his bedroom, motioning for me to follow.

'Who was that?' I asked as soon as the bedroom door had been closed.

'Just some bitch,' he replied bitterly. 'My flatmate is Kenyan. He has a different girl like that back here every day. You know the type: spoilt little rich bitch that wants to rebel against her parents by listening to hip-hop and going out with African men. I don't know how he can enjoy living like that with all those different women. It's not how I could live. I think it's disgusting.'

Christopher's bedroom was like a small box, with a computer in the corner and foreign language dictionaries piled up everywhere you looked. If he had the dictionary of one then he had the dictionary of 50 different languages. On the floor next to his bed, with a bookmark saving his page, was an Uzbek dictionary. Nothing like a bit of light reading to help you drop off in the evening, eh? Dinner was a real treat, but only if you happen to be one of either a daddy bear, a mummy bear or a baby bear. Porridge.

'I know it's not really a typical dinner,' my host explained whilst stirring sugar into the pot, 'but I'm kinda broke at the moment, and hey, this stuff fills you up.'

I couldn't argue with his logic. As we sat and ate the huge bowls of oats in front of us, we were treated – Christopher would use a different word – to the porno sound effects coming from the flatmate's bedroom. The whole appartment seemed to rhythmically vibrate as the squeaky bed banged a soothing beat against the wall. Christopher looked like he was ready to explode with anger but somehow managed to contain himself, although the pulsating vein sticking out of his neck acted as a giveaway to his feelings. Not even the girl's over-the-top moaning was enough to bring the faintest of smiles to his lips. After we'd finished eating and I was washing the dishes, the young rebel came out of the bedroom, again wearing nothing more than a flimsy towel and, en-route to the toilet, put her hand out and introduced herself as Laura. I shook it and then washed my hands. Vigorously. Rejoining Christopher in his room, I found that my night wasn't going to be as comfortable as I might have imagined.

'Did you bring a sleeping bag?'

'Nope.'

'Well, there's your bed,' he said, pointing to the corner of the room.

I looked but saw nothing but a pile of books and a small, bright blue piece of plastic. Closer inspection revealed that the plastic was a deflated beach lilo.

'It's not too bad. I've had a couple of other Couchsurfers sleep on it in the past,' he tried to reassure me. Unsuccessfully.

'I like to get an early night, I hope you don't mind if I turn the lights off at around 10,' he then told me, pacing around the bedroom brushing his teeth.

And so began the most uncomfortable night of the journey. The first hour, from 9 to 10, wasn't too bad as I lay and read a poetry book I'd picked up off of the toilet floor while Christopher perused an English-Moksha (the language spoken in the republic of Mordovia; as if you didn't know) dictionary. But then the lights were turned off, Christopher's snoring began and I tossed and turned on that noisiest of all moist plastics. Minutes turned into hours and still I lay wide awake, without so much as a blanket for comfort. Every time I moved a muscle the sound of my sweaty flesh rubbing against the plastic would make Christopher jump in his sleep, before muttering something in a language I can only assume was

Kalmyk (the language spoken in the Republic of Kalmykia; as if you didn't know), turning over and resuming the cartoon-like snoring.

After a completely sleepless night and another bowl of porridge, I left Christopher's place early in the morning, complete with all my gear. I couldn't spend another night like that, so decided I would be better off trying to log on to the internet somewhere during the day and emailing the other Helsinki residents that had said earlier that they could put me up, to see if the offers were still stood. Failing that, I would sleep rough. Nothing worried me anymore; not now that I was this close to the end of the journey. I jumped on the Metro headed towards the centre of the city, took a seat and then realised that my train wasn't carrying just commuters. Four burly men in black jackets had squeezed in through the doors just as the train was leaving the station and were now making their way through the carriage checking everybody's tickets. I quickly moved to the end of the compartment and crossed my fingers. The train was busy, giving me hope that we might pull in to the next station before they got to me. We didn't.

'Ticket, please.'

'I'm sorry, I haven't got one. I'll just jump off here and walk the rest of the way,' I said.

'Yes, you will get off here. But you will come with me.'

I was marched onto the platform by two of the men, while the other two moved on to the next carriage. I went through the motions, explaining that I had no money to pay a fine, but these boys weren't in lenient mood.

'What's your name?'

'Mike Jackson,' I heard myself saying.

Why the fuck had I used that name? Mike Jackson. Why? They would think I was taking the piss. I was! Why hadn't I said a believable, regular name? Why hadn't I said Russell Baker? Russell Baker is a good, strong, solid name. Mike

Jackson is flamboyant. Men in authority do not appreciate being confronted by flamboyance.

'Mike Jackson? Is that really your name? Mike Jackson?'

My story wasn't believed.

'Yep, Mike, short for Michael, Jackson. Why does nobody ever believe me?'

I laughed, like I was met with this sort of disbelief every time I told people my name. The bigger of the two guys wrote down my details in a little black book and then asked me to empty out my pockets.

'You must have a wallet. And if you don't, then I want to see some identification,' he growled.

I had been clever though, for Mike Jackson is nothing if not quick thinking. As soon as I had seen them enter the train, I'd taken my passport from my back pocket and stuffed it down my sock. Mike Jackson knows that being found in the possession of a passport in the name of Kris Mole would be bad news.

'Follow me,' I was ordered. 'We will see if the police can't sort this out. I don't believe that you are travelling through my country with all your bags, but you don't have your passport on you.'

I was led through a door to a small office, in which a policeman standing behind a desk gave authorization for the large man to search me properly. Every one of my bags was emptied onto a table as I looked on, still insisting that I had left my passport with a friend for safekeeping in the city.

'If we have to, we will call in the British Embassy to sort this out, so just make this easier for everyone and tell me where it is.'

I looked at the policeman's face as the security guard told me this, and knew that it wasn't really going to go as far as a call to an embassy. It was the final move of a desperate man.

'You don't even know for sure that I'm British. You have no proof,' I told them, cockily.

'Right, then we will let you go this time with a warning. Your punishment is that it will take you more than an hour to walk into the city from here. Go!'

I exited the station, stood for a minute, watched the guards disappear down the stairs, gave them enough time to jump on the next arriving train, and then re-entered the station and moonwalked onto the next train, this time making it safely to where I needed to be. *'Shamone!'*

An hour after sending some emails from the city's library I received a text from Gia, a local girl, letting me know that her and her husband would be happy to put me up for the night. Gia's husband Jari met me at 6 that evening in front of one of the city's Metro stations.

Jari and Gia were a fresh-faced, successful couple in their late twenties. They were also two of the nicest people I'd ever met. Throughout the course of the evening and late into the night, they plied me with alcohol and barbecued meat. We sat on the patio and talked like we had known each other for years. By the time I went to bed I had tried every flavour of cider under the sun – apparently Finland is the true spiritual home of cider, and not, as I had always been led to believe, Somerset – as well as getting through a bottle of Disaronno and a jug of apple brandy. These people knew how to host. My bed for the night was the most comfortable not only of the entire journey but of my entire life. And it was a sofa-bed.

A few uneventful days later I turned up at Helsinki Airport to catch my flight to Greece, courtesy of Donatello's Restaurant in Brighton.

Fucking hell, I've made it. Welcome to Athens.

North Cape
Jan Mayen
(Norway)
NORWEGIAN SEA
Scandinavia
Lapland
Tromsø
Kebnekaise
Kiruna
Luleå
Oulu
SWEDEN
FINLAND
Trondheim
Faroe Islands
(Denmark)
NORWAY
Galdhopiggen
Vaasa
Sundsvall
Gulf of Bothnia
Tampere
Shetland Islands
(UK)
Turku
HELSINKI
Aland
Bergen
OSLO
STOCKHOLM
Gulf of Finland
St Pete
Orkney Islands
TALLINN
ESTONIA
Gotland
Stavanger
Wick
Isle of Lewis
SCOTLAND
Aberdeen
NORTH SEA
Göteborg
RIGA
LATVIA
Pskov
Hebrides
Perth
Edinburgh
DENMARK
Oland
British Isles
Glasgow
UNITED KINGDOM
COPENHAGEN
Malmo
BALTIC SEA
LITHUANIA
VILNIUS
ULSTER
Belfast
Newcastle
KALININGRAD
(RUSSIAN FED.)
IRELAND
DUBLIN
Liverpool
Manchester
Hamburg
Gdansk
MINSK
WALES
ENGLAND
Birmingham
NETHERLANDS
AMSTERDAM
BERLIN
POLAND
BELARUS
Cork
Cardiff
LONDON
Rotterdam
WARSAW
CELTIC SEA
Dusseldorf
Leipzig
Plymouth
Southampton
BRUSSELS
Antwerp
GERMANY
PRAGUE
Krakow
KIEV
English Channel
Lille
BELGIUM
Frankfurt
CZECH.REP.
Le Havre
PARIS
LUX.
Stuttgart
Carpathian Mts.
SLOVAKIA
Brest
Strasbourg
VIENNA
BRATISLAVA
Rennes
FRANCE
Munich
AUSTRIA
MOLDOVA
BUDAPEST
CHISINAU
Nantes
BERN
LIECHT.
Geneva
SWITZ.
SLOVENIA
HUNGARY
ROMANIA
LJUBLJANA
ZAGREB
Bay of Biscay
Bordeaux
Lyon
Mt Blanc
Milan
Massif Central
Turin
Venice
BELGRADE
BUCHAREST
CROATIA
BOSNIA & H.
Florence
SARAJEVO
SERBIA
Toulouse
Montpellier
Nice
Pyrenees
Marseille
MONTENEGRO
Bilbao
SOFIA
BULGARIA
Aneto
AND.
Corsica
ITALY
KOSOVO
Vigo
Valladolid
Zaragoza
ROME
PODGORICA
SKOPJE
Porto
Barcelona
F.Y.R.O.M.
Istanbul
Coimbra
MADRID
Naples
Bari
TIRANA
ALBANIA
PORTUGAL
SPAIN
Valencia
Balearic Is.
Sardinia
Olympus
Bursa
LISBON
Sierra Morena
Cordoba
MEDITERRANEAN SEA
Palermo
Messina
Izmir
Anatolia
Seville
ALGIERS
TUNIS
Etna
Sicily
Peloponnese
GREECE
Strait of Gibraltar
Oran
Constantine
TUNISIA
VALLETTA
AEGEAN SEA
Antalya
Tangier
Ceuta (Spain)
MALTA
Melilla (Spain)
Crete
RABAT
Fes
ALGERIA
Sfax
CYPRUS
Casablanca
MOROCCO
Gabes

45. Athens

Mission: Complete!

Days on the road: 162
Distance travelled: 31,350 miles
EU capitals visited: 23

THIS WAS IT. As I walked from the plane towards the baggage collection point, that's all that was going through my head. I had been on the road for almost six months, the past two of which I'd spent with the thought of Greece's capital always somewhere in my mind, always wondering if I would actually make it to this point, and if so, how long it would take me.

I knew I was in Greece as soon as I got into the arrivals hall, not because of the funny script that all the information posts were in, but because everyone just seemed so, well, so Greek. It was a celebration of medallion men, as open shirts failed in their attempts to contain rugs of animal-like chest fur. The pungent smell of strong aftershave was overpowering. Unlit cigarettes hung from the side of every mouth. People stood toe to toe with their arms around each other, smiling and laughing in an overly friendly manner but at the same time only managing to communicate verbally by shouting loudly and aggressively into their companion's ear. To a non-Greek speaker such as myself it was difficult to know if these people wanted to kiss or knock each other's blocks off.

I collected my backpack and exited the hall with nothing to declare. Those hanging cigarettes from the arrivals hall were unlit no more. All around me people smoked. Never mind that we were inside an airport; this was Greece. Smoking was technically only permitted in the seating area of the little café directly opposite you as you emerged into the main terminal building; however, the Greeks had a pretty liberal interpretation of where that area ended, and as much as the waitress walked around telling people they weren't actually inside the designated smoking area, that liberal interpretation was not going to be altered.

'Kris?'

I turned around to be greeted by my final host of the journey. Voula had brown wavy hair and a warm, smiling face.

'Voula. Hi. Thanks for coming to meet me.'

'No problem. I brought a friend with me. She's sitting at the café.'

I somehow managed to find my way through the thick cloud of smoke and put my bum down at the little table where I introduced myself to Voula's friend. Nikoleta had dark olive skin, thick eyebrows, and looked like a girl who didn't care too much for all the superficial things in life. She also had such a genuine openness and friendliness that I immediately took to her. When she spoke it was like listening to a typical Greek restaurant owner.

'Sit down my friend,' she instructed me, loudly.

'Do you want a coffee or something else to drink?' Voula asked.

'I'd love an orange juice. Thanks.'

I discovered that both girls were from Corfu, and were both in Athens studying chemical engineering.

'You seem too nice to be English,' Nikoleta told me.

'Thanks, I think. What exactly do you mean by that, though?'

She laughed and explained that the kind of English she was used to seeing were the kind that came to her father's restaurant on Corfu, drank ridiculous amounts of beer and ouzo over dinner, then went outside to cause a bit of mischief in town.

'Don't worry, I'm exactly like them really.'

I picked up my bags and followed the girls through the terminal to the exit, passing a traditionally dressed Greek Orthodox priest on the way. The bus was packed; there were just two seats available at the back. I stood up and told the girls to take them, but both told me not to be silly and pushed me down into the seat. Nikoleta squeezed in next to me, while Voula went up towards the front and found a little space next to an old lady. As soon as the bus started moving Nikoleta motioned for Voula to come and join us, and she came and somehow managed to get herself into a tiny space between Nikoleta and I, basically sitting on my lap. The drive took a good 35 to 40 minutes. Nobody around us was going to be allowed to ride peacefully home tonight, as these girls talked to everyone. I couldn't understand what was being said, but everyone saw the funny side of whatever it was and the whole back end of the bus was bent over in hysterics throughout the entire ride.

The evening air was warm as we jumped off of the bus; Something I hadn't experienced for a long time, not since Caceres in Spain. Behind me, behind some mesh fencing, stood a couple of soldiers, guns down by their sides. In front of me was what looked like a package holiday resort: white apartment block after white apartment block, all sitting on a huge complex that you had to pass two security guards and go through a gate to get into. This was the student housing area where I was going to spend the final nights of my journey across the continent. Nikoleta went off into her block while I followed Voula up to hers. The dorm was pretty standard, going by most of the other student residences I had seen over the past five months; essentially just a large bedroom with a little bathroom. One thing that this room had going for it that the others didn't was a little balcony complete with table and chairs. There was no telly or computer, just a CD player/radio on the desk in the corner.

'Welcome to the presidential suite.'

Voula indicated for me to chuck my bags down and make myself at home.

'You will be sleeping down here,' she pointed down to the floor, 'but don't worry, there will be a mattress.'

We left Voula's and went down to Nikoleta's, just a couple of buildings away. Nikoleta got on the phone and ordered some food to be delivered, while I sat back on the bed and made myself comfortable. The knock at the door meant that I was finally going to eat something. Two little boxes were put on the table and opened. The first contained five gyros wraps; the second was full of chips. Along with the boxes came cold cans of Heineken.

'You're a hungry boy, so three of the wraps are for you,' Nikoleta let me know.

When I looked at these two girls at that precise moment I saw only marriage material. To be honest, when I looked at the delivery guy standing at the door I saw only marriage material too, so it's fair to say I was just feeling a bit soft at the time. After finishing the food and beers, the yawns and arm stretches started, indicating that it was time for Voula to take me away from Nikoleta's and up to hers to get some shuteye.

It was about 2am when Voula came out of the shower and got into her bed. I got down on my mattress and wondered where the quilt or blanket was. Then I realised: there was no quilt or blanket. There was no need for a quilt or a blanket. I was in a warm country. All I had been given to cover myself was a sheet, and that was going to do just fine. Before turning the light off, Voula told me that she had to get up for a lecture at 8 but that it was only going to be a short one and she expected to be back by 11:30. Did I mind hanging around until that time, or did I plan to go out earlier to see the sights?

'Voula, when you get in at 11:30, wake me up please.'

I slept like a baby. Not the kind of baby that wakes up crying at 3am and wets the bed, but the kind of baby that sleeps, well, that sleeps like a baby. Just after Voula left in the morning, I got up to go to the toilet and on the way back saw something that needed investigating. Strange beams of light were shooting through the tiny holes in the shutters of the patio door. I turned the rotating handle to lift the shutter and was smacked in the face by bright, warm, sunlight. It was just after 8 and it was hot and sunny outside. Could I have chosen a more comfortable city to end my epic venture across Europe in? I don't think so.

I went back to sleep and was woken a few hours later when Voula returned from university. I joined her out on the balcony where we shared a packet of Jaffa Cakes for breakfast. The sun was baking and the shirt was off. Mine, not Voula's. After about an hour of crisping up under the sun's rays it was time to get some lunch. Every student resident congregated twice a day in the huge communal canteen for lunch and dinner. I was invited. As we walked down to the dining hall, I looked around and wondered if I had actually walked into a holiday resort. It was just block after block of bright white building, each one's outside covered with people sitting out sunning on balconies. There were free tennis courts, basketball courts, table-tennis rooms, an area for playing football, and 19-year old girls from Manchester handing out fliers letting you know what daily excursions were planned. OK, not that last part. But all the rest was there. The canteen was like every one I had ever seen: miserable people in white jackets slopping balls of mashed potato onto the plates of the hungry. As we ate I was told a little bit about the place. This particular residential area was built to host the international journalists covering the 2004 Olympics. This meant that not all of the student dorms around the city were anywhere near as nice. Students in Greece get everything for free. All education: free. Accommodation in this lovely complex: free. All meals: free. Another thing that I learnt over this lunchtime chinwag was that it was forbidden for the police to enter the students' residential area. If a police car happened to be chasing a mass murderer and rapist up the street and the criminal then took a quick left turn into the grounds of the university, the police would have to stop the chase.

'Sometimes it has its down side,' explained Voula. 'Like, a couple of times, girls walking in here have been indecently assaulted by guys who know that nothing can happen to them. But overall it works well.'

I was interested to hear more about this law. I sat quietly and listened intently as the girls explained that the rule came about as a result of the Athens Polytechnic uprising of 1973. The uprising was a massive demonstration of popular rejection of the Greek military junta of 1967-1974. It began on the 14th of November 1973 and ended in bloodshed on the 17th after a series of events that included a tank crashing through the gates of the Polytechnic where much of the student population of the city had gathered and occupied the campus. The students had been pissed off in the first place, not just because they were students and had a duty to hate any form of authority, but also because the government had been interfering too much in student syndicalism. They had banned all student elections in the universities, started putting non-elected student union leaders into positions in the national students' union, and were forcibly drafting students into the military. This all led to a strong anti-junta sentiment among the student population and the revolt was inevitable. Ever since then, the 17th of November has been a school holiday in Greece. The campus is also closed on the 15th of November to remember the day the students first occupied the place, and the police and military have been banned from entering university property ever since. After my history lesson and lunch was over, I was to be taken on a tour of the city.

'Um, Kris, do you think it might be a good idea to put something with sleeves on? It might get cold later, and also you might burn. I'm not sure wearing that white vest is such a good idea,' suggested Nikoleta.

'Get cold later? The Greeks and I probably have different ideas as to what constitutes cold. And I won't burn; I will go golden.'

On reflection, I can see I was being a bit optimistic, but I was out in the sun for the first time in Bob knows how long

and I wasn't going to cover myself up to block it out. It was 3 in the afternoon. We strolled down the road to the bus stop, and jumped on a bus packed full of students making their way home, which meant I had to stand having my nose tickled by a guy's dripping wet armpit hair. We travelled into the centre of the city and I emerged into a sea of Japanese visitors clicking away furiously at their super tiny cameras that looked like shrunken credit cards. It was time to be a tourist.

It didn't take me long to fall in love with the city; around two minutes, I think. We headed down the main shopping street, Ermou – 'this is our Oxford Street,' according to Voula – having to stop every minute or so for one of the girls to nip into a clothes shop to look in more detail at something they'd spotted in the window. Not many cars attempted to get down this particular road, as it would have been like trying to drive through the Mardi Gras or some similar street festival. Pedestrians ruled here. I will be more specific; Greek pedestrians ruled here. I was being knocked from one side of the street to the other and then back again. The girls led me away from the main shopping area and up some side streets. This was the Greece I had always imagined: small little streets, lined on both sides by traditional tavernas, where old men with moustaches and hats sat outside at little tables, playing cards, smoking, and drinking ouzo. The Greek flag flew proudly above every doorway. There were no cars, hardly any people, and no noise. We had walked two minutes away from the hustle and bustle of Ermou Street and found ourselves in this tranquil little place straight out of a 1920s novel. Everything was white or light peach in colour: the buildings, the floor, the sky. As we walked up these tiny alleys, the old men would look up and then down at Voula's figure, watching as she moved on and out of their sight, then they'd glance back down to their cards until another young woman happened to stroll past and interrupt their game. I followed the girls up and up and up. The path was steep. The higher we went, the more stunning the view of the city became. The sign pointed us up further still; it had the word 'Acropolis' written on it. As we got to the top, there it was: the Parthenon, right above my head. This was as far as we could go without paying the lady at the gate 12 Euros each to get up close and personal with the buildings of the Acropolis. I wouldn't pay that even if I were there as a regular tourist with cash in my pocket. From where we were standing, we could get a decent enough view of the ancient structures.

We descended down a different path to the one which we had walked up. Along the way there were some beautiful, old, white churches, built into the stone walls. On the front of the prettiest one of all, someone had thoughtfully spray-painted, 'Fuck the Police. Fuck religion.' I smiled at the sentiment. The path followed the perimeter fence to the Acropolis. The sun was still gloriously hot, and I noticed my chest and shoulders were starting to itch. I looked down and realised that I had done what millions of Englishmen before me had succeeded in doing: got burnt to a crisp on my first day in a warm country. I felt proud.

The afternoon was getting late and Nikoleta had to get ready for a late shift at work; while Voula, a couple of her friends and I were going to spend a traditional Greek evening at Nikoleta's place of work, indulging in some traditional local specialities of the food and drink kind.

Elaikon was a busy little taverna. There was only one empty table inside and Nikoleta had reserved it for us. All the tables out on the patio were also full. People were singing, clapping, drinking, talking loudly, smashing plates and being Greek.

'So, Kris, do you like it here? It is very typical,' Vaso, a friend of the girls, asked.

'I love it. This is what I wanted to experience in Greece.'

She then ordered for us all. I looked up to see if I could spot Nikoleta. It was manic. The waiters and waitresses – Nikoleta one of them – were rushing around like blue-arsed flies. How they were managing to get between the packed tables, carrying trays of food and drink without spilling or dropping anything was quite incredible. We were soon joined by a girl I hadn't met yet.

'Kris, this is Natassa. Natassa, this is Kris.'

Now we had met. Nikoleta brought over a jug of steaming hot drink along with four small glasses, and Vaso told her what we wanted to eat. Voula poured the drinks and handed me mine. It tasted like alcoholic Lemsip. After a few of these you might wake up the next morning with a slight hangover, but I would put big money on you not having a sore throat.

'It's called Rakomelo. It's something very traditional here, made from honey and our national drink Raki. It's good, huh?'

'It's alright, yea.'

A table became available on the patio so we took it. The drinks were flowing, food was on its way, and I was sat outside after 10 at night, wearing no more than a t-shirt. Well, I was wearing more than a t-shirt. I had pants, socks, jeans and trainers on as well. This wasn't like one of those nightmares where you suddenly look down to find you're the only naked person in a group of strangers. Why am I always at a bus stop when that happens? Always!

I was talking a lot to Natassa, and found her to be great company. Her mum was an English teacher and this had obviously had a big influence on Natassa because she spoke fluently. Like the other girls, she also had a wickedly sharp sense of humour.

Every time the jug of hot drink in front of us became empty Nikoleta was there to deliver a refill. She also brought us over the huge plate of meat. Every last piece of the succulent pork was devoured and we all arrived back at the dorms in very merry mood shortly before 3 in the morning. That drink may taste like a hot cure for a sore throat, but I tell you what, it packs a punch.

The following day, both Voula and Nikoleta had lectures to attend, so I was left with the keys to Nikoleta's dorm and told to treat it as my own, watching TV or sending emails. All I could think about was getting back home to Brighton the next day on a flight that had just been booked and paid for by another Brighton business, Proto's the greengrocer. Natassa knocked on the door to borrow a hair drier – Nikoleta's, not mine – and asked if I wanted to go with her to vote in the student elections.

'I'm taking the scooter,' she told me.

'When do we leave?'

I wasn't going to turn down the chance to ride around Athens on the back of a Vespa.

'I'll just dry my hair, and then I'll come and get you.'

I put on my helmet, jumped on the back, and we were on our way. The way Natassa dodged in and out of cars was extremely elegant, and the ride was a treat. We got to the student voting centre and it was packed to busting point with energetic youth. Natassa was a popular girl; I just kind of stood in the background like a spare part as people formed a queue to greet her. As she went inside to tick the box and cast her vote, I stayed out on the balcony looking down at all the commotion. There were posters, flags, banners; all trying to persuade the undecided which way to vote. From the looks of the people, my guess would be that this was an election being contested by students from the left, the far-left, the far-far-left, and the maybe-not-really-on-the-left-but-just-love-the-Che-Guevara-look.

I followed Natassa out onto the street, and then jumped on the back of the scooter and my second tour of Athens began. It was one of the best experiences of the whole trip. We went through all the different neighbourhoods, past all of the main sights and attractions, and Natassa gave a running commentary throughout. Our final destination was a hill high above the city that offered a panoramic view of Greece's capital. I stood in awe as Natassa pointed out different places of interest. The whole city of Athens was below me. From here the city resembled a plaster-of-Paris model town that hadn't been painted yet: every building was just as white as the next. The beaches were just a stone's throw away, too.

The following morning I said my farewells to both Voula and Nikoleta and jumped on the back of Natassa's scooter for a lift to the bus stop from where I made my way to the airport. I was in triumphant mood. Finally I was returning home to Brighton. I got in to Heathrow at 3:30pm and was on the bus heading for Brighton an hour later. As soon as we entered the surroundings of the city and the old familiar flower bed that spells out the words 'Welcome to Brighton' passed by outside the window, the cloudy weather that had met me in London passed and the early evening sun of my home town shone brightly. Brighton had never looked more beautiful.

I was met at the bus station by my parents, and the short drive home along the coast road was great: people all over the beach, sitting around on the pebbles, enjoying the early spring conditions, flying kites, drinking cold beers, windsurfing, paddling, chatting, messing about; the sun just above the horizon, out in the direction of northern France.

Acknowledgements

FIRST OF ALL let me take this opportunity to thank every single person that helped me along the way. Those who fed me, watered me, gave me a roof, gave me a lift, handed me a ticket, offered companionship or just put a smile on my face. Each and every one of you made this story possible. Most of you I have kept in touch with and some I have already met up with again since finishing the journey. You are all welcome at my home any time. Well, best to call me first. But you are welcome.

Jon Young. You gave me a chance when everyone else had given up on me. You gave me a place to live, a job, a sensible point of view and direction in my life at a time when I was homeless and on the edge of despair. I obviously never had a real brother, but you come pretty close. And to think that we first met in Warsaw on the Great Euro Freebie Challenge. Thank you, mate.

My heartfelt thanks go to David 'Windy' Baboulene, for all the invaluable advice, support and time that you gifted me throughout my long period of getting this book written. If I ever become half as good a writer as you, I will know I have truly succeeded.

Much love to Russ and Han, for this book never would have been completed without the use of your laptop… And your cooking. I always wrote on a full stomach.

Thanks to my late Grandad and Uncles Graham and Steven, for giving me a place to live while I finished writing this book. Thanks for feeding me and looking after me at times. I hope I have at least made you proud.

Massive thanks to my uncle Michael and his Brighton fruit and veg shop Proto's, for seeing to it that after completing the challenge I wasn't left stranded in Greece. Although, there are worse places to find yourself stranded.

Thank you to Brighton's Ristorante Donatello and in particular Sue, for stepping forward and providing me with that all-important air ticket between Helsinki and Athens.

Thanks to Heather, formerly of the BBC, just for your contact. There was many a day during the journey where I woke feeling cold, hungry and tired, only to be picked up by our exchanging of chatty emails. You were my link to normality; my link to the South of England. You often made me grin. I also greatly appreciate the effort you put into building the pages on the BBC website, sending me audio recordings of my interviews and just being a smiley person; albeit a smile that I never physically saw.

Thanks to the *Shoreham Herald* and the *Evening Argus*, who both did a lot to drum up sponsorships, for which I am grateful. The same can be said of BBC Southern Counties. Thank you.

Thanks also go out to the whole team at Cracow-Life. Without you guys, who knows? I may have died! You all looked after me so well and I remain grateful. If anyone reading this is going travelling in Eastern or Central Europe and in need of some tips, take it from me – these guys piss all over 'In Your Pocket'!

Much appreciation to the artist formerly known as Cat Stevens. Without your anthology on my iPod I don't know how I would have got through the cross-continent treks.

I also have to give a special mention to Miss Briggs, the one person who never stopped believing that this project would come to fruition eventually, when everyone else around me had given up hope. Your words kept me going sometimes.

And finally:

Mia, Philippe, Mr and Mrs Molnar, Line, Liam, Greg, Ollie, Kimi, Julian, Joanne, Andrzej, Jon, Nick, Paul, Hollywood actor Sean Penn, Mark and all at Cracow-Life, Domča, Vlad,

Fubus, Zuzana and family, Vanja and family, Sabrina, Sid, Miroslav, Jasna, Kremi, Adriana, Denisa, Hannes, Sébastien, Alex, Marie, Marie-Amelie, Peter & Mary, Carlos, Celia, Diego, Alex, Marina, Ovidiu, Diana, Alberto, Mara, Isabel, Emma, John, Baijian, Hélène, Marie, Leen, Chermaine, Stephen, Andrea & Benni, Stefanie, Florin, Adrian, Andreea, Max, Cori, Janez, Renars, Liva, Paulis, Elina, Oliver, Christopher, Jari, Gia, Elise, Voula, Nikoleta and Natasa – I thank you all for your hospitality, and I apologise if I have missed anyone out.

2008 Update: I'm very sorry to report that Steve in Alaska, my ever-positive and intensely funny friend who throughout my journey was fighting his own battle with cancer, sadly is no longer with us. He fought like a bull and was kicking cancer's arse for a lot longer than any doctor had expected him to. In the end it got him. Steve really was the most inspirational human you could ever wish to know. RIP big man. Fuck you, cancer!

If you would like to contact me, email me on:
krissymole@gmail.com

Check out my website: **krismole.com**

Also come follow me at: **facebook.com/gatecrashingeurope**

And on Twitter: **@KrisMole**

If you have enjoyed reading this book, tell your friends, and if you have time, write a review of it and paste it all over the internet. You'd be surprised how much of a difference it can make. If you haven't enjoyed it, don't do either of these things. Thank you.

Kris Mole